Dear Dr Chal
You are a Ro

Super Vitality

I wish you were my familys

The Ultimate Guide to Optimal Health, Boundless Energy and Becoming Superhuman!

GP.
Stay Strong Stay Super!

Hari Kalymnios

Hari

2025

Super Vitality
First Published in Great Britain by Kinetic Island Publishing, 2025

Paperback Version: ISBN-13: 978-1-0682831-0-9

Digital Version: ISBN-13: 978-1-0682831-2-3

Also, by Hari Kalymnios

The Thought Gym®
Train the Mind, and the Body Will Follow
(2013)

The Super Journal
The All-in-One Day & Life Planner
(2017)

Working Well
What You Need to Know to Live a Longer, Happier, Healthier Life
(2018)

Super Vitality – Lite Edition
The Ultimate Guide to Optimal Health, Boundless Energy and Becoming Superhuman!
(2025)

WHAT OTHERS SAY ABOUT HARI

"Hari is an inspirational as well as a very educational speaker on a wide range of healthy lifestyle and success topics.... Hari leads by example, which makes him a very convincing speaker and leader... It is impossible not to become healthier in Hari's company." - Svetlana Rakhimova MBA, Independent Researcher

"...Hari's expertise in leadership and energy is obvious and communicated with passion... both entertaining and motivational." – Steve Bustin, Public Speaking Coach

"If you are looking for someone who believes in his topic with both passion and conviction, Hari is your man...We all have much to learn from Mr. Kalymnios." – Janet Tarasofsky MSc, Business Physcologist

"...Hari is the first and only person I would listen to when it comes to health advice, fitness and energy management as he is truly one of the best in his field of leadership & health..." – Anik Petrou, Speaker Booker

"Hari is a truly inspiring guy, he really does live what he believes, one of the few people I know to not only talk the talk but walk the walk...He loves to share his view of the world and always makes me want to get out there and live it better myself. Always full of energy and wanting to help himself and others to reach their full potential." – Aislinn O'Neal, Marketing Expert

"Hari is energetic, engaging, and approachable. He radiates enthusiasm and communicates his breadth of knowledge in an interesting and effective way. My colleagues and I have all thoroughly enjoyed his training. I would certainly recommend hearing what he has to say." – Amanda Zafiris, VP Head of International Marketing

"...I recommend him as someone who is at the very cutting edge of his field, who is very much living his trade, walking his talk and most importantly is someone with a good heart, a hardworking and caring nature and a natural passion for helping people." - Amit Roychoudhury, Pensions & Benefits Manager

This book is dedicated to all those out there who are striving for more, pushing themselves and making a positive impact in the world.

To the gamechangers!

"Change the way you look at things, and the things you look at change."

– Wayne Dyer

Acknowledgements

I would like to thank a few people for helping me with the proof reading of this book prior to its release. Firstly, my mum, who diligently went through the entire book and who made countless corrections to grammar, spelling and more! And who also went through the 'lite' version of the book too and made useful corrections. Secondly, thanks to my dad, who also took a pass at it and helped in many ways.

Also, thanks to Elena Calita and Joe Lake who also reviewed the book and made useful corrections and suggestions. Thanks also to Gemma Sargant who reviewed the 'lite' version of this book and offered valuable feedback.

I would also like to acknowledge my nieces Evie, Lola and Nikita for all offering their suggestions on the book and Minnie and Phoenix for continuing to remind me about how useful children are in teaching adults the principles of wellbeing and living well.

Foreword

Imagine holding in your hands a book that cuts through the noise and unlocks the real secrets to living a long, strong, and vibrant life. In a world overflowing with conflicting advice on health, wellbeing, and longevity, it's rare to come across something that brings clarity, simplicity, and lasting impact.

Over the course of my life—as an Olympic diver, silver medallist, and now as a coach, keynote speaker, and advocate for mental fitness and sustainable high performance—I've been driven by a deep fascination with what helps people thrive. My own journey has taught me that true wellbeing doesn't come from a single practice—whether that's breathwork, meditation, movement, nutrition, or sleep—but from understanding how all these elements interact.

Hari Kalymnios gets that. In this game-changing book, he weaves together decades of insight and lived experience into a clear, actionable framework: *The Leadership BEAT Model*™. I first came across Hari's work back in 2014 through one of his online courses, and we quickly connected over our shared passions for health, mindset, and performance. Since then, I've watched with admiration as he continues to deepen his message and live by the principles he teaches.

What makes Hari's approach so powerful is the way he connects the dots. He brings a rare, big-picture perspective—rooted in science, yet accessible and practical—that helps people take ownership of their energy, vitality, and longevity. He doesn't just teach this stuff. He lives it.

If you're looking for a single, comprehensive guide to building a life of lasting health and vitality, you've found it. This book is more than a collection of tips—it's a blueprint for thriving.

Leon Taylor
Olympic Silver Medallist Diving

Table of Contents

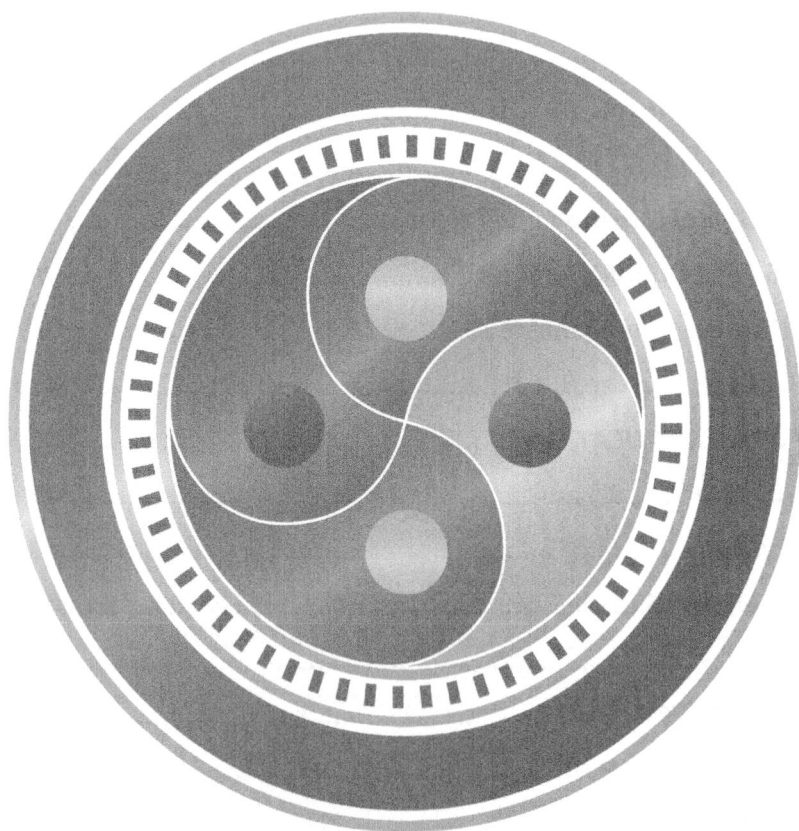

Introduction
And so, it begins…

"You don't have to be great to start, but you have to start to be great."

– Zig Ziglar

It was obvious, and yet it had alluded me this whole time. And my bet is that it's alluded you too. Surrounded by 2000 other people, the realisation was dawning on me, I just wouldn't realise it for another three years.

January 2011 and my life was in the toilet. I'd been made redundant from a good job at the London Stock Exchange. I was directionless, jobless and struggling to get out of bed in the morning.

Was this the catalyst I needed? I couldn't be sure. But I had to try something. Anything.

So, what was the realisation? Well, that's still to come. First, I needed the journey. And my journey really started in that room with 2000 other people.

I was at a personal development seminar by an energetic American – Joseph McClendon III (JMIII) – the Life Strategist Tony Robbins' top trainer. We'd just completed a two-day accelerated personal development training. And then, it was about to be taken to a whole new level.

JMIII explained to us how he'd not had a cold in 27 years and although I believed he was in his mid-30's, from my seat in the arena, he revealed he was in fact 57! That was the start of my journey into discovering what it takes to live a fully optimised and energised life. In the next chapter we're going to look at the discovery I made and how it can be used to accelerate your life, as when you understand it, nothing is the same again.

SUPER VITALITY

Is this book for you? Only if you want to optimise your health, increase your energy, build resilience, and unlock the inner superhuman within you. Only if you want to have the focus, productivity, vitality, and longevity that you are capable of. Only if you want to become the best self-leader you can be. Only if you want to be a change-maker – someone who has a message, idea, or mission to help the world and you need to sustain that mission. You might be a CEO, a business professional, executive, entrepreneur, solopreneur, or freelancer. A coach, consultant, speaker, or personal trainer. A parent or caregiver. Whatever the "role" in life that you currently identify with, this book is for you if you are looking for a way to bring more health, vitality, energy, longevity, and more success into your life. This book is for you if you want to be a change-maker, a leader. Why a leader?

This is my philosophy on leadership. To lead others, the first person you need to be able to lead is yourself. And to lead yourself, optimally, you must be "on point" - mentally, physically, emotionally, and spiritually. To access your own unique superpowers. To become superhuman – and I will explain what I mean by that later. And we are all leaders. The world needs more leaders. More change-makers. People to make the world a better place. Now, more than ever. Even if you will only ever lead yourself. You need to be able to lead yourself to better decisions. To better outcomes. To more success in life (and we all have our own definitions of success).

This book is for you if there is an area of your life where you want a higher level of performance. It's especially appropriate if you are an employer of other people and want to get the best out of them. Your team, department, or organisation. Why? Well, when it comes to assessing performance, especially in many corporate settings, it is based on three primary drivers. Skills (or knowledge), experience and behaviour. Traditionally this is what is thought to equate to performance.

Performance = Skills/Knowledge + Experience + Behaviour

If you want to increase performance, historically you would look at one of the three contributing factors. If you want to increase skills or knowledge, you conduct a Gap Analysis and undertake training. Lacking experience, then you introduce role rotations. If a change of behaviour is needed, then look to giving a person coaching.

Performance = Skills/Knowledge + Experience + Behaviour

£££££ = (Gap Analysis) + (Role Rotation) + (Coaching)

However, there is a missing component to this equation. It's something that at most companies that I've observed, no-one is talking about. Even if you don't work for a big company, and work for yourself, your performance is still ultimately dictated by the missing part of the equation. And that is...ENERGY!

Everything stems from having energy. It's a fundamental part of the fabric of the universe. I'm an Astrophysics graduate, after all. Everything is about energy. $E=mc^2$, remember? If you want to have a competitive edge, to be able to complete your goals, spread your message and complete your mission, achieve your company goals, or live a fantastic life, you need to understand energy. It doesn't matter if you have all the strategies and techniques in the world, if you haven't got the energy to execute on them, you'll never get there. That's why the real equation to increasing performance and results is:

Performance = ENERGY + Skills/Knowledge + Experience + Behaviour

And how do you achieve this energy? That's what this book is all about. Whether that's for you to achieve what you want in your personal life, complete your mission as a change-maker and improve the world. Or even if you just want your team and company to perform better. This book will reveal the secrets to having unbeatable energy and the keys to becoming superhuman.

==========

The world today is changing rapidly. There is an increasing pace of technological advances. A constant stream of information and distractions. More things are competing for our time. When I worked in the corporate world, I would see many people lacking in energy. People are working harder and longer, with burnout, stress, and fatigue ever rampant.

It seems that even with all the world's information a few clicks away, we are still starved of wisdom. As many of us continually chase the latest craze, fad, or app to help reduce our stress, make us more attractive, help us lose weight, increase our productivity, increase our happiness levels, help us find headspace or calm and on and on.

It's been my experience that while tools like apps can indeed help, the reason a person isn't happy, or can't relax, or lose weight is not because they were waiting for that perfect app to help them.

No. There are fundamental principles that we need to understand to help in all areas of our lives. Many of them have been known for hundreds, if not thousands, of years. Yet many people are continually seeking something new and exciting to help them. You might be one of these people?

This book can be thought of as a guidebook or a blueprint. A curation, of all the best practices that I've learnt over the last several decades to help you increase your health, happiness, vitality, and energy so that you might have better focus, productivity, relationships and live a more fulfilling and energised life. This book is more than just that. It's a leadership manual. Not in the usual sense you might perceive a leadership book.

Rather than limit you to the latest leadership tools and techniques. Or simply give you something that's hot today and then obsolete the next. It's going to teach you timeless fundamentals on how to lead *yourself*. How to lead others by being the example. It's going to teach you what you need to know, to think, feel and start to be superhuman. Become a "super leader".

To be superhuman, in my view, is not about being able to hold your breath for 29 minutes (yes, that's been done), or climb Mount Everest in your shorts (yes, that's been done too), or do any other superhuman feat. It's about living at a *super*ior level to the one you might be used to. To operate at a SUPER level. It's about being able to work a full day but have the energy to get up before work and get stuff done. It's about having the energy and vitality to be able to come home and work on that novel that you are writing, or hustle on your side business. Your greater mission perhaps. It's about having energy to play with your children. It's about being able to go shopping all day on Saturday because it's what your spouse wants to do, and for you to remain energised. It's about never being limited on what you can do because of your health, vitality or energy levels.

When you are operating at your best, you can lead - yourself, and others - at your best. I've spent the last 15 years of my life formally looking into what helps people operate at the highest levels – and informally for many years prior to that. What does it take to be a high performer? What does it take to be *super*human?

What does it take so that your health, vitality, energy, focus, relationships, happiness, resilience and longevity all increase? To operate at a level where you are being all you can be. Perhaps pulling away from the masses. The masses who are living life in a way that no longer calls to you. That old way where you might be feeling worn down by the routine of life and business. It might be the old way of suffering from seasonal colds every few weeks or months. The old way of constantly being in a state of low (or high) level stress. It's about ditching the old way of feeling fatigued more often than you would like - and at times when you shouldn't feel fatigued.

In this book, I'm going to share with you what I've discovered. I'm going to share with you the research behind it. The stories, the tips, and the practical steps that you can take to become a super version of yourself. So that you can move forward as a leader. A leader in your business or organisation, your family, and your own body. And more than that, move from human, to becoming *super*human. It's a continued journey after all. Hence *becoming* superhuman and not necessarily *being* superhuman.

This book goes against conventional wisdom when writing a book. And that's to keep the topic narrow. Conversation about one small aspect of a topic. I didn't want to do that. I couldn't do that really. When writing a book about vitality and becoming superhuman, there are a multitude of factors to consider. I want this to be the *only* book that you will ever need when it comes to understanding what it takes to think, feel and be the superhuman self-leader, I know you can be.

How to Read This Book

This book is written in a way that will allow you to both read it cover to cover or to refer to the sections that interest you first. I do advise reading cover to cover though to get a deep understanding of the powerful information it contains. The book can then be used as a reference book to dip in and out of when you need to focus on a particular area. There's also a 'lite' version of this book that runs to around 130 pages, so if you want a pocket guide, or a super streamlined version to get you started, then check that version out too.

At the end of each chapter, I'll give you the key points as well as some exercises or actions to consider taking forward and implementing. While it's not mandatory to complete before going on to the next chapter, I do invite you to take them on board and take action. It will help with fully integrating what you are learning.

Short on Time?

Want to jump to the chapters that concern you right now, and get straight to it, then this will be useful.

If your goal is:

- Improving your **sleep** ....jump to chapter 4.1
- Freeing yourself from **tech addiction** ......look at chapter 4.5
- Tweaking your **diet** ....visit chapter 2.3
- Elevating your **mood** .....head to chapter 1.6
- Changing your **habits** .....review chapter 3.5

Take your time in reading this book. There's a lot to digest. I know that. It's packed with different ideas and themes. As I said, I've done that on purpose. It's the culmination of the best I know when it comes to becoming the best self-leader you can be. Becoming superhuman. And I didn't want to short-change you. My reasoning behind packing it with everything was this. If I were to be hit by a bus and not be around tomorrow, I didn't want to hold anything back. To string things out for another book. I know I'll have more to say in the future. More to write about. As my evolution continues. And as I go deeper into more specific topics. For this book though, I wanted you to have everything. If you could only buy one book about self-leadership, health, energy, longevity, resilience and well-being, then this would be all you would need. Success in this area can be as easy as ABC. First you need to have *awareness* about what you could change. That's what this book will give you. Then you need to adopt a *behavioural change*. Again, I'll point you in the right direction. And finally, you will need to be *consistent*. That's where most people faulter, but by using this book (and supplementary resources in the appendix section) as an ongoing motivational companion guide, it will help you remain consistent in your behavioural changes. The ABC to success!

That all being said. Let's get started with it.

========

0.1 Becoming Superhuman

Finding super…

---

*"I always had a repulsive need to be something more
than human. I felt very puny as a human. I thought,
'Fuck that. I want to be a superhuman."*

- David Bowie

I think it's important to start with my story. It will help make sense of where I'm coming from in writing this book. And it will help explain how the discovery I'm about to share formed.

I'm Hari. Nice to meet you!

I grew up in London and went to school in North London before heading off to study Physics with Astrophysics at The University of Manchester. I graduated from there in 1999 with a First-Class honours degree, but I didn't know what I wanted to do next. My plan, if you can call it that, only extended until I was 21 years old and graduating university. I knew I didn't want to jump straight into a job after university. So, I went travelling. I spent 25 months travelling through Southeast Asia, Australasia, the South Pacific, the USA, Central America, and Mexico.

Travelling was the first time that I had been outside of Europe. And it was a great education. It was more valuable than the three years I had spent getting my university degree. I had hoped that by the time that I returned to the UK I would know what I wanted to do with my life. However, when I came back in December 2001, I struggled. I still didn't know, and after spending a few months lingering about at home, I eventually moved to the Greek island of Crete, where I spent the best part of 2002 at a technical college on a postgraduate program. Somehow, three years after graduating, I was still eligible for a scholarship to a postgraduate program from the University of

17

SUPER VITALITY

Manchester.

When I returned from Crete, in late 2002, I still had no real idea about the next step. The working world seemed daunting. Even though naturally, I'd had jobs throughout university and even when travelling. Now things felt serious. I had to grow up. Become an adult. I wasn't ready for that.

I was lost and felt like I *had* to do something. By random chance I ended up bumping into an old friend from primary school who worked in the local pub. The same pub I used to drink in as a 16, err, sorry, 18-year-old. And I ended up working there. A First-Class Physics with Astrophysics graduate, and I ended up working in a local pub! Eventually that came to an end, as the landlord and I didn't really see eye-to-eye. I then went on to work at my sister's law firm as an office temp. What was supposed to be a three-week long work experience, ended up lasting over 15 months.

The reason I'm sharing this, and why it's relevant, is that all this time, I was expecting someone, or something, to save me. To lead me to where I needed to go. It never came. I carried on drifting. After a brief period of unemployment, after being made redundant from the law firm, I bumped into another old friend (who I knew from my time in the Scouts[*1]). He helped put my resume in front of his boss, who worked for Accenture, at the London Stock Exchange (LSE).

I ended up getting the job and started work in the 'Operations' team. This was a team who were the first line of defence when it came to the IT systems and operated 24 hours a day, 7 days a week. We effectively observed any strange happenings and then after initial diagnosis, called someone more qualified to deal with it.

I worked my way up from Shift Operator to Shift Manager and then transitioned out of the anti-social shift work into other roles within the LSE. I first worked as a Service Manager - the person who sits between the IT department and business and breaks the bad news to the business. Later I became a Service Introduction Manager - the person who is responsible to ensure that when a project team finish their project and hand over to live

---

[*] I was in the Scout movement from aged 6 to 21 and thoroughly recommend getting your kids involved, if you have any. An interesting fact for you. Of the 24 astronauts that travelled to the Moon during the Apollo space program, 20 were once Scouts. And eleven of the twelve astronauts that walked on the Moon during the Apollo space program were once Scouts. And all three members of the Apollo 13 mission. Just saying...

service support teams, everything necessary to support and update the service is in place. I also worked as a Project Manager running teams to deliver new initiatives to the LSE.

All this time, I still didn't feel like I had found what I was uniquely put on this Earth for. I didn't feel that I was in a career. I felt like I was in a job. I seemed to have just fallen into it. I didn't have any real direction or leadership in my life. My life plan had only extended as far as university. Somehow, I spent six years at the LSE. The first three for Accenture, then the last three directly employed by the LSE. I was never unhappy. I wasn't fulfilled either. I felt like I wanted to leave. However, I didn't know what I wanted to do instead.

And then it wasn't my choice. Following the 2008 financial crisis, the LSE made several redundancies from 2008 to 2010. In the middle of 2010, my team was all made redundant. All except me. I think it was due to a technicality (not wanting to report so many redundancies to the press). A few months later, I was able to secure redundancy myself, as I felt that if ever there was a sign to move on, then this was it. So, I took it. I decided to use the redundancy opportunity as just that. An opportunity to finally move to something else. What was that going to be though?

In 2006, I got interested in personal development, psychology, and self-development courses. By 2010, I had already been on a couple of courses, invested in audio programs and read plenty of books. Some of it even stuck and had had a positive effect. I had only really skirted around the topics though.

In 2010, I felt I wanted to take my understanding of one topic a lot deeper. That of NLP. Neuro Linguistic Programming. Effectively, NLP is a collection of tools and a way of understanding how we do what we do. It's a communication method really. Understanding how we communicate with ourselves and others. I decided to go on a course about NLP getting my Master Practitioner qualification. And that set me off down the rabbit hole[†].

What I mean by rabbit hole is that, yes, I discovered some amazing things from NLP. How to change behaviours and get results quicker than previously thought. How to control that voice in my head, understand goals and master my mind to some greater degree. But that's not what I really mean by sending

---

[†] Hopefully you're familiar with the book *Alice in Wonderland*, and my reference to a rabbit hole.

me down the rabbit hole. I ended up meeting some interesting people, who then led me to other interesting events. One such event was the one with 2000 people I spoke about at the beginning of this book. It was the catalyst event.

And it was by going to these events that I got to interact with and observe other people who were high performing people. They helped shift my thinking on many topics. From what it takes to be successful, to what it means to be healthy, to age, to have vitality and to feel energised.

And by going to these events, I learnt about what books to read, which people to pay attention to, which documentaries to watch. The concepts, ideas, and ways to operate in life. I became a student again. This time learning something I was even more passionate about than Physics. Life!

And that set me on a road of exploration and discovery. I started noticing that seven out of ten successful people did 'x', eight out of ten high performers did 'y', nine out of ten talked about 'z'. And on it went. I noticed the patterns. I tested to see how adopting the philosophies affected me. I kept what worked and ditched what didn't. Just like Bruce Lee suggested.

"Absorb what is useful, discard what is not, and add what is uniquely yours."

– Bruce Lee

After several years of taking on board the new practices that I'd been learning, I thought that there must be some pattern to it all. After listing down everything that I had changed in my life on a giant sheet of paper, I saw the pattern. I saw that they naturally fell into just four main areas.

Everything that I had adopted in my life fell into one of these four areas. *The four foundational forces to living with health, vitality, and energy.*

And since making this discovery I've noticed that everything new that I've subsequently learnt, also falls into one of these four areas. I also noticed that some other people came to similar conclusions, albeit not as comprehensively. I guess the truth is the truth. So, several people will arrive at the same destination.

Discovery

The four areas became *The Leadership BEAT Model*™. The subject of this book. Each of the letters from the word BEAT represent an area of focus. In the next chapter, we'll look at what these areas are. Throughout the book, we'll examine each area in detail, understanding what needs to happen in each area to have the health, vitality, energy and longevity you need to lead yourself optimally and be, not only the best self-leader you can be, but the best human – a *super*human.

========

0.2 The Leadership BEAT Model™
The Four Forces for Superhuman Living

> *"When your desires are strong enough, you will appear to possess superhuman powers to achieve."*
>
> *- Napoleon Hill*

The Leadership BEAT Model™. That's the foundation to everything I do now. It's how I optimise myself mentally, physically, emotionally, and spiritually. I know, that when *The Leadership BEAT Model™* is understood and applied, life is never the same again.

When you get it, you find yourself not being at the mercy of circumstances around you. You become your own driving force behind your mental and physical health and wellbeing. You become your own leadership guru.

Figure 1 - The Leadership BEAT Model™

What's the BEAT?

The word BEAT in *The Leadership BEAT Model*™ stands for this: BRAIN, ELEMENTS, ACTIVITY and TRANQUILITY*. These are the four forces that determine lasting long-term success in life. Why? Because to achieve in life, you must have the energy, health and vitality to go out and do the necessary. It doesn't matter whether you have all the strategies, tools and techniques at your disposal. If you don't have the energy to execute on all your ideas, you won't get far.

My study on high performing individuals – *super*humans - if you like, is this. They have a balance from all four areas if they are successful over the long-term. Sure, you can be successful by just focussing on one area, but for how long? A few months? Several years? A couple of decades even? At some stage though, the house will come crumbling down.

Let's look at each section and what it means.

Figure 2 - The Four Forces for Health, Vitality and Wellbeing

---

* Note that tranquility is the more common US and international spelling of tranquillity (British spelling). Due to the international nature of my work, and preference for use, I spell it as tranquility in my model, and therefore also in this book.

B – BRAIN

Everything starts with the mind. BRAIN is a metaphor for your mind, mindset, psychology and intellectual growth and development. How you handle your emotions, the identity you have for yourself, the language you use to describe the world around you. Your beliefs and your values in life.

My first book (and the name of my company) is called *The Thought Gym®*.

Why? I realised that first we must *train the mind, so the rest will follow.* Think about it.

How many times have you known someone to start the gym, go on a new diet or health kick, only to falter and fall back to the old behavioural patterns? If there is lasting change, then fundamentally there would have been a shift in mindset that proceeded it. Until the mindset changes, it's exceedingly difficult to change everything else. To paraphrase the late great spiritual speaker, Dr Wayne Dyer, you must change the way you look at things, for the things you look at to change.

"Change the way you look at things, and the things you look at will change."

– Wayne Dyer

This section, BRAIN, is all about the power of your mind. In my first book *The Thought Gym®*, I go into some depth on the power of the unconscious mind, our values and beliefs. How to recognise them and shift them to be more in line with who we want to be. There are fundamental ways our mind works and when we understand them, we can control how we think and how we show up in the world.

BRAIN isn't only about our thoughts though. It's also about how we feed our minds. How we learn and grow through exploration. How we need that learning to help us feel alive and give us energy.

SUPER VITALITY

Think about it for a second. Have you ever attended the same place of work, day after day, year after year, and then one day, you go to work but this day something is different? It's different because after months of begging your boss, you are finally going on that course that you have always wanted to go on. You're excited. Energised. And yet, you are still going to the same building. Taking the same commute to work. Why? Because learning and growth also gives us energy. If we don't grow, we die. Slowly, maybe? But die, all the same. Everything in nature either grows or dies. It doesn't stay still. If we, as humans, stagnate, and don't learn and grow, we die. Energetically, one day at a time. We'll look at that more in the B - BRAIN section.

"Anyone who stops learning is old, whether at twenty or eighty. Anyone who keeps learning stays young. The greatest thing in life is to keep your mind young."

– Henry Ford

E – ELEMENTS

The ELEMENTS section is all about how you nourish your body. From the inside-out to the outside-in. The elements of old Greek† culture are Air, Water, Earth, Fire and Aether. This section uses those elements as a metaphor for how you need to nourish your body.

---

† I am Greek, so of course, it's fitting!

Air

Air is a metaphor for the power and importance of breath. When it comes to energy, people should first be looking towards the breath from a nutrient perspective. The body needs air more than it needs a coffee in the morning. Think about this. How long can the average person go without food before dying? A few weeks, to a couple of months even. What about water? That's a few days. And what about air? A few minutes, at most. Incidentally, the record for holding a breath is 29 minutes[2]. Now, that *is* superhuman. We don't need to hold our breath for 29 minutes to feel and be superhuman. However, understanding the importance and implications of breathwork will help you feel superhuman.

Water

Water is a metaphor for, well, water. Water is much more complex than just "drink water". There are different classes of water and getting the best quality water into your system is vital if you are to feel energised and vibrant. We will explore more the role that water plays in our health and how much is optimal in this book.

Earth

Earth is a metaphor for the food we eat, as well as our relationship to the earth. Food is a highly contentious issue, and you can get bogged down by the intricacies of it all. I will make it simple for you right now though. If there's one way to understand what is best to eat, it's this: **EAT REAL FOOD**. Everything else is additional. We will cover a simple way of understanding the vital role food plays and how to best make a plate of food up. We will also investigate a recent discovery called 'Grounding' (also known as 'Earthing') and how the physical contact that you have with the Earth effects your wellbeing. Everything from your stress hormone (cortisol) to inflammation (believed to be the primary cause of most disease in the body), to sleep and even jet lag.

Fire

Fire is a metaphor for the sun, being outdoors, nature and the power of light in helping us feel superhuman. Over the last century, the invention and proliferation of the light bulb (thank you Thomas Edison) has brought about great change. We can work all hours, and indoors. The advancement of our society has meant we are working more and more inside with less exposure

SUPER VITALITY

to the sun. A vital source of our health, vitality and energy. Simply stated, we need to get out more. Spend more time outside and in nature. This we intuitively know makes us feel good. In this section, we'll look more into that.

Aether

Aether is what the Ancient Greeks believed was a pervasive energy all around us. Enveloping us. In this context and metaphor, Aether is our environment. From our physical environment - for example, do you feel energised when your house is tidy and has had a spring clean? And, how set up your environment is to promote health and wellbeing. Also, the environment you put on your body (sun creams, lotions, shampoos, make-up and the rest), to the invisible environment so dominant now. The world of EMF's (electromagnetic frequencies) that come from our phones, tablets, Wi-Fi routers, mobile/cell phone towers and even every electrical device in use.

Those are the five components within the ELEMENTS section: Air, Water, Earth, Fire and Aether.

A – ACTIVITY

ACTIVITY is about everything that you do in a day. People may think of ACTIVITY as exercise. Exercise, while important and energising, is not all that ACTIVITY is about. In fact, more than exercise, it's important to incorporate movement into your day. Regular movement. Exercise does not compensate for movement deficiencies, as we'll discover later. ACTIVITY is more than just exercise and movement. It's about everything else you do in a day. Whether you have passion, service, purpose and connection (what I call PSPC). Do you have fun, laugh and surround yourself with energising and inspiring people? Do you also position yourself (your body) for optimal energy? Your posture in this case. The rituals you have. Do they support you?

T – TRANQUILITY

TRANQUILITY is all about how you rest, restore and regenerate yourself. It might be in terms of the more obvious and much talked about topic of sleep. And sleep is important. In fact, I used to suffer in regard to sleep, and so I made it a priority to optimise. I even decided to design a whole course around sleep, which you can learn more about at **https://thethoughtgym.com/supervitality**. Sleep is not the complete picture though.

I know that I can sleep well, but still not be maximising the tranquility I need. TRANQUILITY incorporates subjects such as meditation, fasting, digital nutrition (dieting & detoxing), holidays, massage (and other body work), yoga, tai-chi, qigong, flotation tanks and more.

Figure 3 below gives a visual representation of many of the components that go into *The Leadership BEAT Model*™. As you will be able to see, the philosophy of *The Leadership BEAT Model*™ is both simple yet comprehensive, encompassing many factors that go into health, wellbeing, vitality, energy and becoming superhuman.

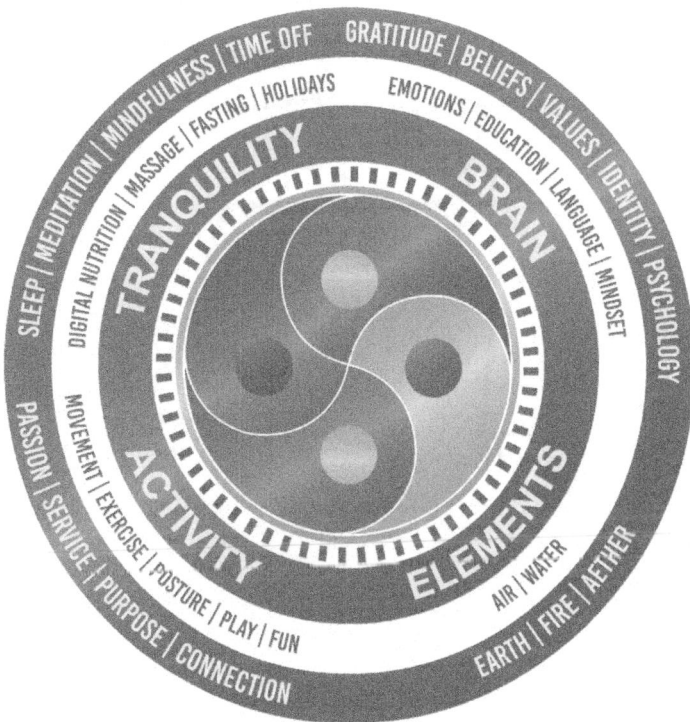

Figure 3 - The Subsections of The Leadership BEAT Model™

SUPER VITALITY

Let's get stuck into the real juice of the book now. I know that there is a lot in here. You might even have your own beliefs and thoughts about what I'm about to share with you. What I would suggest though, is much like I did when learning this information, follow Bruce Lee's wisdom when reading this book (and indeed when learning from both me and other teachers and experts):

"Absorb what is useful, discard what is not, and add what is uniquely yours."

– Bruce Lee

Part 1: BRAIN

Where it all starts…

---

*"All that we are is the result of what we have thought.
The mind is everything. What we think, we become."*

- Buddha

The first section of this model is B, for BRAIN. BRAIN is a metaphor for your psychology or mindset as well as education, learning and growth intellectually.

I worked out many years ago, that everything really starts in the mind. Hence why deciding to name my company *The Thought Gym*® back in 2010. Whatever we aim to do in life first starts with the seed of a thought. And when we fail at something - for example a new health regime, new diet, new habit, it's mostly because we haven't shifted the mindset. We aim to change behaviours without first addressing the mindset behind them. When that happens, we are prone to repeat the same behaviours over and over.

Think about when you've made some drastic change and it stuck - for good. I am willing to bet that there was some fundamental shift in your mindset first. You might not have even been aware of it but something in you must have changed. Especially if the change, suddenly, seemed easy.

I think that this happened for me when I shifted my diet quite dramatically several years ago. More on that later, but for now, suffice it to say, the change was big. It was so far from my normal pattern of eating that people did (and still do) think it must be a challenge for me. The truth is, it never has been. My mindset shifted so much that it's just not in my consciousness to even think about the old pattern of eating.

Do you remember when you were a child? Did you love going into the sweet (candy) shop on the way home from school? Grabbing a Curly Wurly chocolate bar, fizz wiz (classic UK sweets from the 80's!) or whatever else it was for you? Now though... Do you still crave them when you go into a sweet shop? I am willing to bet that you are not even aware that they are there. There is no struggle to avoid buying them. You've just grown out of them. Sure, you might be tempted more today with a Snickers bar, or Twix, but the ones you liked as a child? They are not in your conscious awareness, and you probably could say no to them very easily.

That is what happened to me with my diet. It isn't a struggle for me. I've mentally 'grown out of' the old style of eating. My mindset about it changed.

To understand this concept about thoughts being so fundamental, it helps to understand what I call - *The Thought Cycle.*

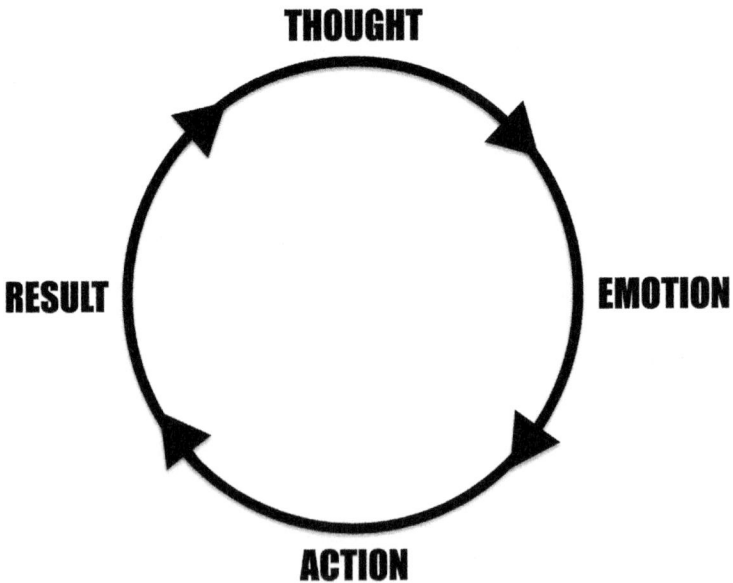

THOUGHT

RESULT

EMOTION

ACTION

Figure 4 - The Thought Cycle (aka The TEAR Model)

If we agree that everything starts with a thought. From the idea for this book, to the laptop I'm writing on right now, to the clothes you are wearing. They were all first an idea - a thought - in someone's mind.

A thought then leads to emotion. Depending on that emotion, you will undertake action. This leads to a result which then will re-enforce the original thought. It helps to understand this by way of example.

34

Let's say you want to run the London Marathon. As we want to raise money for a good cause, challenge ourselves and (for some) prove that we've still 'got it'!

Imagine two people - Robin and Alex. Neither has run a marathon before.

Robin thinks to himself. "Boy this is hard. I've never done a marathon before. I've not even exercised since school! I'm not a runner."

These thoughts lead to an emotion. In Robin's case, it might be one of dread, fear, apprehension or overwhelm.

And the action that Robin then takes? He procrastinates on training. Robin keeps putting it off and coming up with excuses. He goes for a few runs before the big day but nothing significant.

The result? On marathon day, he suffers. He might make it round, but it's painful. He has cramp, finishes slow and then suffers for weeks afterwards.

This then re-enforces Robin's original thought about it being hard. Being no good at running.

Contrast that to Alex. She's never done a marathon before either. Her thoughts go something like this. "Wow, what a challenge ahead of me. I've never run this distance before, but I've always been good at giving new challenges a go. It's going to teach me new skills and disciplines in training for this."

And so, Alex starts to feel good, excited and happy about the marathon.

She then acts. She buys running magazines and joins a running club. She gets the right trainers and partners up with a running buddy. She looks at her nutrition and starts cutting back on her partying, opting to get up for early morning runs instead.

Her result. She runs the marathon and sure it's a challenge, but she makes it round with no injuries. She gets the time she thought she would, and it doesn't take her too long to recover after she has completed the marathon. And her conclusion? Yes, she can turn her hand to anything she wants and make a success of it.

And when the next challenge presents itself, she draws on this result. This becomes a cycle. For both Robin and Alex.

SUPER VITALITY

The Thought Cycle is important to understand as it dictates a lot in life. You can interrupt this cycle at any part of it. The two most usual places are the thoughts or the action part.

We can change what we do and achieve a different result. Imagine you are at a party or business function, and your thought is that it is a rubbish event. Your thoughts are focussed on the fact the person you want to be there, isn't. The food is terrible. The lighting is too bright. You feel bored, frustrated and your result for the evening is that you have no fun, make no new contacts or business.

Imagine though your friend or colleague insists that you dance. You don't want to but are 'forced' to. Suddenly, you start to have fun. Endorphins are flowing, and you think - "well, maybe this is fun!" Your thoughts start towards how great it is that you can hang out with the friends and colleagues who are here. Deepening those bonds, and you can be yourself. And thus, the downward spiral is broken.

It's also possible that you break *The Thought Cycle* at another point in it. You may one day get a fluke win at Golf (or some other game or competition). Whereas once you thought that you were not a winner, and all your past references corroborated that. Suddenly you get a different result. It's a fluke. It changes your thinking though. Suddenly you think you might have a winner's edge. And you begin a new *Thought Cycle*.

The Thought Cycle can lead you to succeed or to succumb.

In the following chapters, we are going to dive more into this. You'll understand what part your unconscious mind plays in all this, how to change and manage your mood at will and more on what role your mindset plays in your success and health.

========

1.1 The Unconscious Mind

Train the mind, and the rest will follow™...

"Our heart glows, and secret unrest gnaws at the root of our being. Dealing with the unconscious has become a question of life for us."

- Carl Jung

Now that we understand *The Thought Cycle*. Let's take a closer look under the bonnet of our minds.

Conscious and Unconscious Mind

You may already be familiar with this idea that we have different minds. Our conscious mind. The mind that makes decisions that we are aware of. The mind we *think* is calling the shots. You can imagine that the conscious mind is like the tip of an iceberg shown in Figure 5. As you can see with the iceberg, what you see above the water, is only a small part of what's going on. Beneath the surface is the bulk of the iceberg. It is what is supporting the bit above the water. Stronger, more powerful, and more dangerous (especially if you happen to be on the Titanic).

Figure 5 - Our Conscious and Unconscious Mind – Iceberg Metaphor

You can think of the unconscious (sometimes referred to as the subconscious) as the part of the iceberg that is submerged. Hidden. It's more powerful than the conscious mind. It makes many of our decisions for us. It holds our habits, beliefs, values and more.

Some things to know about the unconscious mind. Its primary directive is to keep you safe. Secure. So sometimes you might not understand why you've done what you've done, but on some level, your unconscious feels that it is in your best interest.

I often tell my coaching clients to think of the unconscious mind a bit like a 5-year-old child. It can take things personally. It doesn't have a real concept of the future or past like we do consciously. For your unconscious, that time when you were made fun of at school when you were asked to speak up, is still bothering them. Sure, you (as an adult) may have moved on, but you can't figure out why you hate public speaking, or why your throat dries up. Your unconscious is trying to save you from something.

Things to understand about the unconscious mind:

- Safety - its primary objective is to keep you safe and alive.
- Present Day - it acts as if everything is happening in the present.
- Habits - it maintains instincts and generates habits (although needs repetition).

- Perceptions - it controls and maintains our perceptions.
- Literal - it takes things literally (it is a 5-year-old, after all!), and personally!
- Symbolic - it uses and responds to symbols.
- Organised - it stores and organises your memories.
- Emotions - it's the domain of the emotions.
- Serves - it's like a personal butler. It enjoys serving and needs clear orders to follow.

Our unconscious mind really is the driving force behind us. You might have found yourself doing something and then moments later thinking "why did I do that?". Perhaps it was when you bought a packet of crisps or chips? Well, in my case that's sometimes the problem!

I am a lot more conscious of my actions in the moment though, so I don't usually unconsciously buy a packet of crisps or portion of chips. If I do, I'm aware I'm doing it and why. How many people unconsciously on their way to work just stop into a coffee shop to buy their regular coffee. Not even maybe needing it. Just through habit. Then add a croissant to the mix too.

I'm not saying either is good or bad. Just that the actions we take are often mostly driven by our unconscious. That powerful part of ourselves that keeps us ticking. I think I've been aware of the power of the subconscious mind my entire life – even prior to formally learning about it. I remember trying to utilise the power of the unconscious when sleeping when I was around 7 or 8 years old. How did a 7-year-old use his powerful unconscious mind. I used to put my spelling books underneath my pillow when I slept! Yes, it's true. And maths problems and other things I wanted to 'learn' while asleep. I have since learnt that this might have had some benefit. In a couple of ways really. Firstly, it was typically the last thing I would think about before falling asleep, so it would be 'priming'* my unconscious mind for the night. And secondly, even perhaps subtly feeling the books under my pillow, would trigger my sleeping mind to think about what's in them overnight. It's interesting (to me at least) that I used to do this over 40 years ago, intuitively thinking it would do some good. And I have to say, anecdotally at least, that I always performed better when I did it usually getting at least 10 out of 12 on the tests. On the

---

* Priming is the process of seeding your brain with an idea or concept. Advertisements do this all the time. As do mind-magicians (sometimes called mentalists) like Derren Brown to get you to do/say things they want you to.

times I didn't do it, I remember getting no more than 4 out of 10. Go figure.

Cause vs Effect

To be a superhuman self-leader, we must first understand that we must start to take responsibility for ourselves. At some point, we can't look to blame others for what is going on in our lives. It's to do with the principle of (being at) cause or (at) effect.

Sure, we might have had lousy parents (and how you are raised is super important, there's no denying that), but at some point, we must step up and take responsibility. It doesn't mean that you are to blame, but you can still ask yourself how you might have held some responsibility for the situation, or how you can take responsibility from *now* to move forward.

When you become responsible, you become response-*ABLE*. If you take no responsibility, you then have no *ability* to respond. No power to change the outcome, or the future.

Again, it's not about blame. An example I often cite in my trainings is that of a new CEO who comes in and takes over a failing company. Sure, she can't really be to blame for what happened before she even arrived at the company, but she can stand there and address the employees, the shareholders and the public and take responsibility for where the company is right now. Then she can move forward.

Recently I was on my way somewhere important, and I started to get frustrated as everything seemed to be going wrong. The trains were busy, and I couldn't get on. Then there was traffic on the roads and people in front of me at the ticket window were taking ages to get their tickets. I was just about on time, but I still ended up a little flustered on arrival.

Was I to blame for any of that? No. How was I responsible for the situation though? What part did I play? Well, for one, I left too late. I wasn't prepared early enough and didn't leave myself enough time to get there. As soon as I identified what part I was responsible for, I then had a way to fix it. This is the idea behind cause and effect. You can live your life 'at effect' of everything else or be 'at cause'.

You can say that the reason that you're not doing so well in your business is because of the economy, or the government or anything else. But are there people succeeding despite the economy, and under the same government?

Yes. Absolutely. Microsoft, Federal Express (FedEx), General Motors, Uber, Mailchimp, Airbnb and General Electric were all started during recessions. There are countless others.

If you live *at effect* of things, then you buy into some 'story'. Some 'story' that you can't do anything about it. That it's someone else's fault. When you live *at cause* you take responsibility for your life and everything in it. Good and bad. You are the captain of your own ship. You hold the pen, and you are writing your own story.

As change-makers, leaders, and self-leaders, I believe, that we would do well to learn to live *at cause*. And it could well be that there are areas of our lives when we might be *at cause* and other areas when we might be *at effect*. One way to tell is to see if you are making excuses about something. A giveaway is using the word 'because'.

"I'm not successful *because…*"

"I'm not able to make more money *because…*"

On one side of the equation, we have reasons, on the other results.

CAUSE > EFFECT

RESULTS or REASONS

Once we accept to live *at cause* then we can truly make great changes. I'm not saying that the other stuff doesn't play a part. Of course, it does. But if you get bogged down in that thinking, think about whether there are other people out there who experienced the same (or worse) situations but are still succeeding. Chances are, that you will find them.

So that's the first step towards becoming your superhuman self. Learning to take response*ABILITY* and living 'at cause'. Only when you start to be responsible for everything that's happening to you can you have the power to change – can you be RESPONSE-ABLE.

You might be reading this and have said in the past:

"Well, I can't cook decent food because… I don't have time."

"I don't exercise because… I don't know how."

"I'm not where I want to be in my career because… everyone else who gets promoted went to university."

Just reasons. Just excuses.

By picking up and reading this book though, I already know that this is a principle that you - at least on some level - are aware off. You have taken responsibility for your own development by reading this book in the first place. I don't think I need to labour the point anymore. Just be aware of it in case there are areas of your life where you might be living *at effect* rather than *at cause*. As in my experience, we can live different aspects of our lives on different sides of the cause > effect equation.

The H.A.B.I.T. MODEL™

Our unconscious mind is in control of many of our behaviours. These habits form over time. Each time we do something, activity sparks in our brain. Energy fires between the synapses of the brain neurons. The more times events are associated together, the stronger the bond between the synapses. It is like seeing a path that's worn down in the grass in the park from where runners keep running. The more times it is run on, the stronger the path that is created. Another way to understand it, is to look at a copper wire. The wire can be thought of as the carrier of the behaviour. What keeps in the signal of the wire, is the insulating case around it. Our brains have a similar insulating facility called myelin. The more we repeat behaviours the stronger this myelin sheath (copper wire insulation) becomes.

When we keep doing something - either consciously, or unconsciously - we form these strong connections.

I created *The H.A.B.I.T. Model*™ to help you change your habits. It stands for the *Habit and Behavioural Improvement Transformation Model*. Okay, so I might have shoehorned that title to fit the word "habit" as an acronym, but still.

I discovered that there are seven stages in changing a habit. It is based on my own experiences of being successful in replacing habits. I'll share the model and then explain the model with an example from my own life.

Also notice that I say replacing a habit rather than breaking a habit. And it's called the habit transformation because habits can't be broken as such. They can only be replaced with (or transformed to) other habits. In experiments on habits, it has been observed that original pathways still remain, so the way to 'break' a habit is to create stronger alternative pathways[3]. It's as if once the tarmac has been laid to make the road, it doesn't get dug up, so we must build a better, faster more effective road and make it easier to travel along instead of the original road.

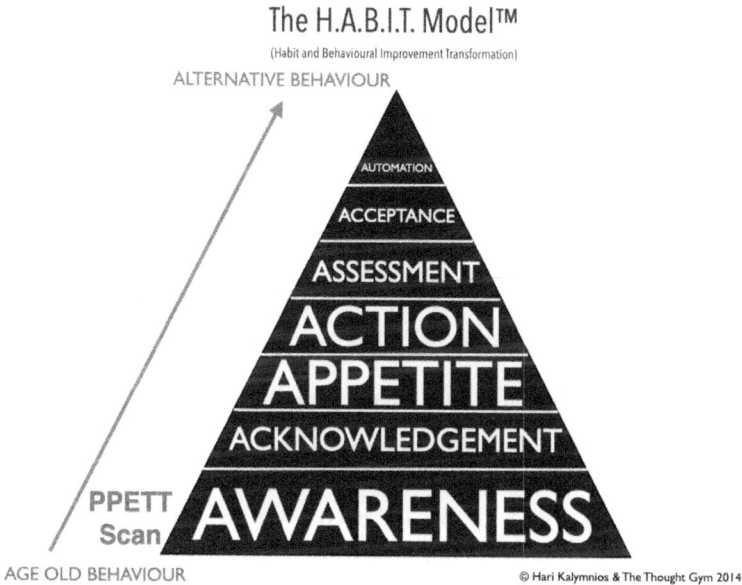

Figure 6 - The H.A.B.I.T. Model

Step 1 – Awareness

To first be able to change a habit, you must first be aware of it. How do you become aware? You see, we're not always aware of our habits. It could be grinding our teeth or always cutting someone short at meetings. It could be grabbing a cookie at a meeting when you shouldn't.

In my case, someone made me aware of something. Since childhood, I used to suffer with my sinuses. As a kid, I had nose bleeds, earaches, a blocked or runny nose and even had my nose cauterised – twice! And then in 2006 my younger sister told me that consuming dairy might be negatively affecting my sinuses. Something that she had recently heard about. I had no idea about that, but her telling me brought it into my awareness. So, the habit I needed to change was consuming dairy.

B - BRAIN

What if you don't have someone else to tell you? How do you become aware? That's where a PPETT scan comes in. If you've heard of a PET scan (Positron Emission Tomography) used in medicine, well, it's nothing like that. A traditional PET scan is used to create a three-dimensional image of the body. This PPETT scan for the H.A.B.I.T. Model is used to help you become aware of what needs to change.

PPETT Scan

- **P - People**
- **P - Place**
- **E - Emotion**
- **T - Time**
- **T - Trigger**

This is how the PPETT Scan works (this is my own spin on the process referred to in the book *The Power of Habit*, by Charles Duhigg).

For the period of a week or so, notice what's going on when the thing happens.

P - People (or pets)

Who is around you - what people (or pets)? Are you always smoking a cigarette when Pete from accounting is around?

P – Place

Is it only in certain places that this thing happens? Are you only smoking when at work, or at the pub?

E – Emotion

What are your emotions at the time that this thing happens? Do you only reach for a cigarette when you are feeling bored? Or stressed? Lonely, embarrassed, relaxed, accomplished? Make a note of how you are feeling.

T – Time

Does this always happen at the same time of day? Is it always in the evening, or morning? Take a note and see if the same time each time this thing happens.

T – Trigger

Is there a specific trigger that is the same each time? Is it every time you come out of a meeting with your boss, or your team?

Once you take a note of the PPETT scan for several days in a row, you will see the patterns. Maybe (in our example above) you only smoke when you get triggered by a stressful meeting. Sometimes you are frustrated, sometimes not. But it's always the same meeting that does it to you.

In my case, had I done a PPETT scan, I would have noticed that my sinuses were worse with certain triggers. i.e., dairy products. Naturally my sinuses were bad at other times too, like when I exercised, but that was on account of all the dairy in my system and that I never really gave it a break. Now that I don't eat dairy, I sometimes play around and consume something that can trigger it. I make a note and now I know what can affect me. Unfortunately, the list is long! Dairy, wheat (and gluten), yeast, sulphites and fried food. Which is fine as I don't consume most of those now anyway - other than very occasionally.

Step 2 – Acknowledgement

Even though back in 2006 my sister made me aware that dairy could be affecting my sinuses. I didn't acknowledge it. I refused to believe it. I often meet people today who come up to me after I share this example with them. And they tell me how they are hearing this news for the first time. That is understandable as I went 30 years without hearing about it. I think the science is unclear on establishing a firm link, but you don't have to wait for science. If you have sinus issues of any sort, just cut out dairy for a month and notice the results of your own experiment.

Even though I had awareness, I still needed to *acknowledge* the potential link. Otherwise, I would be reluctant to change.

I didn't acknowledge the link at first. It took about two years!

Step 3 – Appetite

Once I acknowledged that there was a potential link – which didn't happen until 2008, I had to *want* to want to change my habit of consuming dairy. Even when you become aware, and then acknowledge the potential cause, you still must *want* to change. Have the *appetite* for change.

B - BRAIN

Eventually, sick of constantly being embarrassed by blowing my nose in the yoga classes I had recently started going to, I found the appetite to give it a go. Which leads to the next step.

Step 4 – Action

For things to change, we must act. There are no two ways about it. I had to act. What action? Well, replacing dairy with either nothing, or in the case of my cereal and tea - that I enjoyed at the time - replacing it with soymilk[†].

Having acted, I then needed to complete the following step.

Step 5 – Assessment

To see whether something's working or not, we must *assess* it. Check whether what we are doing is producing the desired result. In my case, did my sinuses improve? In short, yes, they did.

We assess whether the change we are making is working for us. Even then, there are another couple of important steps before we can transform this habit.

Step 6 – Acceptance

We may now be aware of the problem. We may have even acted, changed our behaviour for a short period of time and seen that it worked. Then we must *accept* the new behaviour. In my case, it was to stop consuming dairy. That meant not only different milk in tea and cereal. But also, no more cakes, cookies, and a whole host of other foods. If you want to see just how much dairy is in the food system, just look at the labels of everything you buy. You will find a disproportionate amount of food has milk in it, even when you can't think how or why.

Luckily for me, I did accept it. I know many people who change their diets, discover that the cause of their problems was a result of something they were eating, but still refuse to accept the new alternative.

Once we accept it, we move on to the last step.

[†] I now am aware of the plethora of other milks out there, like hemp, almond, oat, rice, coconut and so on, but I wasn't back in 2008.

46

Step 7 – Automation

For the new habit to truly take form we must make it *automatic*. Otherwise, we run the risk of always finding a challenge to keep it up. If every time I was offered chocolate at work (which I was at the time - repeatedly), I would have to fight some internal battle or make a conscious decision to refrain. I would then tire out my energy reserves quickly. And willpower. Willpower is thought to be a finite resource (although there is some debate about this now in psychology circles. Some stating that willpower depletion only factors in, if you believe it does[4]) and if I kept having to use it to say no to things, by the end of the day all hell would break loose!

To make the habit automatic, you can employ various tools. You will need conscious repetition over some period before it becomes habit. Anything from a few weeks to a couple of months. In one study as reported in the European Journal of Social Psychology, they found it took the 96 participants an average of 66 days to form the new habit to override the old. And anywhere from 18 to 254 days[5].

Ways to Automate

In short, to instil a new habit, you must make it easy to do and automatic. And to replace a bad habit, you must make it difficult to do. There are some ways that this can be done, even using things like the power of a Swish pattern, taken from NLP and that I describe in detail in my first book, *The Thought Gym*®.

Swish Pattern

There are techniques within NLP that can help with automating change. In my first book, *The Thought Gym*®, I describe how to do a Swish Pattern. It's essentially where you take an image (that you would create in your head) of the old habit and replace it with another image of what you want instead. For example, I used to love walking into McDonald's. Even after I stopped eating meat, I would still go in for chips. What I did was to replace the image of the golden arches, so that whenever I saw that image, an image of Muscle Beach in California, USA would jump into my head. The golden arches would transform into someone lifting weights. I know it sounds weird, but it worked.

The following is adapted from my book *The Thought Gym*® to help with understanding the Swish Pattern.

=========

First read it all the way through and perhaps it might be helpful to get someone to guide you through it. Closing your eyes to do this process often helps, so be sure to know the steps first or go to **http://thethoughtgym.com/supervitality** for the guided support.

1. Think of the image that comes to your mind when you think of the habit you wish to change. The 'bad' habit. We'll call this the *Present State*.

2. Associate into that image – in other words, if you're not already looking through your own eyes, step into the image and notice how you feel.

3. OK, step out and clear the screen. Open your eyes and think of something else. Who's your favourite author?

4. Now create a new image to match the habit you wish instead. For example, if your image earlier was the gym and not feeling or looking comfortable in there, change the image to one more inspiring for you like running along the beach feeling happy.

5. Be fully associated into the image – notice the colours, sounds, feelings that you have.

6. Good, now while maintaining that image, step out of it (i.e., become disassociated so you can see yourself in it and you are not looking through your own eyes). We'll call this the *Desired State*.

7. OK, break your state and think of something else. What was the last movie you went to see?

8. Bring back the Present State image (from steps 1 and 2). Now fully associate back into it.

9. Insert a small dark picture of the desired state from step 6 into the lower left corner of the other image.

10. Make sure you can see yourself in that little image.

11. Now for the swish part.

12. While making a swish sound, simultaneously have your Desired State (the one from step 6) become bigger and brighter while at the same time have your Present State image (from step 1 which represents that value) become small and shrink into nothing in the lower left-hand corner.

13. Open your eyes and clear your mind. Think of something else. Who do you most admire?

14. Repeat steps 8 to 13 again, this time a little faster.

15. Keep on repeating steps 8-14, getting faster and faster each time. Do this at least 15 times, remembering to break your state after each time and clear your mind.

Once you've done it at least 15 times, now try and think of that old (unserving) habit and see what image comes to mind. Does the old image appear, or is the change so fast that the new desired image appears? If not, go back and repeat the process until you get it. It takes a bit of practice at first because it's something new and different so persevere. As Pablo Picasso once said,

"I am always doing that which I cannot do, in order that I may learn how to do it."

– Pablo Picasso

For around 20% of people, the image starting from the bottom right-hand side of the screen might work better, so experiment a little and see what works for you.

=========

Creating and Replacing Habits

Some good names to supplement your understanding of habits, in addition to Charles Duhigg and his book, *The Power of Habit*, mentioned above, are the books by James Clear called *Atomic Habits*, and Stanford professor BJ Fogg's book, *Tiny Habits*. I've replicated (albeit with some of my own terminology) James Clear's three-part strategy for creating and replacing habits below, which can be used to make it easier to automate the habit process.

B - BRAIN
Creating New Habits (adapted from *Atomic Habits* by James Clear)

There are three stages to creating a new habit and making it automated. You want to make the new habit:

- **Intentional**
- **Effortless**
- **Enjoyable**.

1. *Intentional*

Be intentional in creating the habit. Do it deliberately. This part of being intentional has three components to it.

1. CIA

CIA stands for Choices in Advance. I go into more detail on this in chapter 3.5 when I talk about rituals. For now, this is about deciding in advance what you are going to do. For example, when I finish my shower, I will drop and do five press ups. Choice (or decision) is made ahead of time.

2. Anchoring

In brief, anchoring is where you attach (or anchor) a new habit to one that you already do. For example, when you make your cup of coffee in the morning (your existing habit), you do five squats (your new habit being 'anchored' to the existing one). See a few pages further on in the section called Habit Anchoring (Stacking) for a fuller explanation.

3. Environment

This means set up the environment for success. For example, I have installed a pull-up bar in the doorway of my office, so I can do a single pull up when I enter or leave the office. I've also placed a rebounder (mini trampoline) between the door and the desk, so I am more likely to use, instead of having it stored away.

2. *Effortless*

Make sure that creating a new habit is easy.

1. Micro habits

Start small with new habits. Rather than asking my clients to go from drinking no water a day (as some are) to two or three litres a day, I ask them to just drink one glass. Or maybe just buy a water bottle. Not even fill it. Just buy it. Think of the smallest possible step you can take and take that.

2. Culture

Be in a culture where it's the norm to do the new habit you want to adopt. If you want to get healthy, then join a company, or group where that's what they already do. And you'll be swept up along for the ride.

3. Advance Prep

If you want to go to the gym in the mornings, then prepare what you need ahead of time. If, like me, you want to juice in the morning, then prepare your vegetables the night before. If I'm going to be in a rush in the morning, it's a lot more likely that I will juice and make my smoothies when I have already set up the vegetables (soaking in water, pre-chopped) and all the smoothie ingredients. All my nuts and seeds are already pre-mixed, and I even have the spoon in the Tupperware ready to use.

4. Environment

Like above, when it comes to environment. Make the environment set up so that you do the thing that you want to do. It's easy for me to walk to the shops to buy food rather than drive, as I've set up my environment so that I don't have a car and I don't need one to walk to the shops.

5. Use technology to automate

Using technology to automate the process can make things effortless. If you want to save for a holiday, rather than having to put money aside each month which will take effort, you can set up an automated payment to come out of your account. Do it on the day you get paid, and into an account that you don't always see online, and before you know it, you will have automated the habit of saving.

3. Enjoyable

Finally, you need to make doing the new habit an enjoyable experience.

1. Reward behaviour

When you do the new thing that you want, reward yourself. Only, not with a gift that might compromise the new habit. For example, if you wanted to get into a new habit of eating healthy, and your habit was to eat two portions of vegetables with every meal, it might not be the best idea to make the reward a piece of cake. Maybe the reward could be something that re-enforces the good behaviour. Perhaps paying for cooking lessons or buying a new healthy cooking appliance you want. Or it might be unrelated, like treating yourself to a 'spa day', or going to the theatre.

2. Track it, to hack it

When the comedian Jerry Seinfeld wanted to write more jokes, he did something simple to help him. He wanted to write at least one joke a day for 30 days. He simply put up a calendar, and for each day he wrote a joke, he did a big red cross to signify he'd done it. Pretty soon he got a string of unbroken crosses, and it was easier to complete the month. Simply tracking the new habit can help embed and automate it. In 2019 I started a 100 Day Challenge group in WhatsApp. With about 50 people in it, the habit was to do 100 push ups a day for 100 days. Later we did further 100 days challenges. At the end of each day, when a person had completed the challenge for the day, they simply put a '100' emoji symbol in the group. Seeing all those emoji's appearing provided a good tracking system, and motivation for others to do their daily habit.

3. Forgive, but don't forget

When starting a new habit, there may be times when you slip up. Forgive yourself. If it's a daily habit, just don't miss more than one day in a row. Or if it's a weekly habit, don't miss more than one week in a row. So, if you wanted to do squats every day for a month, but then you miss a day, it can be tempting to sack the whole thing off. But if you just get back on it, you'll have another opportunity to make it a habit. Even if it's every other day, over the course of the month you'll have done it 15 times. If, on the other hand, you missed two days in a row, it's easy to miss three, then four and before you know it, the whole month has escaped from you. So, *forgive* yourself for missing a day, but don't *forget* the new habit altogether.

Replacing Old Habits

Again, there are three components to replacing the bad habit. These are to make the unwanted habit:

- **Invisible**
- **Impossible**
- **Instituted**

1. Invisible

The first step in replacing the bad habit is to make the habit invisible.

1. Out of sight, out of mind

When I coach people on technology management, one of the big things is the mobile phone. And distractions from it. I simply ask, as one of the first and simplest ways to get a handle on it, to keep it out of sight. Even if it's only behind the screen, instead of next to it. Likewise, if I don't have my bottle of water right in front of me, I'm less likely to drink from it. So, I want it in my line of sight (and reach). Keep things out of sight that you are looking to remove from your habits.

2. See the benefits of making it disappear

Understand and even visualise what your life would be like when you no longer have this bad habit in your life. What is it like to see this habit disappear?

2. Impossible

The next stage is to make doing the bad habit harder than the effort required to do it, or uncomfortable not to do it.

1. Make it hard to do

I have a weakness for chocolates and crisps. So, I make having them hard. I don't have them in the house. If I want them, I don't deny myself from having them. I do, however, need to get off my backside, and walk to the shops to buy them. Made even harder during the coronavirus pandemic of 2020 as social distancing meant big queues to get into even small shops. I had to really think whether I wanted the chocolate. So, make it hard to do the bad habit.

2. Commitment device

Using a commitment device is simply restricting your choice in the future by doing something when you are in sound mind to make the right decision. For example, when I want to make sure I stop mindlessly browsing YouTube videos, I installed a neat piece of software, that removed all the suggested videos from view. So now, I watch what I wanted to watch, or looked up, but don't keep watching for hours. In addition, I have software that means that I can assign certain websites that I can't look at for certain periods of time – even if I reboot my machine. So, when I want to do focussed work, and not distract myself by surfing the web to my favourite websites, I've set it up already to make it impossible. A few years ago, I put in a newsfeed block for Facebook. I thought I would just turn it off, but I didn't. And then I thought a few minutes a week I would turn it off and look at people's latest news. Eventually, this dwindled too. Now, I never turn that blocker off, and only check Facebook for messages and notifications. I don't get sucked into the newsfeed at all. So, use a commitment device to stop you doing the bad behaviour in the first place.

3. Instituted

This step is about instituting commitment into the process.

1. Commitment buddy

When you want to get up early and go to the gym, it's a lot harder to let someone else down than yourself, and so you'll be more inclined to go. During the coronavirus lockdown, I started training my parents via Facetime. My mum then being 69 and dad being 76 and neither ever having exercised. As I was teaching them, I was also training myself. And I told them, that had I not been training them, there was a high probability that I wouldn't be training myself either. The fact that I knew that every day at 10am I had made a commitment to train them, led me to not want to let them down. And vice versa for them too. I'm proud about how they trained with me every day during that time. It was a time of the day that we all looked forward to.

You can also have a commitment buddy who is not directly involved in the behaviour but is watching over you. For example, one time, my friend wanted to stop drinking for two months. He asked me to hold him accountable to this. I added an extra dimension, which was to ask him to make a substantial financial commitment to me. I think it was £500, that if he did drink, he would lose the money, and I could donate it to a charity of my choice. Unfortunately, he declined this, and within a few days had already broken his intended abstinence from alcohol.

I mentioned already about my 100 Day Challenge WhatsApp group. This was a classic example of having a commitment buddy. In fact, around 50 buddies. People in the group didn't want to let others down and were constantly seeing the '100' emoji in the group so it reminded them to do the habit they were after.

2. Commit publicly

This can be a double-edged sword here, as it depends on who is in your social circle. Still, making a public declaration as to your intent can be a big motivating factor, especially if the consequences of not doing it are painful. State publicly what your intentions are, and then you'll soon get sick of people holding you to account on whether you have stuck to your intention.

==========

Habit Anchoring (Stacking)

A great way to introduce new habits is to do something called habit anchoring (sometimes called habit stacking). It's where you anchor (or stack) a new habit onto an existing one. For example, I recently wanted to get into the habit of rolling a massage ball under my feet each day. Why? Well, it helps release tension in the foot after wearing footwear, and releases muscles up the leg. In any case, I kept forgetting or not finding the time to do it. I only needed to do it for a couple of minutes a day. So, what else was I already doing for two minutes twice a day? Yes, brushing my teeth.

I placed the massage ball underneath the basin I used for brushing my teeth. That's another important way to change habits. Make the new habit easy. Visual reminders are one way. Each time I now brush my teeth, the ball is there, and I do about a minute per foot. My electric toothbrush automatically buzzes every 30 seconds to change teeth, so it's easy to swap feet after the second buzz.

Think about habits that you are already doing, and you can anchor (or stack) a new habit on top of.

B - BRAIN
Keystone Habits

Keystone habits are habits that cause ripple effects beyond their own action. I understood that when I skipped certain habits in the morning, it was usually because I had gotten up too late. The keystone habit was going to bed earlier. Even beyond that though, going to bed earlier really came about from not watching TV in the evening. Which meant it was really the habit of watching TV while I was eating if I ate around 7pm or later. If I ate earlier than 6 or 7pm, and I watched something, I was more likely to switch off again for the night, and do something else, like work, read, take a bath, do some yoga or something else. The keystone habit I needed to address was eating late and watching TV, as that trickled over to everything the next day. As when I don't start my day right, it's easier for the rest of the day to escape from me too.

There are other ways that you can shortcut the automation. Having a strong motivator to change. Having a significant emotional event (SEE), can also create a new habit faster. In my case, I was able to picture a future version of me having eaten the dairy and then the ensuing consequences every time that I saw the dairy temptation.

The key in changing habits is to realise this:

1. **Habits take time to form.** We need anything from 18 days to 254 days or even more of repetition to create a strong enough habit[5].
2. **Start slowly – Baby Steps.** I wouldn't try and build in a habit of going to the gym four times a week if you don't go at all. Or going from watching TV every night to watching none. Try just once night a week without the TV. Or going to the gym just once that week. You might think that's too slow. My stance on it is that it is better that it takes you six months or even longer to get to your goal and it becomes ingrained. The alternative is often that you start out strong and burn out. Is that a pattern in your life that you already recognise?
3. **Focus on the process.** Don't get too caught up in what the desired result of the habit is. For example, if it's to eat healthier, then focus on the actions day by day, rather than just thinking about the result.

Quick summary about the mind and becoming superhuman...

1. We have a conscious and unconscious mind. The unconscious oversees most of the decisions that we make each day.

2. We can live 'at cause' or 'at effect' in life. We can find reasons, or results.

3. We are creatures of habit, and these create strong neural pathways. We can transform a habit by going through the seven stages of *The H.A.B.I.T. Model*™ and starting with a PPETT Scan.

Action plan for becoming superhuman...

1. Review *the Thought Cycle* and see if you can identify how this cycle has played out somewhere in your life.

2. Take an inventory of an area of your life, and honestly decide whether you have been living 'at effect' of external circumstances. Decide today to start living 'at cause' instead.

3. Conduct your own PPETT Scan on something that you want to change and notice what are the commonalities.

1.2 The Spoken Word

How your language shapes your world...

"No matter what people tell you, words and ideas can change the world."

- Robin Williams

I wrote about the importance of how language affects us in my first book, *The Thought Gym*®. My thoughts on this are still the same and expressed below in this modified excerpt from *The Thought Gym*® book.

Arguably, the greatest influence on how we think about ourselves comes from our own language. What we hear others say to us, about us and most importantly how we talk to ourselves. We are constantly talking to ourselves, whether we like to admit it or not. These can be empowering or disempowering words depending on what we say. For instance, when you were buying this book, were you asking yourself "Is this worth it?"; "will it work for me?" When you wake up in the morning, you might say something like "Uh, is it time to wake up already?"; "why do I have to go in to work today?" Whether it's conscious or not, you are talking to yourself all the time.

This chapter is all about language and how a change in the way we describe experiences, changes how we feel about that experience. As Shakespeare told us, via Hamlet:

"There is nothing either good or bad but thinking makes it so."

- William Shakespeare

B - BRAIN

Your choice

I'll start with an example. I used to not like doing the ironing. It was such a chore. I used to say to myself "Ah, I HAVE to do the ironing this weekend". But when I made one simple change, the way I felt about doing the ironing changed. I simply changed the *'have to'*, to a *'want to'*. That was it. You see, the ironing is still going to get done but now how I feel about the whole experience is different. Wouldn't you agree that when you say that you *have to, need to, ought to, should do* something, it feels a lot different in your body than saying that you *want to* do it? Try it. Say a few things now and feel the difference.

I started doing it with a lot of other phrases and I started saying things like:

> "I *am* getting up at 6am tomorrow."

> "I *get to* go to the gym."

> "I *choose to* do the housework."

> "I *will be* doing the vacuuming today."

It was such a revelation and so simple!

The decision about using the word "want" or any word, really depends on how it makes you feel. Sometimes if you say, "I want to go for a run", it might mean that you won't. It might mean that you will, and you'll enjoy it. Or for you it might be like saying I want that piece of cake and you really will have it. Or you might resist the temptation and feel lack. That association for you personally to the word "want" is important.

To play it safe, take it a step further and change the word 'want' to a *'will'* or *'am'* phrase. Or *get to.* Or *choose to.* Just like the examples above.

Regardless of what you choose, choose a word that resonates positively with you and shows commitment and certainty in the attainment of the objective. When we have that level of certainty, it takes the stress out of so much. It's done. It's just a done deal, and all that's needed now is to execute on it.

Trying times

Another word that is so small yet becomes so important in your vocabulary is the word *'try'*. We hear it all the time, and whilst we don't notice the real meaning consciously, we do unconsciously. *'Try'* implies a lot of effort with no results. Imagine this scenario; you are a manager at work, and you ask one of your team to produce a report for you and give it to you by 4pm tomorrow. They respond and say: "Yes, sure, I'll *try* and get that to you tomorrow for 4pm." We all know that chances are that it's never going to happen. How many times have you *tried* to lose weight? How many times have you *tried* to eat well, or *tried* to stop eating junk food?

Let's do a little experiment together. If you are sitting down reading this then *try* and stand up (and if you're already standing, then *try* and sit down).

How did you get on?

Did you manage to stand if you were sitting?

Really?

I asked you to *try* and stand up, not to stand up. Do it again. *Try* and stand up.

I do this with my corporate clients and see the same thing over and over. It's what you are doing right now, perhaps?

I bet you are straining while you are sitting there motioning to get up. In reality, you are still sitting there (or vice versa). You see, you're either standing up or sitting down – you can't *try* to do either. Need further proof? If there's a chair near you *try* and pick it up. *Can you?* No. You're either picking up the chair or not picking up the chair. It's like a binary sequence, 0 or 1, on or off.

Did you watch Episode V of the Star Wars movie franchise when you were growing up, or even as an adult? It's called *'The Empire Strikes Back'*. Anyway, there's a great scene in it with the Master Jedi trainer, Yoda, and his apprentice, Luke Skywalker. Luke is undergoing his training and is practising mastering his skills in using 'The Force' to pick up rocks with his mind when suddenly his spaceship sinks into a swamp. Luke doesn't believe they can get it out of there, and Yoda then teaches Luke a valuable lesson.

======

LUKE: "Oh, no. We'll never get it out now."

YODA: "So certain are you. Always with you it cannot be done. Hear you nothing that I say?"

LUKE: "Master, moving stones around is one thing. This is totally different."

YODA: "No! No different! Only different in your mind. You must unlearn what you have learned."

LUKE: "All right, I'll give it a try."

YODA: "No! Try not. **Do. Or do not. There is no try.**"

========

There is so much in that small passage about beliefs and conditioning on what we think. In particular, the last line illustrates the point I'm making.

"Do. Or do not. There is no try."

- Yoda

You either do something or you don't do something - either way you can't 'try' and do it. Now that I've raised your awareness to the word try, I guarantee that you'll hear it all the time and be especially tuned to it when you hear someone say that they'll try and get something done.

When I used to work at the London Stock Exchange, I worked for a very skilled boss, and he was especially good at picking up when people said in a meeting that they would *try* and do something. He wouldn't let them leave until they'd verbally spoken the commitment to getting it done. He wanted to hear them say: "I will get this done by 'X' time." Not just: "I'll *try* and get it done" or agreeing once he'd picked up on the word 'try'. You had to say the commitment back to him out loud. And I've got to say that it works. Once you say the whole thing out loud, it's like something gets registered in your unconscious and because you've made this commitment out loud you find it almost impossible to break.

Does saying that you will do something always mean that you will succeed? Of course not. However, it's more likely that you will persist harder and further without giving yourself the option to quit early. We all know that feeling when we ask someone out to an event, or our party and they reply saying that they will *try* and make it. You don't have much confidence in them coming.

Focus on what you want

How else does language affect what you will do and your progress towards your goals? Choose your words carefully. Using words like "I can't" does not serve you.

"He who says he can, and he who says he can't, are both usually right."

- Confucius

What if you truly can't do something? It might be true to say that you can't run 10 miles, but how could you re-phrase that to better serve you? Here are some ideas:

"I can't run ten miles, *yet*."

"I'm *working towards* running ten miles."

"I'm *in training* to run ten miles."

"I'm *building up my endurance* to be able to run ten miles."

All the statements convey the message that you are currently not able to complete ten miles, but internally, to your unconscious mind, you are instructing it that you will be able to do so in the future. These statements pre-suppose that you will be able to run 10 miles *some*day. If you say you can't do something, your brain will go off to think of all the reasons why that's true. If you say to yourself (and others) that you are working towards something, your brain will go off and search for ways in which to meet that objective. It will do all this unconsciously and it won't take any effort on your part. If your brain works for you in this way, isn't it better to get it working for you and your goals, rather than against?

Here's something else now for you to consider. When you talk about your goals for anything in life or business, state them in the positive and make them positive goals. For an easy-to-understand example, rather than say "I want to lose weight", which is talking about what you *don't* want – i.e., the weight - say what you *do* want. "I want to be fit, healthy and full of vitality". Also, be specific in your outcome as 'lose weight' is so generic. Every time you go to the toilet you 'lose weight'. Your unconscious mind feels like it's succeeded as you've met your goal! Have a specific weight range in mind. I recommend a weight range as you will never be exactly the weight that you want, and your unconscious mind is quite literal, so if you say that you want to be 10 stones, it will think 10 stones exactly, not 9 stones 12 and not 10 stones 2 - but 10 stones exactly. Better to have a weight range of something manageable like between 9 stones 10 and 10 stones 4 (in kilograms that's 62 kg to 65 kg). It's important to have the range as you will always fluctuate in weight – even weighing yourself in the same place and with the same clothes or food in your stomach. When you have a range and you notice that you're going too far to the extreme of the range, you can then take corrective measures.

Another reason why you might consider dropping the word 'lose' is because anything that the body sees as a loss it will fight to retain. Nobody really likes losing anything, do they? Think about it for a second, would you work harder to earn a thousand pounds or to stop someone from stealing a thousand pounds?

In 2004, I learnt first-hand about how you always move in the direction of what you focus on. I was snowboarding in Austria and heading towards a jump when I noticed I was going faster than I was comfortable with, so I started to slow down. This altered my trajectory slightly and I moved off my approach line. As this happened, I noticed a little tree stump around where the jump was and as I focussed on the tree stump, instead of the take-off point, I moved towards it and… BAM! I hit it full force. This resulted in a serious shoulder injury (dislocation and fracture) and about 12 months of physiotherapy; but the point is this. I was focussing on what I didn't want and so, I ended up getting just that! When all I needed to do was focus on where I wanted to go. The same is true of the saying 'lose weight' or anything where you are focussing on the thing you don't want. Saying that you want to lose weight is focussing on what you want to avoid – the weight. The same applies in any business or personal context. If you are saying things like "I don't want to mess up this presentation." You are then focussing on messing up the presentation! Or "I don't want to be poor." "I don't want to miss the flight."

Change the words, change the feeling

Language is one of the primary ways of how we communicate to each other and ourselves and by changing the way that we describe events we can directly change the experience and therefore the emotion that we attach to that experience. By way of example, if I were to miss a bus which meant I was going to be a few minutes late for a meeting I might say all manner of things to myself (or out loud) like:

"Stupid Hari, why didn't I leave earlier?"

"Oh s***, I'm going to be f****** late now!"

How about if you changed some of those words?

"*Silly* Hari, why didn't I leave earlier?"

"Darn it, I'm going to be a wee bit late now."

Can you see how that might feel differently? The words that we choose to describe our experiences *become* our experiences and so we need to choose them wisely. There are estimated to be somewhere between 1 – 2 million words in the English language. Although the average person might be familiar (from a sample of 100,000) with about 50% of them. In the average person's active vocabulary, the number of words regularly used is closer to only 2000. The bible uses 8000 words and Shakespeare used 24,000 – even inventing some himself. Furthermore, there are 4000 words to describe emotional states but amazingly 3600 of these describe negative experiences. It's no wonder that people find it a lot easier to describe their emotions in a negative way than a positive way. Take a minute now to write down all the emotions you feel on a day-to-day basis. Just think over the last week and write them down on a separate sheet.

Pause, and do the exercise.

I'm betting that you wrote down between 8 – 12 words and that 75% of those were negative. I've done this process myself and been in a room with over a thousand people, and that was the average. It's astonishing really considering that there are 400 positive emotions to choose from and we might only be experiencing three or four of them on a day-to-day basis.

I hope that this process has illustrated just how we use our language and how it changes how we represent our experiences by the words that we use to describe them. By changing our vocabulary, it will change what we choose to make our reality and therefore what we can achieve. Spend some time over the next week making a conscious effort to work on the advice given above and notice the change in your outlook to activities and your representation of your experiences.

Quick summary about language and becoming superhuman...

1. Our language and the words that we use become our experience.

2. We all have an inner voice that talks to us – and uses either empowering or disempowering language.

3. Changing the words that we use to describe things will change the meaning and feeling that those things have for us.

Action plan for becoming superhuman...

1. Decide to start paying attention to the words that you use to describe things, situations, experience, and people. Decide from now to eliminate the word 'try' from your vocabulary.

2. If you didn't while reading the chapter, write down all the emotions that you experience daily. Observe how many are positive and how many are negative.

3. Rephrase something that you notice you say on a consistent basis. For example, "I have to get up at 6am." Change it to something else like "I choose/get to/am getting up at 6am." Actively use that new phrase from now on.

1.3 Values

What's important to me is…

"Try not to become a man of success, but rather, try to become a man of value."

- Albert Einstein

What is a value? A value is something that we hold dear to us. We can find out our values on anything by asking this simple question.

What's important to me in [blank]?

You can fill in [blank] with the word 'life', to get your life values. If you want to know what your values are in your career, insert the word career.

For example. Some life values might be:

- Health, family, relationships, new experiences, risk, variety, money, success, work, career, travel, food, freedom, education, love, children, spontaneity, adventure.

When it comes to your career, the values could be:

- Presenting, progression, recognition, being heard, valued, in charge, making a difference, working in a team, having autonomy, variety, similarity.

We have values for all areas of our life. It's useful to know what your life values are, first and foremost. Once you do, it's obvious to understand how and why you make the certain choices you make.

Here's a simple way to find out your values.

B - BRAIN

Take a sheet of A4 paper and write down this question at the top of the paper

What's Important to me in LIFE?

Then list all the values that you hold for that question along the left-hand side with a space next to the value to write what belief you hold about that value. The belief is what you perceive needs to happen for that value to be met.

The reason that you need to write *both* the value *and* the belief you hold for it is because two people might have the same values - they might both put 'love' as a top value in life, but what they believe about love is different. One person might recognise love as when someone does small intimate things for the other, but the other person may believe that love is when they are showered with gifts all the time.

Once you have a list of 10 - 12 values, it's time to order them. I know that they are all important, but this needs to get done. As in reality, you hold some above others.

I suggest writing each value down on a Post-It note. Then imagine that you must throw away one of your values. You can't have it anymore. Decide which one that will be. Then put that to the bottom of a new list. Keep doing that until you have your new order.

The benefit of it being on a Post-It note is that you can move them around a bit until you are happy with them.

When I do this with my corporate clients, I don't tell them they can keep their values. Normally I get them to discard (or swap) their values continually, until there are only two left. Then these become the top two values they have in life.

As you are not in one of my trainings, I'll allow you the complete list to get a good picture of your values.

When you have your list, take a thorough look at it. *Do you live and make decisions by those values?* If not, then I might suggest that you are not living to your highest values. This takes its toll on a person.

If you value 'family' and 'freedom' as your top two values, but you work 80 hours a week, do you really value family and freedom above 'career' and 'success'? You might think to yourself that you *need* to work that much to provide for your family and secure your freedom in the future. *What about today though? What does your family really need? Could you still provide for them and work less hours?* Just a thought.

My personal thoughts are that if you don't have health, wellbeing, or energy (or similar) high on your list (number one or two), then can you really live any of the others to their fullest?

If you value 'family' at number one, but then you are ill, or too tired to spend time with your children and grandchildren, then are you *really* there for them? If you value career, but don't have the energy to perform at the highest level, will you *really* get to where you could do if you were fully healthy and energised?

I believe being able to achieve over the long term starts with health, vitality, and energy. Just as I said at the beginning of this book. So, for me, naturally, health is number one on my list of values.

Over the course of years, when I've repeated this process, I have noticed that my beliefs about what it means to be healthy, fit and energised have changed.

To illustrate; in 2006 when I first did this exercise, my top values were health, security, respect, love.

My top value of health was defined as this:

- **Health**: *12% body fat, run 10k in under 40 minutes, no aches and pains whatsoever.*

The problem came in being able to consistently meet that. I wasn't at 12% body fat, had never (and still haven't) run a 10-km race in under 40 minutes*. And I did have aches and pains from various sporting injuries.

When I did this process again in 2011, things had changed. Health was still top of my values list, but how I described it was different.

- **Health**: *I feel healthy when I'm able to do any physical activity I want to and I'm able to do it freely and with ease.*

That was much easier to meet. And continuing, as I write this book, it has

---

* I did manage a 41-minute run during my last London Triathlon in 2007 though. Which was also the last year I did any real running.

changed again. Health is still a top value but what I believe about it is different.

- **Health**: *I feel fit and healthy when I have the energy to do whatever I want and am not restricted in performing anything on account of not feeling physically able to do so.*

If, in future, I am not able to fit into a single seat in an airplane, then I know I'm way off base!

When you discover what your true top values are, the ones you *actually* live by, it will shed light on why you make certain decisions.

If 'family' is number one for you, but you spend 80 hours a week at work. You may believe that this will meet the 'family' value. You are providing for them financially. But you miss seeing your kids growing up. Miss time with your partner. *Is it worth it?*

I remember once at the London Stock Exchange; a colleague and I needed to go from one office to the other for a meeting. It just started to rain and so for my colleague, Richard, his instinctive action was to hail a cab (bear in mind that we're only talking about a 10 or 15-minute walk, and a cab in London would take just as long).

I had already taken an umbrella with me and the idea of a cab, or even getting the underground (as others often did) didn't even enter my mind. In that context (at least), Richard was more concerned about getting wet and dishevelled than he was about paying £10 for being stuck in traffic in the back of a cab. He placed a higher value on appearance or comfort than I did. I also realised that this was why I cycled to work each day, and he did not, despite him always saying that he wanted to. He would have to carry his bike up a flight of stairs to his flat (not comfortable), wear a helmet (perceived by him not to look good or fashionable), wear a day-glow outfit (urgh!!) and the rest[†]. Whereas I figured that cycling was economical, healthy and a more reliable form of transport. In other words, cycling met my 'health' value by working out, was cheaper than travelling on public transport ('security/money') and I was also guaranteed to know when I would arrive at work each day, and not be at the mercy of the traffic in London (also

---

[†] Interestingly though, Richard recently *did* start cycling to work (a 44km round trip) and is taking part in triathlons. Of course, he's now in a house, not a flat and has two children so I'm sure his values have changed slightly since that time at the London Stock Exchange.

'security').

Here's the interesting thing though. Once I realised just how I was basing my decisions, I was able to better evaluate whether that was always the right approach. To give you an example, I wanted more adventure and risk-taking in my life and wanted to go skydiving, but it cost quite a lot and security (of finances) was a value I prioritised above adventure and risk-taking. However, to fulfil my goal of skydiving I realised that I would have to (at least temporarily) press a 'pause' button on the values above the 'adventure' and 'risk-taking' values. If I always made decisions unconsciously based on how my values were organised, without the awareness of how I organised them, I would be restricting my decision-making ability. This would affect what experiences I would have and affect the quality of my life. The sheer fact that I now have an awareness on how I base my decisions, means that I am now freer to choose and more importantly, able to control my choices rather than letting those choices remain automatic to me. I've used this to great effect in the last few years. One such example was back in 2009 when I decided to hike to Everest Base Camp. The trip was, as I discovered, going to be expensive. I could have put that money to use elsewhere, but I also had a passion for adventure, learning and growing – albeit further down on the list than security. As I was aware of this, I was able to suspend that value temporarily (realising it was inhibiting me) and meet my need for adventure, learning and growing.

Think about your values in life. *Do you live in accordance with the values on your list? Or not? What do you choose to believe about each value? What must happen for it to be met?*

These are all interesting and useful questions to ask yourself. If you haven't already, go back and do the exercise as you will gain a lot of insight. Once you have that awareness you are better able to operate in life more consciously.

This will help you as you operate in your business and personal life. Knowing what you find important to you, and why it's the driving force behind most of your decisions is liberating. You are also able to adjust and pivot on your primary values if you realise that you are not meeting some other values. More importantly, living out of alignment with what we *say* is important to us, for too long a period, creates stress on the body.

Quick summary about what you value and becoming superhuman...

1. Values are things that we hold important to us. These can be specific to any area of our life (e.g., having a set of values just around your career) and what you value in life in general (e.g., health, relationships, success, family, love, adventure, novelty...)

2. Each value has an underlying belief around that value. This is what you believe needs to happen for that value to be true (met) for you.

3. Understanding your top values helps you understand how and why you make the decisions you do. Knowing your values helps you to 'pause' some values, and 'promote' other values. Living out of alignment with your top values will cause you stress in the long run.

Action plan for becoming superhuman...

1. If you haven't already, do the exercise on identifying your top 10-12 values in life and order them. Determine your two highest values in life.

2. Reflect on your top two values in life. *Do you notice whether most of your decisions are driven by these top values?*

3. What values are important to you that aren't being met, on account of ones higher up on the list? Experiment with "pausing" those values to meet lower down values.

1.4 Beliefs

I want to believe…

---

*"Whatever the mind can conceive and believe,
the mind can achieve."*

– Napoleon Hill

What are beliefs? I'm not speaking about religious beliefs here. Beliefs are the rules of our lives; emotionally held opinions which are treated by us as *fact*. They can be empowering such as "I am a great manager/entrepreneur" or limiting like "I'll never be good at leading people". These beliefs - the rules to our lives, have the power to transform us for better or for worse.

People hold on to their beliefs so strongly to the point where, for some beliefs, people are willing to die for them.

There was a time when people believed that the Earth was flat*. Or that you could die if you tried to run a mile in under four minutes. Or that a women's uterus would fall out of her if she ran a marathon. All manner of beliefs. And these shape our world.

Much of our success in life and business is the result of whether we hold any belief in the outcome we're striving towards. IBM (the computer company) didn't believe there was a need for personal computing back in the 1980's and totally missed the opportunity on that one.

The first person who needs to believe, of course, is you. You need to believe in this vision, this idea you might have for the company, department, or world, before anyone else does.

---

* Some still do believe this!

B - BRAIN

Beliefs can be "global" beliefs like:

- Life is…
- People are…
- I am…

Or "conditional" beliefs (if/then):

- If this happens, then that will (or won't) happen.
- If I increase my prices, then I'll lose customers.

Think of beliefs as represented metaphorically by a table. To support the table, it needs legs. For a belief, this is called a reference.

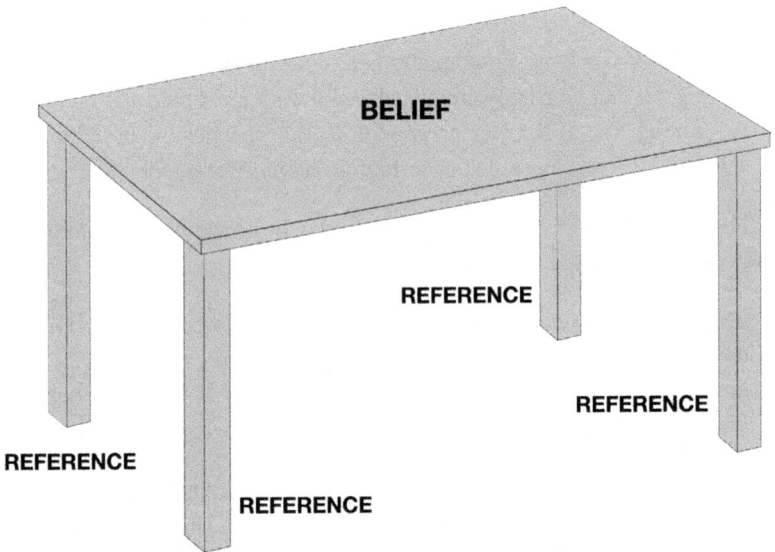

Figure 7 – Reference-Belief Table Analogy

These references are previous experiences, things we've read, heard, or seen from others. Something that makes us believe something is true. In fact, a belief is *not* necessarily truth. It's an opinion really. Not to say it's right or wrong. Just that it is something that you *choose* to accept.

Another way to think of beliefs - which helps me challenge what I might think

74

I *know* to be true is to look at the word beliefs, itself:

Beliefs

What if you focus on what's wrapped up inside that word? Hidden from the outside. What if you choose to see the word like this instead?

Be**LIE**fs

Furthermore, in my trainings I like to suggest the following.

B̲eLIEf̲S̲

What if your beliefs are really lies you tell yourself? Surrounded by 'BS'. BS meaning Big Stories, of course!

We come up with all manner of reasons why they should be true. But they're not necessarily true. Here are some popular beliefs a person might hold.

- You can't start a business in a recession.
- I need lots of money to start a business.
- I don't have time to exercise.
- Getting ill as you get older is natural.

Maybe they *are* 'true', maybe they're not? The point is that we just *choose* them to be true, correct or right. That's not to say they are. We base those conclusions on our evidence. Past experiences. What we hear from others. What we read in the newspapers or books. Social conditioning.

By questioning our beliefs and even changing them, a new world of opportunity opens to us. Some of what's stated in this book might question your current beliefs. And that's good. I always say in my talks not to blindly *believe* what I say. Equally though don't blindly dismiss it. Just because you have ingrained beliefs. Be open. Test things out for yourself. Keep what works and ditch what doesn't.

Sometimes to change a belief you just need to find one reference point that counters your current belief. Let's say you believe it's not possible to reverse your type-2 diabetes or heart disease. Just find someone who has, and that *must* shatter your belief on that. Of course, then you might hold the belief that it's not possible for *you* to change. Just find something in the past you once thought was impossible but then did. It proves that *you can* change.

B - BRAIN

In my talks, I sometimes suggest the following to have more belief in yourself.

When you don't believe in yourself, find someone who
believes in you. And believe in them instead!

What you choose to believe, often becomes your reality. Realise this and start looking for different more empowering beliefs and the references to back them up.

In my first book, *The Thought Gym®*, I outline a process that can take you through exploring your beliefs and start to change how they are represented in your mind. In the interest of not making this book even bigger than it is, I outline the process here: **https://thethoughtgym.com/supervitality.**

To live, lead and have longevity in your life, being aware of how your beliefs shape your world view is critical.

Self-Concept

According to the famous 20th century psychologist, Carl Rogers, your beliefs also stem from your self-concept.

The self-concept is formed of your:

- **Self-Ideal:** How you would like to see yourself
- **Self-Image:** How you really see yourself
- **Self-Esteem:** How you feel about yourself

You can have a self-concept in many areas of your life too. One for playing football for example, but then one also for how you take a penalty. One for how you interact with your family but also one for how you interact with your spouse - both at home, outside, when arguing and so on. We each have many self-concepts for specific areas of our lives and an over-arching self-concept about our lives. These can then feed into our beliefs and therefore thoughts. And remembering *The Thought Cycle* from the introduction to Part 1: BRAIN of this book, our thoughts we know lead to our emotions, our actions, and the results that we get in life and in business.

How I understand it all, is that our thoughts often stem from what we believe about the world, ourselves, situations and so on. Our beliefs about ourselves, are wrapped up in what Rogers referred to as the self-concept. What contributes to a person's self-concept, is how they feel about themselves (self-esteem), how the see themselves (self-image) and how they would like to see themselves be (self-ideal). In the diagram below I have shown how the self-concept feeds into beliefs and therefore how we think.

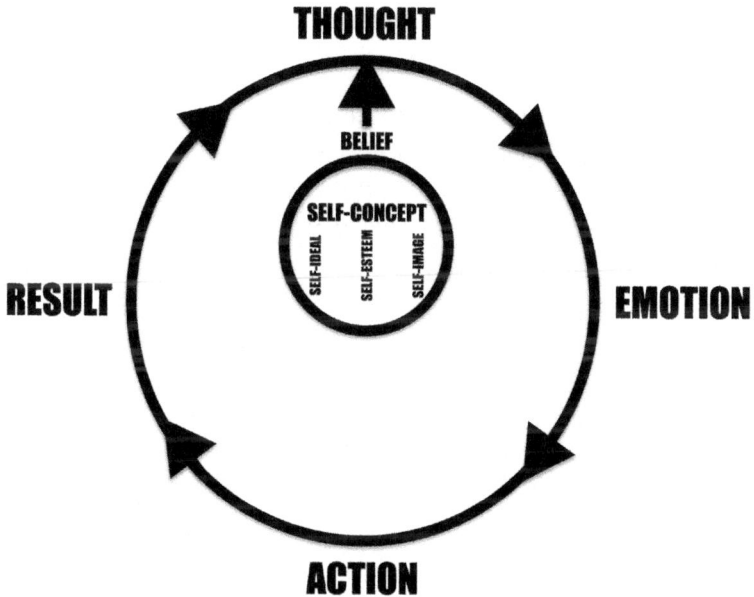

Figure 8 - How the Self-Concept fits into The Thought Cycle framework

Conflict within us tends to arise when (generally) our self-ideal and self-image are not in alignment. For example, we see ourselves as not very successful at leading or enrolling others, but how we *want* to see ourselves is as an amazing and inspirational leader. It's like the situation of living in misalignment with our values. Internal conflict will arise if you have certain values high on your list but are not consistently meeting (or living) to them.

Quick summary about beliefs and becoming superhuman...

1. Beliefs are not fact. They are opinions. We choose them to be the truth based on what we think we know from past experiences.

2. Beliefs can be challenged when you find a past reference that counters the belief. If you find a previous reference that goes counter to a belief, the belief can no longer be true.

3. Beliefs can be 'global' beliefs which generalise all things and people. Or beliefs can be conditional 'if/then' beliefs.

Action plan for becoming superhuman...

1. Think of a belief you hold. For example, it's natural to put on weight as you age. Then find a counter example to this. Is there anyone who's fit, healthy and a great weight and they are older than you? Well then, it's not age that's the determining factor.

2. Over the next week challenge yourself when you hear some statement of fact, or truth. How do you know that to be true? Is it *really* true, or just commonly held opinion?

3. Visit **https://thethoughtgym.com/supervitality** and look at the process to changing beliefs.

1.5 Reframing

What you see is what you get…

"Change the way you look at things, and the things you look at will change."

- Wayne Dyer

Reframing must be one of the most important skills that you can learn if you want to enjoy life more. People who are happy and enjoy life have been shown to be healthier and live longer[6]. The concept of reframing is to look at something from a different perspective. It's not the same as positive thinking or just sticking your head in the ground and ignoring what's going on.

The way I like to explain it is to imagine that you are in a house with windows and doors. And you spend your whole life looking out through just one of the windows. That's the view that you will see. Your perception of reality will be *based* on that view. If you move to another window, or even open the door, how would things look differently to you? It's the same situation out there. You are just taking a different viewpoint on the situation.

It's worth taking a side note here to talk about stress. We all experience stress. Most of the time we are experiencing too much negative stress. Most visits to doctors' surgeries (GP's or primary care physicians) are fundamentally stress related[7]. Here is the thing though. It's not that stress is bad for us. Sometimes we know we perform better under stress. It's really about our *interpretation* of the stressor that matters[8]. If we think the stress that we are feeling is good for us, then experiencing the 'stress' means we will likely get stronger. Or that we care about what we're doing. It has a different effect on the body. In fact, a little stress helps us get stronger and grow. When the scientists were creating the *Biosphere 2 Ecosystem* – a self-sustaining mini-Earth inside a giant bubble – they couldn't figure out why the trees weren't growing. Even when they had

79

everything the scientists thought they needed. Sunlight, soil, water, air. Later it was realised what was missing. Stress. In the form of wind[9]. The trees wouldn't grow because they didn't have the wind creating a stress on them. So, we do need stress, to grow and develop. It's just that chronic (long-term) stress tends to have a detrimental effect on the body and mind.

How you look at things determines what you see and experience. When looking to be our superhuman selves, we need to know this. Let's say you've just lost your job as a high-level executive that you've been in for 30 years. You could see that one way. You've been rejected by an ungrateful and unappreciative company. Tossed out the door, so to speak. Or you could decide that this was the push that you needed to pursue the business you have always wanted to. Or to spend time with your children or grandchildren.

The key comes back to language really. The way you speak to yourself in this situation. Here are some questions you might like to ask yourself.

1. *Where's the lesson in this?*

2. *How can I grow from this?*

3. *What's not perfect about this yet?*

4. *How can I use this situation to my advantage?*

5. *What am I missing here?*

6. *How must X [person] have seen this situation?*

7. *What would I have done in X [person's] situation?*

There are plenty of questions that will get you looking through a different window. A few things to note in the questions above. Some are presumptive. "Where's the lesson" implies that there *is* a lesson. And that means that the unconscious mind will *search* for that lesson. If you don't assume there is one, you won't find it.

The third question implies that although things are not perfect right now, they will be in the future. The last two take the frame of the other person. Based on their experience, beliefs, restrictions, skills, talents, and commitments, would you have made that decision? If you had the same upbringing and resources at your disposal, the chances are that you can see how they might have come to that conclusion.

The Power of How

A powerful word I like to use is '*how*'. Whenever I ask myself *how*, I usually find a way. Whether that's figuring a better way to stack my pots and pans into my cupboard. Or how to maximise my learning time on my commute*.

The Power of How. It's worth remembering – and using daily.

The meaning of any experience depends on how we decide to "frame" it. By that I mean, that nothing really means anything when out of context. We can change how we decide to look at it.

What does a whisper mean?

Well, nothing on its own. It's just a whisper. In the context of a large room full of people whispering back and forth will take another meaning. Or a parent whispering to child at night before they go to bed, it takes another meaning. Or a wife whispering to her husband when in bed together.

There are many different types of "frame". For simplicity, the way I like to teach it is just to consider a "frame" as a point of view.

And reframing, is just choosing to focus on some other element.

You could see it raining and think that your afternoon is ruined. Or you focus on what that means instead? Re-frame it to mean something else. The plants get watered saving you time later. You might frame it to mean that you are now incentivised to stay in and write the report that you've been putting off for the last week.

The three main types of reframing are *content, context* and *time*.

For example:

"I am too slow at making decisions."

Content Reframe:

"You think you're too slow. It's not that you are too slow, it's that you are

---

* I listen to audio training programs when walking and then read from a Kindle device on the trains. Kindles, I find are better because they are easier to get in and out of the bag or pocket quickly when travelling and allow easy one-handed reading (freeing up the other hand to hold on to the train rail).

such a caring person."

Slow = Caring

Context Reframe:

"You would be the ideal person to advise others about making major investments"

Slow = Asset

Time Reframe:

"Just think how much quicker you are now than you were when you first started doing it six months ago."

Slow = questioning belief and showing progression

A Magic Way to Cope with Stress – and a key to happiness

In the world of business, and as leaders we must learn how to reframe continually. Where most people might see obstacles, a great leader will reframe it to see opportunities. The reality is that there is very little that we are in control of in our lives. And most people will stress about things over which they have no control. The economy, whether someone likes them or not, whether they will get the promotion, what a certain world leader might or might not do, past regrets and whether our local sports team will win or lose. We can't control any of this. Even the promotion. All we can do to influence the promotion, is our best effort. Prepare, develop our skillset, be helpful to others, practice interview skills, have a good track record and so on. We can't control whether we are given the promotion though.

The idea that people worry about things they cannot control is nothing new. It's a leading principle of the ancient philosophy of Stoicism. In addition to our efforts, we can control how we *look* at things though. To manage the stress that come up in your life and work, I find the following a useful thing to remember. I call it the *Stoic 3C* (which I believe I heard on a podcast once from author Craig Ballantyne).

Control what you can control.

Cope with what you can't, and

Concentrate on what's important.

In the big scheme of your business, or your life or your relationship – *did what just happen really matter? Could you really control all aspects of the experience? Can you control how you look at it – how you frame the experience? Can you cope with what you can't control and reframe the experience?*

This might all sound like semantics, but it's not. It's how we shape our reality. We are doing it in a certain way anyway, so why not do it in a way that serves us? Nothing means anything except for the meaning that we give it.

"There is nothing either good or bad but thinking makes it so."

– William Shakespeare

Quick summary about reframing and becoming superhuman...

1. How we *frame* our experience is just our perspective on it. Each person has a different perspective, or frame, depending on several factors.

2. We can choose to reframe how we look at things and this will lead to a different meaning for us. We can look through the window at the field, or through the door. Both will give us a different view of the same thing.

3. Stress is either good or bad depending on how you perceive it to be. Most people stress about things that they cannot control. Learn to control what you can control and cope with what you can't, while concentrating on what's important.

Action plan for becoming superhuman...

1. Take a sheet of plain paper. Write down all the things in your life that you spend your time thinking (or worrying) about. Now circle only those things that you have 100% control over. For example, if you have written that you worry about what secondary school your child will get into, you don't have 100% control over that. You don't even have control about how much they might have to study. What you do have control over is supporting them. Offering them opportunities, for example tutoring (it's up to them whether they take advantage).

2. Decide to focus on doing your best to focus only on those things you *can* control. Learn to cope with what you can't. And remember to always concentrate on what's important in life.

3. The next time something happens that goes against your expectations, reframe it to something positive.

1.6 Master Your Mood

Why you feel the way you feel...

---

*"Realising that our actions, feelings and behaviour
are the result of our own images and beliefs gives us
the level that psychology has always needed for
changing personality."*

- Maxwell Maltz

If you want to show up as your best self in the world, as the best leader you can be, would it be useful to know how to do that? Most people think that how they feel is just how they feel. Sometimes they feel great. And sometimes not. They just got out on the wrong side of the bed.

Let me ask you a question. *If you're not in charge of how you feel, who is?* Your boss? Your shareholders? The taxi driver? The weather?

No.

We are in charge of how we feel. This might be a revelation to you. It might be difficult to accept. Especially when we are used to saying things like:

"She/he makes me so mad!"

The truth is that the other person has no real control over how you feel. *You* create the feeling within you. Your mood or your state may be *influenced* by external situations, but really, it is *you* that is creating it.

It comes back to this idea of cause and effect. If you are living 'at effect' then sure, the other person *will make* you angry, upset or feel a certain way. If you live 'at cause' then you will recognise that *you* are the one *creating* the emotion inside of you.

85

B - BRAIN

And really there are only three things that contribute to how you feel. All beginning with the letter 'A'.

And when you get this. I mean, *really* get it. You will be liberated and be in control of how you feel at any given moment in time.

And why is that important?

Well, imagine being able to show up to present to the board of your company in any way you want? Or what about leading a meeting? Pitching to investors? Even show up for your friend's party at the pub feeling just the way you want. Or even a networking event? We know how much people usually love those events. Any social event, in fact.

How you manage your mood will affect what happens.

I remember when I first *really* got this concept. I had heard it before (although not as the three A's that I am about to explain. That's my unique presentation of the concept), but it never really sunk in. This time, I was walking to my local underground station on a grey London autumn day. Initially I was thinking about how miserable the day was. It wasn't a miserable day, of course. The day doesn't have emotions! And why should the weather dictate whether I was happy or not? Suddenly I heard this idea that it is *I* that create my mood, and everything clicked. How these three things I'm about to share with you are really dictating my mood. And I felt liberated. Really! I know it sounds crazy, but it's amazing too.

So, are you ready? I've built it up quite a bit now. I do that purposefully so that you really take note.

The three things that dictate your mood (or state) at any given moment in time are:

ATTENTION

A

SSIGN   **CTION**

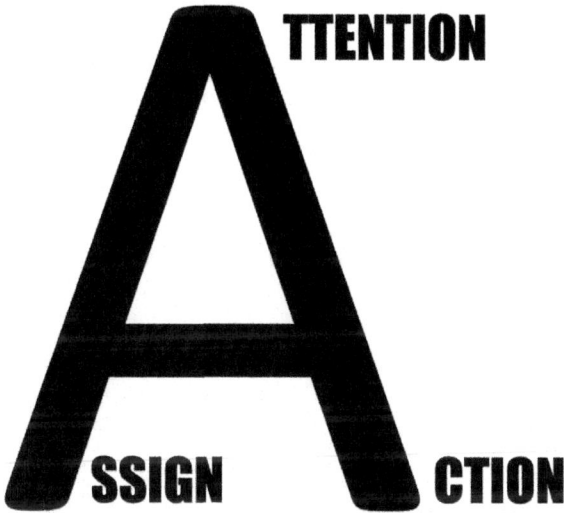

Figure 9 - The Three Things That Dictate Your Mood or State

Attention

This is the first thing that dictates your mood. It is what you *decide* to pay attention to in the moment. You might be paying attention to the fact that it's raining, or that the air conditioning is too hot or too cold. Maybe that you're 40 and still haven't 'made it'. Or that you are getting divorced.

There are billions of bits of information around us at any moment in time. You could even start paying attention to how your right big toe is feeling inside of your shoe or sock right now.

In London, it's easy to pay attention to the rain. It's often raining! So, let's continue with that example. I could be with you and I'm paying attention to the fact it's raining. You might be paying attention to the fact that you're in my company. Or that you're visiting London. We're both at the same event but are having a different experience.

If you're about to go into a pitch and you start paying attention to the fact that this is the 23rd pitch that you've done (and the others have all been unsuccessful), or that you haven't finished that public speaking course yet, so you won't be any good, how do you think you're going to feel? Whereas, if you go in and pay attention to the fact that you know your numbers, you know

87

your product, customers, and skills. You're passionate and raw, bursting with energy and determination, do you think you'll feel differently?

Once we decide what we are paying attention to – and granted, mostly this is unconscious until you recognise this framework - we must do the next 'A' in the framework.

Assign

We need to *assign* a meaning to it or *assign* language to describe it. I might say:

"It's bloody raining again!", or I might say

"The sky is crying".

Do they feel different to say? Yes. It's the same thing that I'm paying attention to. But the words assigned are different. We already know that language is a critical component in this mindset section. The words we use to describe our experience *become* our experience.

It could be the same with you for something else. Let's say that 'John' at work did something you didn't like. You might say:

"I'm absolutely furious with John for doing that!"

What if you assigned the following language? Would it feel different to you?

"I'm slightly peeved with John for doing that!"

Do you sense the feeling change? I expect so. Try it out for yourself. You'll soon get it.

The other thing is the *meaning* that you assign to what you are paying attention to. For some, the fact that it's raining might mean that their plans are ruined. Or that their commute home will be tougher now because they are cycling or walking home. For me, the meaning I assign to the rain is one of saving me some time. *Why?* I am rubbish at watering my plants and so when it rains it means that they are getting watered. And I save time because I don't have to water them for a few days.

We can both be paying attention to the same things yet derive different meanings from what we are paying attention to. Or we could both use different language to describe what we're paying attention to, which will have a different feeling inside each of us.

In the example earlier - of pitching to a group of investors - what if you assign the meaning to the 23rd pitch that you are getting the pitch better and more eloquently refined? Or that your non-polished public speaking skills will benefit you as potential investors will see you as a passionate, non-robotic presenter.

It's up to you what meaning or language you *decide* to assign. Each option will have a different outcome for you.

Action

The last thing that determines your mood in any given moment of time is the physical actions you take with your body. How you are standing, your facial expressions, your posture.

The physical actions of your body also dictate how you feel. You know this intuitively to be true, I'm sure.

Have you ever been to a party or function and been sat there miserable and not having a great time? Then a friend grabs you and forces you to dance. Pretty soon, you're in the swing of things and you feel different. Even if that feeling is embarrassment! It's still not the same feeling.

Science is now proving that the physical actions we take change our inner physiology. The hormones within us dictate whether we are stressed, calm, confident, unsure, or assertive.

In her popular TED talk[10], Amy Cuddy, a social physiologist from Harvard University, talks about the experiments she undertook investigating how posture can affect cortisol and testosterone levels.

Cortisol is often thought of as the stress hormone, although there's more to it than that. And cortisol isn't necessarily bad. We release more of it in the morning to wake up, for example. That said though, in most stressful situations though, there will be a cortisol rise. This results in a fight, flight or freeze response in our body. An inbuilt response evolved from our ancestral days when we were encountering a lion, and not a slew of emails. This rise in cortisol can be useful short-term, for example to run away from that lion. However, when not required, or functioning incorrectly, cortisol (excess or depletion) may lead poor decision making[11], unwanted tension in the body including bone and muscle breakdown[12], increased blood pressure[13], severe fatigue[14], and a whole host of other deleterious issues[15], if left unchecked. And according to the US Centre for Disease Control (CDC) stress amounts to 75% of all doctors' visits, while the Occupational Health and Safety news and the National Council on compensation of insurance, state up to 90% of all visits to doctors are for stress-related complaints[16]. Dr Rangan Chatterjee (who starred in the brilliant BBC series *Doctor in the House*) believes that 80% of what he sees as a GP (General Practitioner) from patients is in some way stress related[17].

Testosterone is a hormone responsible for many physical changes that occur (specifically in males), like building muscles, strong bones and getting taller[18]. However, it is present - and vitally important - in both males and females. In addition to physical changes, testosterone has psychological implications. Attributes such as confidence, assertiveness, and optimism.

In Amy Cuddy's experiments, she found that adjusting the participants posture, to one she calls 'power-posing' led to dramatic changes in cortisol (stress) and testosterone (confidence) levels. A 'power-pose' is one of keeping open body language. The classic standing posture might be one that you can picture Superman or Wonder Woman making. Hands on hips, chest puffed up, head upright, legs hips-width apart. Of course, there are other 'power-pose' positions. In a chair this might be leaning back slightly or just sitting upright. The opposite of this, a weak pose, would be anything that closes the body off. A collapsed chest, closed posture and hunched over.

What Cuddy found was that high-power poses lead to an *increase* in testosterone in the body by an average of 20%, while those in a low-power pose had a *decrease* of 10%. Again, a high-power pose also led to a *decrease* of cortisol by 25%, whereas those in a low-power pose had their cortisol levels *increase* by 15%. The poses were executed for only two minutes.

The idea that changing your physical posture affects your mood is nothing new really. It's been spoken about and taught for years. I quote Amy Cuddy's work as it has become very popular due to her TED talk[10].

When you fully grasp the magnitude of this section it will truly liberate you. You will understand that how you feel, your mood or your state, is just a result of these three things. What you pay *attention* to, the language or meaning you *assign* to what you paid attention to, and your physical *actions* of your body.

Knowing this, and consciously taking advantage of it, will be a game changer. You will be able to show up for any meeting, conversation, or event in the way that you want to. Simply remember:

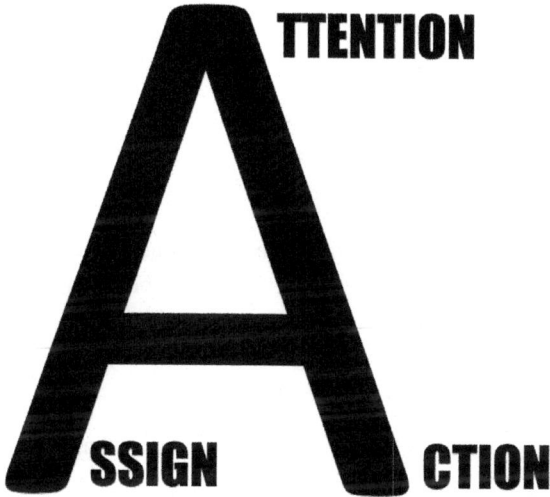

ATTENTION

ASSIGN   **ACTION**

Figure 10 - The Three Things That Dictate Your Mood or State

Quick summary about how and why we feel the way we do and becoming superhuman...

1. Only three things really dictate how we feel at any given moment in time. What we pay *attention* to, the meaning or language we *assign* to what we pay attention to, and the physical *actions* of our body.

2. Knowing this information means that we can effectively control how we want to show up in life. We don't need to leave it to some mystical force or waking up on the right side of the bed!

3. Two minutes of power posing is enough to make a difference of 30% in testosterone levels and 40% in cortisol levels, between that of high power and low power posing.

Action plan for becoming superhuman...

1. Next time you are self-aware and feeling a way that you don't want to, ask yourself:

- *What am I paying attention to right now?*
- *What language or meaning am I assigning to that?*
- *How are the physical actions of my body contributing? Do I need to move or stand differently?*

2. Based on what you recognise from asking yourself the three questions above, decide upon new meanings for what you are paying attention to. Or start to place your attention on something else. If needed, move your body in some way. Even if it's just putting a smile on your face.

3. The next time that you must give a presentation, or speak up at a meeting, spend at least two minutes in some form of power-pose. An open body language posture. Even if you are sitting in a chair.

1.7 Identity

Who am I?...

"As a man thinketh in his heart, so is he."

- *James Allen*

As we continue along our journey for health, vitality, and energy, we must look at the concept of identity. It's the essence that defines who we are and shapes our actions. In this chapter, we will delve into some of the pioneering works of Robert Dilts' neurological levels of change and Maxwell Maltz's principles of inner change preceding outer change. By examining these theories and understanding their application, we can embark on a transformative journey towards a healthier, more vibrant self.

The Significance of Identity in Well-being

Identity is the amalgamation of our beliefs, experiences, values, and aspirations, ultimately shaping our perception of self and influencing our choices. When it comes to health, vitality, and energy, our identity becomes a guiding force, directing our actions, decisions, and habits. The frameworks presented by Robert Dilts and Maxwell Maltz explain the profound role of identity in our journey towards well-being.

Robert Dilts' Neurological Levels of Change

Robert Dilts, a pioneer in the realm of personal development, introduced the neurological levels of change—a model that dissects transformation into distinct layers. This model comprises six levels: Environment, Behaviour, Capabilities, Beliefs and Values, Identity, and Purpose. By exploring these levels, we can grasp the intricate layers that constitute our identity and influence our health choices.

1. **Environment**: This level encompasses our external surroundings— the physical spaces, communities, and influences that shape our experiences.

2. **Behaviour**: At this level, we engage with our habits, actions, and behaviours. It's where the tangible outcomes of our identity and beliefs manifest.

3. **Capabilities**: This layer reflects our skills and competencies. While improving capabilities can empower us, sustainable transformation delves deeper.

4. **Beliefs and Values**: Dilts' model acknowledges the potency of our internal constructs—beliefs and values. These influence our decisions and actions, but transformative change extends beyond them.

5. **Identity**: At the core of the model lies identity—the essence of who we are. True transformation requires a shift in self-concept and self-perception.

6. **Purpose/Mission**: The pinnacle level is purpose—the driving force behind our actions. Aligning with our purpose ignites unwavering commitment.

This is perhaps best illustrated with an example. Using figure 11 as a reference point. Let's say you have a smoker, and they want to quit smoking. You could change the environment in which they smoke. For example, if they always smoke when they are in the pub, then taking them out of that environment will likely lead to them changing. However, it's not the strongest levels of change. As soon as they are back in the pub, they are likely to smoke again. However, if you go up a level and give them new behaviours to do, such as chewing gum, or Nicorette patches, or a vape, then they probably won't smoke.

Again though, when they are tested, they are likely to smoke if we consider that maybe they smoke because it calms them down. In that case, the change of environment won't work, and neither will the chewing gum. They might need new skills to manage with the stress or anxiety. By teaching that person calming or confidence techniques it will empower them to make quitting smoking last longer.

It's not the end of the story though. Above skills and capabilities is the level of values and beliefs. If, for example, that person believes that smoking is cool (because they used to see the 'Marlboro Man' adverts or look at pictures of James Dean smoking), then they are likely to still want to smoke. Or they believe that they need to smoke to be in with the 'in crowd' at work to get the best projects (a bit like that episode of *Friends* when Rachel takes up smoking because she believed she would get the better projects at work). If you ultimately believe that smoking is benefiting you in some way, then even if you take the person out of the environment, or give them new skills or behaviours, they will still end up smoking.

The better levels to work on are that of identity and purpose. How you see yourself. If you were once a smoker, but now consider yourself an ex-smoker, that is different from seeing yourself as a non-smoker. What do I mean? Well, an ex-smoker, still has a lingering identity, or a conflict of some sort in their identity, as being a former smoker. It means they might be more likely to smoke again compared to someone who didn't see themselves as a smoker at all.

A classic example I give in my workshops is that of my dad. My dad took up smoking at 18 years old and only stopped on the morning of his triple heart bypass surgery 40 years later. What happened with him was quite interesting though. He had no cravings or withdrawal or anything. In an instant, his identity shifted to that of a non-smoker (rather than ex-smoker). You can put him in a smoky environment with other smokers and give him a drink or two and still he wouldn't be tempted to smoke. Fundamentally his identity shifted.

In addition, if you consider that your purpose on Earth is to be a guiding light of health and wellbeing, then there's no way you'll smoke because it goes against your fundamental purpose.

The neurological levels of change by Robert Dilts illustrates well that to get permanent and lasting change, really the change must be at the levels of identity and purpose. Otherwise, if you change the lower levels but still fundamentally believe something different about who you are as a person, then the change is likely not to end up being permanent.

Dilts' model reveals that genuine change transcends surface alterations. It calls for a profound re-evaluation of our self-concept and values—a transformation that mirrors Maxwell Maltz's paradigm.

NEUROLOGICAL LEVELS OF CHANGE

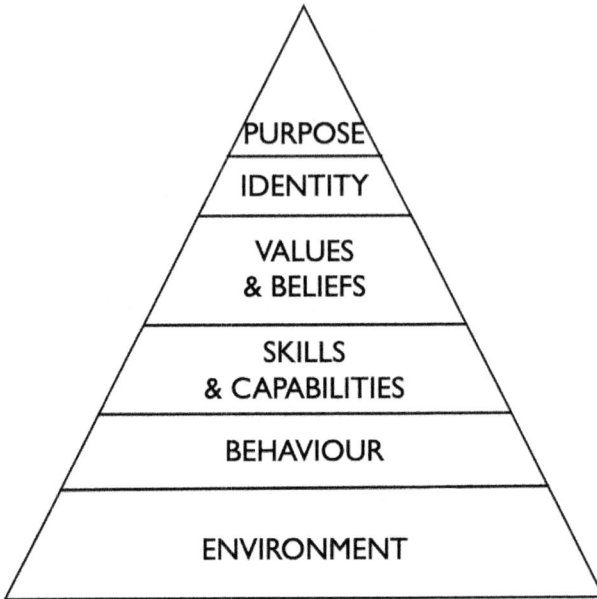

Figure 11 - Robert Dilts Neurological Levels of Change

Maxwell Maltz's Inner Change as the Precursor to Outer Change

Maxwell Maltz, a visionary plastic surgeon in the 1960's, recognised that altering physical appearances didn't always result in inner contentment. His insights led him to explore the realm of inner transformation, focusing on our self-image. Maltz's seminal work, "Psycho-Cybernetics," emphasized that our external reality mirrors our inner world.

Maltz's ideas seamlessly harmonize with Dilts' framework, emphasizing that lasting change begins by reshaping our self-concept and inner beliefs. He introduced the notion of "self-image," the mental portrait we hold of ourselves. Maltz observed that individuals with positive self-images often achieved greater success, highlighting the intimate connection between identity and outcomes.

Consider the example of adopting a healthier diet. Our default habits may lean towards convenient but less nutritious choices. This aligns with Dilts' levels of environment and behaviour. However, true transformation—a burst of change—occurs when we challenge these defaults and redefine our identity as individuals who prioritize health. This is what happened to me in 2011 and so the changes to my habits were straightforward, as I had a fundamental shift in identity about who I was. Even when I'm put in an environment that is non-conducive to healthy habits, or something stressful happens or my capabilities are altered (e.g., being injured), I'm still going to find a way to make a healthier choice.

Sustainable transformation involves navigating each level of Dilts' model, reshaping the environment, behaviour, capabilities, beliefs, and values. However, the crux of the matter lies in the shift of identity—a burst that catalyses enduring change, like what happened with me around my health and diet, and to my Dad with smoking.

Maltz's assertion that inner change leads to outer change is also profound. By reshaping our self-concept and embracing a positive self-image, we set the stage for identity-driven transformation. The transformative burst ignites a departure from the familiar and propels actions aligned with our newly defined identity.

Visualise your future self—immerse yourself in the mental canvas of your desired identity. I have a process in *The Thought Gym*® that can guide you through an identity change process and has been reproduced for you at **https://thethoughtgym.com/supervitality**.

To bring about identity change start with embracing practices that challenge your habits. Step out of your comfort zone, adopt habits in alignment with your envisioned identity, and affirm your transformation with unwavering determination. As Maltz advocated, internal shifts precede external change. This alignment triggers bursts of transformation, injecting vitality, energy, and a steadfast commitment to your evolved identity.

Ultimately, embarking on the journey towards health, vitality, and energy involves unearthing the layers of identity that guide our choices and actions. Robert Dilts' neurological levels of change and Maxwell Maltz's principles of inner change leading to outer change offer profound insights into this transformative process. In this intricate dance, our identity acts as both the compass and the destination, leading us toward a life characterized by radiant well-being, renewed vitality, and boundless energy.

Quick summary about identity and becoming superhuman…

1. There are multiple levels that change can happen at. Robert Dilts talks about environment, behaviours, skills & capabilities, values & beliefs, and then finally the levels of identity and then purpose (or mission).

2. The most effective way to affect change (although also the hardest) is at the level of identity or purpose.

3. Changing the outer you won't be effective in the long run, unless you change the inner you first.

Action plan for becoming superhuman…

1. Review the identity process detailed in my first book *The Thought Gym*® (and also available here: https://thethoughtgym.com/supervitality).

2. Do something this week that steps you out of your comfort zone or aligns with the identity of the person you want to become.

3. Write down a positive affirmation detailing your new identity and have it somewhere you can say it out loud each day.

1.8 Education

If you want to earn more, learn more…

"I have never let schooling interfere with my education."

– Mark Twain

I believe that we have a lot to learn from babies. They haven't been jaded or conditioned by adults yet, and they intuitively know what to do to be happy. They also live in the present moment - something many of us adults spend years trying to master again through meditation, mindfulness, yoga, and other practices. They don't harbour grudges, and they just move on when things happen, when many of us would think about the situation for hours, days, weeks, or years to come.

And it was by observing babies that I realised another important thing about health, vitality and most of all, energy. You can get energy from learning and growth.

Think about it. Have you ever gone into work, the same place that you have done for years and years, but on this day, you feel different? More energised. All because you are due to go on a course that you've been pestering your boss about for months. It's in a subject you're really interested in. Even though you are going to the same office, you feel lighter, more energised. That's the anticipation of learning something new.

Everything in nature (another great teacher of mine), either grows or it dies. If we don't grow, then we tend to feel stagnant and de-energised. Read books, go to events, talks and seminars. Listen to audiobooks and podcasts. Maybe even take a college course that interests you. It doesn't even need to be in your area of specialism. Sometimes you can get new ideas from fields far removed from your day-to-day specialism.

B - BRAIN

In terms of your health, by learning new skills you can help to create and strengthen connections in the brain[19]. And by doing this, you can ward off typical diseases of ageing like dementia, it's reported[20]. Dr Denise Park a neuroscientist from the University of Texas enrolled 39 volunteers of advancing age. Randomly assigning them tasks from digital photography to quilting. And others simply leisure activities like listening to classical music or word puzzles. After a 3-month period, the researchers found that those engaged in more complex activities - such as learning Photoshop - showed improvements in memory compared to those who engaged in social activities or non-demanding mental activities at home[20].

In the last decade neuroscientists have made significant advancement in understanding the brain. Even though we haven't even really scratched the surface. The brain has a neuroplasticity to it. Meaning that it's malleable. It can learn new skills and adapt. Even at later stages in life. It's not fixed. We also continue to grow new brain cells throughout life. A process called neurogenesis. Something I was always told at school wasn't possible and that as we age our brain cells die off and don't get replaced. The good news is that they *can* come back, at least in certain areas of the brain, like the hippocampus*. Exercise is a good option for neurogenesis[21]. As is learning, in particular spaced learning[22]. Learning over time, rather than cramming in one go.

I don't know whether you really need to be convinced of this. Just think about it. Don't you feel more alive when you are learning and growing?

I, for one, do. It wasn't always the case though. For a long time after university, I didn't want to learn really. I associated learning with lack or missing out. I felt I had spent too much of what should have been my social time in studying. I did well in high school achieving 10 A's and A*'s in my GCSE's†, and then AABC in my A-levels. At university, I continued to study hard and eventually was awarded a First-Class Batchelors of Science degree in Physics with Astrophysics from The University of Manchester. Then I was done. I didn't want to take another exam again, and equated learning to exams, and having to put in too much effort at the expense of other things.

---

* The hippocampus is a brain structure embedded deep in the temporal lobe of each cerebral cortex. It is an important part of the limbic system, a cortical region that regulates motivation, emotion, learning, and memory.
† I did in fact get 11 GCSEs, but the 11th, which I obtained when I was just 14 years old (instead of 16 years old) was a B...in Greek – and I'm Greek!

Eventually, I realised that the learning only really starts when you *leave* formal education. And that we must keep growing and learning. If we are to be successful in business and our careers, many paths will have further study and exams. I took a few exams when I worked in IT (Information Technology) for the London Stock Exchange (passing my ITIL[‡] and PRINCE2[§] exams). Really though, the learning came when I decided to pick up books again for my own personal benefit. I really got into reading non-fiction during travelling around London on the underground. From 2011 to 2014, I read 200 books, averaging about a book a week. Then I slowed down as I left corporate employment and didn't travel as much on public transport. I also decided that I didn't need to 'inhale' more and more knowledge, so slowed my reading down. I still spend a good hour a day though learning in my field. That might be podcasts, magazines, webpages, audiobooks, or other materials relevant to business, health, leadership, psychology, mindset, resilience, and wellbeing.

To help me focus on making learning a part of my day to day, I created an easy to remember acronym (I do love a good acronym).

A.B.L.E. - Always Be Learning & Evolving

And I ask[**] myself if I am being A.B.L.E. on a day-to-day basis.

If you prefer, you can remember thinking about babies and how they operate. I call this having the **E3 Baby Mindset**. Why?

When I observed babies, I noticed that they were doing three things as they went about their day.

E3 Baby Mindset - Exploring, Enjoying & Evolving

If you've ever had a young baby or infant, you will be able to see the truth in the *E3 Baby Mindset* quickly. They are continually *exploring* their surroundings, people, new shiny lights, and objects. Everything. They are also

---

[‡] ITIL – Information Technology Infrastructure Library. A qualification for IT professionals.
[§] PRINCE2 – PRojects IN Controlled Environments (version 2).
[**] Sometimes I like to think of 'ask' as 'always seek knowledge'. Another way to remember to continue to learn and grow.

having fun in doing it. They *enjoy* it. Adults often miss that part out. We need to have fun too. Especially when learning, as it not only helps us learn better, but it encourages us to seek out and learn more. It creates a positive association to the learning experience. And of course, lastly, babies *evolve* through completing the first two stages.

Think about *A.B.L.E.* and living with an *E3 Baby Mindset* in your life and you will be adding more of a spring in your step, as well as providing a fertile ground for your brain to develop and stay sharp as you age.

You might consider this a 'growth mindset'. Carol Dweck, in her popular book *Mindset* popularised the terms 'growth mindset' and 'fixed mindset'. Those with a 'fixed mindset' seeing their abilities, skills, intellect, and talent as fixed and strongly tied to their identity of self. This can result in not stepping up to try new things as much, believing that you can't learn something and lead to self-limiting behaviour. Those with a 'growth mindset' don't see their abilities, skills, intellect, and talent as fixed, but something that can growth and expand. Their current knowledge and skill level are not an indication of where they can go. It's just where they might be starting from.

Choosing to adopt a 'growth mindset' will allow you to take more opportunities to better yourself. To fail and try again. Knowing that you will improve with a decent amount of practice. And continuing to learn as you age will only assist in your wellbeing[23,24].

Quick summary about learning and becoming superhuman...

1. Growth and education are vital for our health, vitality, and energy.

2. Remember to think whether you are being A.B.L.E. (Always Be Learning & Evolving) and living with the E3 Baby Mindset (Explore, Evolve, Enjoy).

3. Our brains are malleable – neuroplasticity – meaning you can "teach an old dog, new tricks". They are also able to create new brain cells – neurogenesis.

Action plan for becoming superhuman...

1. Find a podcast on a subject that subject that interests you and subscribe to it. You can find a selection of podcasts I like at the end of this book.

2. Continue your learning and growth once you finish this book by committing to another book. Again, a suggestion of books to deepen your knowledge are suggested at the end of this book.

3. Check out some courses at a local higher education institute, or online faculty like EdX.com, Coursera.com, Udemy.com, Masterclass.com, Mindvalley.com or Curious.com.

1.9 Gratitude

Live with an attitude of gratitude…

"Often people ask how I manage to be happy despite having no arms and no legs. The quick answer is that I have a choice. I can be angry about not having limbs, or I can be thankful that I have purpose. I chose gratitude."

– Nick Vujcic

I attended a personal development event called *The YES Group* in January 2011 and at the end of the event, the speaker, as part of the Q&A segment mentioned something about gratitude. I had heard about this practice before in some form or another. Most notably the maxim to "live with an attitude of gratitude", but not really done anything practical with it. We all say we are grateful but what do we do to cultivate it. And why should we?

The speaker suggested that we spend the next 30 days writing in a gratitude log. Which is to say, regularly writing brief reflections on moments for which we're thankful, at the end of each day. Just three things. And so, I did.

And you know what I noticed?

I became happier. Much happier. This lines up with the work by many researchers on gratitude. Research by UC Davis psychologist Robert Emmons, the world's leading scientist on gratitude, and author of *"Thanks! How the New Science of Gratitude Can Make You Happier"*, showed that simply keeping a gratitude journal can significantly increase well-being and life satisfaction[25].

Furthermore, Emmons states that people who practice gratitude on a regular basis report the following benefits[26]:

Physical
- Stronger immune systems.
- Less bothered by aches and pains.
- Lower blood pressure.
- Exercise more and take better care of their health.
- Sleep longer and feel more refreshed upon waking.

Psychological
- Higher levels of positive emotions.
- More alert, alive, and awake.
- More joy and pleasure.
- More optimism and happiness.

Social
- More helpful, generous, and compassionate.
- More forgiving.
- More outgoing.
- Feel less lonely and isolated.

We are brought up from a young age (and indeed it's part of our evolution) to look for the negative in the world. The danger out there. Is that a lion's print near the cave? Was that branch broken before we left for the hunting trip? Seeking out the negative, or noticing things that shouldn't be there, literally helped us survive to this day. It's useful. It helps us. That's why we're acutely tuned into it. So, it's not necessarily bad, but does it serve us to overly focus on it? No, not really.

And when it comes to job successes, only 25% of job success is based on IQ. The other 75%, of job successes are predicted by your optimism, social support, and your ability to see stress as a challenge instead of a threat[27].

Most people follow the pattern of 'If...then..." when it comes to happiness[*].

- If I get the promotion, then I'll be happy.
- If I get the partner of my dreams, then I'll be happy.

Also sometimes thought of as the 'Have-Do-Be' approach to happiness.

- When I *have* my degree, then I will be able to *do* the job I want, and then I will *be* happy.

---

[*] Not just happiness. Many other emotions follow this principle too.

- When I *have* secured the promotion, then I will be able to *do* what I want (e.g., buy a house) and then I will *be* happy.
- When I *have* more time, then I *do* more volunteering and then I will *be* happy.
- When I *have* 'so-and-so' as my spouse, then I will *do* more excursions, and I will *be* happy.

It's never ending. There is always the next thing, and the next thing. You'll never be happy. As opposed to the way it really is, according to many spiritual teachers I've learnt from, and what I've come to realise myself. Which is 'Be-Do-Have'.

- When I'm *being* happy, I *do* more things like excursions, and I end up *having* the relationships I want.
- When I'm *being* happy at work, I *do* a better job, and I end up *having* a promotion.

The idea is first to *be* the kind of person that does the thing you want to do, and then you'll end up having what you want (or perhaps need) in life. I know this can be a challenging concept to get your head round, so just sit with it for a while and think carefully about it.

As Shawn Achor describes in his funny and informative TEDx talk[27] on positive psychology (viewed over 26 million times on the TED platform up to May 2025), if you can raise someone's level of positivity in the present, they will experience a happiness advantage. Meaning their brain at positive performs significantly better, than at negative, neutral or stressed. Your intelligence, creativity and energy all rise. Not to mention other business outcomes like superior productivity, which increases by 31% compared to negative, neutral or stressed. You become more resilient; there is less burnout and less turnover.

When you do as I suggest and write down three things that you are grateful for each day, it re-wires your brain to scan the world for the positive rather than the negative. Researchers from the Harvard T.H. Chan School of Public Health analysed data from more than 70,000 women and found that being optimistic seemed to beat all the usual factors associated with good health (such as marriage and socioeconomic background). Being optimistic lessened harmful effects of conditions like diabetes, high blood pressure, high cholesterol levels and depression[28].

And the good news? Optimism can be learnt. One way is writing down three things that you are grateful for each day. Other ways include keeping in your mind your 'best possible self' – the version of you that has achieved all your goals. And a third way is to keep a log of little acts of kindness that you do for others. It should be noted too, that genetic factors only play a small part in whether someone is optimistic or not. According to The SAGE Encyclopaedia of Lifespan Human Development, twin studies report this to be around 25% - 30%[29]. That means that up to 75% of whether you are optimistic is in your control. And chances are that you will still have some of that 25%, it's unlikely to be 0% optimism. That means you could top up and be 80-90%, even if your natural genetic inclination is only around 5-15%.

Feedback

And then there's school. When we might get seven out of ten correct on our spelling test, we (or our teachers and parents) often get us to focus on the three we got wrong. That's not to say you don't want to improve, but by focussing on what you got right and encouraging the behaviours you want to see more of, you get better results. This has been shown when it comes to giving feedback and developing people. If you can focus on the positive, and then, if you need to show the improvements needed, you rather highlight what needs to happen to get it right, instead of what was wrong[30].

Here's a basic model I developed for giving feedback.

Good-GO-Great!

Good

The first thing is that you want to focus on what was good. What you liked in what they did. And here's an important note. Your mindset when entering this conversation with the person is that you *really are* focussed on what they did well. You are not saying nice things, just because you want to soften them up to dish the blow. No. You are just looking at the good. Tell them what you liked.

G.O. – Growth Opportunities

The focus on the areas of growth for the person. Where can they stretch themselves? What would make them even better next time they did the thing? It's important that this is not the 'constructive criticism' part. I hate that phrase. As soon as most people hear that they will go into a defensive mode. And then, because they will go into essentially a 'fight-or-flight' mode, they will not take in any of the 'constructive criticism' anyway. And then they'll continue to do the thing that you don't want them to do. It's important that you approach this area from your own mindset perspective as the growth part. Even though your instinct is to just tell them all the things you perceive they did 'wrong'.

And when it comes to giving the growth opportunities, expressing them in the positive. Rather than saying, I liked your presentation, but you spoke too quietly. Instead, perhaps say, I liked your presentation, and you could have had even more impact if you projected your voice more. Both are saying the same thing – they need to speak up, but which would you rather hear? And notice the change of the word 'but', to 'and'. The word 'but' negates what precedes it.

- *I can see your point of view, but...have you considered it this way?*
- *I understand what you're saying, but...I think this...*
- *I like your red top, but....it would look good in blue.*

The word 'and' is a building word. You still want the thing you said before to count – if you meant it. You *can* see their point of view; you do *understand,* and you *do* like their red top. If you use the word 'but', you negate all that, and the person just hears the second part of the sentence. The word 'and' builds onto the sentence.

- *I can see your point of view, and have you considered it this way?*
- *I understand what you're saying, and I think this...*
- *I like your red top and it would look good in blue.*

Sometimes you do want to use the word but[†].

- Okay, so you didn't get your point across, *but* your passion and research really shined through.
- This is going to be a tough day of learning, *but* the skills you will learn will be worth it.

[†] Note too, that often delegates I teach, change 'but' to 'however'. 'However', is just a fancy word for 'but'. A 'but' with bows on it.

Great

And then finish it off with something that was great in what they did. Again, my view is that 80% of the feedback should be with what they did good and great and what you want them to repeat and build on. The other 20% should be where they can grow and stretch themselves and make things even better and more impactful.

The same goes for when we give feedback to ourselves. We can often be our harshest critics.

NEWS – Never-Ending Wasted Stress

And then there's the news. What I like to think of as *Never-Ending Wasted Stress* (NEWS)! It's hardly representative of what really goes on. If a 30-minute news segment accurately reported the good and bad 'news' in the world, you'd find the bad parts were only a small fraction. Instead, they know that bad news keeps people glued to the set, and so most of it is negative. News, by definition, must be uncommon, or unusual. Otherwise, it wouldn't be news. However, if you read the newspapers and watch the news continuously, you'll be surrounded by a one-sided approach to the world. And it's 99.9% negative. And you'll start to think that everything is like that in the world. Even if consciously, you know better, subconsciously you'll think differently. So, it's understandable why you might have a slant towards the negative.

What happens when you start to keep a gratitude journal is that you start to seek out the positive in the world. And sure, at first, it can be hard to write those three things down. Especially if you are not in a good place in life. However, you eventually find so much to be grateful for. In the beginning you might find that you write the same three things each night. I encourage you not to though. Find new things to be grateful for. And not just obvious things, like family, or house, car (although it's good to write those down from time to time). You might be grateful for a blue sky (in London, we always are), or the smell of a rose, or that someone held a door open for you that day. It could be anything. That you have access to free libraries. The internet.

"Gratitude is the sign of noble souls."

- *Aesop*

As you start to do this, it will start to re-pattern your brain. The neurons in your brain will start to fire differently and different connections made between them[31,32]. Every time you express gratitude or self-compassion through journaling, verbal appreciation, or giving you're creating a new neural pathway which will lead to greater happiness, compassion, and appreciation[31]. As a result, you will become happier. I guarantee it. It's one thing I suggest to all my coaching and corporate clients for shifting their perspective on the world in a relatively short period of time.

On the BBC programme, *The Truth About Personality*[33], Dr Michael Mosely, undergoes training in Cognitive Bias Modification to see if he could become more positive over a 7-week period. He underwent this training along with mindfulness training, due to scheduling restraints. The Cognitive Bias Modification had him reviewing pictures of people expressing positive, negative, or neutral emotions and then trying to pick out the positive ones. Training his brain to see the positive. After the seven weeks were up, there was a significant improvement in his readings from before the experiment. Of course, this might also have been due, in part, to the mindfulness. However, I believe that keeping a gratitude journal is a similar, and effective way to remove negativity bias. And more pleasant than staring at a computer screen of random people.

Being grateful can therefore change your view on the world and make you happier. So, what? Does that make you superhuman? Well, it does make you healthier. Being happier has been shown to improve your physical health[34], live a longer life[35], and more[36].

According to a 2014 study published in *Emotion*[37], having appreciation (or gratitude) can help you win friends. It can also help you sleep better according to a 2011 study published in *Applied Psychology: Health and Well-Being*[38]. I can certainly attest to that one.

Furthermore, Dr Robert A. Emmons from the University of California and Dr Michael E. McCullough from the University of Miami have done a lot of the research on gratitude. In a 10-week study[25], with three groups, Group 1 writing things each day they were happy or grateful for, and Group 2 writing

B - BRAIN

daily irritations. While Group 3 just wrote about events that had affected them (positively or negatively). After ten weeks, those in the gratitude group exercised more and had fewer visits to the doctors. Of course, this isn't conclusive. However, just a few searches will find plenty of studies supporting the benefits of gratitude. For example, in another study from 2006 published in *Behaviour Research and Therapy* found that Vietnam War veterans with high levels of gratitude experienced lower rates of PTSD[39].

You don't need to take my word for it, or any study for that matter. Just give it a go for 30 days.

To start with I suggest picking either first thing in the morning, or last thing at night (or both if you are an over-achiever). Write down (my preference for this is to write it down) three things that you are grateful for. That's it. Why write it down, rather than think it? Firstly, you are more likely to remember to do the practice if you have a pad and pen by your bed. Secondly, there's something more concrete when you write things down rather than just thinking them. And lastly, it will also be like keeping a little journal of what's going on. I've recorded over 15,000 things that I'm grateful for, across several journals. Having them easy to view serves as a nice reminder. I remember even being able to find three things to be grateful for on the day that I returned home from a trip abroad having to cut it short due to injury. I was on crutches because I had torn my meniscus and upon opening my front door, I found my girlfriend of four years ready with her bags packed announcing she was leaving me! I still did my gratitude log that night.

In early 2019, I managed to rope my family into doing this. We have a family WhatsApp group for communications, and I suggested that we use our group for gratitude too. For 30 days, I suggested that we write down three things that we're grateful for and share it in the group. Not everyone decided to do it, but a few of us did, and even those that decided not to do it, occasionally jumped in. After 30 days, people just continued to do it, so we kept it going. What's been nice about this practice is that we've been learning more about each other's day and general feelings. Perhaps it's something to consider in your family?

Some people might think that they have nothing to be grateful for, but trust me, I bet they do. I bet you have plenty to be grateful for. For one, you can read. Besides, if a person is not grateful for what they currently have, what makes them think they will be grateful in the future when they finally do get what they think they want.

112

> *"The happiness of your life depends upon the quality of your thoughts."*
>
> - *Marcus Aurelius*

A slightly more advanced practice is the future gratitude part. After doing the gratitude log for around six months, I added another list on the other side of the page. Writing down three things that I'm grateful for in the future *as if I already had them*. By doing this, you engage the brain to almost see and feel things that you want in life. Like a mini visualisation of the future you want to create. To start with, so as not to be overwhelmed, I normally just recommend people stick to writing three things to be grateful for in the present.

Gratitude practice is part of an overarching field of positive psychology, with leading authority Martin Seligman spearheading much of the movement. Positive psychology, deviated from traditional psychology in the way that rather than looking at people who were depressed and so on, and asking what's wrong with them. Instead, researchers in the field of positive psychology are more concerned with looking at what makes people happy[40]. Makes sense really. What you focus on, you tend to get. So, if you want to be happy, focus on what happy people do, not what unhappy people do.

Quick summary about having gratitude and becoming superhuman...

1. Gratitude is good for your health and wellbeing. It will make you happier and healthier, and more pleasant to be around.

2. Just spending a few minutes each day expressing gratitude can alter your brain structure in a matter of weeks.

3. We are wired to seek out the negative in the world, so we must actively cultivate our appreciation muscles.

Action plan for becoming superhuman...

1. Start a daily gratitude log. Keep a notebook and pen by your bed and write down three things each evening before going to bed that you can be grateful for. They can be large or small, the same things or different things. Commit to doing this for 30 days (as a minimum).

2. Once you have fully embedded the habit (after a few months), you could consider also writing a future gratitude log.

3. Text, email or speak to someone and tell them one thing that you are grateful to them for.

Part 2: ELEMENTS

Elemental my dear Watson…

"Earth, water, fire, and wind. Where there is energy there is life."

- Suzy Kassem

The second key area identified in *The Leadership BEAT Model*™ is that of ELEMENTS. This section is all about how you decide to nourish your body. From the inside and out. And the requirements for nourishment fit into metaphors from the Ancient Greek notion of the five elements. Air, Water, Earth, Fire and Aether.

Air

Air is a metaphor for the power and importance of breathing. When it comes to energy, many people turn to food, coffee or (tragically) energy drinks. I

115

like to keep things simple. An acronym I use is K.I.S.S. Most people think of this acronym as Keep It Simple, Stupid! I like to think of it at Keep It Solution Simple. To paraphrase a quote often attributed to Einstein:

"Everything should be as simple as possible, but no simpler".

– Albert Einstein

Meaning that let's not complicate things unnecessarily. Think about this. How long can the average person go without food? A few years ago, I would have said about four hours! I personally have done over a week, but that was with juices, so I was still getting nutrients. The average person, before they die, can go weeks without food, even a couple of months.

What about water? How long can the average person go without water before they die? A few days.

What about air? How long can you go without air before you die? A few minutes only.

So, it stands to simple reason that if air is the most important thing for life from those three things, then it's where we should start when it comes to increasing our health, vitality, and energy levels.

Water

Next up we have water. As we've seen it is number two on my list above when it comes to surviving. Water is often thought of as just water. It's so much more complex than that. And there are many different types of water that we can look at consuming. It's essential for life and having enough of it is super important to our health, vitality, and energy levels. We are roughly 70% water. The Earth is roughly 70% water. These are clues as to how important water is to us. We'll dive into water (pardon the pun) in more detail in the chapter on water.

Earth

Earth is a metaphor for the food we eat, and our relationship with the Earth itself. Does our food come from the earth, or from man? That should tell you something (remembering K.I.S.S.). My summary on food - and we'll go into it in more detail in the chapter about food is this: **EAT REAL FOOD**. Everything else is nuance. If it was made in a plant and not from plants, you shouldn't eat it. If it has a marketing campaign, a celebrity endorsement, or advertising behind it, you shouldn't eat it. If it comes in a packet, be weary. If it's built for shelf-life, instead of self-life, then don't eat it. If it can outlive you, stay away.

Again, we'll explore in more detail in the chapter on food. As well as a simple approach to eating that everyone can adopt (no matter what your ethical, or other dietary inclinations). In short, when it comes to the first three things I've just mentioned – Air, Water, Earth, it's really about *O.W.N.-ing* your life. O.W.N. stands for Oxygen, Water and Nutrients. Just thinking about that and focussing on those three things, will be a great place to start.

In addition to the food that we get from the Earth, the Earth section is about our physical connection to the Earth. In a practice called 'Grounding' or 'Earthing', we'll explore the latest discoveries about how direct physical contact with the ground (earth) can affect our health and well-being.

Fire

Fire is a metaphor for our relationship with the sun and being outdoors in light and in nature. In recent years we've become weary of the sun, and as a general population we are spending more time indoors and under artificial lights. The sun is key to life on this planet. It's vitally important to us for many reasons that we will explore in that chapter.

Aether

Aether is the what the Ancient Greeks believed was a pervasive energy all around us. A bit like 'The Force' from the Star Wars movies. Enveloping us. In this context and metaphor, Aether is our environment. From our physical environment - for example, do you feel energised when your house is tidy and following a spring clean? Also, is your environment set up for things like movement? Consider the environment that you put on your body (sun creams, lotions, shampoos, face creams, make-up). Aether also covers the invisible environment so ubiquitous now. The world of electromagnetic frequencies and radiation (EMF/EMR).

========

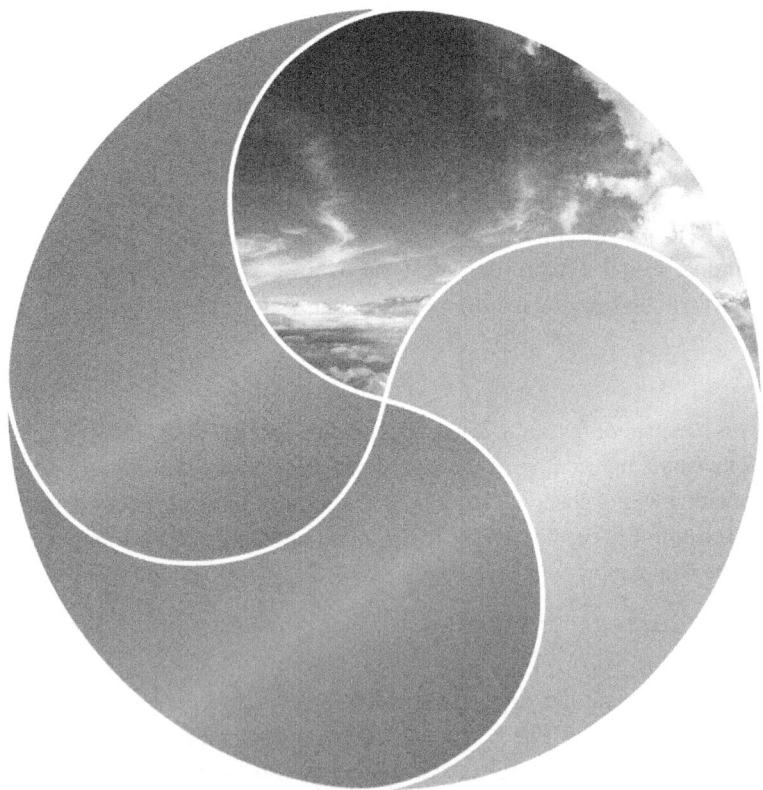

2.1 Just Breathe (Air)

I just gotta breathe man…

"If you know the art of breathing you have the strength, wisdom and courage of ten tigers."

- Chinese adage

Breathing is something that we take for granted. We've been doing it since the day we were born. And while as infants we were actually pretty good at it, we've gotten progressively worse at it. At least from my experience from testing this out with hundreds of people in audiences around the globe and by observing people day-to-day.

When we think about how to feel more energised in the day, how many of us turn towards something like food, or coffee? Or some other substance?

If you think about it simply. I asked in this section's introduction. How long can the average person go without eating food? Hours? A day? It's actually a few weeks to even longer. Mahatma Gandhi famously went three weeks without food at the age of 74. Sure, you'll become weaker and more nutrient deficient but…you'll be alive.

And water? How long? That's in the order of days. Even up to a week by some estimates. If you have watched the movie *'127 hrs'* starring James Franco (and based on a true story), then for him, it was about 127 hours[*]!

What about breathing? How long can a person go without breathing? Well, not very long is the answer. The order of minutes. 29 minutes and 3 seconds

---

[*] In the movie, the character that James Franco is playing, Aron Ralston, gets his arm caught in between some rocks when out canyoneering by himself and can't get it free. He runs out of water, and after 5 days realising no help is coming (he didn't tell anyone where he was going), he relents and, <SPOILER ALERT>, unappealingly, cuts through his own arm to get free.

if you are Vitomir Maričić of Croatia who took the world record for breath-holding in June 2025[†].

But the rest of us. *Significantly* less time[‡].

It stands to reason that if breathing is the most important thing for survival, then it's got to be a place to start when it comes to increasing energy.

Our brains demand up to 25 per cent of the oxygen we breathe in[41], so concentration, focus and cognition can suffer with reduced breathing efficiency.

And not only that, but breathing well can help with[42-44]:

- Releasing stress.
- Reducing anxiety.
- Stimulating the parasympathetic nervous system response (your rest and digest part of your autonomic nervous system).
- Muscle relaxation.
- Lowering blood pressure. As your muscles let go of tension, your blood vessels dilate, and your blood pressure returns to a normal level.
- Lowering your pulse.
- Boosting your immune system.
- Trigger endorphin release, in turn improving feelings of wellbeing and providing pain relief.
- Stimulates the lymphatic drainage system of the body. The body's natural 'sewage' system for moving toxins around and out the body.
- Improves attention and focus.
- Modulation of insulin production.
- And a lot more…

[†] This is with the use of oxygen in preparation for the breath hold. Without it, the pure breath hold record (static apnoea) is 11:35 minutes.

[‡] Most people without training would struggle to get to a minute. Unless you are Tom Cruise who trained to hold his breath for a Mission Impossible film and his record is over six minutes, repeatedly doing underwater shots that lasted four minutes! I have done some basic training on breath holding and increased my own from 40 seconds to over 4 minutes in just a few minutes of training.

Awesome, right? So, what does 'breathing well' really mean? In short, it's breathing lightly but deeply into the belly (not chest) and in and out through the nose.

Diaphragmatic Breathing

Most people breathe incorrectly, from what I've discovered from my own observations and research into the subject. Think about your breathing right now. Are you breathing into the belly or the chest? If you are hunched over at work, are you even able to position yourself to breathe deeply?

An overwhelming large portion of the population breathes shallowly into the upper chest. Even when asked to take a full and deep breath in my wellbeing workshops, delegates will puff up their chests, yet nothing of their abdomen moves.

When people breathe into the chest, they immediately restrict the amount of oxygen they can get into their body. They also turn on their sympathetic nervous system (the fight/flight/freeze) component of the autonomic nervous system (ANS). The ANS has the role of perceiving your internal environment and then, after processing the information in the Central Nervous System (CNS), regulating the functions of the internal environment.

Let's keep it solution simple (K.I.S.S., *remember?*)

Picture a balloon being inside a bird cage, and the balloon inflating (see figure 12). Of course, the balloon will be restricted by the sides and floor of the cage. It won't be inflated to its full capacity. It's a bit like that with the lungs. The cage is your chest, ribs and back. And if you just breathe into the upper portion of your body, neglecting the abdomen, then it's like you've put a fixed floor in your own bird cage. But luckily for you, your actual floor is moveable. And it's called your diaphragm.

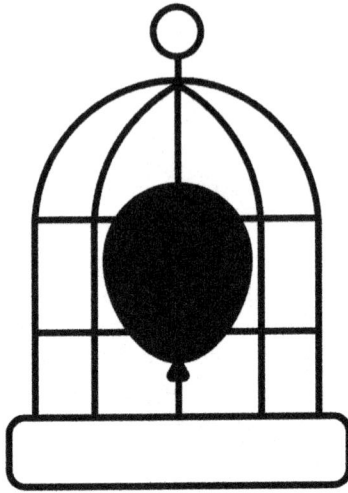

Figure 12 - The Bird Cage Metaphor for Breathing

When you breathe into the belly first, you allow your diaphragm to contract and pull the lower part of your lungs down. This allows you to reach more of your full capacity of breath. Now obviously you are still breathing into the lungs, but the effect of the lungs expanding down, is that your belly will ever so slightly protrude outwards.

When you take a full breath, your belly will come out more. You will also have your chest rise afterwards, and even your ribs and back expand out a little too. Effectively it's **belly-chest-back-ribs** breathing.

If you are a parent or spend time around young children you might notice how babies and toddlers automatically breathe this way, into the belly. Then somewhere along the line, for a variety of reasons, as they get older and spend more time in chairs at school, many will also start to breathe into the chest.

Have a go at this little exercise.

1. Place one hand on your belly, and the other hand on your chest.
2. Take a normal breath for a few times.

Where are you breathing into? Is your belly moving?

If not, spend some time focussing on the hand that is on your belly and then moving it outwards as you breathe in. You might find that you are forcing it out. Try to resist this and stay focussed. Eventually, the belly will relax more than being forced out each time you take a breath in.

If you've cracked it and are ready to have a go at taking a deep (diaphragmatic) breath, then try this.

1. Take a deep breath in and focus on (releasing) your belly.
2. Then notice as your chest then rises.
3. And then try and fill air into your back.
4. And now the space between your ribs.

Chances are that you would have found that quite hard.

The most important step is 1, then 2. If you can get 3 and 4 in as well, when you need some full deep breaths, then all the better. Day-to-day, when you catch yourself, you'll want to bring attention back to belly breathing. Over time, you will do it more and more naturally as you go about your day.

Yes, I know that this sounds quite simple. Just breathe. It *so* important though.

Nasal Breathing

We want to breathe into the nose, as it's designed for breathing more so than the mouth.

Dr Maurice Cottle, who founded the American Rhinologic Society in 1954, says that the nose performs at least thirty functions, all of which are important supplements to the roles played by the lungs, heart, and other organs[45].

The nose has a four-stage filtration system, as opposed to the mouth which hasn't got any. First, the hair filters out the particles in the air. Then, the mucous has an enzyme that kills viruses and bacteria. Next, the turbinates (ridges of tissue on the inside of your nose) and sinuses warm and condition the air and produce nitric oxide (which improves lung function). Finally, as the air enters the lungs it goes over the last two filters: the adenoids and the tonsils.

In addition to that, nose breathing imposes much more resistance to the air stream than mouth breathing, resulting in a 10-20% increased oxygen uptake[45]. Also, if you breathe in and out through the mouth you will expel more water[46]. This, in addition to being more dehydrating, can cause a dry mouth increasing the acidification of the mouth, and might even result in more dental cavities and gum disease[45]. Mouth breathing also causes bad breath due to altered bacterial flora and is proven to significantly increase the number of occurrences of snoring and sleep apnoea[45]. Mouth breathing is also thought to create dental malocclusions (misalignments) and craniofacial bone abnormalities[47].

Nose breathing is also more likely to activate the abdomen, whereas when you mouth breathe, you're more likely to breathe into the chest.

Over-breathing

As counterintuitive as it might sound, but many people, according to Patrick McKeown, author of the excellent book *The Oxygen Advantage*, have a problem with *over* breathing. In that their respiration rate is high and they are drawing in oxygen but at the expense of carbon dioxide. Carbon dioxide is thought of as simply the waste product when it comes to breathing. No so. It's vital to have carbon dioxide to allow oxygen to be carried from the blood stream to the cells where it's needed. It doesn't matter if your blood oxygen saturation is high if it's not going to where it needs to - the cells.

A metaphor to help you understand this. Imagine that the streets of a city are the veins and arteries. Instead of transporting blood cells, they are transporting cars. So, cars = blood cells. These 'cars' carry 'passengers'. In this case, the 'passengers' are oxygen molecules. Now these oxygen molecules (our 'passengers') want to get off, and head to a 'club', or a 'theatre', or 'cinema'. But to get into the 'cinema' or 'theatre', which is, in this metaphor, a cell in your body, you must buy a ticket. Imagine that there is only one 'person' selling tickets to get in, it will take a long time, and you won't bother staying, so you get in your car and drive off. Searching for another 'club' or 'theatre' to get into. The person selling the ticket, is *carbon dioxide*. The more 'ushers' you have ushering people in, the easier it is to get into the place you want – the cell. So, you *need* carbon dioxide to allow oxygen into the cell. Over breathing, saturating the blood with oxygen, is only going to create more and more cars with passengers (in our metaphor) but none getting into the venues.

So, we need to become carbon dioxide tolerant and not over breathe. Patrick McKeown talks about breathing *light and right*. I like to say light and deep. So rather than a deep breath meaning inflating your lungs and puffing up your chest, shoulders and back. It means deep down. Like having depth in a swimming pool – a shallow end and a deep end. Low down into the abdomen. But soft, or light.

The Wise Old Man

In some of my talks I tell the story of a friend of mine whose dad (at the time) was 100 years old. His son (my friend) was 30. Yes, that means his dad was 70 years old when he was conceived. When my friend asked his dad what the secret was to his long life, his dad simply replied:

"Breathing"

So simple. My friend's dad had been a lifetime practitioner of martial arts and disciplines like qigong, so when he said breathing, it was more than just a flippant statement about how you obviously need to breathe to stay alive. It was about the power of breath for longevity.

The Science-y Bit

We are made up of an estimated 30 trillion cells[48][§]. And these cells need fuel. That fuel isn't coffee or Red Bull though. It's adenosine triphosphate (ATP). ATP is made inside the cells. In an area called mitochondria[49]. The mitochondria take the energy from food, but they need oxygen to extract the energy. Without the oxygen, we don't get the energy locked up inside what we eat.

Oxygen is vital for our survival. It's vital for our energy. Without it we die. That much is easy enough to grasp. I want to drive the point home though.

In the early part of the 20th century, Nobel prize winner Otto Warburg did some experiments on cells. He concluded cancerous cells gain their energy primarily from non-oxidative breakdown (without oxygen) of glucose. In contrast to healthy cells that generate energy from oxidative breakdown. His experiments concluded that by depriving cells of oxygen it promoted anaerobic cells which lead to cancer[50]. Now if that's not a reason why you

---

[§] Note, that estimates vary widely from 10 trillion to 100 trillion. In this paper, they report 3.0×10^{13} (30,000,000,000,000) human cells with 3.8×10^{13} bacterial cells in the human body.

want to make sure you get enough oxygen then I don't know what is.

Furthermore, Dr Harry Goldblatt from the Rockefeller Institute did research on cells from rats[51]. Rats not known for developing cancer. He divided the rats into three groups. One was a control group, the other two had cells removed from them. One set of cells were deprived oxygen, and the other cells given what they required. Then he injected the cells back into the rats. The control rats were fine. The rats that had had cells removed, given what they needed and then re-inserted were also fine. The rats that had the cells re-injected into them that had been deprived of oxygen ended up developing cancerous tumours.

A Yogic Approach

I practice yoga[**]. In yoga, one aspect is that of 'pranayama'. The word pranayama can be broken up into two parts. Prana meaning life force or vital energy and ayama which can be interpreted as expansion (or to set free[††]).

So, *pranayama*, means expansion of your life force. Our life force is the breath. Our spirit, in fact. The root of the word spirit is spiritus (which is Latin for breath). When we expand our breath, we expand our life force.

Within pranayama there are many different techniques and ways to breathe. Some activate your sympathetic nervous system (fight or flight), but most that are taught in classes are there to activate the parasympathetic nervous system (rest and digest). This is because we are already in a hyper state of tension or stress most of the time, for most people. In fact, researchers from Boston University School of Medicine discovered that yoga and breathing can be better than drugs for lifting depression[52].

The simple way, for the purposes of this book, and your own benefit, is to remember that you activate the relaxation response by exhaling for longer than you inhale. This will stimulate the vagus nerve and activate your relaxation response. The word vagus stems from the word vagabond, as it is a wandering nerve which touches every major organ in your body travelling from the gut to the brain. Ninety per cent of the fibres in the vagus carry

---

[**] Yoga in the West is seen as a physical practice whereas in reality, yoga is a whole integrated system of living. In the West we focus on the asana part of yoga which is the physical aspect of yoga. Asana means seat.

[††] Yama however means control. Ayama is the opposite, meaning to free or expand. So, it could be interpreted as controlling the breath too. As with many ancient and translated traditions, it could be open to interpretation.

information from the gut to the brain, and not the other way around as you might think[53].

The Routine

Here's my approach to day-to-day breathing to help get you on the right track. And really, you don't need to know much more than this to get some amazing benefits.

Each morning after showering, I make sure I take ten deep breaths into through the nose and down into the belly. Allowing the belly to inflate slightly.

As I breathe deeply, the chest and back might also start to rise. Sometimes I visualise the space between the ribs expanding too. I then exhale strongly through my mouth for double the duration that I inhaled. Blowing out all the steam from the bathroom. This part serves two main purposes. One, it clears my bathroom full of steam. And two, it helps me imagine I'm a bit like Superman blowing out my 'Arctic Breath'! Well, I have always been into superheroes!

I then repeat these breaths ten times.

Breathing in like this will allow for maximum oxygen to come in and energise. As well as the right balance of CO_2 to be in the body. CO_2 is essential for us as proper levels will help trigger our red blood cells to release the oxygen they are carrying.

Then I aim to do that routine a couple more times later in the day. As a good way to remember it, do it just before lunch and then just before dinner too. It's best done on an empty stomach as you are using the belly.

Most clients I coach, or audiences I speak to, can find breathing into the belly unusual. Even difficult. Stick with it though. I always suggest that whenever you happen to turn your attention to your breath, think about breathing into the stomach. Over time, this will become more natural and like second nature. You won't have to forcibly think about breathing into the stomach.

If you can manage to breathe into and out of the stomach throughout the day and then take three sets of 10 breaths a day too, you will be well on your way to a healthier, less stressed, and more energised you. The *ten-breath exercise* is also a great thing to do to destress at any point during the day.

E - ELEMENTS

Whenever I catch myself getting stressed, I just remember to breathe deep into the belly, and then long out the mouth or nose. I usually breathe in and out through the nose, unless I'm doing the morning ten-breath routine, when I have lots of steam to remove from the bathroom.

Real Supermen

Once you start to explore the power of breathing you can spend a lifetime learning about it. For example, I mentioned earlier the breath expert Vitomir Maričić, who holds the record for the longest breath hold at over 29 minutes. Yes, it's possible by undertaking years of training for people to experience truly superhuman feats like this. And another ambassador for breathing is Wim Hof. He's also known as the 'Ice Man'. He has spent years working on breathing techniques and now teaches them to others. Wim Hof has multiple world records. He has also climbed to 22,000 feet altitude on Mount Everest (the Death Zone) wearing nothing but shorts and shoes. Wim is proving to people all the time just how we can control our autonomic nervous system[43], previously thought impossible – hence the name autonomic. Wim's breathing techniques have been studied intensively, and research is showing just how turning our attention to our breath and breathing in different ways can help with reducing chronic inflammation[54] and therefore possibly help with inflammatory conditions like rheumatoid arthritis and inflammatory bowel disease. Breathing techniques were also used when Wim Hof was deliberately - as part of a university experiment - injected with E. Coli and showed that the bacteria did not affect him significantly. Furthermore, these techniques and results have been replicated with others. Others who spent merely days learning the techniques and not decades like Hof originally had to do. I often do some Wim Hof breathing techniques for energy and immune support, and I've also noticed an increase in my breath holding after just a few sessions from 45 seconds to over 4 minutes[‡‡].

Simple Breathing Exercises

Box Breathing

This is a simple breathing exercise designed to created balance and focus, and I first heard about it from former Navy SEAL, Mark Devine. Called Box

---

[‡‡] Typically, I do three rounds of his technique and on average the opening rounds are around 2.5 minutes and end up at around 3-3.5 minutes for the breath holding part. I have reached over 4 minutes on times when I'm particularly focussed.

Breathing as the pattern resembles that of a box. Simply inhale for a count of four[§§], hold for four, exhale for four, hold for four and then repeat. Repeat as much as time allows. I would recommend at least four cycles.

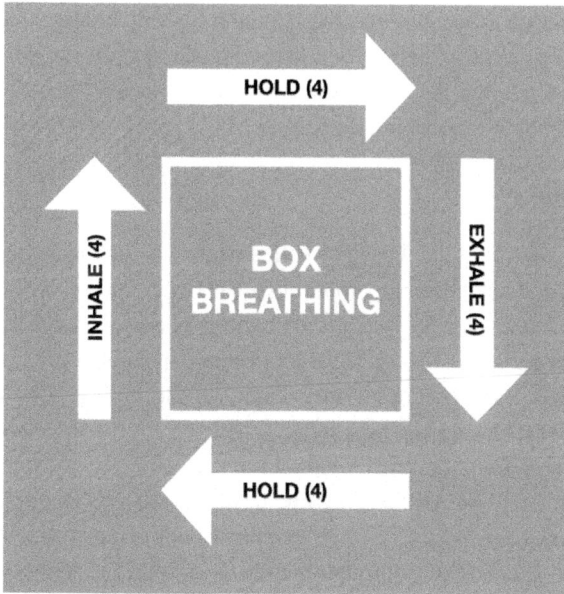

Figure 13 - Box Breathing

Breath of Fire

This is a yogic breathing practice. Simply sharply inhale. This is a quick, forceful inhale into your lungs. The inhale is of medium intensity but without over-exerting yourself. Exhale. Without pausing, exhale with an equally matched level of force as your inhale. Be sure the inhale is the same length and depth as the exhale. Continue these dynamic inhales and exhales without pausing. The inhales should seamlessly merge into the exhales, and vice versa. Once you are comfortable with the flow of the breath, bring your attention to your core muscles. Begin to use your core to power the breath. To end your Breath of Fire practice, draw in a long and deep inhale and slowly release your hands down by your side.

[§§] This does not have to be four seconds. Your counting could be quicker or longer than once per second.

4, 7, 8 Breathing

This breathing practice invites you to inhale for a count of four, then hold for seven and then exhale for a count of eight. As with Box Breathing, this does not have to equate to seconds exactly, although typically this is what is taught. Whatever your count is though, you keep the pace the same. This breathing can help with calming the nervous system and relaxation. Good to do when stressed or wanting to relax before bed.

1:4:2 Breathing

I'm not sure what this one would be called exactly. I first heard about it over 15 years ago and have been incorporating ever since. This is one that I would typically use in the morning for a bit of power or energy. Breathe in for a ratio of 1 (e.g., four seconds), then hold for four times that amount (i.e., 16 seconds) and then exhale for twice what you inhaled for (so in this case it would be eight seconds). Hence 1:4:2 breathing. Whatever your first inhale lasts for, work it out from there. I normally have an inhale lasting between 3-5 seconds so, at the top end, I would hold my breath for 20 seconds and exhale for 10 seconds. Remember to breathe into the belly (abdomen) and I inhale through the nose, and exhale either through the nose or mouth. Usually, I am doing this breathing technique after my shower in the morning in a steamy bathroom. In that case, I like exhaling through the mouth. Not only does it allow more release of carbon dioxide, but I like to see the steam being blown out.

The retention part of this breathing technique can be quite challenging for some people. Including feeling lightheaded with it. Start small and slow. And maybe do while sitting down first.

I would aim to complete 10 rounds of this 1:4:2 breathing technique. If you want to really be an over-achiever with this, I suggest doing it three times a day, 10 rounds each time. Once after the shower and before eating breakfast (if you eat breakfast), then once before lunch and then again once before dinner.

Re-Lease Breathing

The re-lease breath is my go-to when meditating, but also whenever I feel stressed. Very simple to do. On the inhale, imagine saying the syllable 're' in your head. On the exhale, say the syllable 'lease'. If I'm meditating, I keep the inhale and exhale roughly the same. If I'm feeling stressed, or nervous, I tend to extend the exhale to at least twice the inhale. I probably do this breathing technique more than any other. When I'm getting frustrated waiting in a queue, or in traffic, is another good time to practice it. You can also replace the word 'release' with other two syllable words that suit you. 'Let go', 're-lax', 'all good', 'I'm safe', 'I'm strong', 'all healed'. You get the idea.

Wim Hof Breathing

The Wim Hof technique is one that stimulates the sympathetic nervous system really. As opposed to many techniques taught in yoga classes and other places which aim to stimulate the parasympathetic nervous system. Remember, the sympathetic nervous system is the fight-flight-freeze response, and the parasympathetic nervous system is the rest & digest part. Most people are over activating their sympathetic nervous system much of the time, which is why it's so popular to do breathing techniques to counter that.

The Wim Hof technique will help you stay calm and relaxed when the body is crying out to be stressed. It's best learnt and taught either through the app, or the online training course Hof offers, or through accredited trainers. That said, I'll give the brief overview below, so if you are curious, you can find out more.

NOTE: Never do this technique, or any other breath holding techniques in or near water, while operating machinery or driving, or in any situation when you might endanger yourself or anyone else. You can do this technique sitting on the couch or a chair or lying or sitting on the floor.

1. Inhale deeply and fully. Fill the lungs as much as possible. I start with the belly, then move to the chest, ribs and back. Wim Hof doesn't seem to care whether you breathe in through the mouth or nose. Through the mouth will more rapidly activate your sympathetic nervous system, I believe. It also dries me out, and I find it uncomfortable. I breathe in through the nose. I can get plenty of air in that way. Other people will need to use the mouth to get it all in.

2. Let the air go. Notice this isn't an exhale in the traditional sense. Yes, you are exhaling in that you are letting some air go, but you are not emptying the lungs. Think of it as more of a sigh out.

E - ELEMENTS

3. Repeat the inhale and sigh out 30-40 times.

4. On the last sigh out (after the 30-40 cycles), hold your breath. You are not holding on the inhale, but after the release of breath.

5. Hold for as long as you can through a slight level of discomfort. Note that you might get an urge to breathe quite soon if you are not used to it***. Often this urge passes as you become more cognizant of this desire to go into fight or flight. The body thinks you are in danger – which technically you are as you are not breathing. If you combine this with the 're-lease' mantra (saying), or some other calming saying, I find it's more comfortable.

6. When you have a strong desire to breathe, then take a big inhale and hold your breath (on the inhale) for 15 seconds. Then exhale fully – everything from your lungs.

7. Repeat steps 1-6 for another 2-4 rounds.

I normally do three rounds in total. When I started doing this technique my breath hold was around 45 seconds. Now it's often (by the third round) in the 3-3.5-minute region. A couple of times even over 4 minutes. This technique isn't really supposed to be designed for increasing your breath hold – there are other techniques for that which free divers use.

From what I understand, it's more about creating a stress response in the body, but then being able to control it. This kind of breathing is good for immune system boosting, inflammation reduction and stress management. It's also quite energising.

Again, I recommend downloading their free app†††, which is the best way to start for free, or following a guided video on YouTube.

1:2 Breathing

This might be the simplest breathing exercise I teach people. It is good for de-stressing and activation of the parasympathetic nervous system. Simply exhale for double your inhale. Like many techniques listed, inhale through the nose, and into the belly. Exhale through the nose (or mouth) for twice the

---

*** I also use a swimming nose clip to ensure I'm not having to hold my nose, or have any air seep in. It's not important to have a nose clip though.
††† Just look up 'Wim Hof breathing app' and you'll find it.

132

inhale length.

If you inhale for four seconds, then exhale for eight seconds. That's it. Do a few rounds of this to start to feel more relaxed and able to think clearly again after a stressful episode. Aim for at least five inhale/exhales. After that you should feel very different. If time allows, and if it's needed, do more.

There are as many breathing techniques out there as there are people, so you could spend a lifetime just on breathwork. That said, most of us don't have a desire to do that, and a few techniques will be ample. Or simply just learning to breathe in through the nose and into the belly.

If nothing else, just take one conscious nasal-belly breath a day. And then maybe work up to two, then three, and eventually (it took me over six months) you might find that you naturally start to breathe into the nose and belly.

)

Quick summary about breathing and becoming superhuman...

1. Most people are not breathing correctly. They breathe shallow (into the chest) which activates the fight or flight response easier.

2. If you want to breathe well, focus on breathing in and out of the nose, and in and out of the belly.

3. Breathing affects every aspect of your wellbeing, from stress levels to focus and attention. From your energy levels, and concentration to your immune response and blood pressure.

Action plan for becoming superhuman...

1. **General Breathing Technique:** Day-to-day, and throughout each day, try to focus on:

1.1. Breathing in and out through the nose and breathing into your belly, taking diaphragmatic breaths.

1.2. Breathe lightly and naturally, not trying to force the breath, or over breathing.

1.3. For the first few days or weeks, it might feel a bit forced as you re-adjust to breathing into the belly and not chest but stick with it.

2. **Energising Breaths:** Several times a day, for example after showering, before lunch and before dinner, take some energising breaths:

2.1. Take a long inhale into the belly, counting in your head – 1, 2, 3 ... up to where it's a comfortable challenge.

2.2. Exhale deeply (nose or mouth) for double the number you got up to. E.g., if you counted to 5 on the inhale, count to 10 on the exhale.

2.3. Repeat each cycle 10 times.

3. **De-stress 'Releasing' breaths:** This technique is one I use *a lot* when I find myself beginning to get stressed out a little.

3.1. Find a quiet, comfortable place where you can be undisturbed for 5 – 10 minutes. Set a timer running.

3.2. Notice any areas of the body that feel tense.

3.3. Inhale deeply into the belly while saying (in your head) the first part of the word 'release' (so, saying *"Re-"*)

3.4. Exhale deeply (with attention on the tense area of your body) while saying (in your head) the second part of the word (*"-lease"*).

3.5. Inhale *"Re"*, exhale *"lease"*

3.6. Continue to do this until the timer alerts you.

3.7. *Tip*: If you are at work, then you can take a quick break away from your desk and use a cubicle in the washroom.

3.8. *Optional*: You can substitute the word *"Re-lease"* with *"Let go"* or *"Re-lax"* if you prefer. Or create your own winning combo.

2.2 Liquid Gold (Water)

Go with the flow…

"Be like water…be water, my friend."

– Bruce Lee

While breathing is foundational to our survival and energy, coming in a close second is water. The surface of the planet is covered in 71% water[55]. The body is around 60% water[56*]. If we want to be feeling like we are superhuman every day, then we need to be drinking super well each day.

In fact, just a 2% drop in body mass from water leads to up to a 20-40% drop in performance[57]. Researchers at the Human Performance Laboratory (University of Connecticut) found that even mild dehydration – just 1.5% - altered peoples energy levels, mood, and clarity of thought[58,59]. Conversely, being hydrated can have the effect of alleviating depression and crankiness as well as headaches and sleepiness.

Water is sometimes known as H_2O (or di-hydrogen monoxide – sounds scary). Two hydrogens atoms covalently bonded with an oxygen atom. But water is not just H_2O. Water is a universal solvent which means that other substances can dissolve into it. And there are many other substances that come along with that H_2O. Pure distilled water may be H_2O, but the water most of us will encounter has many different minerals that we need for our body, dissolved into it.

The first time I really appreciated the importance of water – or the detrimental effects of a lack of water rather – was when I was 18 years old. I was on my

---

* As babies we are closer to 75% water. According to H.H. Mitchell, Journal of Biological Chemistry, the brain and heart are composed of 73% water, and the lungs are about 83% water. The skin contains 64% water, muscles and kidneys are 79%, and even the bones are watery at 31%.

Gold Duke of Edinburgh (D. of E.) Award hike. A four-day (3-night) expedition through wild country in Wales, UK. One thing I didn't realise going into it was that we would have to find our own natural water sources from the land. My friend, Prakash, and I were woefully underprepared as we didn't realise this, and so didn't bring any water purification tablets with us.

After a particularly horrendous and arduous rainy first day hiking in Wales, which involved clambering over tussocks, getting stuck in swamps, and being left soaking wet, we got towards the end of the day. Prakash, myself and the other five members of our group ended up about an hour out from camp and huddled together in a mosquito-laden bog and out of water. I got so desperate I put my water bottle into the bog desperate for a drink. What I pulled out was dirty, green and with bits floating in it. I couldn't bring myself to drink it. We carried on to camp, thirsty, wet, and tired. We couldn't cook our evening meal, as we needed water for that too.

The next day, I woke up wet, cold, tired, and thirsty. The only liquid I had on me was beer! Don't ask me why I decided that four cans of beer would be more useful than water purification tablets[†]. I opened the can of beer and took a gulp. I almost vomited. Beer at 6am is not the best idea! I got very close to quitting the whole hike that day, were it not for Prakash convincing me to just do a few minutes, and then another few minutes. As it turned out, we later found a good stream, the weather became warm and sunny and the rest of the hike, although having several more challenges, ended up being successful.

After that experience, I never took water for granted again. I was used to having to fetch water from distance from my days as a Scout on camps. This was a whole new level of appreciation. And when I went on my 25-month travelling adventure around the world, I was always very aware as to whether I had clean drinking water with me.

What water does, other than hydrate us?

Water is important for the maintenance of our DNA[60,61]. And it facilitates reactions in our mitochondria[62] - the power houses of our cells. The mitochondria are where ATP is produced - your energy. The liquid portion of your blood - the plasma - is also 90% water, and the blood is used to transfer oxygen, nutrients, antibodies, and waste products. And continuing with waste

---

[†] Prakash, I'm sure, is still probably the only D. of E. participant to carry a bottle of Martini Rosso with him on the hike.

removal, the lymph fluid is mostly water. The lymph fluid is part of your lymphatic system which is effectively the sewage system for your body. So, the lymph helps keep you clean and healthy and needs plenty of water to do it.

Water is also needed for digestion and the digestive secretions[‡]. You might already realise this, but if you are constipated, leave the pharmacy-bought laxatives, and go for hyper-hydration instead. It will help[63].

Water is also needed for the cerebrospinal fluid of your central nervous system, and your brain stem. In fact, the cerebrospinal fluid is about 99% water[64].

You need water for your synovial fluid (the protective cushioning between your joints)[65]. When the synovial fluid wears through, that can cause joint problems like arthritic conditions. And water is needed for your hormones to work properly, and your body uses water as a pathway to transmit neurotransmitters (brain signals).

Water is vitally important. And if you are anything like the 90% of people I come across, then you may not be drinking anywhere close to enough. In my experience, most people are living in a state of chronic dehydration. How do I know this? Well, most people I interact with go significant portions of time (we're talking sometimes hours) without drinking anything close to hydrating - and no, coffee doesn't count. Nor do energy drinks, or alcohol.

Water makes up around 73% of your brain[56]. And often, if someone has a headache, it's going to be resolved with proper hydration[66]. Water dehydration can also often be mistaken for hunger. And in a study by the University of Washington, they claimed that one glass of water shut down midnight hunger pangs for almost 100% of dieters[67]. I know from my own personal experience too, that if I'm hungry but first drink a large glass of water, I don't feel so hungry. If you want to know whether you are hungry or dehydrated, then just try it out for yourself. We can go much longer without

---

[‡] I don't recommend drinking with meals though. I recommend giving it 30 minutes either side of a meal with no drinking. Others will argue that drinking during meals is fine. I'm not stringent with this, so I guess you can see for yourself if it affects positively or negatively your experience. I wouldn't gulp through lots of liquid during a meal though, even if I was drinking. Just a few sips.

food than we can water, so my bet is, that if it's outside normal mealtimes, then it's dehydration (assuming a decent diet of course).

In fact, researchers at the University of Illinois found that people who drink up to three glasses of water a day eat 205 fewer calories, and their sugar intake drops by nearly 18g and their cholesterol by 21mg a day. Overall, the 18,311 adults participating in the survey were drinking an average of 4.2 cups of water a day (way less than I would recommend, mind you), and researchers found significant difference in the diets of those drinking just one glass a day compared to those drinking more. Just adding an extra glass a day will make a significant difference to your health, the researchers say[68].

Water, oh brother!

"Water is the driving force of all nature."

– Leonardo Da Vinci

Water isn't just water. Water is a liquid crystal[69]. You might have heard of liquid crystals when talking about television sets and smartphones. They transmit and store information or energy. As does water[69]. When it's cooled and solidifies you can see the crystalline structure of water. Water is the most valuable substance, other than air, we have on this planet. In fact, our future deep space explorations are currently dependent on finding water on other celestial bodies, to enable us to reach out even further to the stars. It's that important.

Not all water is created equal though. And while it's just important to drink more water, it's also best if you drink the highest quality water that's available to you at the time. Don't be too fixated about it, just do the best you can with what's available.

Water has a structure, but sub-optimal water can have a coagulated structure and actually be clumped together so that not all the water gets into the cells where it's needed[70]. The bridge between the cells and water being allowed into pass is called an aquaporin. These aquaporin's only allow the right sized molecules through. So, you could be drinking water, and still your body doesn't absorb it well[70].

If you don't drink the optimal water, not only will you be potentially absorbing substances that you don't want. You may also not feel as hydrated as you could be. Over two hundred substances (in addition to water) were found in normal tap water by the Environmental Protection Agency (EPA) in 45 US states[71].

In 2008, the Associated Press published an investigation that found that 41 million Americans were drinking water that was tainted with pharmaceuticals – ranging from anti-depressants to muscle relaxants and who-knows-what in between[72]. In fact, 56 different pharmaceutical chemicals were found in the water supply in the US, stretching from Southern California to Northern New Jersey[73]. To say nothing of all the chemicals intentionally put in there to treat water and make it safe. In treatment plants, water is moved to a chlorine contact tank and this is where it's mixed with a solution of sodium hydrochloride and this is the same chemical that's in bleach[73]. They are bleaching your water. Water from the tap, is not just water. It's water and…a whole host of other dissolved substances.

A comprehensive study of the drinking water of over 28 million Americans detected a widespread level of pharmaceuticals and hormonal active chemicals in the water supply[74]. Nineteen municipalities were monitored over the course of a year. This is what was found in their water – albeit in small, and deemed safe, amounts. But present, nonetheless.

- Antibiotics: Amoxicillin, penicillin, tetracycline.
- Pain relievers like Tylenol/Paracetomol, aspirin, ibuprofen, naproxen (which is used to treat pain associated with arthritis), and prednisone.
- Mental health prescriptions like Valium and Prozac
- Caffeine and nicotine.
- Pesticides like atrazine (one of the most widely used agricultural pesticides in the United States).
- Lead, arsenic, and hormone replacement medications such as estrone.

I must stress, that these were in *safe* amounts. This isn't to scare you, but merely to bring awareness to you that regular water might not be just the water you think it is.

The biggest thing that is put in to treat tap water is chlorine. A bleach, but also an antibiotic[75]. Antibiotics kill bacteria. They don't discriminate between good and bad bacteria. Antibiotic means anti-life. These days it's becoming more and more recognised how important our own bacteria, within and on us, are for our health. Especially the bacteria in our guts[§] which is where most of our immune system is located[76], and which is also responsible for producing 90% of the serotonin[**] in our bodies[77]. The chlorine is in 'safe' and 'responsible' amounts, but we are drinking it all the time. *Can it really be a good idea to be consuming antibiotics daily – even if in small amounts?* I don't know the answer to that, but my intuition says I'd rather not be a guinea pig.

The second biggest chemical found in many tap waters (though thankfully hardly any in the UK or Europe) is fluoride. Which according to the National Research Council (NRC), fluoride can cause damage to the brain[78]. In fact, *Lancet Neurology*, also published an interesting piece of research concluding fluoride to be toxic to the brain's development too[79]. Like much research, highly contested, and while it's true that you can usually find research to back up any point of view, it's something to think about.

In chapter 7 of the National Research Council's (NRC) 2006 "Fluoride in Drinking Water: A Scientific Review of EPA's standards" – after a request by the Environmental Protection Agency (EPA) to examine fluoride, the research found dementia-like effects when exposed to fluoridated water[78]. The NRC also notes significant risks to your thyroid, bones, and bone cancer with exposure to fluoride in chapter 8 of their scientific review of the EPA standards[78]. Harvard scientists found a direct correlation between fluoride and a dangerous form of bone cancer called osteosarcoma[80]. Their conclusion:

"Our exploratory analysis found an association between fluoride exposure in drinking water during childhood and the incidence of osteosarcoma among males but not consistently among females. Further research is required to confirm or refute this observation."

Why is it in there? It's not there to kill anything. It's not a pathogen. It's there as medication. Yes, effectively a medication because it's thought that fluoride can help with cavities in teeth. Fluoride applied topically to teeth, *could* potentially be helpful[81]. Ingested from the water supply? I haven't seen any research to suggest that drinking fluoride helps with teeth cavities. Millions of people around the world are being 'medicated' without their knowledge or

---

[§] We have bacteria all over us and inside us, but the gut is an important place for a good balance of bacteria to be maintained.
[**] Serotonin is the 'feel good' hormone.

consent. I was totally shocked when I discovered this. Thankfully, unless you're living in the United States or in a place where they still fluoridate water, it isn't a big concern for you. Check with your water provider whether they add fluoride to your supply[††].

Which Water[70]?

What do we do about which type of water to drink then? We've had the scary stuff, so let's look at what we can do about it.

Which types of water can we consume? Let's look, but before we do, know that you just need to do the best you can with the situation at the time. When you can, get the best, but if you're thirsty and at your friend's house and they don't have what you need, it doesn't mean don't drink any water. In your own home, or place of work – somewhere you drink most of your water, you take a bit more time and effort to get it a little better.

In reverse order of quality, we have...

Bottled Water

Bottled water's only requirement is that it is as good as tap water. Not exactly comforting knowing what we now know about tap water. The Environmental Working Group (EWG) did a test on ten major US brands and found 38 different contaminants including nitrates, arsenic, Tylenol, caffeine, and industrial chemicals[82].

What about the bottle? Most bottled water is stored in plastic. When looking at plastics – especially the disposable kind used in most bottled water, we're looking at substances called xenoestrogens. Foreign to the body[‡‡]. BPA you might have heard of, as many reusable bottles are now BPA-free and by law all baby bottles need to be too. BPA stands for bisphenol A. BPA is an industrial chemical that has been used to make certain plastics and resins since the 1960s. As water is a universal solvent, substances that it encounters can dissolve into it. Including things from the plastics. And although BPA-free is great, there may be other things that have yet to be considered that are dissolving into the water and not good for us either, such as polyethylene terephthalate (PET or PETE), which poses a cancer threat[83]. And if you re-use the plastic bottles, then it can leach chemicals such as DEHA and benzyl butyl

---

[††] There is a proposal to fluoridate much more of the UK water supply.
[‡‡] Xeno is taken from the Greek word xenos, which means foreigner or stranger.

phthalate (BBP), an endocrine disrupter[84]. Plastics also photodegrade[85]. Which means that light can break them down. This affects the quality of the water too (no matter the original source).

Am I saying never buy bottled water? Or only buy it in glass? Sure, glass is better. Perhaps invest in a bottle for yourself, whether that's BPA-free plastic, glass, or a stainless steel one and take quality water from home with you, and then fill up as you need to, from the best sources around. It's not always going to be possible to have pure filtered water when out and about, but do what you can, when you can.

And that moves us on to the next type.

Filtered Water

Filters are popular these days. Many people use something like a Brita filter. Which incidentally is owned by Clorox[86]– a company that specialises in cleaning and disinfecting products. The water suppliers put chlorine in the water, and then a company that sells disinfecting products also sells a product that takes it out. Well, in fact, Brita filters don't remove chlorine, they just remove the taste of it[87]. You're still getting it.

These filters do something. They work – a little, and they are better than nothing. But let's look at another option.

Distilled Water

Distillation makes the water into H_2O. Which is *pure* water. *Did you ever drink that pure water in your chemistry lab at school?* I did. It tasted funny to me. Well, water, as we mentioned in the beginning of this chapter, isn't just H_2O, it's H_2O *plus* lots of other naturally occurring minerals.

Distilled water is a bit of a scavenger, as it doesn't have the dissolved minerals of other water. And minerals that the body needs. So, it might start to take them *from* the body. Minerals in the body could start to bind to that distilled water. I did go to a talk once from someone who swore by distilled water for curing some chronic joint pains he had. He had tried lots of other things and this was the only thing that worked. It makes sense if there is a build-up of calcification in places, then I can believe that distilled water could help alleviate the condition. Whether it's a good thing to have all the time, or just cycle through, or make sure you add minerals back in elsewhere, I don't know for sure. Even the speaker himself didn't suggest (from memory) to exclusively drink distilled water 100% of the time. I've yet to go extended periods on distilled water, so I can't speak from experience, but it is something I might experiment with in the future to see if any little joint niggles disappear.

I do own a distiller. And at home, when I'm able to put the water in a glass bottle, I use it. Just to see if I notice any difference. I don't like putting it into plastic bottles though, so don't drink it away from home. I probably only consume 10% of my daily water intake from distilled water. There is some dispute about whether it's good or bad. Some people having drunk it exclusively for decades swear by it. I might attempt a 24 – 48-hour water fast on it someday to see what happens. Currently, I can neither recommend, not caution against it.

Purified Water

Purified water doesn't really mean anything other than the water has been put through filtration, so it's a non-term really.

Alkaline Water

Most natural water sits around a pH of 7.0, or thereabouts. The pH scale is one of acidity and alkalinity (pH stands for potential Hydrogen). With 0 being very acidic and 14 being very alkaline. We have different pH values for different parts of our body, but the blood has a pH of 7.365[§§] and will always stay extremely close to that value[88]. Or else we'd get very sick. Regardless of what you put into your body. As we will discuss in the 'Earth' section later, to keep the blood at roughly 7.365, your body will work hard to maintain balance if it is overly stressed[***].

The idea of alkaline water is that the pH is in the range of 8.5 – 9.5. The theory being that by consuming more alkalinity, the body will be better balanced. Water can be naturally high in alkalinity or artificially alkaline created by a water Ioniser. In the case of using an ioniser, the water is being alkalised by a machine. The water is being 'charged' with electricity and creating a disassociation of the water – splitting the water molecules apart. More OH- and less H+. The result is two streams of water. One alkaline, and then a wastewater which is acidic. The machines that do this can also be flipped around to create an acidic water, with alkaline water coming out the waste

---

[§§] Generally, the range is 7.35-7.45.
[***] This could be through diet, but also other environmental factors like pollution and stress.

pipe. Acidic water can be useful as a cleaning water – for example spraying it on surfaces and wiping with a cloth, or even taking off make-up.

In terms of drinking ionised alkaline water, this is an artificial water, as we are using modern technology to create this system of alkalinity. There is a lot of debate about benefits (or harms) of alkaline water. Some people saying that it can, in fact, be damaging. Some saying that if it's naturally alkaline, then yes, it's great. At the same time saying that artificially created alkalised water can be damaging for the body. If the water is naturally alkaline, then it's due to the compounds in it (e.g., magnesium, potassium, calcium, sodium). The body then gets those beneficial minerals that it's looking for. If it's artificially alkaline, then it won't have these in there. But the body is expecting them because of the alkalinity.

In some counties – Japan comes to mind – alkalised water has been used and ionisers sold for many decades and approved as medical devices[89]. In one double-blind placebo controlled four-week trial, the researchers concluded that ingesting alkaline water on a daily basis improves health and exercise capacity, even in healthy people[89].

It can be hard to separate fact from fiction when it comes to the alkaline water industry. It might be that ionised alkaline water is good for treating conditions when used in the short-term. Long-term it could be that natural alkaline water is what is needed. It might be that purported benefits of alkaline water are due to the molecular hydrogen and not any of the other claims[90].

If you choose to use alkaline water, it is recommended that you gradually build up the amount of alkaline water you drink slowly, as it can create a detoxification process in the body – and produce headaches. I bought a water ioniser machine in 2013 and have been using it since then. I vaguely remember something like mild headaches happening in the first few days (but not all day), and then my body must have adapted to it. I also have three filters that the water passes through before it gets to the ioniser (and there's one in the ioniser, so effectively my water passes through four filters and the ioniser). I consume about 20-30% of my daily water through the ioniser, but if I'm drinking herbal teas (which I often do), I tend to fill the kettle up directly from the (triple filtered) tap water, and not ionised water.

I think that there is too much uncertainty and controversy around alkaline and ionised alkaline water for me to specifically recommend drinking it or not. You would be best off looking into both sides of the arguments and concluding for yourself. Currently I'm happy to use artificially ionised alkaline water – at least until my machine breaks, and then we'll see.

Reverse Osmosis

Reverse Osmosis (RO) water is water that passes through a tight membrane - 0.0001 microns. Compare that to bacteria which is 0.4 microns. Effectively it's removing lots and lots of things in the water – pharmaceuticals and the rest. You're effectively getting blank water again. This might be okay for some people, and not for others. And the machines can be expensive too (just like ionisers).

Mineral Water

Mineral water that you buy or get from wells (sometimes labelled as 'artisan' water), is really water from underground aquifers (lakes). This water has gone through the normal hydrological cycle which can take hundreds, if not thousands of years, and it comes to rest in these aquifers. We head down there and pull out the water. It's clean but it might not really be "ready" yet. We are going to get it, rather than it coming to us, through the rocks and coming out of a spring. And because it hasn't gone through the rocks it might have a higher mineral content and total dissolved solids (TDS) than you might like. And it's possible that there would be too many minerals in your body. It's fine for most people, but just be aware, it might not be the absolute best choice. Leading on to…

Spring Water

The best choice if you can get your hands on it. It would have gone through the natural earth-water cycle and is primed and ready for us. Of course, it's not easy to harvest your own spring water for most people, but you could use a resource like findaspring.com to find one. I used it to locate one in Hampstead, North London, but I have to say it had a strong taste of copper to me, so I wasn't a fan. Not 100% sure why that was, but I think it was the piping used to deliver the water. It's a good idea to make sure that the spring you are drinking from is safe to drink from. If it's been tested and shown to be safe, all the better. As you can possibly be exposed to things you don't want to with raw natural springs. When I led a retreat in Turkey in 2014, we were fortunate enough to be very close to a natural spring. And the water was amazing.

E - ELEMENTS

Of course, you can also buy spring water. It's an option when out and about but might be cost prohibitive as a daily option. Although I'm sure there are companies that will deliver great spring water. Hopefully in decent bottles that are made from glass and re-usable.

So, the best options would be safe spring water harvested yourself, then store-bought in glass, then you could look at mineral water, reverse osmosis, and alkaline water. For me, I drink around 30% of my water as alkaline water, about 10% as distilled and the rest as triple-filtered water[†††].

The above list isn't even exhaustive, as there are waters like Hydrogen water (which may well be the most promising, but I've only just started to use hydrogen water so it's too early for me to comment), different tree waters, fat water, protein water, coherent water and by the time you're reading this there may be even more.

Spicing Up Water

If you want to make your water a little better and add a bit of 'structure' into it, you could consider adding in some salts – sea salts, Himalayan salts, or some other kind of rock salt. Salt can have some 60+ trace minerals in it[91], so you're giving the water some power back and alkalising it a little.

You could also consider squeezing in some fresh lemon juice. Lemon has a natural fit with water. Lemon has what is called an anionic orbit[92]. Its atoms are spinning in a reverse way to other foods. It's spinning in a way that parts of your digestive tract do, or that your saliva spins. So, it's good at cleaning you up a bit. That's why many people drink lemon in their water (and adds a nice taste). It also adds some ions in there. My first drink of the day is normally 400ml of warm water, followed by 400ml of hot water lemon. Both are great for your digestion and bowel movements.

In addition, you could use various fruits and vegetables to liven up your water. Just chop them up and leave them in the water. The flavour will seep out into the water and change the taste. Especially good if you are someone that

---

[†††] Each canister is devoted to addressing a different set of harmful chemicals, heavy metals, chlorine, chloramines, and over 100 additional contaminants.

148

doesn't like drinking water much. Many water bottles come with infusers now to make the whole process a lot easier[‡‡‡].

Alternatively, try drinking hot water. Yes, just plain hot water. Without the tea, coffee, milk, or sugar. My mum never used to like drinking water, and was chronically dehydrated in my view, but a few years ago she got into the habit of drinking hot water and loves it. I even bought her a little flask that keeps the water hot and that she uses that all day every day now. Keeping her hydrated and doing her body a lot of good.

Water bottles

Just a quick word about water bottles. I've gone through many, many, *many* water bottles and own quite a few even now. I have ones for the house made from glass, ones to travel with made from BPA-free plastic in sizes ranging from 700ml to 2.2l, ones to take hot water with me, collapsible ones, and many others for all manner of things.

What I would say is buy a design that you like, and that will encourage you to drink. Ideally, it should be BPA-free and free of other toxins. Think about what size you are happy to carry around with you, and where you'll be using it. I'm out and about a lot so I carry a 1.5l bottle normally with my water in from home, as I would rather fill up as little as possible when I'm out. If I head to the gym, I often take the 2.2l bottle with me if I'm doing two hours or more of training. I prefer to see the water level too, so unless I'm taking hot water with me, I don't like using the stainless-steel bottles as I can't see what's in them. Glass is too heavy and fragile for me when travelling.

If you are just going to work and they have decent water there, you might only need a smaller bottle. Keep it near you throughout the day and in your line of sight. This is important, as if you can't see it often, you'll forget to drink from it regularly. Out of sight, out of mind. Set a little challenge for yourself, such as whenever you respond to an email you have a rule that you take a sip of water. Or you decide that you'll finish one bottle before lunch, fill up, and finish it again before leaving for the day.

Experiment with the kind of bottles you use too. I've had clients in the past who found that they didn't like drinking out of bottles that they couldn't see into. I'm the same. I would rather a bottle I can see the water line in full, rather

---

[‡‡‡] Again, consider things like cucumber which won't leave an acidic residue to sit on the teeth all day.

than a stainless steel one, or one with just a slither of visibility. When my client changed bottle styles their drinking amount immediately increased.

How Much Should You Drink?

It depends. There are many factors that can influence how much you need to drink. From the ambient temperature and humidity, whether you speak a lot for your job (we lose a lot of water through exhaling), your activity levels, whether you've exercised and what type of exercise you do. Also, whether you work in air-conditioning and a whole host of other factors, such as your weight.

In terms of an actual quantity or formula, there are a wide range of opinions on the matter. Here's my view and formula (rule of thumb) for the minimum amount you should be aiming for, based on what I've researched and experimented with.

> *Half your body weight (in 'pounds') in fluid ounces.*

If you are used to the US system, then that's easy enough. If you weigh 180lbs, then you should aim to drink 90 US fluid ounces a day. That's about 2.7 litres.

If you were to measure in kilograms, then an approximate formula is

> **0.033 x weight (kg)**

For example, 180lb is around 82kg. So that would be 0.033 x 82 = 2.7 litres. Or 1/30th of your body weight. An easy way to think of it is to divide your weight (kg) by three and then again by 10.

I still think that is a little on the low side. I'm 80kg and have been drinking between 3 – 5 litres of water a day for the last several years with noticeable improvements in my alertness, focus, energy, skin complexion and more. If I drink less than three litres I don't feel as super. And of course, if I'm exercising a lot that day, it will be even more.

What about hyponatremia?

Hyponatremia. This means drinking too much water. Yes, too much of anything can kill you. Even water. You do hear of these extremely rare times when a marathon runner will die from hyponatremia. It's when a person has had so much water that the levels of sodium in their blood are extremely low. Most of us consume enough salt each day[§§§], and we aren't running marathons each day. And even if you are running marathons, then hopefully you will also be fuelling yourself appropriately with food too and taking in enough water to replace what you're losing. The training you do will help you gauge this.

That being said. If you drink 500ml of water right now, but you believe you should be at three litres based on the calculations above, then take your time getting to that level. A few weeks at least. Just start by increasing incrementally. You might decide to increase by 500ml in week one. Another 500ml in week two and so on. Until you hit your target.

How do you know when you've hit the daily target that you have set yourself? Don't rely on drinking water from a glass. It's not as easy to keep track of in my experience. As mentioned already, invest in a purpose-built BPA-free (and other toxins free) plastic water bottle. With a bottle that you refill, you can easily keep track of how many times you need to fill and consume that bottle each day. Some bottles even have a number dial on them to mark off how many times you have refilled them.

Set yourself a target throughout the day. For example, if you're aiming for four litres, set a target of drinking one litre of water before the workday starts. Then another litre by lunch. One more litre before finishing work for the day, and another litre in the evening. Give or take. Having micro-goals like this (for many areas of your life) can really help keep you on track.

What counts as water?

Well, water of course. Then (non-caffeinated, non-fruit) herbal teas. Oh, and sparkling water, though be cautious with sparkling water as carbonated drinks have been shown to increase the hunger hormone ghrelin, which could contribute to weight gain[93]. That's about all I would count. If you can't water

---

[§§§] Even if you don't actively add it, most things in a packet will have salt in it.

your plants with it, you shouldn't water your insides with it. Just think of it in those terms.

Coffee, tea, soda-pop (fizzy drinks), cordials and fruit juices don't count. Neither do store-bought flavoured waters. Nor bottled smoothies. Even the 'innocent' looking ones[****]. You'll be overdosing on sugar in no time[††††]. Even if they say naturally occurring fruit sugars. Exercise caution. Oh, and just in case I must spell it out, NO – alcohol doesn't count towards your daily limit either.

Low-to-no sugar vegetable juices *could* count though. Just watch out for sugar content in those too. The World Health Organisation (WHO) recommends that adults have less than 25g (6 teaspoons) of free sugars a day[‡‡‡‡]. A 500ml bottle of cola has around 53g sugar (12 teaspoons), and a Venti White Choca Moca Frappaccino (whatever that is) has a mega 74g. That's practically 19 teaspoons of sugar. *Before* you add any of your own. And 500ml of flavoured water can still have around 43g of sugar (over 10 teaspoons). So, don't rely on those kinds of beverages to make up your water intake.

What about 'experts' who say you get a large quantity of your water through your foods? Well... I juice vegetables pretty much every day. And I can tell you, I get around 400ml of juice from five portions of low sugar vegetables. In any case, less than 30% of adults tend to reach five portions of vegetables and fruit a day[94]. I'm sure that the human body can extract more from vegetables than the juicer can, but not *that* much more. Plus, more importantly, you can't measure it. And as management guru Peter Drucker once said:

"You can't manage what you can't measure."

– Peter Drucker

[****] Did you know that the smoothie brand Innocent is now owned by Coca Cola?

[††††] Do I *never* drink store bought smoothies? No, very occasionally I might if I have a need for one. Honestly though, I would say that's around 5-6 times a year only.

[‡‡‡‡] Free sugars are defined as the type of sugars that are added to food, as well as sugars that are naturally present in honey, syrups, and fruit juices, not sugars in milk products and whole fruit & vegetables. The sugar in fruit juices is considered free sugars too. Sugar in smoothies depends on the intensiveness of the processing method, whether the skin of the fruit was included and whether fruit juices are also added.

The Pee Test

So, how do you know when you've got enough in the tank? Well, there is a super-simple check that you can do to monitor your body's levels of water throughout the day. It's the best (and easiest) way to know whether you need to drink more water or not. It's called *The Pee Test*. Just look at the colour of your urine: it should be *virtually* clear. Just the slightest tinge of yellow on occasion, that's ok. Anything darker and you really need to drink some water as soon as possible.

It's how I gauge my hydration levels throughout the day – every day. I look at my urine and make sure it appears clear when it comes out. When the urine rests in the bowl, there will be the slightest hint of colour, but not much. If it's yellow when I'm peeing, I know I need to drink some more water[§§§§].

Clear pee, clear skin, clear thinking – All clear!

Water is liquid gold. It really is. Make sure you capitalise on this substance to boost your productivity, increase your focus, give your skin a lift, raise your energy and ensure great health.

[§§§§] Slight caveat here is that sometimes, depending on what I've eaten, I could know I'm hydrated but the pee will be coloured. I usually know that this colour is coming from the food, and so don't worry about it then. Usually, the next time I'm going to the toilet the thing causing the colourisation has passed through.

Quick summary about hydration and becoming superhuman...

1. Most people are walking around each day in a state of chronic dehydration.

2. Water is essential for every aspect of our being. From our focus and energy levels, to what our skin, hair and nails will look like.

3. There are many different types of water, but the important thing is to make sure you commit to drinking an amount that's right for you and gives you an 'A' on *The Pee Test*.

Action plan for becoming superhuman...

1. Commit to buying a decent water bottle that you will be happy to carry around with you and use every day. Whether it's stainless steel, glass, or a BPA-free plastic bottle.

2. Use the formula given to get an estimate or how much water someone of your weight should consume at a minimum. Consider the other factors that will increase this amount.

3. Steadily, and slowly, increase your water intake until you get to your desired volume while using *The Pee Test* as a guide ensuring a virtually clear stream each time you go to the toilet.

2.3 Third Rock from the Sun (Earth)

Mother Earth, Gaia...

"Tell me what you eat, and I will tell you what you are."

- Jean Anthelme Brillat-Savarin

Earth is a metaphor for both the food that we eat, and our relationship with the Earth. If you want to perform at the highest level, then you need to get the nutrition part sorted.

Food is a very complicated and divisive subject. And you can get bogged down for years in endless studies, arguments, debates and more. I like to keep things simple and save you the effort. There are many approaches that might work. And remember that just because something works for your body one day (or year) it doesn't mean that you must eat that way forever. A lot of people into food can get their whole identity wrapped up into what they do or don't eat. It has almost become a religion for many.

Before I reveal my philosophy to eating, let's just keep it simple.

Food can seem to be a highly complex subject. Proteins, fats, carbohydrates, calorie counting and on it goes. Who has time to count calories, carbs, or anything else for that matter. I don't know anyone that succeeds in measuring things in that way, over the long haul.

When it comes to food, things are always changing. Foods, diets, and styles of eating fall in and out of vogue with the seasons. Though there are a few fundamentals that most experts agree on.

1. **Eat plenty of vegetables**. Have a little fruit. I advise setting a target of at least eight portions of vegetables per day and two portions of fruit. Effectively a 4:1, veg to fruit ratio.

2. **Eat real food**. In other words, if it was made by man don't eat it. If it was made *in* a plant, and not *by* a plant, don't eat it. If it has an advertising campaign convincing you to buy it, don't eat it. If it sits in the middle aisles of the supermarket, then be cautious[*]. Eating processed food has been shown to lead to participants in one study to eat on average 500 calories a day more than when eating real food. And put on about 1 kg in two weeks[95].

3. **Limit your sugar intake**. The World Health Organisation recommends less than 25g (6 teaspoons) a day for adults[96]. And for children, it's far less than 25g[†]. Most people are getting over 100g a day. In fact, those children under five years old shouldn't really have any.

4. **Don't be afraid of fat**. Even saturated (if it's coming from things like avocados, coconuts and similar). Sixty per cent of the non-water weight of the brain is fat[97‡]. Fat also creates essential hormones in your body[98]. Fat is also a cleaner source of energy, and longer lasting, for your body than carbohydrates[99]. Just stay away from hydrogenated fats, processed fats and oils (like sunflower oil) and use oils that have high smoke points[§], if you are heating them.

---

[*] The middle aisles are where most of the processed junk sits.

[†] The WHO recommends less than 5% of your calories to come from sugars. For a diet of 2000 calories, 5% is 100 calories. Sugar is a carbohydrate where 1g equates to 4 calories (for fat 1g equates to 9 calories). So, 100/4= 25g.

[‡] Also note that you may also have heard that the brain is also 85% water. This is also true when in the body. When out of the body, most of the weight (60%) of the brain is fat.

[§] The smoke point is the temperature at which the oil starts to break down. E.g., extra virgin olive oil = 160°C, coconut oil = 177°C - 232°C, ghee = 252°C, avocado oil = 271°C

5. **Chew slowly**. Most of us chew too quickly and not enough. Aim for 25 chews before swallowing. Yes, 25. This starts to release more saliva and hence enzymes in the mouth to break down the food[100-102] and lead to a beneficial effect on the body, for example becoming more satiated[103]. Not to mention helping you become more mindful whilst eating - even the taste of the food might change for you.

Okay so that's the general guidance. But I know that some people like a more structured approach, a 'diet' to follow. To help people I developed a principle-led system called *PANLO 80/20*. It's a non-dogmatic approach to eating - which involves no calorie or micro/macro-nutrient counting - that you can follow whether you are a typical Western 'eat everything' foodie, Paleo disciple, vegan advocate, vegetarian or into something else. If your focus is health, then I believe that the *PANLO 80/20* approach is an inclusive and easy way to think about food.

So, what is *PANLO 80/20,* and will it get you energised and feeling superhuman? Absolutely. But don't take my word for it. Read on and then test this for yourself.

PANLO 80/20

I call my approach to eating *PANLO 80/20* because the *PANLO* stands for the five areas, or questions, to consider when choosing food.

P – Plant Based

Is the food plant-based?

Every nutritional expert worth their salt, that I've come across, universally agrees that vegetables are good for you. In fact, they are *super* for you. Full of fibre, micronutrients, antioxidants, protein, fats, and carbohydrates. Most experts will attest that we should all be eating more plants. Our diets should be plant-based regardless of whether you choose to eat animals or consume animal products, the overwhelming evidence and consensus is that getting your greens in, is very good news.

So, the first question I ask is:

"Is what I'm about to eat plant-based?"

I.e., loaded with vegetables above and beyond anything else. It doesn't have to be plant-*only*, but heavily weighted towards plants. The first criteria and what I believe (through experience, observations, and research) is key, is that the food is plant-based.

A – Alkaline

Is the food alkaline in nature?

You may remember something of the pH (potential hydrogen) scale from high school biology and chemistry. It's a measure of acidity (0) to alkalinity (14) with 7 being neutral. We mentioned it in the chapter about water.

The body has different pH levels depending on the organ we're talking about[104], but one of the best indicators of health, is healthy blood. The blood has a pH around 7.365 (give or take a narrow band). It will stay in this range regardless of what you do, because if it deviated too much you would get seriously ill. Eating alkaline won't turn your body alkaline, but you are giving your body an abundance of nutrients to support its ability to maintain homeostasis[105].

When you consume lots of acid-forming products the theory goes that the body must work harder to maintain that healthy range - homeostasis. It draws on nutrients from elsewhere in the body (like the organs – kidney, liver, skin, bones, and so on) to neutralise the acidity. And that it takes significantly more alkalinity to neutralise the acidity that comes in[106]. Our diets should therefore be tilted towards alkaline items. Not 100% alkaline, but as I'm about to explain, it's very easy to create acidic load in the body and so I recommend that roughly 80% of the diet should be alkaline.

Acid can be created in the body through several ways. Foods like sugar, meat, dairy, processed foods, soda's, coffee, alcohol and even many fruits. Also, you can create an acidic environment through stress, pollution, hard or excessive exercise and a lack of sleep.

It's impossible to avoid creating some level of acidity in our bodies. Our diet should therefore be moving towards alkalinity. You can pick up a copy of an acid-alkaline food chart I have compiled (see Appendix) at **https://thethoughtgym.com/supervitality**.

I'll be the first to admit that there is some controversy over the idea of an 'alkaline diet'. However, when you do focus on foods considered alkaline (mainly vegetables for example), and eliminate items considered mostly acidic (soda, alcohol, processed foods, fast food, for example) most people will undoubtably feel better. Whether it works for the reasons touted, or it works just because it introduces more real foods in the guise of vegetables, does it matter?

In terms of my approach here, for one I'm not promoting an 'alkaline diet' as you might read about in the press. I'm explaining the *PANLO 80/20* approach (not diet) that I take to eating. Most vegetables are alkaline, making it easy to recognise whether you are skewing towards alkaline or acid in your food choices. Especially if you are looking for plant-based foods based from the 'P' in *PANLO* anyway. Some fruits, like tomatoes, avocados, lemons, and limes are also alkalising. Lemons and limes, although acidic, have an alkalising effect on the body[107]. Other food items that are acidic tend to be many grains, beans, nuts, and seeds. That doesn't mean you don't eat them. They can be great for you (depending on the grains you eat and how you prepare the beans), but they just make up the 20% of the balance.

N – Natural

Is this food in its natural state?

Does the food look like something you would find in nature?

We are living in an ever-increasing *un*natural world. How most people eat, move and exercise are not natural patterns anymore. We stay awake later than we should, not following the natural rhythms of nature and forgetting that we (everyone and everything on this planet) are part of one symbiotic system. All to our detriment.

When it comes to food, *does what you're about to eat look like it came from nature?*

Could you recognise it in a field?

If not, then minimise the consumption of it.

For example, if I'm cooking a curry and it's full of broccoli – I can recognise that as broccoli. I don't see many chicken nuggets roaming around in fields anywhere. I don't see many veggie-burgers or meat burgers unless on a shop shelf or in a restaurant. Even when I make a homemade pizza, I'm piling on around five portions of vegetables including a whole head of broccoli, courgettes, peppers, and onion. All of which I can recognise as real food –

albeit on top of an 'unnatural' pizza base (but most of the pizza that I'm consuming is natural looking).

Think simple.

Does it look like nature gave it to me?

Even grains aren't as nature presents them to us. They are processed by man. This isn't about eating nothing unnatural but just get some awareness over it. You can't go into a supermarket and buy a gluten-free vegan brownie and think that it's healthy or natural. It's not. Okay, you might find a 'healthy' homemade brownie (full of superfoods like spirulina and chia) being sold at a market by some artisan baker, but it's still not a naturally occurring brownie.

Again, to stress. I am not advocating that you *never ever* have anything unnatural. I eat things that are not natural quite often. Just limit that which isn't natural in your diet, as far as is practically possible.

L – Live / Lightly Cooked

Is this food live or lightly cooked?

Cooking food has benefits. It softens it for us to chew on and releases other nutrients sometimes not available in raw food[108]**. However, introducing more live (raw) and lightly cooked (e.g., steamed, stir-fried, steam-fried) food, I believe is a good idea. In the 1920's Edward Howell, MD, promoted the idea that the enzymes available in raw foods help us to break food down without the need to produce as many enzymes on our own. And, that by keeping foods rawer it protects their 'life-force'. While some people feel his work has been discredited, and don't buy into it, I'm open to these ideas. I am not fanatic about eating raw at all. Again, this is all part of *PANLO 80/20* so will become clear to you by the end of this chapter. Plants are living things and so cooking can 'kill' them. Maybe picking them from the ground already starts that process but cooking probably advances it. It's plausible that the energy that we might have gotten from the plants might then be diluted by cooking, and we end up not taking as much. To be honest, I haven't done significant research into this and can't conclusively say. However, looking up something called 'Kirlian photography' will show you images of the

---

** Some nutrients are in fact more accessible after boiling or steaming. This is true for several antioxidants: ferulic acid (found in, for example, asparagus), lycopene and beta-carotene (found in orange and red coloured vegetables e.g., sweet potatoes, tomatoes, and squash).

'energetic field' of plants before and after cooking[††].

Better still, start introducing more live foods (salads, steamed veg, raw veg) and decide for yourself whether you start to feel like you have more energy. Again, I don't believe you should be 100% raw at all. I think that 50% - 60% is a good range to experiment with. Whenever I've upped my raw food intake, I do find an extra bit of energy. In the winter months I prefer a little less raw/lightly cooked foods though.

O – Organic

Is this food organic?

Lastly, I consider whether the food is organic or not. I'm not super religious about this, but it is an ever-growing presence for me now. I have a weekly organic vegetable delivery from local farms which I use to fuel most of my meals in the week. I can often taste the difference in the food and discovered that, for me, organic hummus tastes better compared to regular hummus.

Think about this. If there are products (like Monsanto's *Ready Round Up*) being sprayed onto farmland to kill insects and bugs, then the plants are being sprayed with things that are designed to kill. The food is being sprayed with something poisonous[‡‡]. This gets into the soil and the plants absorb this. *Do you really want to eat that?*

As part of my long post-university travels, I visited Vietnam for about a month in 2000[§§], and on my visit there I got to see the effects of another product Monsanto made. It was called *Agent Orange* and it caused massive birth defects in children as it was used by the US as part of their military campaign against Vietnam during the Vietnam War. Granted, Agent Orange was *meant to be* (horrifically) destructive to humans but *do you really want to be eating food sprayed with products made by the same company that also makes products like that?* During my time in Vietnam, I visited many museums awash with images and the stored remains of young children that were

---

[††] Kirlian photography is a technique for creating contact print photographs using high voltage. The process entails placing a sheet photographic film on top of a metal discharge plate. The object to be photographed is then placed directly on top of the film. Kirlian photography is a little bit 'out there' and certainly has its critics, but it does make me pause for thought.
[‡‡] Glyphosate is one such chemical, and you really don't want to consume that.
[§§] I was back-packing for over two years all around the world and it was the best education I ever received.

affected by Agent Orange. Images I can still vividly picture to this day.

Of course, I'm not suggesting that "conventionally" grown food (the label used to describe non-organic food) is like that. Not even close. But when I can, I prefer to eat food that hasn't been sprayed with chemicals designed to take life.

There is some evidence coming through to show that organic food has more antioxidants and less toxic residue[109]. Some further evidence showing that people eating organic have reduced cancer risk too[110].

There was also an interesting experiment with one family where they ate non-organic and then went organic for two weeks. Before the experiments there were significant levels of pesticides in their urine. After two weeks. Virtually none[111]. Are you sure you want that in your body?

Rather than be super strict with this, at home, when I can, I buy organic. If my food runs out, and I do a local shop, I'll get what's there. If I'm out with people at a restaurant, I'll eat what's there and the best choice.

At work, when you are in the lunch canteen or out with your mates, there isn't always going to be a choice on the matter. Don't get caught up with that and certainly don't be one of those people who say, "I refuse to eat it unless it's organic!" When you can though, just think about introducing more into your weekly shop. In your own home, however, where you are King (or Queen) of your own Kingdom (or Queendom), why not think about it?

And if you can only buy a few items organic, and the rest non-organic, then the following two lists might be useful to you. Known as the *Clean Fifteen* and the *Dirty Dozen* and taken from the Environmental Working Group website, EWG.org. The Clean Fifteen are those conventionally grown foods that are considered okay, and the Dirty Dozen are ones you should look to getting organic when you can[***].

*** These lists are updated yearly, so you can just do an online search for the latest recommendations.

Clean Fifteen:	Dirty Dozen:
Avocados	Strawberries
Sweet Corn	Spinach
Pineapples	Nectarines
Cabbages	Apples
Onions	Grapes
Frozen Sweet Peas	Peaches
Papaya's	Cherries
Asparagus	Pears
Mangoes	Tomatoes
Aubergines	Celery
Honeydew Melons	Potatoes
Kiwis	Sweet Peppers
Cantaloupes	
Cauliflower	
Broccoli	

80/20

That's what *PANLO* is about. Plant-based, alkaline, natural, live or lightly cooked and organic. What about the *80/20*? This simply means do *PANLO* as much as you can. Four meals out of five, or 75-80% of your plate.

And with the *PANLO* idea, I would rarely get all five *PANLO* principles checked off. If you can aim for three or more principles (or letters) from *PANLO* for 80% of the time, then you will notice a big change.

I'm on a mission to get the *PANLO 80/20* idea more widespread as it allows for more flexibility than most other styles. It covers the essential elements, and you can still be *PANLO 80/20* while being vegan, Paleo, Keto, vegetarian or pretty much anything else[†††].

For each meal ask yourself:

1. *Is this food **plant-based**?*

2. *Is it **alkaline**?*

[†††] Although, granted, probably not that easy if you are a nose-to-tail carnivore!

E - ELEMENTS

3. *Does it look like something I would recognise in **nature**?*

4. *Is it **live**/raw or just **lightly** cooked?*

5. *Is it **organic**?*

Aim for three or more answers being 'yes' and you're good to go!

Figure 14 - The PANLO 80/20 Plate

Additional Considerations

It's worth mentioning here other important considerations when eating. While we want to focus on getting good things into the diet, it's also worth eliminating certain foods. Taking a step-by-step approach is a good idea. An idea I heard from Lucas Rockwood's podcast was this idea of 1+1. What 1+1 means is that you focus for a period - say 21 days - on introducing one good new thing into your diet, for example an extra portion of broccoli at each meal, but at the same time you focus on removing one bad thing from your diet, for example, fizzy drinks. And keep going until the balance works out well for you, and you want to stop. Below I list a few things you might want to consider dropping from your diet or severely limiting as many people feel better for doing so.

Foods to Consider Removing

Dairy

What's wrong with dairy? It's got calcium in it right? All those celebrities promote it, don't they? Milk moustaches and the "Got Milk" campaigns? We've been told to have it since we were kids.

Where to start with dairy? Here are a few popular arguments against it.

Intolerance

Most people in the world - estimates around 75% - are in fact intolerant (to one degree or another) to milk[112]. After the age of about five years old, most people stop producing lactase[113] - the enzyme that is needed to break down the sugars in milk - lactose[‡‡‡]. Most of the world's population don't drink milk. In fact, not being able to digest lactose is the norm, and so some scientists call for it to be called lactose *persistence* in people that *can* consume lactose, as that's the uncommon situation, not lactose 'intolerance'.

Dairy consumption is a Western behemoth of a concept that has been brainwashing generations. Forget what I say though. The best thing is to test it for yourself. Most people find that their health improves by eliminating dairy. Personally, I used to suffer from sinus issues my entire life. From nose bleeds to blocked and runny noses, earaches and even having my nose cauterised twice. All I know, is that when I decided to temporarily remove dairy from my diet in 2008 for Lent[§§§], my issues with having a runny or blocked nose, and difficulty in breathing through my nose almost got completely disappeared. I'd say about 80%. The other 20% improvement came from removing gluten from my diet in 2012. Together with egg, peanut, soy and fish, wheat (which contains gluten) and dairy account for about 90%

[‡‡‡] In fact, recently I learnt that one of my nieces (at the time 7 years old) was, like me, identified as lactose intolerant. Whether this was always the case and just picked up, or simply because she was of that age, I don't know.

[§§§] I'm not religious, however I find Lent is a good finite time to run experiments that either remove or introduce habits.

of the allergies out there[114].

Other people report improved digestion, less bloating, sinus, and earache improvements, no more IBS (irritable bowel syndrome), eliminating usual headaches and more energy amongst other things.

It's Acidic

Another potential reason to avoid milk is that it in fact creates an acidic forming environment in your body[115]. The body then must deal with the acidic load to keep your blood at pH 7.365. This means that your bones may use calcium and phosphorus to buffer the acid[116]. Losing calcium and phosphorus may weaken bones over time and not allow them to regenerate as they are meant to. It might also result stripping vital nutrients from elsewhere in your body too. Liver, kidney, lungs, heart, skin and so on.

Just remember - there is a prevalence for acid to enter our inner environment. And an acid-alkaline balance is required, and you shouldn't be all of one or the other. And because it's so much easier to acidify than to alkalise, I suggest you just remember:

Acid = Bad

Alkaline = Good

Osteoporosis

Following on from acidic influences that milk instigates, countries with lowest rates of dairy and calcium consumption have the lowest rates of osteoporosis[117,118]. Granted, advocates of dairy products will say that correlation doesn't mean causation – and it doesn't. They might also point out that these cultures might have more exposure to Vitamin D (sunshine), which is essential for bone health. And they are less sedentary. All these points are true and valid. However, it's something you might like to consider. Furthermore, studies show that women who drink large amounts of milk have a higher incidence of bone fractures than those that don't[119].

Also, studies of calcium supplementation have shown no benefit in reducing fracture risk[120]. As this study reported in the British Medical Journal concludes:

"Dietary calcium intake is not associated with risk of fracture, and there is

no clinical trial evidence that increasing calcium intake from dietary sources prevents fractures. Evidence that calcium supplements prevent fractures is weak and inconsistent." Calcium intake and risk of fracture: systematic review.

Vitamin D appears to be much more important than calcium in preventing fractures[121]. And hip fractures are more common in people who consume more dairy products and take in high levels of calcium[122].

Cancer Link

The main protein in milk is called casein. It's a substance that is also used to make certain glues[123]. *Would you want that in you?* Aside from that, when researchers were studying the effects of casein on cancerous cells, they found out something interesting.

When the subjects (rats) were exposed to a carcinogenic substance (called aflatoxin) the rate of cancer growth would increase if they were also consuming a diet of 20% protein (casein)[124].

When they were switched back to a diet of 5% protein (casein) - the rate of growth slowed. Up to 20% - it increased again. Down to 5%, it decreased again. It was as if it were turning on and off cancer growth like a light switch.

Interestingly though, when the rats who were on the plant-based protein mix of 5% were then given a diet of 20% plant protein, their cancerous cells didn't increase.

The tipping point for the cancerous growths seemed (for animal protein) to be in the region of 10% - 15%.

What else?

Research shows that higher intakes of both calcium and dairy products may increase a man's risk of prostate cancer by 30 to 50 per cent[125]. Plus, dairy consumption increases the body's level of insulin-like growth factor-1 (IGF-1)[126] — a probable cancer promoter[127].

Bear in mind that even the World Health Organisation (WHO) recommends less than 10% of calories to be taken from protein****, but most Western adults

****The WHO states 0.66g protein per kg. If I weigh 80kg that's 53g protein. There are 4 calories in a gram of protein. So that's 212 calories. An 80kg person might require around 2500

consume 20 - 30 % of their calorie needs from protein, with the vast majority of that from animal protein[128].

Antibiotics and Perpetual Impregnation

For a cow to produce milk, like a human counterpart, she must be impregnated, all the time. Otherwise, they won't produce the milk required. *How are they impregnated?* Well artificially, of course. *Doesn't that sound pleasant?*

Coupled with the fact that (if you are in the US) there is now widespread use of antibiotics in cows bred for milk which means all sorts of problems. For example, antibiotics become more widespread and then when we need them, they don't work. Not to mention the thought of whether you really want to have milk from a cow that needed antibiotics to make it "safe" to use.

Antibiotics have also been known (by farmers for years) to increase the size of the animal – i.e., make them fat. *Could this also be a reason for a nation's rising obesity rates?*

Oh, and did I mention bovine growth hormones are also used - although thankfully only really in the US.

Weening

Don't you think that it's strange to consume milk past the weening ages, which are from birth to around two years old? We're the only species that I know of on Earth that consumes milk past infancy. And not even from our own species. But from a species whose milk is perfect.... for *their* young. Not our young. Nature gave us the perfect food for infancy - breast milk - from a human. And when you consume dairy, it's not like that's the milk from just one cow. There might be milk from 100 different cows going in a bottle of milk. If you don't think that it's weird to drink and have ice cream and other dairy products made from another species, would it be weird to have ice cream made from human breast milk?

That's right - a store in Covent Garden used to sell ice cream made from human breast milk[129]. It eventually stopped trading after some members of the public complained. Despite tasting either the same or, for some people, better

---

calories a day. I am 80 kg and maintaining my weight eat around 2800 calories a day. 212 calories out of 2500 is less than 10%.

than 'regular' milk.

Why are we so disgusted with taking milk from other humans, but perfectly happy having it from other species?

Bizarre, when you give it some thought, I think[††††].

Fake Claims

Despite what you might think, there are no scientific studies proving the benefit of consuming milk and dairy products. Although advertisers would have you believe otherwise.

The Federal Trade Commission (FTC) in the US recently asked the UDSA to investigate the scientific basis of the claims made in the "milk moustache" ads[130]. Their panel of scientists stated the truth clearly[131]:

- Milk doesn't benefit sports performance.
- There's no evidence that dairy is good for your bones or prevents osteoporosis — in fact, the animal protein it contains may help cause bone loss.
- Dairy is linked to prostate cancer.
- Dairy causes digestive problems for the 75 per cent of people with lactose intolerance.
- Dairy aggravates irritable bowel syndrome (IBS)

Simply put, the FTC asked the dairy industry, "Got Proof?" — and the answer was NO!

Plus, dairy may contribute to even more health problems, like[131]:

- Allergies (I had since childhood, until giving up dairy)

- Sinus problems (I had since childhood, until giving up dairy)

- Ear infections (I had since childhood, until giving up dairy)

- Type 1 diabetes

- Chronic constipation

[††††] I believe the breast milk ice cream company started trading again a few years later, this time selling tubs of the ice cream.

• Anaemia (in children)

Just look up what Dr Walter Willet has to say about dairy's "scientific claims"[132]. He's the second most cited scientist in all medical literature and the head of Nutrition at the Harvard School of Public Health.

Compare the amount spent in the US on advertising for the milk moustache ads in the 1990's - $190 million - to that which the National Cancer Institute did in promoting vegetables and fruit - $1 million. Just because someone has a bigger marketing budget, does it make their statements true?

"If you tell a lie big enough and keep repeating it,
people will eventually come to believe it."

– Joseph Goebbels[‡‡‡‡]

Final words on dairy

I could go on about milk for a while, so let's leave it there. But suffice it to say, I think you can do without it. And your body will thank you for it. If you don't believe that, then that's fine. What I would ask you to consider, is a 30-day experiment without it and see what improvements you notice. There are many alternatives to animal milk these days including: Coconut, Almond, Hazelnut, Hemp, Rice, Soy, Quinoa, Oat, and some that I've not even heard of.

Look out for unsweetened varieties, particularly around almond and hazelnut. I used to use coconut, almond and sometimes hazelnut. Now, I rarely use any milks. I would only use them in my smoothies and now I've moved towards mainly water in the smoothies.

Occasionally I might make my own almond milk (or other nut milk), or if in a rush, I might buy some. There are plenty of non-dairy alternatives for you. In both milk and cheeses. You can look up how to make your own nut cheeses and other non-dairy cheeses. Far better and healthier than store-bought vegan cheeses, in my experience. Remember, just because something is 'vegan' it doesn't mean it's healthy for you. Still, they are getting better tasting, and

---

[‡‡‡‡] This quote is attributed to Joseph Goebbels, but there is some discrepancy about this. He was Adolf Hitler's propaganda minister in Nazi Germany.

although personally I'm not a big vegan cheese fan, if it's a big stumbling block for you, you could hunt around for some that work for you – at least some of the time. Experiment and see what will work for you.

Wheat/gluten

According to Dr Alessio Fasano, from Harvard Medical School, everyone is, in some way affected by gluten. One randomised clinical study published in Alimentary Pharmacology and Therapeutics concluded that short term exposure to gluten induced feelings of depression too[133].

Fasano asserts that the ingestion of gluten causes micro-tears in the gut lining for everyone. The protein 'zonulin' is interfered with by gluten, and zonulin is the only known protein to regulate human intestinal permeability[134]. While this might not be disastrous for everyone (much like tears of muscle fibres build strong muscles), it can be for many people[135]. They just don't realise it. I was like that. For years I consumed wheat (and therefore gluten) and couldn't imagine going without bread, pasta, biscuits, croissants, or anything else that had gluten or wheat in it.

What is gluten?

Gluten is one of the proteins found in wheat. It is also, in a slightly different form, found in rye, barley and oats. Although technically speaking oats don't have gluten in them, but because of how they are grown and processed, they are often contaminated with gluten, unless otherwise stated. Gluten is the substance that gives dough its elasticity and helps it rise, keep its shape and a chewy texture. There is also a different kind of gluten found in other grains, like rice, but usually when people are talking about gluten, they are talking about the proteins found in wheat, barley, rye, and oats.

What's so wrong with it?

The problem with wheat, is that our body can't really digest it very well. When you think of gluten - think glue. Gluten is the glue that holds the produce together essentially. It contains proteins that are resistant to digestion[136].

The major problem is that since the 1960's wheat was re-engineered to help solve a growing food crisis and make it grow faster[137]. The problem was that there wasn't much research done on what the effects would be. As a result, the wheat that we see today (after much manipulation over the years) is a far cry from what was seen 60 - 100 years ago. In fact, wheat today has many more chromosomes than the early varieties[138]. Five percent of the proteins found in modern wheat are brand new[139]. Wheat really isn't real wheat. Even before the manipulation of the strands of wheat by food scientists our bodies weren't well adapted for it, but now, not only is it effectively an alien substance to the body. It's EVERYWHERE! In places you wouldn't expect to find it. Sausages (especially vegetarian ones), stock cubes, burgers, cakes, biscuits, cereal, dips, sauces, facial products, shampoos, conditioners and obviously pastas and breads. And many vegan products.

Wheat also contains phytates which bind with health-boosting calcium, iron, magnesium, phosphorous and zinc in the intestinal tract, preventing these minerals from being absorbed properly. If you eat wheat excessively (which most people do, as it's in everything, let alone the pasta, bread, and cereals) you could end up with mineral deficiencies, which make you hungry all the time, and a whole host of other things as described below.

Gluten also contains amylase-trypsin inhibitors[136] which are shown to cause inflammation[140] in the digestive system. Wheat germ agglutinin is a type of lectin found in wheat that is also linked to autoimmune issues and inflammation[141].

Possible Health Problems of Gluten

Below I've listed some health problems that have been linked to gluten[139]. Having a link does not imply causation at all. It only states that there seems to be a link, and other factors are certainly at play. In other words, it doesn't mean that if you consume gluten, you will get the condition, nor does it mean that everyone with the condition will be a gluten consumer, or even if they are, that removing gluten will remove the condition.

It's up to you to decide whether you believe this or not. What I can say is that most people I've spoken to who have removed gluten from their diets have experienced health benefits[§§§§].

[§§§§] Caveat to this of course, is not just starting to buy lots of processed food that are labelled as 'gluten-free' and thinking this is doing you good. A small amount to transition, but often these gluten-free products are worse as they contain many more ingredients and might exacerbate the problem, rather than alleviate it.

Digestive	Neurological	Skin	Musculoskeletal
Irritable Bowel Syndrome	Multiple Sclerosis	Hives	Chronic Fatigue
Gas	Autism	Alopecia	Arthritis
Pancreatis	Neuropathy	Dermatitis	Joint Pain
Constipation	ADHD	Psoriasis	Low Bone
Gastroparesis	Brain Lesions	Moles	Density
Heartburn	Balance Issues	Itchy Skin	Osteoporosis
Lactose	Epilepsy	Eczema	Poor endurance
Intolerance	Cerebellar Atrophy	Rashes	Fibromyalgia
Villous atrophy	Schizophrenia	Acne	
Diarrhoea		Dark circles	
Canker Sores		under eyes	
Bloating			
Esophagitis			
Chronic Sore Throat			
Autoimmune	**Mental/Emotional**	**Kids/Babies**	**Other**
Rheumatoid Arthritis	Dementia	Digestive Issues	Melanoma
Hashimoto's	Mental Fogginess	Colic	Hypoglycaemia
Addison's	OCD	Fatigue	Anaemia
Type-1 Diabetes	Ups & Downs	Poor	Poor Endurance
Crohn's Disease	Depression	Growth	Asthma
A1 Hepatitis	Anxiety	Eczema	Cystic Fibrosis
Sjogren's	Irritability	Poor Sleep	Infertility
Scleroderma	Headaches	Ear	Colon Cancer
Lupus	Migraines	Infections	Nutritional
		Crankiness	Deficiencies
		Esophagitis	(B12, Iron, Folate, Vitamin K)

Personally, the main benefit I found was that my sinus issues cleared up. It was a combination of dairy and gluten. Cutting out dairy got me 80% of the way there and gluten the final 20%. I also didn't feel bloated or heavy after meals anymore when I cut out gluten. I used to get earaches, and these disappeared. And I was more alert, and my focus was better. I also used to have dark circles under my eyes, but shortly after given up gluten a good friend commented how they used to notice them and now they don't. Generally, I feel better.

That's not to say that I'm 100% gluten-free now. There was a period of several years when I was very strict. Now I might have it on a rare occasion, but that's a far cry from before, when it would be three times a day. But still nothing heavy like pasta, or bread.

Recently I ordered a plant-based burger at a restaurant, and I forgot to request the gluten-free bun. I realised before I took a bite, but I thought I wouldn't bother asking them to change it. Curious to see how I would react to eating regular bread. It was a bad idea, as before I had even finished it, I felt pain in my stomach. Later my nose felt blocked and worsened by the next morning. I also developed an earache. And I became quite tired and spaced out. These types of reactions don't happen all the time for me. Usually, it will be one or two of them and a little milder. It depends on what I'm having, how much and from what brand.

As a population, we now eat around four times the levels of wheat that we ate in the 1950's (and that's when it was a bit easier for us to digest it)[139]. Wheat also contains lectins (another type of protein) which causes inflammation and cell damage[139*****]. Inflammation is now being suspected by many to be the root cause for many illnesses and diseases in the body.

Wheat also creates a large amount of visceral adiposity - in other words "belly fat"[142]. This is by far the riskiest area for fat to develop as vital organs sit in that area. It also causes inflammatory chemicals to be released which stress the body, prevent weight loss, signal the body to add more belly fat and produce oestrogen, which increases breast cancer risk[143,144].

Remember that manufacturers will use other words too, other than wheat so look out for the following too:

Corn starch Edible starch Vegetable protein	Food starch Modified starch	Rusk Thickener

***** Lectins are present in many plants as they act as a natural defence for the plant. There are ways to prepare or cook them to remove most or all the lectin's issues.

Remember that buying gluten-free products isn't really the answer. *Are they PANLO?* Nope. They are a good transition food but ideally eating gluten-free means eating things that are naturally gluten-free. The emphasis being on the word *natural*. And as manufacturers start to offer more gluten-free options, I suspect that we will find another heavily used ingredient in our diet. People tend to think they eat a varied diet but upon closer inspection it normally consists of wheat (gluten), dairy and meat (and that meat tends to just be chicken, cows, and pigs). Many products are being made with substances like soy and corn, so they are everywhere too. And people may start to develop intolerances and problems with them all. I'm hypothesising that as we continue to limit the foods we are exposed to and use one food for the basis for other foods, it's plausible that we will end up developing more intolerances in the future. Any time we put too much emphasis on a particular food group, that's what I suspect we'll find.

Sugar

I'm not sure I need to say much about sugar. I will start with the fact that the World Health Organisation (WHO) currently recommends that we don't consume more than 25g (6 teaspoons) of free sugars per day for health[145]. Free sugars are those found in fruit juices (and some high sugar vegetable juices), processed foods (check on smoothies). Those that are easily absorbed. The average American in 2017-2018, consumed 68g (17 teaspoons) a day, even more for children[146]. Remember these are averages, so there are people consuming way more[††††††].

Look at the packaging of anything you buy. Really scrutinise the label if it's something that you buy regularly. It's worth the time investment up front. You will see that it is likely loaded with sugar. I'm very aware of all these things, and read labels all the time, but I can still quite easily go over this limit. When reading the labels, be aware that the ingredients are listed in order of their quantities. And sugar is often labelled under different names so that it can be put in there several times on the list. Otherwise, it would appear as the number one ingredient!

What is Sugar?

Before sugar enters the bloodstream from the digestive tract, it is broken down

---

[††††††] And these data are from several years ago, and the problem is getting worse, not better.

into two simple sugars:

Glucose - found in every living cell on the planet and what our body doesn't get from food, it produces. It's the primary fuel for our brains too[‡‡‡‡‡].

Fructose - Our bodies don't produce this in a significant amount and so far, there has been no physiological need identified for having it.

Fructose is only metabolised in any significant amounts by the liver. Which is fine if we have a little. From the odd bit of fruit here and there, or during/after a workout session. What happens here is that the fructose turns to glycogen and is stored in the liver until we need it. Neat, eh?

Fructose —> Glycogen

But… once the liver is full of glycogen (very common), eating a lot of fructose overloads the liver and turns the fructose into fat.

Fructose —> Fat

Because of the fibre in fruit, it's unlikely that you will be able to overload on fructose from fruit, but you can from fruit juice. If you are going to consume a moderate amount of fruit (good for phytochemicals, antioxidants, and vitamins & minerals), then make sure that you eat it, not drink it - or at least, drink it with the fibre still intact.

I personally recommend that you go much heavier on the vegetables, rather than the fruit. More like 80/20 or 90/10 in favour of vegetables. And aim for at least eight to ten portions of vegetables a day. UK recommendations are currently a woeful 5-a-day, although I heard rumours of it increasing to 7-a-day. Here's hoping. Japan recommends 17[147]. And even the BBC reported in 2017 how ten portions of veg a day was associated with health and longevity[148].

Non-Alcoholic Fatty Liver Disease

When fructose gets turned into fat in the liver, it is shipped out as VLDL (very low-density lipoprotein) cholesterol particles. However, not all the fat gets out. Some of it can lodge in the liver. This can lead to Non-Alcoholic Fatty Liver Disease (NAFLD), a growing problem in Western countries that is

---

[‡‡‡‡‡] Although there is an argument for the brain being able to run on something called ketones, which are beyond the scope of this book.

strongly associated with metabolic diseases[149]. Being metabolically unhealthy means markers like insulin, blood pressure, cholesterol, waist circumference, triglycerides, and weight are out of normal ranges.

Studies show that individuals with a fatty liver consume up to 2-3 times as much fructose as the average person[150].

Insulin Resistance

Insulin is an important hormone for the body. It allows glucose (blood sugar) to enter cells from the bloodstream and tells the cells to start burning glucose instead of fat. But having too much glucose in the blood is highly toxic and one of the reasons for complications of diabetes, like blindness.

One feature of the metabolic dysfunction that is caused by the Western diet, is that insulin stops working as it should. The cells become "resistant" to it. I.e., insulin resistance. Insulin resistance is thought to be a leading cause of many diseases. Including metabolic syndrome, obesity, cardiovascular disease, and especially type-2 diabetes.

Several studies support the view that sugar consumption is associated with insulin resistance, especially when it is consumed in large amounts[151].

Eventually, as insulin resistance becomes progressively worse, the pancreas can't keep up with the demand of producing enough insulin to keep blood sugar levels down. Blood sugar levels increase and leads to type-2 diabetes.

People that drink sugary drinks have an 83% greater increase in type-2 diabetes than those that don't[152].

Cancer

Insulin is one of the hormones that helps maintain any uncontrollable and multiplication of cells - which is what cancer does. Many scientists believe that having highly elevated insulin levels can contribute to cancer[153].

With sugar promoting an acidic environment in which cancer seems to thrive and you have a perfect mix for cancer to proliferate if you consume too much sugar.

> *"Cancer, above all other diseases, has countless secondary causes. But, even for cancer, there is only one prime cause. Summarised in a few words, the prime cause of cancer is the replacement of the respiration of oxygen in normal body cells by a fermentation of sugar."*
>
> *- Otto H. Warburg, Nobel Prize winner*

Satiety

A study of fructose versus glucose drinkers showed that the satiety levels (how full one feels) were affected negatively in the fructose drinkers than glucose drinkers[154]. And fructose didn't lower the hunger hormone - ghrelin - nearly as much as glucose did[154].

Fructose prevents your brain from accepting the satiety hormone leptin - the protein that's vital for energy expenditure and intake. So, you keep wanting more and more and more and…. Well, you get the picture.

Remember that even people in Brazil eating sugar canes all day long are still consuming fibre as part of that process. Just like you do when eating fruit. And the fibre acts as an indicator that you are full, so you don't overdose on sugar.

Drugs

Sugar activates the same pleasure receptor sites in the brain as does cocaine[155]. *Isn't that something to think about?* Sugar releases masses amounts of dopamine (feel good hormone, and known as a 'seeking' hormone), just like drugs do[§§§§§].

Heart Disease

For years, people were blaming heart disease on saturated fat. And so 'low-fat' this and that came in, but with no effect. Heart disease kept on rising. Now

---

[§§§§§] Dopamine is also released during online activities like social media scrolling, but more on that in the chapter on Digital Nutrition.

the theories are pointing towards the magic white stuff - sugar - as the culprit.

Studies show that large amounts of fructose can raise triglycerides[156], small, dense LDL (low-density lipoprotein), and oxidised LDL (very, very bad), raise blood glucose and insulin levels and increase abdominal obesity... in as little as ten weeks[157].

These are all major risk factors for heart disease.

Not surprisingly, many observational studies find a strong statistical association between sugar consumption and the risk of heart disease[158].

Inflammation

When your blood sugar rises, your body produces greater numbers of pro-inflammatory molecules called cytokines. In addition, high blood sugar levels cause your body to produce molecules called advanced glycation end products (AGEs). These are destructive molecules that trigger inflammation. As we mentioned above, increased sugar can increase visceral fat. Visceral fat, in addition to giving you an unsightly belly, also produces pro-inflammatory chemicals[159-161].

Levels of Consumption

Added to all this, we are consuming ever-increasing amounts of the stuff. See the graph below and it's obvious that something's got to change[162].

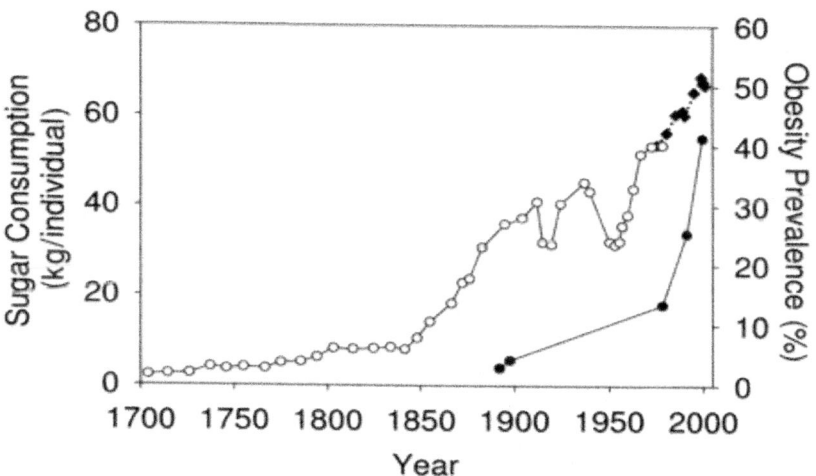

Figure 15 - Sugar intake per capita in the United Kingdom from 1700 to 1978 (○) and in the United States from 1975 to 2000 (♦) is compared with obesity rates in the United States in non-Hispanic white men aged 60–69 y (•). Values for 1880-1910 are based on studies conducted in male Civil War veterans aged 50–59 y.

Source: Johnson RJ, et al. American Journal of Clinical Nutrition, 2007. NB: The two dips in the early and mid 1900s resulted from World Wars 1 and 2 respectively.

You, as an individual have the power to affect your own habits and then, in turn, hopefully positively influence others. First start with yourself.

Sucrose

Sucrose is really a combination of fructose and glucose. Sucrose is 50% fructose and 50% glucose. High Fructose Corn Syrup - used ubiquitously in everything it seems and under a million different names - is more like 55% fructose and the rest glucose. It's been the suspect in countless health issues and should be avoided like the plague.

Other names for sugar

Watch out for how they hide sugar in processed foods. Other names they will use - often in combination, as the order of ingredients is the order of the quantity in the product, and they don't want sugar to be listed first. Some other names for sugar in products are:

Agave Nectar	*Ethyl Maltol*	*Maltodextrin*
Barley Malt	*Fructose*	*Maltose*
Beet Sugar	*Fruit Juice*	*Malt Syrup*
Brown Sugar	*Fruit Juice*	*Maple Syrup*
Buttered Syrup	*Concentrate Galactose*	*Molasses*
Cane Juice Crystals	*Glucose*	*Muscovado Sugar*
Cane Sugar	*Glucose Solids*	*Panocha*
Caramel	*Golden Sugar*	*Raw Sugar*
Corn Syrup	*Golden Syrup*	*Refiner's Syrup*
Confectioner's Sugar	*Grape Sugar*	*Sorbitol*
Carob Syrup	*High-Fructose Corn*	*Sorghum Syrup*
Castor Sugar	*Syrup*	*Sucrose*
Date Sugar	*Honey*	*Sugar*
Demerara Sugar	*Icing Sugar*	*Treacle*
Dextran	*Invert Sugar*	*Turbinado Sugar*
Dextrose	*Lactose*	*Yellow Sugar*
Diastatic Malt		
Diastase		

Better Sugars

While it might not be possible to avoid sugars. And they do make some foods much tastier; there might be a scale on which we can look at sugars. Here is a list adapted from Dr Marilyn Glenville's book, *Natural Alternatives to Sugar.*

Verdict - OK

- Maple Syrup – A natural sweetener for cakes but buy organic.
- Barley malt syrup (extract) – A natural sweetener which might not suit all recipes.
- Brown rice (malt) – Changes the texture of baked goods, use sparingly.
- Stevia – use in moderation and only as pure stevia (often it is mixed with other things as it is many more times sweeter than sugar).
- Whole cane sugar – a natural unrefined form of whole sugar.
- Palm sugar – a natural sugar alternative for cooking as well as in drinks.
- Coconut (palm) sugar – tastes a bit like brown sugar and useful substitute for white sugar. When possible, buy organic.

E - ELEMENTS

- Yacon syrup – Use instead of liquid sweeteners like honey and when possible, buy organic.

Verdict – Not so OK

- Fructose – fine in fruit (within limits) but not as a white powder.
- Agave – Up to 90% fructose.
- Honey – a simple sugar that affects blood glucose quickly.
- Molasses – May contain high levels of pesticides and other chemicals.
- Xylitol – Hard on the gut and very processed.
- Sorbitol – Heavily processed and negatively affects digestive system.
- Evaporated cane juice – Another processed sugar from partially refined sugar.

Overall, I don't use sugar in my cooking, as I rarely do any baking. I think the last time I made a raw vegan chocolate cake was in 2012. That might have called on blending up some dates. Or something like date syrup or maple syrup. I recently also found a bar of chocolate sweetened with erythritol, which is a sugar alcohol (anything with -ol at the end of it is an alcohol derived sweetener). Apparently, it doesn't raise blood sugar and has 70% the sweetness of sugar. I personally found that when I ate that bar of chocolate in the evening (and I normally stop eating things like chocolates at 4pm as they stimulate me too much to sleep later), it had no adverse effects on me getting to sleep and I didn't feel wired like on regular vegan chocolates.

Conclusion

Regardless of where a particular type of sugar sits on any 'health' scale, it is still sugar. Sugar is sugar is sugar. Start to adjust your pallet to not desire it. Avoid sugar when possible and limit it to less than 25g per day. Your taste buds change over a matter of days and so eventually you will get used to fewer sweet foods[163,164].

Meat & Fish

The issues surrounding eating meat and/or fish can be very contentious. Where everyone has an opinion. It's an issue that is beyond the scope of this book really. I'm not here to tell you to stop eating meat or fish. Just to do it with awareness. I don't currently eat meat and haven't since 2011. It wasn't that I watched a documentary about the industry or had any health reasons to stop. I didn't have any friends who convinced me. I didn't go to a talk or watch any YouTube videos on it. I just gave it up for seven weeks over Lent in 2011******, and then went back to eating lamb on Easter Sunday. I felt tired, and then something sparked inside of me. I realised that over the previous seven weeks I had more energy, could eat more but not feel stuffed, needed less sleep, and felt lighter. I decided to only eat meat when I was out and about rather than buy it for the house. The next day I went to a friend's barbecue, and they were serving horrible burgers. And so, I decided not to have it for a while. And 'a while' is still going on. I dropped fish from my diet in 2012 but didn't even realise it until 2013. I woke up one day and realised I hadn't eaten fish for six months! And it didn't (and still doesn't) call to me to eat it.

I currently feel better for not eating meat or fish. Can you be healthy and eat meat and fish? I believe so, yes - absolutely. Are we meant to eat them? Maybe. There is a natural cycle to life, but as pre-historic humans we only ever used to get the leftovers from another animal's kill. Not until we created spears and were able to hunt would we have killed for ourselves in most cases††††††. And then there's the whole argument about our teeth, intestines and so on. There are convincing arguments both ways out there in the world, so I won't go into them here. You can investigate it yourself if you like.

Regardless – even if you choose to believe the argument that we are omnivores (as opposed to natural plant eaters as some would say) and *can* eat meat, does it mean we *should*? And just because we once did eat meat and fish, does it mean we still have to? The world has evolved, and many people might now be able to live healthily without meat and fish. Both meat and fish eating have massive implications for the environment as well as the welfare of animals and fish, and for humans too – especially conventional practices[165]. Meat production seems to have double the carbon footprint of plant-based foods[166]. And contributing to more greenhouse gases than transportation[167].

I know that some of these data and calculations are contested, and there are arguments to be made about sustainable farming however, the fact remains that in most cases what is being put on the supermarket shelves is not natural.

****** As I mentioned earlier, I'm not religious, but I do find Lent a useful period to make changes.
†††††† Although Christopher McDougall in his excellent book, *Born to Run,* makes the convincing argument that our ancestors in fact wore down animals to death, by chasing them. It could well be true, but the fact remains, there are many other animals out there better suited to hunting than humans, when we don't have tools.

Most supermarket meat is inhumanely raised and killed. Full of hormones, antibiotics and who knows what else. Fed on a diet that is not the animal's natural diet. Fish is often farmed, and they swim about in their own faeces – not exactly a pleasant thought. Or full of mercury because we've poisoned the waters.

Average meat consumption worldwide has doubled since the 1960's too[168]. And that's an average, so richer nations would have seen more than a doubling. How much should we eat? Estimates vary, but a good rule of thumb would be about an open palm sized portion. That's if we eat it at all. You can certainly survive without it. Even thrive. In my first book – *The Thought Gym*® – I go into why I am conducting this long-term experiment, but I think the real reason is that I feel better – physically, mentally, emotionally, and spiritually. I found (as is the story with other athletes) that my endurance increased, my recovery time reduced, and I currently feel lighter and more mobile without meat, than with it.

If you choose to eat meat, then I would suggest finding clean sources, that are fed on their natural diet, without unnecessary medication being used and allowed to roam free. Eat more organ meats too – as they are more nutritionally dense. Speak to local farmers. Anything that you are going to eat regularly deserves a bit of time invested up front. Yes, it will be more expensive in the short term, but a couple of things about this. Firstly, eat less of it and spend more on it. You'll spend the same overall. And secondly, as with many things regarding health, and things being more expensive, I always say you:

Pay now, or pay later

What does that mean? Well, pay now with your wallet, or pay later with your health (and medications, surgery, and pain).

Will I ever eat meat or fish again? Well, technically I've never said that I've given them up completely. I'm just conducting an experiment. I just didn't eat them yesterday, or the day before, or the day before that. Will I eat meat or fish tomorrow? Maybe. I'll listen to my body and conscience on that one. If I feel that my health requires it, I'm open to it. It just doesn't call to me right now. I do recognise that as we age and go through our different life seasons and experiences our bodies will desire and need different things, so I'm not here saying that I will never *ever* eat these things again. If I do, I hope that knowing what I currently know, I would do it with a bit more consideration.

We certainly can't survive as a planet with the way things are going. Yes, people are looking into other options from lab-grown meats to insect proteins and everything in between. These solutions, we hope, will be more sustainable and kinder to the environment, so we'll see how all that develops.

Could you, however, cut down a little? It might be that you decide to only buy organic and naturally fed animals. For me, it's much easier to say no altogether. If I were someone who only ate hormone-free and antibiotic-free grass-fed beef that had roamed around free, and then I got hungry after a few drinks, I'm not sure I could say no to that dodgy hot-dog vendor outside the station on the way home one night. Or when I'm at a friend's house for dinner, turn to them and tell them I can only eat organic grass-fed meats!

As I heard the author, Jack Canfield, once say:

"100%'s a cinch, 99%'s a bitch!"

– Jack Canfield

It's easier for me to be 100% committed to something than 99%[††††††]. It doesn't leave room for debate or deliberation. Constantly wondering whether today will be the day that I allow something to creep in. And then it becomes easier for more to creep in too.

You might be different? In fact, I'm sure you are. We all have our own view on how to do things. This is just mine, as I am today.

Other things to consider avoiding or eliminating

Refined Carbohydrates: breads, pasta, croissants and so on. All these will spike your blood sugar, have little to no nutritional value and will make you hungry again soon after eating them. Not to mentioned devoid of fibre and bleached. If you've eliminated gluten, as I suggested above, then that should take care of this anyway.

[††††††] Would you rather be married to someone that was 100% committed to monogamy or 99% committed?

Processed Foods: which really includes refined carbohydrates above too. These can be laden with salt, sugar, bad fats, preservatives, and other ingredients detrimental to your health. To be avoided. If having them, take a super close look at the ingredients label and see that it's the *least* bad option available. And try and surround the processed food with as many vegetables as possible.

Fizzy Drinks: I don't think I should really have to say this, but obviously fizzy drinks, energy drinks and so on are a definite no-no. Regardless of whether they are full versions with sugar or some derivation, or diet versions with Aspartame or some equally as harmful sweetener, STAY AWAY. You simply can't hope to become your superhuman self if these things are in your house or part of your diet. Am I saying never? Well, yes really. I guess if I'm being 100% honest, I think I have had three or four cans of coke in the last five years, so maybe not never. If you can limit them to once every few months, then you'll be ok.

Fruit Juice: this isn't as bad as coke. But only because of the nutrients it contains. Many of the gains are offset by the amount of sugar. It can take around eight oranges to make a glass of orange juice that is consumed in 20 minutes. *Can you eat eight oranges in that time, or even an hour?* You would be full up after a couple of oranges. And it would release sugar much slower into your body then through just juice.

Vegetable Oils: Once touted as healthy options, these are mostly detrimental. Overly processed and oxidised they are not good for the human body and can even be carcinogenic. I even put a word of warning on olive oil. Extra virgin olive oil (in fact just olive oil too) is good for us when not heated to its smoke point. As it starts to break down and becomes carcinogenic[169]. When using oils for cooking, choose cold-pressed (not heat treated) oils, stored in dark glass bottles (to reduce oxidisation and plastic leeching) with high smoke points (the temperature at which the oil breaks down). I use coconut oil mostly for stir frying (sometimes olive oil), and then cold-pressed rapeseed oil or olive oil for covering potatoes. On salads it's avocado oil or extra virgin olive oil.

Caffeine: It's a stimulant. Yes, it's been linked to some great things like mental awareness, increased cognition, and athletic performance boosts[170]. On the flip side it's acidic, interferes with the receptor sites in your brain to signal tiredness which doesn't allow the brain to properly register it's time to flush out toxins. It's also mildly addictive. And most people are drinking too much and too late on. Caffeine can have a half-life of 3 - 8 hrs. Meaning that if you drink a cup of coffee at 2pm, then quite possibly by 10pm you still have half the caffeine in your system. To put it another way, it's like drinking half a cup of coffee at 10pm. I, for instance, thought that if I needed a cup of caffeine each morning to wake up, then something was wrong elsewhere.

Occasionally I do have caffeine. Usually as matcha tea (a concentrated green tea extract) every other month or so when I feel like it. I just don't have it every day. It's a substance that loses its effectiveness over time, and if by coming off it you get headaches and withdrawal symptoms (like many do) then you might be addicted. The headaches will pass after a few days though. When I gave up tea and coffee what I noticed was that it wasn't the drink itself that I missed. It was the ritual of making something hot. Hanging out in the kitchen at work with colleagues or heading to a shop to buy a drink. A bonding experience. You can still have all that though. Just make a cup of something different. A nice herbal tea or even just hot water. When I head to these popular coffee chains now, many have started to sell turmeric lattes which I love and so I buy those on rare occasions as a bit of a treat. Be warned though that the Starbucks version is a latte with turmeric. Meaning, that unless you specifically ask, they will add coffee in there. I got caught out once as I just assumed it would be turmeric and plant milk. And I instantly knew something was up when I got a bit hyper. Now I know to ask first and double-check.

If you do use caffeine, use it intelligently. Perhaps cycling on and off it for periods of time. And don't rely on it to become functioning in the morning. Drink water first thing in the morning, not coffee. I suggest waiting a couple of hours before having your first coffee or tea and then stop all caffeine by 12 or 2pm.

Alcohol: I'm sorry to say, but alcohol is a toxin, and it doesn't help you become superhuman. Sure, you will read headlines about the great benefits of compounds like resveratrol in red wine, but what they won't tell you is that you would need to drink about 40 litres *a day*[171] to get the estimated benefits[§§§§§§]. In the UK about a fifth of adults drink more than the recommended 14 units a week[172]. I know people for whom drinking alcohol

---

[§§§§§§] Resveratrol is not an essential nutrient, and no recommended amount exists, but animal studies suggest 500mg would be needed to provide health benefits. Red wine contains 12.59 mg per litre, so do the maths. Even though a study showed as little as 40 mg might be beneficial, that's still three litres. Think about the damage that would do elsewhere.

is a daily occurrence*******. I don't think I really need to go into the effects of alcohol, but suffice it to say, you won't be doing yourself any favours.

You might think you need it to relax (I would suggest looking at the TRANQUILITY section for tips on that), or to sleep (again, look at the TRANQUILITY section), but alcohol's not the only option. Am I saying that I never drink. No. I do drink. Very infrequently though. I might go two or three months with nothing to drink, and then I might have two evenings in a week when I do drink. In terms of getting drunk, that's even less frequent. It does happen though. Three or four times a year though. Not three or four times a month. I have never really been able to physically take the after-effects of drinking alcohol. Although I don't get stupid when I'm drunk, or have memory blackouts, or even get sick during the evening. The next morning, it's a different story. I'm always ill. I must have vomited from alcohol over 200 times in my life. That's not good. My body was telling me that it's just not designed for it. I took a long time to listen!

It's not even about getting drunk. The problem is that many people drink 'by default'. Automatically. A glass of wine every night with the meal†††††††. Or hanging out with colleagues after work in a pub or bar, going to networking events with free booze available. You might think that this is okay, but I do take another view. You can't be your superhuman self if your body is always working to process alcohol toxins, or the food that inevitably gets eaten on account of drinking. Or the dehydration, or the poor-quality sleep. Or the need to have to 'take it easy' the following morning or anything else that it is for you.

That said, as I mentioned, I do drink. I just choose *carefully* when I do decide to drink. A special occasion, and they happen *occasionally,* remember? Or when I know I really have nothing on the next day and want a total day off. It's April now as I write this, and I think I've had three glasses of alcohol since New Year's Eve (which was a bit of champagne). When I do drink, I look to get the best alcohol possible. As 'clean' as possible. Not too complicated or not much processing. I tend to avoid beer (mostly these have gluten and yeast in them which can trigger my sinus issues) and wine (I find

---

******* Although generally there are not that many people like that in my close social circles anymore.
††††††† I used to do this too. And maybe there's nothing wrong with that. I know of some super health-conscious people that do enjoy that. Still, I can't help but know that even one drink for me negatively affects my sleep. And bad sleep affects everything. So, I can't in good conscious suggest that it's okay to do that. Your choice, of course.

the sulphites and 75+ preservatives and additives they can put in wine, and not on the label, affect me too). Usually, I stick to vodka with soda water, and a wedge of lemon. Or if it's available and appropriate, a glass (or two) of champagne. Occasionally cocktails, although the sugar content in some cocktails can keep me up at night.

So, I'm not saying be tee-total and never *ever* drink. Just be a bit more aware about how often you drink. Why are you drinking and what is it compensating for? What kind of alcohol are you drinking and are there better options? Can you intersperse each drink with water? Just be a bit cautious and mindful with it.

That might seem like a long list of things to eliminate. But remember that eliminating them also means eliminating all the bad effects from them too. Eliminating poor health, low energy, and a whole host of other things. Plus, there are still tons of things that you *can* consume. Focus on what you will gain, rather than any perceived loss and it will make the transition easier.

Supplements

I am often asked about supplementation. Whether I think people should take them or are they necessary. My views have evolved over time, but below are my current thoughts.

Should we all be taking supplementation. Not necessarily. Ideally, we would get all our nutrient needs from food, and I'm the first to suggest *food-first*. It's called *supplementation* after all, and not *substitution*. There are a couple of problems with this ideal.

1. Our **soil is way less nutritious** than it was even 70 years ago. Our soil has depleted massively, as reported in Scientific American[173]. This is due to mono-cropping, over-farming, use of harsh pesticides, chemical in the environment and more. An excerpt from the Scientific American article:

    "A landmark study[174] on the topic by Donald Davis and his team of researchers from the University of Texas (UT) at Austin's Department of Chemistry and Biochemistry was published in December 2004 in the Journal of the American College of Nutrition. They studied U.S. Department of Agriculture nutritional data from both 1950 and 1999 for 43 different vegetables and fruits, finding "reliable declines" in the

amount of protein, calcium, phosphorus, iron, riboflavin (vitamin B2) and vitamin C over the past half century."

2. We are **not living natural lives** anymore. The way nature intended. We aren't exposed to the sun, or the earth. We have more stresses in our lives - from emails, commuting, smart phones, EMF's, harsh chemicals in shampoos and other toiletries, chemicals in the atmosphere from pollution, poor (although "non-lethal") municipal water supplies, and on and on. All these things deplete our ability to use and maintain the nutrients we get into the system.

If we were living a normal "natural" lifestyle, then yes, it should be possible to thrive without supplements.

Different people may require different supplements at different stages of life too. And we don't necessarily need a multi-vitamin, as you won't need to take everything.

DISCLAIMER:

That said, please DO NOT take this as any form of medical advice. Please seek the council of a trusted expert to give you personalised advice. The information below is to raise your awareness as to what I currently personally take (although this changes over time) and why you might want to *consider* what you take if anything.

It's also worth getting comprehensive blood work done to see if you are deficient in anything. Conduct some research though, as some traditional tests might not be as reliable as your General Practitioner (GP) or primary care physician thinks.

I would also really look at your supplements. I wouldn't just buy any brand. Make sure that they are not synthetic (i.e., they come from whole food sources when appropriate to the supplement) and don't have fillers, binders, anti-caking agents and bulking agents in them. Ensure that they are non-GMO, free from wheat, gluten, dairy and other allergens, additives, and preservatives.

Super green blend

The first thing that I recommend everyone consider is some form of super green blend. This will typically be a blend of various super foods. For example, spirulina, wheatgrass, alfalfa grass, barley grass some greens like broccoli extract and lots of other things depending on the brand. Normally the way I consume these super greens is to blend them into my smoothie in the morning. The blend I have been using the last few years – Amazing Grass – have some nice flavours and so it tastes nice even when mixed only with water. I consume it this way if I'm travelling and not able to take a blender with me.

Why take super greens?

Simply put, we just don't consume enough greens. Greens are good, but the nutrient profile these days is so much lower than in the past (see above). It's good to cover your bases. The blend I use has the equivalent of around nine portions of vegetables & fruit in it. It tastes nice and is easy to consume. So why not? The super greens I use also have an ORAC rating of 15,000.

ORAC stands for Oxygen Radical Absorption Capacity. Effectively it's a measure of how good a food is at neutralising free radicals. You might have heard of free radicals as being bad for you. The truth is that free radicals are a natural part of being human. They aren't bad per se. We just tend these days to overload our body with these scavengers that can do our bodies damage. When we're looking for food high in antioxidants, we're looking for food to neutralise the free radicals.

By comparison, a half-cup of broccoli has an ORAC rating of around 500. What number of ORAC do we need a day? Estimates vary, and I don't think there are any government guidelines on this but according to Nutritionfacts.org we should be aiming for 8-11,000 ORAC per day[175]. And the thing is that you can eat five servings of fruit and vegetables a day and get anywhere from 2,000 to 30,000 units. It depends on the vegetables and fruit that you are eating. So, it's not as easy as you might think.

Even though I juice vegetables every day and have a large vegetable smoothie every day too, I still like to have my super green blend. Plus, I find it makes my smoothie taste nicer. In fact, I never make my smoothie without a super green blend‡‡‡‡‡‡‡.

---

‡‡‡‡‡‡‡ If you want to know more about my superfood smoothie, head to **https://thethoughtgym.com/supervitality** for a demonstration.

E - ELEMENTS
Vitamin D3

Vitamin D3. Also known as the sunshine vitamin, as we would normally get it by being exposed to the sun. The trouble is that most people live their lives indoors (including those living in hotter countries). And when we are outdoors, we have been conditioned to lather ourselves with sunscreen. We need 20 - 40 minutes (depending on skin tone) of direct sunlight a day[§§§§§§§]. During the hours of 11am - 4pm, or when the sun is strongest[********]. We also need sunlight to help with the immune system, which is why it's better to get the sunlight from nature.

We can't always do that. I've read that you can store your Vitamin D from the summer months, but I've also read the opposite. My advice is to take a Vitamin D3 supplement (there are other forms of vitamin D, e.g., D2, but most of the studies have been done on D3). Typically, Vitamin D3 is from animals, although I take a plant-based Vitamin D3, and these are widely available.

Also, to note that Vitamin D it isn't a vitamin at all, but a potent neuroregulatory steroidal hormone that influences at least 1,000 of your 25,000 genes[176].

The need for Vitamin D

Vitamin D is *crucial* for our bones. If you just take calcium for bones, it won't be absorbed properly without this vitamin. Calcium also needs vitamin K2 (see below).

So, adequate vitamin D intake is important for the regulation of calcium and phosphorus absorption[177], maintenance of healthy bones and teeth[178], and is suggested to supply a protective effect against multiple diseases and conditions such as cancer[179,180], type-1 diabetes[181], and multiple sclerosis[182].

In addition to its primary benefits, research suggests that vitamin D may also play a role in:

1. Reducing your risk of multiple sclerosis, according to a 2006 study published in the Journal of the American Medical Association[183].

2. Decreasing your chance of developing heart disease, according to

[§§§§§§§] See chapter 2.4 for more on sun exposure times.
[********] If your shadow is longer than you are tall, then the sun is probably too low.
192

2008 findings published in Circulation[184].

3. Helping to reduce your likelihood of developing the flu, according to 2010 research published in the American Journal of Clinical Nutrition[185].

In addition, research has shown that vitamin D might play an important role in regulating mood and warding off depression[186,187]. In other research in people with fibromyalgia, researchers found vitamin D deficiency was more common in those who were also experiencing anxiety and depression[188].

It could also help with obesity. Researchers from the University of Athens Medical School gave Vitamin D supplements to obese and overweight children and adolescents (half received placebo). By the end of the year, the supplement group had lost significant amounts of body fat, and their body mass index (BMI) – a common, if questionable, marker for obesity - dropped[189].

Vitamin D also helps with irritable bowel syndrome (IBS) say researchers at the University of Sheffield who tested 51 IBS patients and found that 42 of them were deficient in Vitamin D. Those with the worst symptoms of IBS having the lowest levels[190]. And another study from John Hopkins, Duke and Stanford universities stated that high doses of vitamin D3 could help MS (Multiple sclerosis) sufferers too[191]. It may even help with rheumatoid arthritis[192].

In summary, Vitamin D is super important for health. Yet most people don't get enough. It would certainly be wise to check levels though, so you don't have too much Vitamin D. Most people would find they are lacking the vitamin though and this lack may influence many conditions, including:

Cancer	Crohn's disease	Hearing loss	Infertility
Hypertension	Cold & Flu	Muscle pain	Asthma
Heart disease	Inflammatory	Cavities	Cystic fibrosis
Autism	Bowel Disease	Periodontal	Migraines
Obesity	Tuberculosis	disease	Depression
Rheumatoid	Septicaemia	Osteoporosis	Alzheimer's
arthritis	Signs of ageing	Macular	disease
Diabetes (T1 &	Dementia	degeneration	Schizophrenia
T2)	Eczema &	Reduced C-	Insomnia
MS	Psoriasis	section risk	

E - ELEMENTS

How much to supplement?

That's a good question and there are many differing opinions. I suggest a bit of research into this, as the European Foods Safety Authority recommends about 15 micro-grams (600 IU - International Units)[193], although may have increased that to 100 micro-grams (4000 IU). I currently take 4000 IU. I've had my Vitamin D levels tested a few times and they've been bang in the right range, so currently it looks like it might be right for me. In addition, one study showed that a dosage of 4000IU for four months achieved a 10 per cent reduction in arterial hardness when tested on a group of 70 African Americans aged 13 to 45, who were also overweight or obese. So, it could be that high doses of vitamin D might reduce those first signs of heart disease – the stiffening of arteries[194].

Is this too much?

Dr Reinhold Vieth, one of the world's leading experts on vitamin D toxicity and metabolism, cites a study on his website about this[195]. The study from Canada found that a dose of 2909 IU per day is needed for 97.5% of Canadians to achieve the current blood level recommended by Health Canada. They went further and determined that doses of 3094, 4450, and 7248 would be the doses required for normal weight, overweight and obese participants respectively. If all that it too much, then the article from Dr Reinhold Vieth's site states that you start off by taking 35 IU per pound (of body weight) per day or 75 IU per kilogram per day[196]. For me that's about 5,600.

It's confusing, I know. The thing to remember though is that you are more than likely Vitamin D deficient. You can get your blood levels tested and then supplement if needed. And then get them checked again. Part of the problem lies in the fact that recommended blood levels can differ too. I would hope that your General Practitioner (GP) or primary care physician would be best placed to advise you.

Vitamin K2 (MK-7)

Alongside Vitamin D3, you might consider also taking Vitamin K2 (MK-7 is the form I recommend). K2 works in conjunction with calcium and D3 for bone health. Vitamin K2 (MK-7) activates matrix GLA protein (MGP) to bind excess calcium and promote arterial flow and flexibility.

Vitamin K1 is found in leafy green vegetables such as broccoli, kale, spinach, and brussels sprouts. Vitamin K2 is found in high concentrations in fermented
194

foods including sauerkraut, hard cheese and natto – which is a traditional Japanese dish made with fermented soybeans.

Scientists don't know whether high vitamin D intake is harmful when vitamin K intake is inadequate. Evidence suggests it might be a concern, but a definite conclusion cannot be reached currently. Much of what I've researched suggests taking K2 alongside Vitamin D3 so that's what I'm currently doing.

Vitamin B12

The next vital vitamin that I take is Vitamin B12. It's vital to having enough energy, and very low B12 intakes can cause anaemia and nervous system damage. If you are plant-based, as I am, then you won't really be getting any Vitamin B12.

Yes, there is some in fortified foods, nutritional yeast, and some algae like spirulina (although I'm not 100% sure on the human bioavailability of this). Two varieties of edible algae (dried green (Enteromorpha sp.) and purple (Porphyra sp.) seaweed (nori)) have been found to have active B12, but other algae have inactive B12-analog compounds that have no apparent benefit in animal metabolism. Some varieties of mushrooms and some foods made with certain fermentation processes have very small amounts of active B12.

Supplementation is cheap and easy. Taking fortified foods is an unreliable option as you'll have to really be "on it" to ensure you get adequate amounts each day.

I simply take a supplement that I place under my tongue (sublingually), and it dissolves in 20 minutes. I do this once or twice a week. It's recommended (if taking B12 weekly) that you take at least 2,500mcg a week. I take 5,000mcg twice a week. You can't really take too much as it's just excreted in urine, being a water-soluble vitamin. If you take something daily, then 250mcg per day. Even though the maths doesn't add up, it's due to how it's absorbed[†††††††]. My regular blood tests indicate that my B12 levels are optimal.

[†††††††] See https://nutritionfacts.org/video/daily-source-of-vitamin-b12/ for a good explanation. For more on B12 check out: https://nutritionfacts.org/questions/what-is-the-best-way-to-get-b12/

And as a side note, because it's often the "elephant in the room" when it comes to strict plant-based diets, how can we eat only plant-based if there are deficiencies. A few thoughts on that.

1. B12 isn't made by animals (or plants) in fact. It's made by certain bacteria, some of which line the guts of certain animals. Humans also make B12 in our colon, but it's too far downstream to be utilised.

2. So, aren't we meant to eat animals? It's likely that the B12 conundrum has a valid point here. We may have evolved millions of years ago from plant-based animals into humans, to ones who, to survive, started to eat animals, insects, bugs etc. This might have changed our physiology. Who knows for sure? The fact is though, that just because we have adapted to eat animals, does it mean we *should*? Technology has advanced so we don't live in caves anymore, wait months for a message from our family, and certain diseases like Polio aren't much of a problem. With our ability to get all we need without the need to kill animals, why do it then? If you have a problem with taking B12, then think about what other modern creations you would be happy to relinquish? iPhone, car, house, bed, beer, etc. We evolve - it's what being human is about. We can adopt, adapt, or avoid new advances, but they are still there.

3. Being on a whole foods plant-based eating protocol typically has more nutrients in it than any other diet - especially the standard Western diet. Many are likely to be deficient in more vitamins and minerals being on the standard Western diet, than a plant-based diet due to low vegetable consumption and other factors.

4. As we age, even animal eaters lose the ability to produce and absorb B12, and people over the age of 50 or 60 should consider supplementing with it[197]. In fact, in the US Farmington Offspring Study, 1 in 6 animal eaters, between 26 - 83 years old, were B12 deficient[198].

It might be that humans can reabsorb the B12 that is produced, and that deficiencies might take years to show up[199]. My advice, especially if vegan or plant-based, is to supplement.

B-Complex

A B complex vitamin is a dietary supplement that delivers all eight of the B vitamins: B1 (thiamine), B2 (riboflavin), B3 (niacin), B5 (pantothenic acid), B6, B7 (biotin), B9 (folate), B12.

I started taking a B-Complex in 2016 even though I consume about 10 - 20 portions of vegetables a day, so chances I'm deficient in many vitamins and minerals is low these days. In fact, recent blood tests showed no vitamin or mineral deficiencies. And B vitamins are important (and cheap). As with B12, B vitamins are water-soluble and excreted if too much is taken.

These essential nutrients help convert our food into fuel, allowing us to stay energised throughout the day. While many of the B vitamins work in tandem, each has its own specific benefits — from promoting healthy skin and hair to preventing memory loss or migraines.

In addition, many people take a B complex vitamin to help increase energy, support brain health, enhance mood, improve memory, ease stress, stimulate the immune system, and boost hair and skin health.

It is also said to enhance heart health, alleviate anxiety, and soothe skin disorders.

Each B vitamin is essential to certain bodily functions:

1. B1 and B2 are important for healthy functioning of the muscles, nerves, and heart.
2. B1 helps the body make new cells. May help prevent kidney disease in people with type 2 diabetes and reduce the risk of cataracts.
3. B2 is important for red blood cell production and fighting free radicals. May prevent migraines.
4. B3 helps regulate the nervous and digestive systems and helps convert food into energy. May boost HDL cholesterol and lower cholesterol levels.
5. B5 breaks down fats and carbohydrates for energy and is responsible for the production of hormones.
6. B5 and B12 are required for normal growth and development.
7. B6 supports the immune system, helps the body produce hormones, and aids the body in breaking down protein. Also helps to regulate levels of the amino acid homocysteine (an amino acid thought to contribute to heart disease when it occurs at elevated levels). May protect against heart disease, relieve PMS symptoms, and alleviate pregnancy-related nausea.
8. B7 is involved in the production of hormones. Is associated with healthy skin, hair, and nails.
9. B9 helps cells make and maintain DNA and promotes the growth of

red blood cells. Also help to regulate levels of the amino acid homocysteine. May help prevent breast cancer, colorectal cancer, and pancreatic cancer, as well as decreased risk of birth defects when taken by pregnant women.

10. B12 helps regulate the nervous system and plays a role in red blood cell formation. Also help to regulate levels of the amino acid homocysteine. May prevent confusion in older adults and reduce levels of homocysteine.

Some good reasons to make sure you're getting enough vitamins in.

Probiotics

Probiotics are bacteria that line your digestive tract and support your body's ability to absorb nutrients and fight infection. There are as many bacteria cells in your body as human cells[48,200]†††††††.

Historically, we had plenty of probiotics in our diets from eating fresh foods from good soil and by fermenting our foods to keep them from spoiling. However, because of refrigeration and dangerous agricultural practices like soaking our foods with chlorine, our food contains little-to-no probiotics today, and many foods contain dangerous antibiotics that kill off the good bacteria in our bodies.

Study on the gut (micro-biome) is a new focus in nutrition science and medicine, but it's getting more into mainstream media. It's thought that what happens in your gut could be responsible for many biological factors, from your mood, ability to gain or lose weight, your immune system (80% of your immune system is in your gut[201]) and dozens of other bodily functions.

Why are our micro-biomes so bad?

Well, we have too many antibiotics prevalent in our world. Antibiotic, quite literally, means anti-life. It's like taking a neutron bomb to the Amazon rain forest and blowing it up, and then not even planting any new trees (which would be probiotics in this metaphor). The micro-biome is like our own little rain forest in our stomachs. In fact, we have a micro-biome on our skin, eye lashes and elsewhere. The gut is super important though. With 300 – 500, 1000 and even 2000 species of microorganisms in there[202-204]. And as

---

††††††† Historically it has been quoted as around 10 times as much bacterial cells as human cells, but more recent estimates approximate it as 1:1 (give or take).

mentioned, there are just as many of these microbes' cells as human cells. These microbes have 360 times more protein coding DNA than we do[205]!

It has been found that probiotics have an anti-inflammatory potential and likely:

1. boost the immune system[206]
2. prevent and treat urinary tract infections[207]
3. improve digestive function[208]
4. heal inflammatory bowel conditions like IBS[208]
5. manage and prevent eczema in children[209]
6. fight food-borne illnesses[210]
7. halve bone loss (in the elderly)[211]

Many people with health issues, such as thyroid imbalances, chronic fatigue, joint pain, psoriasis, autism, and many other conditions don't realise that these illnesses may originate in the gut[212].

Over 40 diseases have potentially been linked to bacterial imbalance. Including depression[213], arthritis[214], IBS[215], and cancer[216].

By adding more probiotic foods into your diet, you may see the following benefits:

1. Stronger immune system[217].
2. Improved digestion[218].
3. Increased energy from production of vitamin B12[219].
4. Better breath because probiotics destroy candida[220].
5. Healthier skin, since probiotics naturally treat eczema and psoriasis[221].
6. Reduced cold[222] and flu[223].
7. Healing from leaky gut syndrome and inflammatory bowel disease[224].
8. Weight loss[225].

New studies underway may prove that probiotics can[212]:

1. Reduce flu and cold.
2. Reduce overuse of antibiotics.
3. Treat kidney stones.
4. Treat colic.
5. Prevent cavities and gum disease.

6. Treat colitis and Crohn's disease.
7. Combat antibiotic-resistant bacteria.
8. Treat liver disease.
9. Battle cancer[226].
10. Manage autism.
11. Lower cholesterol.
12. Fight bacteria that cause ulcers.
13. Improve acne.
14. Lose weight.

Here are the top seven probiotic killers that can prevent your body from getting all the tremendous probiotics benefits it needs[212]:

1. Prescription antibiotics.
2. Sugar.
3. Tap water.
4. GMO foods.
5. Grains.
6. Emotional stress.
7. Chemicals and medications.

It's probably a good idea to try and get your probiotics from fermented food, when possible, like sauerkraut, kimchi, kombucha, Coconut kefir, Natto, Miso. I do buy sauerkraut or kimchi when I remember, but to cover my bases I supplement.

It's probably a good idea to rotate through different strands and brands, and cycle on and off taking them from time to time. There is some debate about how much is absorbed and makes its way into you, but to cover my bases I still take them.

Magnesium

This mineral is responsible for over 600 bio-reactions in your body (that we know of)[227]. In other words, a deficiency in magnesium (as 80% of people are estimated to be[228]) means your body can't do well, or at all, 600 processes that it needs to, to make your body function well. A 2018 review of magnesium's role in neurological disorders found a direct link between magnesium and depression. The lower the levels, the more severe the depression[229].

The recommended daily magnesium intake for adults is 420mg for men and 320mg for women[230]. Magnesium deficiency is often misdiagnosed because
200

it does not show up in blood tests as only 1% of the body's magnesium is stored in the blood[231].

Why are we so deficient?

Well, with more stress in our life, more magnesium is used up. It's like a buffer to stress[232]. The blood needs magnesium to be constant to supply co-factors for enzymatic reactions. Why isn't it in food? Well, the usual reasons really. Agro-business, mono-cropping, soil depletion. We need to consume greener and chlorophyll rich foods. Our cardiovascular system, digestive system, nervous system, muscles, kidneys, liver, hormone-secreting glands, and brain all rely on magnesium to accomplish even the most basic tasks.

And scientists believe it may play an important role in preventing, ameliorating or treating dozens of health conditions including asthma[233], autism[234], heart disease[235], eclampsia[236], epilepsy[237], HIV/AIDS[238], multiple sclerosis[239], PMS[240], and lupus[241]. It also vitally important for the nervous system heart rate, blood pressure and brain function[229].

It's so important that the body can draw on magnesium from bones, tissues, and other places so that it can be distributed to more important places[242].

Magnesium also assists digestion, relives tensions, it's an anti-stress mineral and it relaxes nerves, activates enzymes important for protein and carbohydrate metabolism[243].

Magnesium is needed for the production and transfer of energy. It modulates electrical impulses across cell membranes[243]. A calcium-magnesium balance is needed for bone health. Calcium will leach out the bones if there isn't a proper balance[244].

It's also needed for muscle contraction and relaxation, nerve conduction and keeping vertebrae in proper position[245,246].

Also, I can first-hand attest that magnesium (especially Epsom salt baths) is beneficial for great sleep and recovering from muscle soreness from exercise. I use a spray every night before going to bed, and when I have time, a magnesium (Epsom) salt bath.

Why topical?

It's the most effective way of getting into the blood stream by-passing the digestion system. Otherwise, the intestines and kidneys may filter much of it and it can cause stress to the kidneys, if taken orally[247]. It may also create digestive distress (bowel intolerance) when taken orally. Also, when done topically or trans-dermally, you can spray it directly on affected areas.

Omega-3, EPA/DHA

The next supplement I take is an Omega-3 supplement. There is a plethora of information on the benefits of taking consuming Omega-3 oils. Traditionally we think of fish for Omega-3, but there are many issues with fish. Not least of which is the high levels of mercury in most fish, and over-farming of fish with depleting supplies. If you eat fish, I encourage you to investigate sourcing the smaller ones and these should ideally be line-caught and wild. The acronym, *SMASH* (which I first heard from author and physician, Dr Mark Hyman), is a good way to remember the good sources of fish for Omega-3's.

S - Sardines | M - Mackerel | A - Anchovies | S – Salmon | H - Haddock

Fish get their omega-3 from algae, so why not bypass the middleman (and the mercury and micro-plastics in the ocean) and go straight to the source?

You can get Omega-3 from nuts and seeds, but it's the ALA form (alpha linolenic acid). And although currently the only "essential" one is ALA, with the others being EPA (eicosapentaenoic acid) and DHA (docosahexaenoic acid), more research and importance is being placed on EPA and DHA.

Your body can convert ALA (from the nuts and seeds) to EPA and DHA but not very effectively in most people. Human conversion of ALA into EPA ranges from 8% to 20%[248]. Conversion of ALA to DHA ranges from 1% to 9%[248]. My recommendation, if you don't eat fish, is to supplement with an EPA/DHA Omega-3 and then you don't have to think about the ALA conversion at all.

Why do we need Omega-3?

It's needed for brain development, healthy bones, and joints, and the prevention of heart disease[249]. In addition:

- Blood fat (triglycerides). Fish oil supplements can lower elevated triglyceride levels.

- Rheumatoid arthritis. Fish oil supplements (EPA+DHA) can curb stiffness and joint pain.
- Reduces depression and anxiety.
- Supports baby development.
- Improves issues around asthma.
- Helps with ADHD
- Can help with Alzheimer's disease and dementia.
- Needed for eye health.
- It fights inflammation.
- Helps with autoimmune diseases.
- (Possible) cancer risk reduction.
- Improves sleep.
- Improves skin.

A quick note on Omega oils, as there are other types of Omega oils including 6, 7, 9 and 11 to name a few. Most of us are familiar with Omega-3 and possibly Omega-6. Often Omega-6 gets a bad rap. It's not all bad. What's bad is having too much of it. The ratio of Omega-6:Omega-3 that most professionals think is good for reduced inflammation and most benefits is somewhere around 3:1 (Omega-6:Omega-3), with some suggesting even lower ratio of 1:1. Most people tend to be in the 15-25:1 ratio. So not great at all. Omega-6 dominance is mainly because of vegetable oils being used everywhere in cooking and processed foods. You can, of course, get Omega-6 oils from nuts and seeds directly, although it's unlikely (if you are avoiding processed foods and oils) that you will get too much, unless you are eating copious amounts of nuts and seeds. A handful a day is all I would recommend. In fact, one study showed that Omega-6 could prevent premature death and protect against heart disease[250].

So, we do need all types of Omega oils, but it would be wise to know what your ratio of Omega-6:Omega-3 is, because this is likely to be quite off. I don't eat many processed foods or buy vegetable oils or cook with them – instead usually using coconut oil, water or sometimes a dash of organic cold-pressed rapeseed or olive oil. And I still had a ratio of 5:1 as opposed to 3:1 where I'd like it to be. So, it is worth getting tested. Although it's usually an expensive test (~£100) and most likely isn't covered by your health provider.

Since first testing, I have increased my amount of Omega-3 supplementation, while trying to limit even further any possible excessive sources of Omega-6 and on retesting found an improvement.

Grapefruit Seed Extract

Another supplement I take is called grapefruit seed extract. It's a liquid supplement and I take around 12 drops which I drop into my daily cold-pressed vegetable juice. It is a substance derived from the seeds, membranes, and the pulp of grapefruits. And it's used as a broad-spectrum, non-toxic, antimicrobial product. It is known to be highly effective for fighting infection and promoting health. Grapefruit seed extract is used as a purifier, antiseptic, and preservative[251].

I started taking it when an old friend of mine mentioned that she never got colds since starting to take it. That seemed like a good enough reason to me. Even though I was already pretty good in not developing colds, I started taking it and it's served me well so far.

It can be useful for fighting candida (yeast) overgrowth which does affect large numbers of people. Candidiasis, referred to as "candida," is a fungal infection that can affect men and women of all ages in various parts of the body. It most commonly occurs in the mouth, ears, nose, toenails, fingernails, gastrointestinal tract, and vagina. A Polish study published in 2001 found that a 33 per cent grapefruit extract has a potent anti-fungal effect against Candida albicans strains taken from patients with candida symptoms[252]. Grapefruit seed extracts anti-fungal properties help it combat candida infestations by killing the yeast cells that have taken over in the body.

Grapefruit seed extract also is used as a general antimicrobial. Benefits can be experienced when it's taken by mouth for bacterial, viral, and fungal infections, including yeast infections.

It's a strong taste, especially when put into plain water. In my juices I don't notice it, so daily I take it that way. If I'm feeling less than 'superhuman' then I might dilute it in water and gargle it before drinking it.

Other Supplements

There are a handful of other vitamins and minerals I might supplement with year-round or periodically including Zinc, Vitamin C, Quercetin and

Astaxanthin. However, the ones above I consider more applicable for most people.

Summing Up

So that seems like a lot, but I think most people reading this, as a minimum, should be on Vitamin D and Magnesium. Also, a good probiotic and Omega-3 would be a good idea. The B vitamins might be less essential for some, as too the Grapefruit Seed Extract.

Depending on individual circumstances you might have other needs like Iron, Zinc, Iodine, Selenium, amino acids, or any number of factors.

Without getting tests on absolutely everything, it's hard to know. My recommendations above come from understanding that most people will have Vitamin D and Magnesium deficiencies, as well as some level of poor gut bacteria, and too high amount of Omega-6 and Omega-9, and not enough Omega-3.

As ever, you decide. Don't be so proud to think you should get all your needs from food to close yourself off from considering supplementation. Yes, we *should* get it all from food. We should also play in the dirt, walk barefoot, get lots of sunlight, sleep when the sun sleeps, and rise when it rises. We should not be using artificial light or be hooked on smartphones. There's a lot we *should* be doing and *shouldn't* be doing. But see the world, and your life, as it is. Keep an open mind. Experiment and test. Measure and track. Then you can see for yourself.

Practical Ways to Increase Vegetable Intake

There is evidence to suggest that we should all be aiming for many more vegetables and fruit in our diet. In fact, ten portions or more[148]. Personally, I consume anywhere from ten, all the way up to 20 or more portions of vegetables a day[§§§§§§§§].

How is that possible?

My 'secret' really is my breakfast (or first meal of the day, as sometimes it's closer to lunchtime when I have this). What I call 'frontloading'. If I can

---

[§§§§§§§§] I think my record was close to 50 one day, when I was feeling ill and had lots of wheatgrass shots and other vegetable juice drinks.

frontload my day with great nutrition, then I know I'm on the winning track. Even if the rest of the day goes badly. The key is in my daily vegetable juice and vegetable smoothie. These have varied over the years but below I'll list a typical day.

Vegetable Juice

Typically, I make 400 - 500 ml of cold-pressed********* vegetable juice. This normally comes from 400 – 600g of vegetables. 1 portion = 80g, so that is 5 – 7.5 portions going into juice extraction. Yes, fibre is important. And I get it throughout the day and in my smoothie too. In the juice however, I'm looking to get an injection of nutrients into my system and not overload my digestive system.

If starting out, I'd recommend adding a bit of fruit in there if you are not used to this kind of taste. I rarely add fruit in my juices unless using up fruit that might spoil. Typically, my juice would be like this†††††††††.

1. Lemon; half a lemon with the skin off, but white plinth still intact
2. Ginger; 1 – 2 cm (skin on if organic, otherwise off)
3. Cucumber; 4 – 6 cm
4. Celery; 1 – 2 stalks
5. Broccoli; 2 – 4 cm of stalk
6. Kale; small bunch
7. Spinach; handful
8. Mixed leaves; handful
9. Bell pepper; half
10. Zucchini; 4 – 6 cm
11. Tomato; half
12. Parsley; pinch
13. Coriander; pinch
14. Mint; pinch

********* Cold-pressed juicers use a slower mechanism and provide a higher yield than what is known as a centrifugal high-speed juicer. And the juices taste better for longer, although I advise drinking within 15 minutes. Centrifugal ones tend to be cheaper though, and I used one when starting out for the first three years before upgrading to a cold-pressed slow juicer.
††††††††† It might vary day to day depending on what I have in, but I would always look to include lemon. Otherwise, it will taste very 'earthy'.

I've been juicing since 2012 and didn't start off with that many things, so I wouldn't advise you to put that much in if you are brand new. Start small and simply. Start with 60% vegetables and 40% fruit and move the ratio over the subsequent few weeks. Your taste buds will change. I would also look to avoid high sugar fruit and vegetables. I don't usually juice things like carrots and beetroot for that reason. Occasionally, I might. Just not every day or week.

I find it easier to make my juices and smoothies with a variety of ingredients rather than just one or two, as I don't need to buy lots and lots of the same thing. If I were making just cucumber juice, then I would need to buy tons of cucumbers each week. This way, my fridge looks normal with a great variety of vegetables rather than stocked with just one kind. Plus, I can make food dishes with the vegetables too, as I buy things I can use for lunch and dinners easily. I do mix it up from time to time, and have less ingredients, and maybe just two or three. *Flexibility within the framework* – that's the key!

Juices are great to get a large amount of nutrients into you, in a short amount of time and without feeling too full. I also use smoothies all the time.

Smoothies

In addition to juicing, I also make smoothies. These have the added advantage of containing plenty of fibre allowing for a slower release of sugars and helping you feel full. And as you'll see below, I also add plenty of other ingredients to make these smoothies... super smoothies!

Bear in mind when you read this, that when I started making smoothies in 2012 it was very simple. Banana, spinach leaves, a super green chocolate blend and a non-dairy milk[‡‡‡‡‡‡‡‡‡‡]. Now it (usually) resembles the following:

1. Lemon; half a lemon with the skin off, but white plinth still intact
2. Ginger; 1 – 2 cm (skin on if organic, otherwise off)
3. Cucumber; 4 – 6 cm
4. Celery; 1 – 2 stalks
5. Broccoli; 2 – 4 cm of stalk
6. Kale; small bunch
7. Spinach; handful
8. Mixed leaves; handful
9. Bell pepper; half

[‡‡‡‡‡‡‡‡‡‡] I might still on occasion make a chocolate based one. Usually on the weekend, or if my nieces are around.

10. Zucchini; 4 – 6 cm
11. Tomato; half
12. Parsley; pinch
13. Coriander; pinch
14. Mint; pinch
15. Coconut fat; 1 heaped tablespoon
16. Avocado; half – including half the stone/pip
17. Turmeric root; 2 – 4 cm
18. Turmeric powder; 1 tablespoon
19. Cinnamon; teaspoon
20. Salt; pink Himalayan
21. Pepper; red and black pepper corns grinded
22. Goji berries; 1 tablespoon
23. Chia seeds; 1 teaspoon
24. Hemp seeds; 1 teaspoon
25. Nuts & Seeds; 3 tablespoons – almonds, brazil, hazelnut, cashew, walnut, pecan, sunflower, pumpkin, flax
26. Supergreen blend; 1 tablespoon
27. Spirulina; 1 tablespoon
28. Medicinal mushroom blend powder (Lion's Mane, Ashwagandha, Reishi, Chaga, Cordyceps); 1 teaspoon
29. Sprouts; teaspoon
30. Berries; frozen blueberries, around a dozen
31. Banana: 1 or 2
32. Ice cubes; 4
33. MSM[§§§§§§§§§]; (methylsulfonylmethane); 1 tablespoon
34. Water; 0.5 – 0.75 litre
35. Oat milk; 0.25 – 0.5 litre

Some of the things above I might cycle in and out of the smoothie, but it's about 80% the same most days. It's a lot, I know. I don't know anyone else that might mix so many different things in together. Some might not think this would be good for the body to digest. I guess it depends on how it sits with you. I built up to this over many years. Step-by-step. I'm not suggesting that you go from no smoothies to this one in one go. Or ever. Perhaps limit it to

---

[§§§§§§§§§] MSM is a chemical in animals, humans, and many plants and has anti-inflammatory and antioxidant effects and plays an important role in making collagen and glucosamine, both of which are vital for healthy bones and joints, and in the production of immunoglobulins, which help your immune system.

just 3 – 6 ingredients. That might be better for you. This is just what I do, and I know I feel great for it.

The above typically makes around two litres of smoothie. Which is what I would have each day[**********]. Usually one litre from around 9am – 11am, and then the second litre around 2pm. It really depends on several things. Sometimes, if I am getting up early the following day and don't have time to make anything, I might have one litre the day I make it and then one litre the next day. It doesn't taste as fresh the next day, but you can store it in a glass container with no air in it to limit oxidisation. Then the day I'm going to drink it I might add half a lemon and a banana to it and re-blend. It gives it a bit of spark and tastes pretty good again[††††††††††].

Nutrition Facts

I have never counted calories or anything in my life, but because many people were asking me about my smoothies (as they would often see me out and about with them), I made a video about making it. I measured my typical quantities and noted the amount of protein, fats, carbs, and calories. To my best calculations, this is what my two-litre smoothie will give me:

- Protein ~ 40g
- Fat ~ 75g
- Carbohydrates ~105g
- Sugar ~22g
- Calories ~1200

Yes, it's a LOT. I know. I quite often only eat one other meal for the rest of the day. Although sometimes two or even three. I don't give myself super strict rules, except for trying to leave at least 12 hrs from my last meal of the day to the first meal the next day. Usually, it's 16 hrs or more. More on that in the section on intermittent fasting in the 'TRANQUILITY' section.

What about the sugar content. Twenty-two grams of sugar sounds a lot when the WHO recommends only 25g of free sugars a day. Well, technically these aren't free sugars as they are being absorbed complete with their fibre, as well as the added fibre from the other nuts and seeds. And the cinnamon helps with

---

[**********] Although many days I give up to 50% of it to other people like my parents or friends.
[††††††††††] As I write this (May 2019) I'm experimenting with just one litre each day as I'm training less due to injury and frankly, I want a bit of a break. Flexibility within the framework, remember? We don't have to do the same thing all the time.

blood sugar balance too. I typically won't have any other sugar in the day and most of that sugar is from vegetables or the berries which isn't the same as typical fruit sugar.

However, if we take a 500 ml portion – quite a large portion compared to what the average person would have - it has around 5.5g of sugar in it. Comparing this with some typical drinks people consume:

- Hari's Super Smoothie   (500ml) = 5.5g
- 'This Water' lemon/lime bottled water   (500ml) = 42.6g
- Pret-a-Manger Orange Juice   (500ml) = 51g
- Coca Cola   (500ml) = 53g
- Innocent Smoothie   (500ml) = 68.6g
- Starbucks Venti White Choca Moca   = 74g
- Burger King Super-Size Coke   = 79.5g

And remember that (except for the Innocent smoothie) none of those have fibre to slow down the sugar spike and they are free sugars.

I've tested having no smoothie on certain days, and I do struggle. I get hungry and don't perform as well. I really think the juice and the smoothie are the secret sauce for me.

Experiment a little and see what works for you. If you want to see a video of me making these drinks together with a fuller explanation as to why I include various ingredients, then head to **https://thethoughtgym.com/supervitality**.

Which is best? Juicing or Smoothies?

People do seem to get fixated on whether one or the other is better. I like them both and each have their benefits and drawbacks as detailed below.

- Juicing
  - Pro's
    - Assimilate nutrients very quickly.
    - Can consume more nutrients as not too filling.
    - Can use up vegetables and fruits before they spoil.
    - Refreshing.
    - Energising.
  - Cons
    - Cleaning the machine can be a chore for some

people[‡‡‡‡‡‡‡‡‡‡].
- High amount of waste 'fibre'[§§§§§§§§§§].
- Need a lot of vegetables so could be expensive (though much cheaper than store bought juices).
- Smoothies
  - Pro's
    - Can pack in more than just vegetables and fruit, such as proteins and fats from nuts, seeds, coconut, avocado, as well as herbs, spices and minerals like turmeric, cinnamon, salt & pepper.
    - Keeps you full for longer, if done right.
    - No waste as everything is used.
    - Easier and quicker to wash up.
    - Uses less vegetables and fruit for comparable amount of product[**********].
  - Cons
    - Takes longer to prepare (if you're doing it my way).
    - Might be *too* filling.
    - Need a high-quality blender to blend the tough ingredients.
    - More expensive in terms of additional ingredients.
    - Hard to make small portions (if combining lots of ingredients).

If I could only afford to buy either a juicer or a blender, I'd go for the blender. It's more versatile usually (depending on the type you buy[††††††††††††]), and then I can get in all the extra ingredients that keep me full and feeling fantastic. You can also make juices from it by either using a nut milk (or cheese cloth) bag and extracting all the fibre or diluting in lots of water so it's more like a juice[‡‡‡‡‡‡‡‡‡‡‡‡]. When I've had to spend time away from my juicer and only blended for a couple of weeks, I really miss the simplicity and refreshing taste of juices. Usually, it's easier for me to buy a store-bought juice I'm happy with rather than buying two litres of smoothie!

[††††††††††] This is where listening to podcasts can really make it less of a chore.
[§§§§§§§§§] Although this can be composted or made into food products.
[**********] Although you must use water or some other liquid to liquefy it.
[††††††††††††] For information, I currently have a Vitamix blender and love it. I have been using it since 2013 and they come with multi-year warranties. They do cost a small fortune though.
[‡‡‡‡‡‡‡‡‡‡‡‡] The nut/cheese cloth bags are a bit messy though, and technically if you do the second way of just putting lots of water in there to dilute it's not exactly a juice (and doesn't taste as nice in my experience).

Meals

Juices and smoothies increase my vegetable intake, but because I am plant-based in my eating, I tend to have a lot of vegetables in my meals. I might eat one or two meals a day (after my juice and smoothie). This might be lunch and dinner, or sometimes I'll have what I call 'linner' which is combined lunch and dinner around 3pm – 5pm§§§§§§§§§§§§, if I'm only eating one meal that day.

Each meal will be loaded with vegetables. Typically, 400g or more, which is five portions. This might be a stir-fry, a curry, roasted veg, steamed veg or something similar. I then combine it with more filling carbohydrates like sweet potato, rice, quinoa, buckwheat, rice noodles, buckwheat noodles, lentil pasta************, amaranth or some other naturally gluten-free food.

By eating lots of vegetables and following the *PANLO 80/20* approach allows me to eat a further five to ten portions of vegetables each day on top of what's contained in the smoothie and juice.

So, when you take that all into account, the juice, the smoothie, and the plant-based meals it's quite easy for me to rack up the number of portions of vegetables I mentioned. Getting 10 – 20 portions of veg in a day is quite common for me. Occasionally I might even have a wheatgrass shot (yes, it really is a type of grass that has gone through a juicing process) which is super good for you and the equivalent to ten portions of vegetables.

I know, not everyone can do, or would want to do, what I do in this regard. There isn't any published research that I know of that says that eating 15 portions is significantly better for you than eating ten portions. So, don't be as crazy as me and go as high as 20, but I would strongly recommend aiming for at least ten portions of vegetables (800g) a day.

Frequency of Food and The Body

I just want to touch on a more 'woo woo' topic, purely because I want this book to cover as much as possible to help you. And that is this idea of frequency. Everything in the universe emits a frequency. Frequency is measured in cycles per second, otherwise known as Hertz (Hz). Nikola Tesla

---

§§§§§§§§§§§§ My mate likes to call it 'dunch' but as that can sound a bit too much like brunch, and as I also first started calling it linner, I'll stick to linner.
************ More protein too as made from lentils.

has a quote I often think about when trying to understand how things work. Tesla was unbelievably smart. Albert Einstein was (allegedly) asked by reporters what it was like to be the smartest person on the planet. To which he responded, "I don't know, ask Nikola Tesla".

"If you want to find the secrets of the universe, think in terms of energy, frequency and vibration."

– Nikola Tesla

When it comes to food and the body, everything has a frequency. So, each organ of our body has a certain frequency[253]. For example:

Brain Frequency	- 72 – 90 MHz
Human Body	- 62 – 78 MHz
Heart Frequency	- 67 – 70 MHz
Liver Frequency	- 55 – 60 MHz
Pancreas Frequency	- 60 – 80 MHz
Disease Start at	- 58 MHz

Food has a frequency too. Everything does. The higher vibrational foods are perhaps the ones you might expect. Vegetables, fruits, nuts, seeds. Below that it would be vegetables cooked in boiling water, milk, fridge butter, eggs not freshly laid, honey, cooked fish, peanut oil. Below those cooked meats, sausages, coffee, (black) tea, (regular) chocolate, jams, processed cheeses, and white bread. And lastly, the lowest are products like margarine, alcoholic spirits, refined white sugar, and bleached flour.

Do you have to believe any of this? Not really. But if you notice, all the foods that tend to be 'high vibration' also tend to be more 'alkaline' but also more nutrient dense, high in fibre, and generally have nutrition experts recommending them. Whether they are doing that because of nutrient content or other reasons, there seems to be a pattern to recommending similar foods. Real foods. Colourful and mostly plants.

Mindful Eating

It's also worth mentioning mindful eating as a practice. So many people think about food all day and then when they come to eat, they rush the whole process. Whether that is watching TV while eating (and I'll hold my hands up to this one, as I'm guilty of this one when eating alone), or just stuffing their faces in between emails at work.

I believe that we should enjoy the process and pay attention to our food. It's a ritual of our culture and by being mindful we can learn to slow down a bit and pay more attention to the present moment. Which is a good thing to relax you a little. Eating when stressed is not a good thing as the hormones in your body will be different (think cortisol) and these could influence the food you are eating. I think it's better to eat something not as healthy but be relaxed and enjoy the process. Rather than be stressed about whether that salad that you are being served is organic or not.

Part of mindful eating is to chew food more. Most people, in my experience, almost inhale their food and are swallowing chunks of the stuff. I know we often feel in a rush to get everything done, but my recommendation is to chew for longer. Next time you eat, count how many chews you take. I would guess it's around ten. Aim to work up to 20 – 25 chews if you can.

The digestive process starts from the secretion of saliva which has digestive enzymes in it[254]. When you chew, you start to allow the food to be broken down more and be more easily absorbed in the body. You might also start to notice different flavours and subtleties in the food.

I'm still working on this on an unconscious level, i.e., I must consciously think about counting my chews to get up to 20 – 25 chews before I swallow, but when I do, I am more mindful in my eating, and it seems to me the food sits better with me. I would also suggest not drinking anything (if you can) while eating your meal, or for the 30 minutes prior and post eating. I'm by no means perfect with this, and drinking is part of the meal process. However, as you start to get ready to eat, the stomach secrets digestive juices, which can be compromised by drinking too close to pre or post food.

Give it a go and see for yourself for the next week.

Real Talk

I want to be real here. Am I saying that I'm perfect and always eat just real food. No. It's not about perfection. It's about doing the best you can. Sometimes I like to eat the odd bit of 'processed' food. For example, there are some great vegan burgers in supermarkets these days. I do look for ones that have the least amount of ingredients in them, and that are all recognisable ingredients. If I can get those, then I will. Sometimes I might buy something more 'experimental'. It's all okay. It's not about being 100% perfect.

I occasionally eat gluten-free bread which is sometimes full of tons more ingredients than a regular piece of bread. Would I advise eating that every day? No. It can be a useful transition food, or when over at friends or just because you fancy it, but it's still heavily processed. I enjoy vegan ice cream on occasion, and vegan & gluten free cakes, chocolates, and brownies. I still have a major weak spot for crisps[††††††††††††] and chips (French fries). So yes, you might see me walking down the street tucking into a bag of crisps. It's OK. Chill.

Earthing

The other part of the EARTH section of *The Leadership BEAT Model*™ is to do with a 'discovery' called *Earthing* (also known as *Grounding*). This is to do with our relationship to the Earth. We live un-natural lives now and have lost touch with many of the practices that we once did in our history. The practice of *Earthing* is simply this. Getting into physical contact with the earth or soil daily.

[††††††††††††] Crisps in the UK are known as 'chips' in the US.

E - ELEMENTS
Why Earth?

In his book, *Earthing – The Greatest Health Discovery Ever?* Clint Ober goes into more detail on this, but I'll give you the abridged version.

The Earth is teeming with negative electrons that can be transferred to us when we physically touch the ground. A rarity these days unless you happen to live in sunny climates and near to the beach or lovely parks. Certainly, in London, where I'm from, we can go months without getting our skin in contact with the ground, by walking barefoot.

These negative electrons are natural antioxidants. They bind to the free radicals in our body. The things we don't want too much off. Everyone is obsessed with drinking orange juice to get lots of antioxidants when the Earth's surface is full of them[255]. Twenty to thirty minutes a day is what we need.

Studies on *Earthing* are still in their infancy but are promising in showing that *Earthing* can reduce inflammation, lower cortisol, reduce DOMS (delayed onset muscle soreness) and improve sleep[256-261]. I suspect that time will show that it can be beneficial for more things as in effect, it is helping the body get back into balance. Clint Ober's book *Earthing* goes into some fascinating examples of how *Earthing* has helped people, including Tour de France cyclists, recover and even repair from injury.

Researchers at the University of California at San Diego tested grounding on a group of 16 massage therapists (who regularly suffer from aches and pains) during a six-week period. Four weeks of grounding and two weeks without. Over that six-week period their pain, physical function, anxiety, depression, fatigue, and sleep patterns were assessed. During the weeks of grounding, the therapist's reports improvements in these areas. Biomarkers of inflammation, blood viscosity and heart rate variability (HRV) all improved[259]. Of course, it's a small trial, but it's encouraging and in line with many other studies. And think about yourself for a moment, don't you feel great walking barefoot in the park or on a beach?

City Living

Living in London (or another city) it's not easy to always walk barefoot on the grass, so is there another way to *earth/ground*? It turns out, yes. There are products that mimic the effect of touching the ground, and have, according to research presented in Ober's book, the same beneficial effects.

216

2.3 Third Rock from the Sun (Earth)

More products are coming out, but I personally have a grounding sheet, mat, and strap. These products work by connecting to the earth part of a traditional plug socket. If the electrics in your house are properly grounded (and one would hope they are, but you can check by purchasing an inexpensive device that plugs into the sockets and will tell you), then you are still drawing up the negative electrons from the Earth.

I know this sounds crazy. There are studies to back this up though[257-261], but personal experience is always far more convincing.

When I first got my grounding sheet, I should have been having a more troubled sleep. Why? As I mentioned in the chapter on gratitude, one time I returned home from a few weeks away to find my long-term girlfriend with her bags packed and ready to move out and leave me. The night she left, and the subsequent nights, I slept like a baby. I didn't want the break-up to happen, so I don't think it would have been relief at the ending of the relationship. Not only did I have great sleep, but more vivid dreams and what was (upon sleep tracking) deeper and more restful sleep.

At the same time as all this, as I previously mentioned in the chapter on gratitude, I also sustained a serious knee injury (tearing my meniscus) resulting in being on crutches for around eight weeks. I used a grounding strap attached to my knee overnight and when working at my desk. On the days I used it, I felt less pain than when I didn't. Was it the placebo effect? Maybe. Although my experience echoes the experience of others in studies relating to pain and *Earthing*[259,262].

In the past few years, whenever I've had other injuries, I've used the mat or strap on the site of injury and it always seems to heal quicker or I am in less pain, compared to when I don't use it. Of course, this is all anecdotal and you might not believe it. That's fine. Like I said, experience is the biggest convincer, so if you are curious about it, I would suggest reading the book or researching and investing in something for yourself, to test it out. Why not just spend 20-30 minutes a day walking or sitting barefoot when you can?

Quick summary about earth (and eating) to becoming superhuman...

1. Most experts will agree that most of us need more plant-based foods to thrive. Aim to make 80% of what you eat *PANLO* – plant-based, alkaline, natural, live, and organic. Eat real food, and don't be afraid of healthy fats.

2. It's easier to frontload your day with nutrients from plenty of vegetables. For example, having juices and/or smoothies based around vegetables. Supplement where necessary, but don't use supplements as substitution for a healthy diet.

3. We've lost our connection to the Earth over the last few decades and its associated health benefits. Spending time each day in direct skin contact with the earth is good for us. Grounding products can help fill the gap if being on the earth directly isn't easy.

Action plan for becoming superhuman...

1. Add an extra portion of vegetables to each meal you eat for the next week. Gradually continue to do this until you are consuming ten or more portions of vegetables and fruit a day. Remembering the 4:1, veg to fruit ratio. Keep in mind *PANLO 80/20* at each meal.

2. Practise mindful chewing, noticing how many times you chew food before swallowing. Aim to build up to 25 chews.

3. Whenever possible, get into contact with the earth – even for just a few minutes. Consider buying an 'earthing' product.

2.4 The Great Fireball in the Sky (Fire)
Just look up…

"The sun is the most important thing in everybody's life, whether you're a plant, an animal or a fish, and we take it for granted."

- Danny Boyle

When I was developing *The Leadership BEAT Model*™, a lot of the learnings came intuitively. This section is one. I realised that I always feel so much better when I'm in the sun and outdoors. Not rocket science exactly. I suspect you feel the same. I knew it was important to include though. To the point that I can do other things right - like eating, drinking water, exercising and sleep and if I'm feeling "off BEAT" it might well be coming from this section.

And then I started looking into sunlight a bit more, and light therapy in general. There's a lot out there about its benefits and even more is coming. We're just scratching the surface right now. It's obvious when you think about it though. The Sun gives everything life on this planet. In fact, we are really consuming trapped sunlight when we eat. If you eat animals, then they have eaten the grass (or other animals that have eaten the grass/plants). The plants are trapping the energy of the Sun in them. That's what we are getting when we eat. We also need to absorb the sun directly.

Most people will be aware that we need exposure to sunlight for Vitamin D. Technically a hormone. But why? Well, Vitamin D is essential for being able to absorb calcium (for strong bones[263]). Without enough vitamin D, it won't matter how much calcium you get. You won't be able to reap the benefits.

Vitamin D has a role to play in cancer prevention too[180]. Data collected from both in vitro and in vivo studies are highly optimistic regarding its potential in prevention and regression of colorectal, prostate and breast cancers[179].

Vitamin D has many important roles in calcium and phosphorus metabolisms, the prevention of the cancer, therapeutic effects of autoimmune disease, and the protective effects on the atherosclerotic cardiovascular disease and diabetes[264]. There's even been a statistical correlation made from researchers between obsessive compulsive disorder (OCD) and latitude (i.e. how much sunlight people were getting)[265].

And it's important if you have kids to allow them to play outside and get lots of Vitamin D. Researchers from John Hopkins University found that children born with reduced levels of Vitamin D run a 40 per cent increased risk of hypertension between the ages of three and 18, and they are more than twice as likely to become hypertensive if their Vitamin D levels are consistently low at birth and early childhood[266].

Researchers from Karolinska University Hospital in Sweden reviewed nearly 30,000 Swedish women (aged 24 – 64) whose levels of sun exposure were tracked for 20 years. Frequent sunbathers had a lower risk of developing heart disease or dying from any disease prematurely compared with those who avoided the sun[267]. There is probably a law of diminishing returns if you spend too long in the sun to the point of burning, of course. The point is, we shouldn't be afraid of the sun. *Use*, don't abuse, it.

So how much sun do we need?

It really depends on so many things. The time of day, time of the year, position on Earth you are at (your latitude*), your skin colour, how much of your body is exposed, susceptibility to burning and more.

Some experts believe that we get enough Vitamin D in the summer months and can store it for the winter. And yet I've heard the opposite from other experts too. However, even in the summer, and even at the equator and in sunny regions, people can still very easily be vitamin D deficient. Our modern lives mean that we generally spend way too much time indoors. So even if it's sunny outside we don't really experience it.

A rule of thumb that you might consider is to spend half as much time out in

* If you live above the 37th parallel, then except in summer, the sun won't be strong enough. The 37 parallel is essentially anywhere above Greece, Italy, Spain, southern borders of Utah, Colorado, and Kansas, and the northern borders of Arizona, New Mexico, and Oklahoma.

the strong sun, as it takes for your skin to change colour. Strong sun would typically be from 11am - 4pm depending on where you are. Or making sure that your shadow is shorter, than your height. In other words, if you have a long shadow, then the sun is probably too low for significant vitamin D production. In addition, let's say that normally, without sun cream, your skin would start to change shade after 40 minutes. Then you would want to spend 20 minutes in the sun. Ideally every day or every other day.

Dr Sharad Paul, a geneticist and skin cancer expert, suggests exposing 20% of your body surface (that's about a t-shirt and shorts amount) for a minimum of 20 minutes a day to get enough vitamin D. After that time, your vitamin D absorption, by the skin, gets saturated[268]. We can get a bit more technical. The formula for finding out your burn time is to divide a quantity of minutes by the UV index for the day. For example, redheads are typically called type-1 and have a 67-minute burn time. Those with blonde hair and blue eyes are type-2 with a 100-minute threshold. Mediterranean people, like me, would be type-4 and have 300 minutes as a threshold. And on it goes. You can find the UV index from the weather reports, but in all honesty, that might be a bit much to be thinking about. About 20 minutes and if you are super easy to burn, just make sure it's not 20 minutes all at once.

I still believe that for vitamin D, it's essential to supplement all year-round (see the section earlier in the book on supplements for more detail). Yes, it's less important to supplement in the summer if you are exposing enough of your body surface area, but it's best to just get into the habit and keep it up[†]. And it's rare that you would get enough sun exposure most days in the summer. Just your face and arms aren't enough. You'd need to expose most of your torso.

[†] It is possible to get too much Vitamin D though, so you do need to be a bit mindful, and perhaps get tested. It's also important to supplement with Vitamin K2 when supplementing with Vitamin D.

E - ELEMENTS

Shinrin-Yoku

The 'FIRE' section is not just about sunlight, but also, it's about being outdoors more. We've detached ourselves from nature and our environment. And if you are anything like me, and you live a busy life in the city you're more likely to be surrounded by a concrete jungle rather than a real jungle.

The Japanese have this principle they call Shinrin-Yoku. Forest bathing would be the approximate English translation. I like that – *Forest Bathing*. What this is about, is getting into nature. There are studies that show that being out in nature can reduce oxidative stress in the body after a walk in the woods[269]. A 2017 review of 127 studies showed the physiological benefits including lower levels of cortisol, lower pulse rate, lower blood pressure, greater parasympathetic nervous system activity and lower sympathetic nervous activity compared to walkers in city environments[270]. Another study of 498 Japanese residents reported lower feelings of hostility, depression and anxiety as a direct result of time spent in the forest[271].

Researchers from the University of Exeter looked at the health and lifestyles of 20,000 people. Time in woodlands, town parks, beaches and other natural areas will all reap rewards provided that you spend 120 minutes a week in nature (these two hours need not be all at the same time but can be spread out)[272].

There's something about being in nature that is beneficial for us. Whether that's the fractals[‡] that only seem to appear in nature that calm us down. Or the energy that is given off by plants. Or the fact you are away from pollution, cities or whatever. It's not totally important to know in order to take advantage of it.

Again, don't get bogged down in the studies and the science of it all, but think about this intuitively. *Do you feel better when you get to spend time in parks, forests, by the sea or lakes, mountains, fields or anywhere else in nature?* My guess is yes. Sure, there is science to support this. You don't need to wait for more and more science to do it from today[§].

There may be another reason why being outdoors is good for us - *dirt*. Bacteria. Being exposed to our local environment and the thousands of species of bacteria. These bacteria are our 'tenants'. They live in our property – our body. It's known as the microbiome. It's in our guts, on our skin, pretty much all over and in us. Although we often think about the gut. And these 'tenants' of ours can help with our own immune system if we have a good variety of them, and an abundance of the good kind[273]. We've lost touch with that. Children today don't tend to play in the dirt as much as children of previous generations. They typically spend too much time indoors, and being sedentary, on their devices, and so aren't exposed to the variety of bacteria that their grandparents might have been exposed to. This has health consequences, and we would do well to get out more into nature to allow these little bugs back into our lives. Perhaps plan a picnic in nature?

Even if you live in a city, hopefully there are parks that you could visit. If so, I invite you to create a little 'rule' that you walk through a park once or twice a week. Even consider a monthly trip out of the city – even if it's just for a couple of hours.

In fact, an NHS Trust in Scotland (Shetland) is now even starting to prescribe getting into nature for chronic disease management[274].

[‡] A fractal is a never-ending pattern. Fractals are infinitely complex patterns that are self-similar across different scales. They are created by repeating a simple process over and over in an ongoing feedback loop.

[§] Since writing this chapter, we have experienced the Sars-Cov-2/Covid-19/Coronavirus pandemic and lockdowns worldwide. And since then, it has become more and more obvious to people that the things that I've been talking about for over a decade, including nature, sunshine, connection to people and so on, are important for health and wellbeing. Not just diet, exercise, and sleep.

E - ELEMENTS

Light Therapy

In addition to being outdoors in the natural sunlight and nature, there is more research being done on light therapy (using laser light, red, infrared, near infrared, blue light, full spectrum light and others) to promote healing and health. Sometimes referred to as photobiomodulation. Our bodies have evolved over millennia to respond to the light-dark cycle of the planet. The problem is that we have moved away from that to a large extent. Especially in the winter in northern climate cultures when there is no light at the beginning or end of the day when we are going to, or coming back from, work. I remember when I worked in central London, I could sometimes go a whole week without having daylight on my skin or seeing daylight, let alone the sun. And I was someone who made a big effort to, at least, get out during lunch.

In 2017, I started using a Seasonal Affective Disorder (S.A.D.) light box during the winter. What these do is produce an intense light that mimics the sunlight you would get in the darker months, when all we see most days is grey cloud – at least in the UK. The S.A.D. light box produces about 10,000 lux** when about 30 cm away from it.

I must say that I use this every day now during the darker months, so that I can get light into my eyes first thing in the morning. Not only does this help me wake up and kick-start the cortisol in my system, but it also helps me sleep in the evening. I don't even use it exactly as directed. Which is to be 30cm away from it for 15 minutes. I am typically 1 – 2 meters away as I have it on while I'm waking my body up exercising on a rebounder (mini-trampoline). I will be on the rebounder for 15 – 25 minutes and then do some simple stretches or exercises. I might be in front of the light box for 30 – 40 minutes. And then again in front of it after breakfast for the first 30 – 60 minutes of my day, when I'm 80 – 100 cm away from it.

I've noticed more energy in the morning, increased alertness and feel my sleep improved too. Anecdotal perhaps. But experience is the best teacher, so judge for yourself.

Research is starting to show promise that light can be used to treat insomnia, attention deficit hyperactivity disorder (ADHD) and dementia[275-277]. Studies

---

** Lux is the unit of measurement for light brightness. My lux app on my phone only registers up to 32,000 lux and a sunny day in London goes beyond that. Even a cloudy day can be around 10,000 lux – similar to the light box. Inside office buildings it might be only about 100-200 lux. That's two orders of magnitude less.

are also indicating that it might improve function in patients with Parkinson's disease[278-281].

There are even companies developing technology which shine light into the ears, as there are photoreceptors on the brain[282], which could possibly be used for S.A.D., jet lag and perhaps even more conditions. There is even an argument to be made that light therapy can be used to boost things like testosterone production[283], with studies dating back to 1939[284]!

Light therapy, or photobiomodulation, is still a much evolving therapy, and there are researchers looking into the different effects that different wavelengths of light have on us. Certainly, the prognosis looks good for the treatment of pain[285], inflammation[286], boosting mitochondrial function[287], increasing collagen[288] (the proteins that make your skin young and elastic, which we lose as we age). Even wound healing[289]†† and eyesight[290].

Since 2019 I've been experimenting with using red and near infrared light too. I have another couple of light boxes (in addition to the S.A.D. one) which emits red (660nm wavelength) and near infrared (IR) light (850nm wavelength). I typically use this now when meditating for 15 minutes in the morning shining it on to my face and upper torso. Then I will do some mobility exercises and have it shining on the rest of my body targeting different areas for a few minutes each. When I work from home, I have it under my desk and shine it on my knees and legs to help with healing a knee surgery I undertook to repair a torn meniscus in October 2019‡‡.

Red and Infrared light therapy has thousands of scientific papers examining potential benefits. Benefits being explored include reducing inflammation, speeding up healing, improving exercise and recovery, boosting testosterone, stimulating collagen production, improving circulation, improving mood and more. I certainly feel more energised after using my red/IR device.

In general, though, you want to mimic nature. Get nice blue light (or full spectrum light) in the morning and daytime, and towards the end of the day limit blue light exposure. That means limit light from lamps, bulbs, TV's, phones and so on. Personally, I make sure that after dusk I am wearing blue-

---

†† Yes, this was in mice, but now the Star Trek healing devices of the 23rd and 24th century, where they point a light and a wound heals up miraculously, don't seem too far-fetched.
‡‡ I originally tore my meniscus in 2015 and healed non-invasively. Then in December 2018 I tore it more significantly creating a bucket-handle tear, that had flipped in-between the knee and so needed surgery to put back into place.

light blocking glasses, which I've owned since 2015. I have found these extremely helpful for inducing sleepiness and extending my deep sleep. More on sleep improvement strategies in the chapter on sleep.

Quick summary about light and becoming superhuman...

1. Humans are meant to have appropriate light exposure as part of a natural light/dark cycle to thrive.

2. Being exposed to daylight, nature and being outdoors is great for our health and wellbeing, reducing stress and anxiety.

3. Even if we can't always get into a natural light/dark pattern (which is usually best), there are technical solutions that can be used such as light boxes, and other forms of light therapy. Both for day-to-day solutions, but also potentially in the treatment of health issues.

Action plan for becoming superhuman...

1. Aim to expose yourself to daylight every day, especially in the mornings. Expose yourself to sunlight when you can (even on a cloudy day) without sun cream, for 20 minutes, being mindful of your skin type.

2. Spend regular time in nature – Shinrin-Yoku. Even if that's walking in the park 2–3 times per week. When you can, explore the countryside.

3. If you live in a country where the winters are dark and long, and you are not out much during the day, then consider a getting and S.A.D. light box, or Infrared light box. It may help you with your alertness, energy levels, mood, sleep and more.

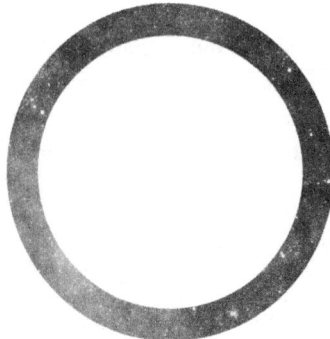

2.5 The Space Between Us (Aether)

It's not what we see that matters…

"Its energy surrounds us, and binds us, luminous beings are we. Not this crude matter. You must feel the force around you…everywhere…"

– Master Yoda (from The Empire Strikes Back)

Aether is a metaphor for the environment that envelops us. From having a tidy desk or house to having your environment set up to get you to move more as well as what we put on our skin and hair, to the invisible waves interacting with us from moment to moment.

Physical Environment

I'm sure you've heard of Feng Shui - the Japanese practice of arranging your environment in a certain way for energy to flow well. Without exploring the details of that practice here, what I do feel, as you might too, is that a clean, tidy, and organised environment helps me to feel more relaxed, at peace, able to concentrate and have focus. Beyond just being clean and tidy, when there are inspiring pieces of furniture or pictures around, doesn't it make you feel great?

According to Marie Diamond, the celebrity Feng Shui expert, when you have chaos around you, you are more likely to be in Beta brainwaves (15 – 30 Hz), which means you're less likely to be in an inspired and visionary state. If you are in an organised environment, it's easier to get into Alpha brainwaves (9 – 14 Hz) – which is better for relaxation, creative visualisation and moving plans forward[291].

And let's not forget plants too. Having plants can add many benefits. NASA's

227

E - ELEMENTS

1989 Clean Air Study[292] identified several plants able to remove toxins (formaldehyde, benzene, xylene, ammonia, and trichloroethylene) from the air. For example, English Ivy, Spider Plant and Chrysanthemum.

If you can, set up your environment in the best way possible. Think about plenty of natural light, some plants and decorated in a way that makes you feel relaxed, yet focussed and comfortable. If you do, I'm sure that you will notice a pleasant uplift in your energy levels.

A good way that I've found for what to think about when setting up your environment are the first four elements.

Air: Is the space clear from clutter? Is there fresh air coming in and windows and doors that can open?

Water: Perhaps adding in water features like mini desk-sized waterfalls or fountains. Water soothes us. Maybe, like me, you use water in a diffuser.

Earth: Are you able to put plants, and greenery around? Or at least nice paintings or pictures of nature? Perhaps a little bit of grass to walk barefoot on?

Fire: Is there lots of natural sunlight? Do you have an open space to go to?

228

Part of your physical environment is also about whether it is set up for you in a way to serve you, beyond being just being tidy or organised. Does your company, office space or home environment get you feeling superhuman? Do you have something that can get you moving more? We need to move regularly, which we'll cover in the ACTIVITY section, but for now, have you set things up to enable that to happen. For example, are the lifts more awkward to get to than the stairs, to encourage stairs usage? If you work from a home office, you could consider putting a pull up bar in the doorway and each time you walk under it doing one pull-up. Or, if you are like me, you have a mini-trampoline (rebounder) close at hand that you can jump on while making phone calls. It might be to use a standing desk to encourage movement while working. There are endless possibilities for setting up the environment to support you. From being clean, tidy, and organised, to encouraging movement, creativity, and collaboration between colleagues*.

For an example on how your environment can affect you, a study from Cornell University even showed that if your kitchen is messy, then you will be more inclined to overeat[293].

Sound

Think about how sound can affect your health and wellbeing. I'm sure we've all been frustrated with unwanted noise. I remember at university my housemate, whose room was directly beneath mine, used to play his music. It wasn't always loud, but there was a lot of bass that he would use. The sound and the vibrations would really disturb me and not allow me to concentrate. Even today, my walls are a bit thin, and I can sometimes hear the neighbours. I did explore investing in thousands of pounds in soundproofing solutions but in the end, I spent a few pounds on construction-style ear defenders. They seem to do the job well when it gets noisy – which thankfully is rare anyway.

Unwanted noise is linked to shorten lifespan. The European Environment Agency estimates that environmental noise contributes to 48,000 new cases of ischaemic heart disease a year as well as 12,000 premature deaths. In addition, they estimate that 22 million people suffer chronic high annoyance, and 6.5 million people suffer chronic high sleep disturbance. As a result of aircraft noise, they estimate that 12,500 school children suffer reading

---

* I believe that Apple's new headquarters was instructed by the late Steve Jobs to facilitate this kind of accidental interaction between colleagues.

E - ELEMENTS
impairment in school[294].

Conversely though, sound can be used for benefit too. Perhaps you work well with classical music, or subliminal sounds and affirmations. Sound (or Gong) baths and chanting are often used in yoga and meditation centres and retreats for wellbeing. It might be the sounds, or more accurately, the vibrations that heal and soothe the body. In fact, writing this reminds me of one of my favourite quotes of all time (also mentioned earlier), and something I often think about when looking at certain situations.

> *"If you want to find the secrets of the universe, think in terms of energy, frequency and vibration."*
>
> *– Nikola Tesla*

Personal Environment

Most people don't give a second thought to the environment of their body and what they put on themselves. The average American woman uses 12 products a day – nearly 200 chemicals, according to the 2004 survey by the Environmental Working Group[295]. Chemicals like parabens, sodium laureth/lauryl sulphites (SLES & SLS) are prevalent in shampoos, conditioners, creams and so on. These are not natural things to be putting on our bodies. Some experts in this area even champion the idea that if you can't put it *in* your body (i.e., eat it) you shouldn't put it *on* your body. And I'm inclined to agree. It makes sense. What you put on your skin gets absorbed into your body. And people are absorbing high levels of dangerous chemicals from popular sun creams and sprays[296] that may lead to cancers or developmental and reproduction issues.

Here are the main ones that you should look out for and avoid:

Sulfates: Such as sodium lauryl sulfate (SLS) and sodium laureth sulfate (SLES).

Found in shampoos, body wash, oral hygiene products, cleansers, makeup, skin care serums, topicals, hair styling products and hair colour.

Linked to cellular damage, reproductive disorders, kidney damage, respiratory problems, and skin, lung, and eye irritation.

Phthalates: Such as dibutyl phthalate, diethyl phthalate, dimethyl phthalate, fragrance, MMP, MEP, MiBP, DMP, DEP, DiBP.

Found in deodorant, anti-perspirant, perfumes, fragrances, hair products, skin cleansers, makeup, moisturisers, lotions, and spray tans.

Linked to endocrine system disruption, cellular damage, reproductive disorders, birth defects, hormonal changes, early-onset puberty, thyroid abnormalities and are suspected carcinogens.

Phthalates are a terrible by-product from our dependency on plastics. In 2004, the US Centre for Disease Control tested 2,540 people and found that 97 per cent had measurable phthalates in their body[297].

Triclosan: Triclocarban

Found in sanitizer, antibacterial products, body wash, deodorant, antiperspirant, hair products, toothpaste, mouthwash, and teeth whiteners.

Linked to heart disease, heart failure, reproductive disorders, hormonal changes, thyroid abnormalities, endocrine system disruption, muscle function disruption and skin irritation.

Parabens: Any chemical ending in -paraben, such as methylparaben or propylparaben.

Found in cosmetics, makeup removers, deodorants, antiperspirants, lotions, spray tans, sunscreens, shampoos, cleansers, and body wash.

Linked to breast cancer, tumours, endocrine system disruption, reproductive disorders, hormonal changes, and thyroid abnormalities.

A study by the US Centres for Disease Control and Prevention measured parabens in urine samples from 2,548 men, women, and children. Nearly all (99.1%) had methylparaben, and 92.7% propylparaben, with almost halve the samples containing ethylparaben (42.4%) and butylparaben (47%)[298].

In addition, antiseptics found in toothpaste, shampoo, lotions, and eye drops contain compounds known as quaternary ammonium salts, or "quats". And quats are included in mouthwashes, nasal sprays, lozenges, and household cleaners as well as many other products. And these have been found to affect our mitochondria – the cell's powerhouses. Quats also interrupted oestrogen signalling which could affect a woman's reproductive cycle and fertility. This research, from the University of California, Davis was only tested in test tubes (in vitro). However, there is a desire to now test in animals[†] and therefore know more about possible impact of quats on human health[299].

Researchers at the University of Alberta in Canada found a direct link between a changed gut microbiome and the number of times that disinfectants were used around the home. And, in the study, infants that live in homes where standard disinfectant were used were twice as likely to have higher levels of gut microbes known as Lachnospiraceae, which are linked to weight gain. Their weight was checked from age one until aged three, and those with raised levels of Lachnospiraceae as infants, had a higher BMI by the time they were three. Those that lived in homes that used eco-friendly cleaning products weren't affected[300].

It can be tricky to find something, but it's worth it in the long run. I say to everyone, if it's something you are going to be using a lot, whether a cleaning product for the house, a body product or food, it's worth spending time up front to make sure it's not harmful to you. Researchers in Norway from the University of Bergen even concluding that chemicals in household cleaning products are so dangerous that the lung damage has been compared to smoking 20 cigarettes a day[301].

Sadly, many factors are working against in becoming superhuman. There is Kryptonite[‡] everywhere. We must be careful, if we are to become the best leaders we can be, that we have things working for us.

There are apps which can also help. At the time of writing, *Think Dirty* is an app on iPhone/iPad which can be used to scan barcodes and give you a rating on the product that you are using. This will allow you to see how many harmful ingredients are contained within it.

What about when you go away, on business trips and holidays? What do you do then? Well, most people take their own products, but if you don't, I wouldn't worry about it. The odd use here and there isn't going to matter too much. In the long term, and where you have control, why not stack the cards in your favour.

As reported by the European Environment Agency, according to some estimates, about 6 % of the world's disease burden — including chronic

---

[†] Note that I am not a supporter of animal studies but am merely reporting the process here.
[‡] The fictional meteorite, Kryptonite, is Superman's main weakness.

diseases, cancers, neurological and developmental disorders — and 8 % of deaths can be attributed to chemicals[302]. More than 300 million tonnes of chemicals were consumed in the EU in 2018 and more than two thirds of this amount were chemicals that are classified as hazardous to health, according to Eurostat. Over 20 000 individual chemicals have been registered in the EU under the Registration, Evaluation, Authorisation and Restriction of Chemicals (REACH) Regulation[302].

As these numbers keep growing.

Control what you can control.

Cope with what you can't, and

Concentrate on what's important.

The above is a phrase (I first heard author Craig Ballantyne say) well worth remembering for everything in life, but especially in this chapter and the chapter on food. We can get quite uptight about things if we allow ourselves to. If we just focus on controlling what we buy for our house, that's a start. Then we might start looking to whether there is anything we can control outside of the house. Like the restaurants we chose for food. The places we spend time in. The products we use to clean our house and ourselves.

Electromagnetic Frequencies (EMFs)

EMFs are all around us. From more natural one's like the rays from the sun and the fields generated by the earth and humans (yes, we generate fields). To more recent EMFs like light bulbs, electrical appliances, radio, telephone towers, Wi-Fi, Bluetooth and more.

The thing we must remember is that we are all electromagnetic beings, and we are affected by these waves. There isn't really a question about that. The question is how *much*, to what affect, and can we do anything about it. A major $30 million 10-year study concluded that radio frequency radiation from mobile networks do cause cancer[303]. It was using less powerful 2G and 3G networks and done on rats to control exactly how much radiation they were exposed to, rather than relying on a human questionnaire.

I recommend picking up a copy of the books *Radiation Nation* and *EMF*d* as well as watching the documentary *Resonance – Beings of Frequency* to go deeper into this. For now, know that having an EMF enabled device directly on you negatively affects your biochemistry. For example, researchers in Finland found that just 33 minutes of mobile phone use suppressed glucose metabolism in the brain, suggesting a lack of food for brain neurons which would lead to concentration, learning and memory problems[304]. And it's been shown since 2004 that mobile phone radiation has the ability to alter human DNA[305].

And if you are male and reading this, know that several studies show negative effects on sperm count and quality with exposure to mobile phones[306]. If you have teenage kids, take special note, as researchers from the Swiss Tropical and Public Health Institute, concluded that radio frequency electromagnetic fields caused memory problems in adolescents after using a mobile phone for just a year[307].

Furthermore, it appears that magnetic field non-ionizing radiation[§] dramatically increases the risk of miscarriage by almost three-fold[308]. The US National Toxicology Program (NTP) concluded their $25m research project exposing mice and rats to 10-minute bursts of mobile phone radiation. Their conclusion? Mobile phones are a definite carcinogen (in the animal studies) and damaged the DNA in the brain of the subjects[309].

Now, I don't expect anyone reading this (me included) to give up their mobile phones. They are here, and here to stay for the foreseeable future. However, how can you reduce the impact that these waves have on you? Here are some quick tips:

1. Carry your phone in a bag and not directly on your body.
2. Use a case that can shield you from the EMFs when you do have to have your phone on you. A Faraday cage is effectively what you can carry the phone around in, and what I use most of the time.
3. Don't put your laptop on your lap. If you do, use an EMF shield[**].
4. Put the device into airplane mode whenever you can (this has the added benefit of saving battery and you won't be disturbed. The

---

[§] Magnetic fields (MFs) are emitted from both traditional sources that generate low frequency MFs (e.g., power lines, appliances, transformers, etc.) and from emerging sources that generate higher frequency MFs (e.g., wireless networks, smart meter networks, cell towers, wireless devices such as cell phones, etc.)

[**] Many of these EMF shields aren't doing what they say they are, so you'll need to do your homework on proven products.

mobile phone in my opinion is for me to *reach out* to the world, not for the world to *reach in* and disturb *me*).

5. Turn your Wi-Fi connection off overnight (you might not be able to prevent your neighbours signal entering your house, but you can control your own). Maybe even consider an old school ethernet connection too.

6. Never, *never* sleep with your phone anywhere near your head. Ever[††].

7. Use your phone on speakerphone when speaking on it. Never hold directly to the head unless just for the briefest of moments, and still a few centimetres away.

8. Use headphones that are wired, or better still, air-tube headphones that convert from digital to analogue and use pressure waves to deliver the sound.

9. Stay away from Bluetooth headphones where the receiver is built directly into the earpiece[‡‡].

The book *EMF*d* by Dr Joseph Mercola goes into lots of granular detail on the effects of EMF's, 5G technology and personal solutions that you can implement in your own environments above and beyond what I mention in this chapter. I have to say, Mercola's book is quite overwhelming - even for me - but it's there for you if you want to take a deeper dive into all of this.

I know that we are living in the 21st century. We all have busy lives that are increasingly dependent on technology. And trust me when I say that the irony is not lost on me that I am writing this while using a laptop. Albeit with the Wi-Fi turned off, as I'm on a train and hoping it saves me some battery. My phone is in my bag, on airplane mode. If you were ever to call me and I wasn't expecting your call, you would be lucky to reach me as my phone is usually on silent when not in airplane mode.

[††] There may be an argument to have it in airplane mode, but I've had phones in the past where even on airplane mode there had been a signal!

[‡‡] Sorry to all you Apple Airpod users, but the Bluetooth signal from one headphone to the other is passing right between your ears. Happy with that?

Quick summary about the environment and becoming superhuman...

1. The physical environment that you create for yourself can determine your motivation, creativity, energy levels and more, so ensure that you have set it up for success.

2. What you put on your body is just as important as what you put in your body. Many products are full of un-natural chemicals that could negatively affect you. While they may be deemed safe, no-one has ever tested all the variety of combinations of chemicals that people end up putting on them.

3. EMFs are ubiquitous in our environment. Some are naturally occurring and others man-made. The long-terms effects of so many of these are not fully understood and that which is understood is not publicly widespread knowledge. Although we shouldn't overly stress about them, we should control our immediate environment.

Action plan for becoming superhuman...

1. Set your physical environment up for success. Tidy your space, organise your things or do a bit of a spring clean – even if just your desk area.

2. Buy one product for either cleaning your house, or yourself that is free from harsh chemicals like parabens, SLES, SLS. Whether that is a shampoo, multi-purpose spray or a piece of make-up.

3. Take one action to clean up your EMF junk. Be that turning off your WiFi router at night, turning your phone into airplane mode when it is on you, or keeping it off your body altogether. It could be just using earbuds instead of using the phone directly against your head.

Part 3: ACTIVITY

What you do in a day...

"All growth depends upon activity. There is no development physically or intellectually without effort, and effort means work."

- Calvin Coolidge

This section is about the third part of *The Leadership BEAT Model*™ – ACTIVITY. We all know that exercise is good for us and important for a variety of reasons. Humans are designed to move. And regularly, with intermittent periods of resting. Modern culture in the developed world has flipped this on its head. Most people spend much of their time stationary and then move ever so slightly.

The exercise drum has been beating loud and hard for decades. The number of options for exercise out there are too many to even begin to list. And yet, many people simply don't exercise enough. And we know it's great for us. To list just a few of the benefits:

239

VITALITY

1. Improves mood.[310]
2. Maintains and improves bodyweight.[311]
3. Good for muscles and bones (especially as we age).[312]
4. Increases energy levels.[313]
5. Reduces stress.[310]
6. Reduces the risk of chronic diseases, including up to:
   - 65% lower risk of death from cardiovascular disease.[314]
   - 50% lower risk of type 2 diabetes.[315]
   - 50% lower risk of colon cancer.[316,317]
   - 20% lower risk of breast cancer.[317,318]
   - 30% lower risk of early death.[314]
   - 83% lower risk of osteoarthritis.[317]
   - 68% lower risk of hip fracture.[317]
   - 30% lower risk of depression.[317]
   - 30% lower risk of dementia.[317]
   - a 35% lower risk of coronary heart disease and stroke.[317]
7. Can help the brain and memory (improves executive functions).[310]
8. Can help with relaxation and sleep.[319]
9. Promotes a better sex life.[320]
10. Live longer.[321]

I shouldn't need to sell you on that. In fact, when I mention ACTIVITY is the third component, most people will naturally assume I am talking about exercise. This section is not just about exercise, although exercise is important. It's about all the activities that fill up your day. From the exercise you do, yes, but more importantly, regular movement - whether structured or unstructured. It's also about how you spend your time, your routines, and rituals. Do you have people that engage and inspire you in life? Give you energy or drain your energy? What about giving yourself in service to other people. Do you have fun? Play? Laugh?

ACTIVITY looks at all those activities that can occupy your day.

=========

3.1 Exercise
Move it, or lose it...

"Physical fitness is not only one of the most important keys to a healthy body, it is the basis of dynamic and creative intellectual activity."

- John F. Kennedy

We are designed to move. In fact, we're designed to move most of the time interspersed with rest throughout the day and more significant rest at night. We have that reversed now because we spend a lot of time sedentary and not moving and then when we get to bed many of us have trouble sleeping. You have probably heard about getting 10,000 steps a day[*]. The reality is that it can be more nuanced than just saying that. Although, debate aside, I do believe it's a good, albeit imperfect, measure for most people to look at step count. Sadly, a 2010 study of over a thousand Americans measured how much the average adult walks over a 24-hour period. The study found that the average number of daily steps was 5,340 for men and 4,793 for women. The technical definition of 'sedentary' is less than 5,000 steps per day[322]. Then there is also an argument to take 10-minute bouts throughout the day, rather than shooting for the 10,000 steps number. Again, another good idea. I'm all for it. Just move. Move often. It doesn't have to be intense. That said, what are the overall guidelines on how much we should move to stay healthy.

How much do we need to move?

Here's the current (UK) guidelines on exercise:

---

[*] My personal goal is 12,000 steps a day minimum. Although there is some debate about the validity and origins of this 10,000-step number.

A - ACTIVITY

- Adults should be active daily[†].
- Over a week, activity should add up to 150 minutes of moderate intensity – in 10-minute (or more) chunks.
- Perform muscle strengthening activities at least two days per week.
- Incorporate balance and co-ordination exercises at least two days per week.
- Minimise sedentary time (get up and walk around a bit, have a stretch).

This might sound like a lot to do, but in fact there are plenty ways to utilise your time efficiently, which we'll look at in the next chapter. For now, let's talk about exercise though. And I have a distinction to make here.

Intentional vs. Integrative

Let's look at the day of a typical person working in a large cosmopolitan city. They might spend eight hours in bed, 30 minutes eating breakfast, spend one hour commuting in to work, eight hours at their desks, one hour at their desk eating lunch, one hour commuting back, 30 minutes at dinner, then a couple of hours watching TV or being online in the evening. That's 22 hours out of a 24-hour day. Which amounts to 92% of the time being sedentary.

And you might be thinking that you're okay because you go to the gym for an hour a day. Well, you are only one hour better off. Which is 4%. And a study from 2012 indicated that exercising after work isn't enough to prevent disease. Long periods of sitting were associated with diabetes, cardiovascular disease, and death - even for those who got exercise at other times of the day[323].

Obviously, I'm not saying *don't* go to the gym or do exercise. It's great for all the reasons (and more) stated earlier, but it doesn't make you a whole lot less sedentary over the course of the day. And recent research shows that the active "couch potato" can still have compromised metabolic health[324]. The same study goes on to report that each one-hour increment in TV time[‡] was found to be associated with an 11% and an 18% increased risk of all-cause and cardiovascular disease mortality, respectively. Furthermore, relative to those watching TV for less than 2 hours/day, there was a 46% increased risk

---

[†] And I would assert that that needs to be throughout the day, not just one small period when you can squeeze it in.
[‡] Note that the study was looking into "active couch potatoes" and so investigated TV watching while sitting.

of all-cause and an 80% increased risk of cardiovascular disease mortality in those watching four or more hours of TV per day. This was independent of traditional risk factors such as smoking, blood pressure, cholesterol and diet, as well as leisure-time physical activity and waist circumference[324].

So clearly normal exercise is not the complete answer. The answer is to get as close to our natural rhythms as possible. Regular movement. In a review published by the International Journal of Behavioural Nutrition and Physical Activity, breaking up periods of sitting every half hour was recommended. This can prevent the catabolism (the breaking down of tissue) known to occur during sedentary periods[325].

Years ago, people wouldn't even know what you meant by saying the word 'exercise'. They'd look at you and say "huh?" For them it was just living. Ploughing the fields, walking to the store or to fetch water.

That's the difference between what I call 'Intentional' exercise - going to the gym, playing football, running, attending a spin class. And 'Integrative' exercise, which could be anything that gets your heart rate up or gets you moving in different and moderately challenging ways. This could be taking the stairs (especially if taking two steps at a time) which is proven to increase health[326], cycling to work, getting off the bus or train a stop earlier, parking your car at the far side of the car park, walking up the escalators instead of just standing still, gardening and house cleaning to name but a few. Or short periods of high-intensity exercise (interspersed in the day), which has been shown to boost memory and increase BDNF (brain-derived neurotrophic factor) – a protein that keeps brain cells healthy[327].

The opportunity for 'Integrative' exercise is everywhere. By integrating movement and exercise into your day, it will be much easier to meet the national guidelines. Without the exercise taking up all your time. Not only that, but if you break up sitting with moderate intensity breaks you will significantly reduce your glucose and insulin levels, thus reducing the risk for diabetes[328].

We'll look at 'Integrative' exercise in the next chapter, for now let's take a closer look at 'Intentional' exercise.

Intentional Exercise

And if you are exercising - I am into exercise in a big way, so I'm not against formal exercise by any stretch (pun unintentional but welcome) - what's the

243

best type? Here's the answer.

The one you'll stick to. That's it. The one that you enjoy and can perform consistently. That's the best exercise. If you want to determine what exercise to choose, then I suggest doing the following process.

Think about an exercise that you currently do or are interested in. Going through the list below, score the exercise out of the number in brackets. Score it a '1' if it meets that component, '0' if it doesn't. The last two criteria are scored out of '5' and '8' because they are more important an influence as to whether you will stick to the exercise or not. Why have I created this selection process? Because there is no one best workout, but there are the best workouts for you. And in my experience the best ones tend to meet the following criteria. What I call the *S9 Sport Selection Criteria.*

S9 Sport Selection Criteria

1. **Strength** (+1) - *Does the exercise increase your levels of strength?*
   o   As we age our bone density decreases but that doesn't mean that your bone strength needs to decrease. Regular strength building activities are vital to allow a maintenance of muscle mass and bone strength as we age.
   o   *Some examples:* Yoga, weightlifting, calisthenics (bodyweight), resistance bands.

2. **Suppleness** (+1) - *Are you becoming more flexible because of doing this exercise?*
   o   Ever noticed how bendy and flexible children are? When we age, we become naturally stiffer (mostly because of modern life). If you don't use it, you lose it. We all need to incorporate frequent stretching into our physical routines.
   o   *Some examples:* Yoga, gymnastics, ballet, Brazilian Ju-Jitsu, Capoeira.

3. **Stability** (+1) - *Is your balance improving with this exercise?*
   o   As we get older the risk of falling increases (and therefore fractures), but this need not be the case if you continue to work on your balance.
   o   *Some examples:* Yoga, slacklining, gymnastics, obstacle course race training (and Ninja Warrior).

4. **Size/Shape** (+1) – *Will this exercise give you the type of body you are after?*
   o A swimmer's body is different from a sprinter's. A weightlifter's to a yogi's and a dancer's to a bodybuilder's. What kind of physique are you aiming for? This will have a bearing on what you might end up doing.
   o *Some examples:* Weightlifting, calisthenics (bodyweight), Cross-Fit, yoga, swimming, running[§].

5. **Speed** (+1) - *Does this exercise increase your speed, require pace, or get your heart racing?*
   o Is it important that you keep your speed up as you age? To keep the fast twitch muscles active. It might not be a big thing for you, but something to consider.
   o *Some examples:* Sprinting, cycling, rollerblading, football, basketball.

6. **Stamina** (+1) - *Is your cardiovascular endurance improving?*
   o If your goal is to be able to cycle from London to Paris, then you will need some level of stamina. Or if it's to complete the London Marathon. Maybe even just be able to spend eight hours with your significant other shopping? If so, you might want to consider incorporating some exercise that increases your stamina.
   o *Some examples:* Running, cycling, swimming, walking, rollerblading, rowing, skipping, boxing, football.

7. **Skill** (+1) - *Does it challenge you in some way? E.g., the movements performed.*
   o Performing new complex movements (such as dancing) may aid in keeping the brain youthful and functioning well[329]. The added benefit in the moment is that skilled activities might require some level dedicated in-the-moment focus which can help take you out of whatever is otherwise occupying your mind. For example, the horrible day at work you've just had.
   o *Some examples:* Dancing, Olympic lifting, Cross-Fit, boxing, kettlebells, Thai boxing, Brazilian Ju-Jitsu, obstacle course racing,

---

[§] Every sport (or exercise) will lend itself to developing a particular type of build, although this also depends on your body type and genetics.

qigong.

8. **Spirit** (+5) - *Does it enliven your spirit?*
   o In other words, do you enjoy it? Or does it make you happier, more connected, more "in balance"?
   o ***Some examples:*** Yoga, dancing, Frisbee®, tai chi, qigong.

9. **Significance** (+8) - *How does this exercise meet your needs for what you consider to be significant (or important) in an exercise?*
   o It's important that the exercise you choose meets your need for significance or you won't do it enough. This is about what you consider the most important aspects of the exercise.
   o ***Some examples***: Being outdoors, being able to do it regardless of the weather, being with people, doing it by yourself, following a grading system, being close to home, having the flexibility to do the exercise whenever you want.

Add up your scores now. It should be out of 20. The closer to 20 you are, the more likely that the exercise you've chosen is well rounded and a good fit you. You'll notice that the last two - *Spirit* and *Significance* - have more importance assigned to them. That's simply because if you don't enjoy it and it doesn't meet what you deem to be significant (important) for you, then you simply won't do it in the long-term.

Ideally, you would score points in most of the categories and the last two would have several points. If not? Then it might be time to re-evaluate what kind of exercise you do. Truth be told, it's unlikely that any one exercise will meet all the criteria fully which is why it's a good idea to have more than one to follow. If your thing is running, then are you really doing much to increase strength, suppleness, and stability? I aim to get a variety of different exercises. Currently these include cycling, boxing, Thai boxing, yoga, weights, bodyweight conditioning, kettlebells, Capoeira, swimming, and walking.

For me, yoga is my foundational exercise. It complements everything else. I like to think of it like the cement (or pointing) in the brick work to the house. Sure, the windows, the doors, the walls, the roof easier to admire. In this metaphor, that's all the other exercises. However, without the pointing keeping the bricks in place (the yoga), it all comes crumbling down. Yoga doesn't do everything for the body – as is obvious looking at the S9 Sports Selection Criteria above, but it does make everything else better. My recommendation is that although you can learn some basics online, nothing beats having an experienced teacher guide you through the subtleties of the movements. Try out many different styles, teachers, and studios to see what resonates with you. Commit to going for at least 6-12 months to get the basics before transitioning to online classes – but still maintain a teacher-led live class on a weekly basis if you can.

Many people have become accustomed to thinking of exercise in terms of things like 'going to the gym' or 'running'. If playing Frisbee®, or ballroom dancing is more up your street, then go for that too. Getting some *'Intentional'* exercise into your day or week will pay dividends and it's enjoyable too!
It's not the only thing to look out for as we'll discover in the next chapter.

Quick summary about exercise and becoming superhuman...

1. As humans we are designed to move regularly, with some periods of rest and recovery. We have that flipped on its head – to our detriment.

2. There are a few criteria that you could consider when doing 'intentional' exercise, but the main thing is to make sure you enjoy it and can access it easily.

3. 'Intentional' exercise can take many forms including things that you might not ordinarily consider. For example, dancing, playing Frisbee® or walking the dog.

Action plan for becoming superhuman...

1. Look at how much 'intentional' exercise you get in a typical week. *Does it meet the current government guidelines?*

2. Decide on an 'intentional' exercise pursuit you could try (if you don't already have one). Assess it against the S9 Sports Selection Criteria to see how it stacks up. Consider introducing a complementary exercise to make up any shortfall.

3. Consider signing up for an event in your chosen exercise to provide motivation. This could be a yoga workshop or retreat, a triathlon, a grading, or a public dance show.

A - ACTIVITY

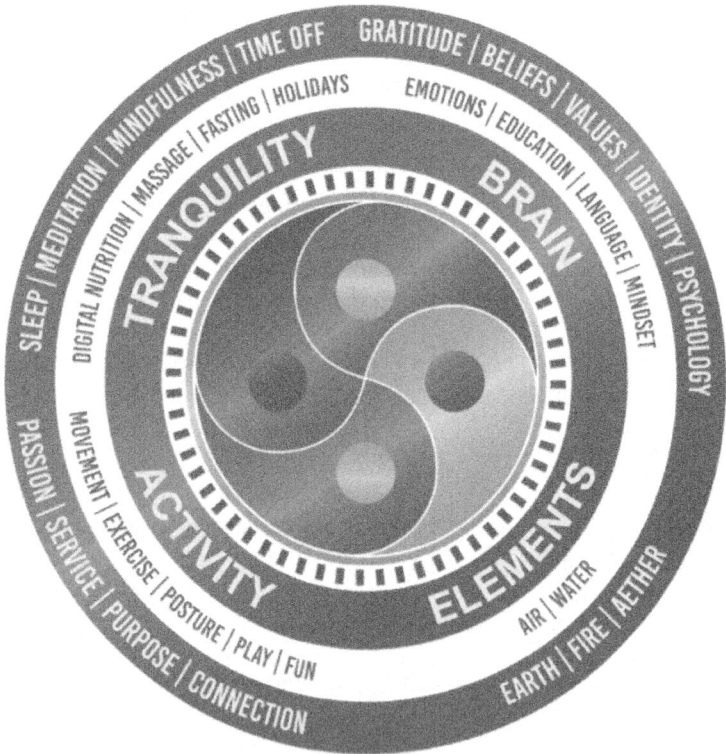

248

3.2 Movement

I like to move it, move it…

---

*"To me, if life boils down to one thing, it's movement.
To live is to keep moving."*

- Jerry Seinfeld

We learnt in the previous chapter, that just by doing some 'Intentional' exercise, as great as it is, even if done every day, won't necessarily make us that much less sedentary. And being sedentary is a big health problem right now, with the average Briton sitting for almost nine hours a day[330]. The way that we live our lives now is so out of balance with the entire of human history. We're becoming fragile creatures when we are not really meant to be that fragile. We are resilient by nature. Survivors. And yet, we can injure our back bending over to pick up an envelope.

Simply stated, we need to move more. Exercise is great and to be encouraged. Movement, however, is essential and mandatory.

The Research…

- Researchers from the American Cancer Society have found that women who spend 6 hours or more of free time sitting per day have a 10% greater risk of getting cancer than women who spend less than 3 hours of free time sitting per day[331].
- Each hour of sedentary time per day on average associated with a 14% increase in coronary artery calcification burden. Independent of exercise activity and other traditional heart disease risk factors[332].
- Research has shown that sustained deformation of a fat cell (i.e., from sitting) can lead to the cell to produce more lipids (fat) at a faster rate[333].

- Eighteen subjects were given text and emails to read (sat or walked at a treadmill desk). Ten minutes later those walking had higher percentage right when recalling[334].

- Blood flow to the main artery of the legs (femoral) was impaired by as much as 50% in just one hour. Breaks at 30, 90 and 150 minutes (in a 3-hour period), were able to keep the flow well[335].

- Sitting on exercise ball (versus chair) burns 4 calories per hour more. 2.5 lb a year. 1 kg[336].

- Stanford psychologists have discovered that when people walk, they increase their creativity by 60 per cent compared to when they sit[337].

- Evidence out of Sweden that found a direct correlation between fitness levels and IQ[338].

- Professional footballers are alarmingly sedentary in their leisure time, and comparatively more so than non-athletic groups of a similar age and older[339].

- Sedentary behaviour increases the risk of certain cancers[340].

- Sitting leads to heart disease[341].

- Sitting is linked to obesity[342].

- Sitting is linked to diabetes[343].

- Sedentary habits are associated with higher risk of developing depression[344]

Use every opportunity to move. And make sure that you don't experience extended periods of time without moving. Ideally, we would get up and move every 25 minutes or so. At least once per hour. Swapping just 30 minutes of sitting for any activity even, can reduce your chances of an early death by up to 35 per cent[345]. And sitting for too long claims over 60,000 lives a year in the UK according to researchers from Queen's University, Belfast[346].

There is a shift in some workplaces towards standing desks – and it's a good start in recognising the problem that decades of sitting down has created. It's still, however, one sedentary position. Albeit using slightly different muscles. Researchers from Texas A&M Health Science Centre School of Public Health found that giving up the chair can reduce back pain and discomfort and boost productivity by nearly 50 per cent. As well as burning more calories, improving overall attention and thinking[347].

And even if your job already involves standing, *how much do you move from that position? Do you need to crouch or squat regularly in your job?* Chances are no. And yet, that's what we did for aeons of human history. We moved a lot. We jumped, climbed on things, crouched down, hung from things and so on. To survive. Now, we don't have to do that to survive, or do we? Our stationary nature has made us a population of people who aren't surviving well at all these days.

Every time your butt hits a chair, electrical activity in your muscles stops. In addition, the energy your body uses reduces from an average of 99 calories per hour, to 78 calories per hour. Doesn't sound like much does it? Over an eight-hour workday though, that's 180 calories. Assuming 240 working days in the year, and that's 43,200 calories. Not only that, but when you sit, levels of fat-burning enzyme lipase fall by 90%[348]. Sitting around all day ultimately leads to weaker muscles and bones and will make it harder to do everyday things. Plus, there's an increased risk of heart attack, stroke, and Alzheimer's by being sedentary. The simple way around it is to move more. Walking for an hour a day can reduce the risk of heart attack and stroke by as much as 50%[349]. Even just sitting for 20 minutes less each day is enough to maintain muscle mass and improve our overall health. After a year, those 20 minutes translated to signs of reduced risk for type-2 diabetes and heart disease discovered researchers from the University of Jvvaskyla in Finland[350].

An easy way to encourage yourself to start to move more is by following the advice in chapter 2.2 about drinking more water. The more you drink, the more you'll find it a convenient reminder to get up and go to the toilet (i.e., move). A double win. And if you want to really amp it up, you could decide that every time you get up to go to the toilet you do 20 air squats (squatting without any weight on you), or ten push-ups, or ten jumping jacks. Of course, check the floor is clean before you get down to do those push ups!

Integrative Movement

As an alternative to 'intentional' movement, which is deliberate and more traditional, I use the term 'integrative'. 'Integrative' movement describes any movement that can be integrated into what you are already doing. Going about your day as usual, and doesn't require you to change clothes, or go to a special venue.

Integrative Movement Suggestions

Here are some simple suggestions that could get you moving more each hour and each day.

A - ACTIVITY

- Stand up whenever on the phone.
- Do some exercise every time you go to the toilet (e.g., push-ups, air squats, jumping jacks).
- Walk over to colleagues to ask them a question rather than email or phoning them.
- Take the stairs. Even if you can't make all the flights at first. Take as many as you can then get the lift (elevator) the rest of the way up. Walk down.
- Have walking meetings.
- Invest in a standing desk.
- Hold standing meetings. The added benefit here is that meetings will become more effective and shorter.
- Cycle, walk or run to work*.
- Get off the bus or train a stop earlier.
- Take a walk at lunchtime.
- Park the car at the furthest point in the car park.
- Walk up the escalators.
- Do some (elbow) dips when waiting for copies to come out of the photocopier, or when waiting for the kettle to boil.
- During TV ad breaks do some light exercise.
- Set a reminder on your phone or computer to get up and move†.
- Volunteer to give up your seat more often on trains.
- Squat instead of bending over when picking things out of low cupboards or off the floor.
- Learn to put your shoes and socks on without sitting down, but by balancing on one leg.
- Take the stairs two or three steps at a time.
- Order less things online and instead go out to the shops for them.
- Do some chair yoga while at your desk.

One study looked at the links to energy levels and cognitive function. They looked at the difference between sitting all day or doing one bout of exercise in the morning or micro-bouts throughout the day. The researchers concluded that in addition to the beneficial impact of physical activity on levels of energy

---

* Okay, so you might have to change clothes for this one.
† I often use a timer on my computer that is set for 40 minutes and when the timer is complete, the software will play Bob Marley's *Get Up, Stand Up*, during which time I'll go make a cup of herbal tea, do some pull ups, or press ups, squats or jump on a rebounder (mini trampoline) or even take a quick walk round the block.

and vigour (which both the one bout and micro bouts did), spreading out physical activity throughout the day improved mood, decreased feelings of fatigue and reduced food cravings (which one bout of exercise didn't) compared to the sedentary group[351].

Furthermore, researchers from Stanford University discovered that walking boosted creativity in participants by 60%[337]. Think about that next time you're tempted to stay at your desk for lunch. You'll be more creative at work in the afternoon. And amazingly it didn't matter if participants walked outside or on a treadmill staring at a blank wall. They still all boosted their creativity.

The Power of How

We looked at the power of how earlier in the book if you remember? I find it a useful approach. Your mind is a bit like Google. If you type in a question, you will get an answer back based on what you type in. If you type in "why can I never find time to exercise?" your subconscious mind will run off and find out all the reasons why that's true. If you ask a better question like: "how can I integrate more exercise into my day?" or "how can I make exercising fun?" or "how can I adapt what I'm currently doing each day to bring more movement into my life?", you will get a better answer.

I use the *Power of How* all the time. One time I bought a few extra pots and pans despite my cupboards already being full (or so I thought). I asked myself: *"how should I arrange this cupboard, so everything fits in?"* And you know what, I found a way.

Make sure you use the *Power of How* wisely and ensure that any questions that you put into the Google of your subconscious will bring you back the answers that will positively serve you.

A.S.E. Training™

We have a playground around us to use. If you are in a driving city, then you have more creative work to do. Integrate some *A.S.E. Training*™ into your day. What is *A.S.E. Training*™?

A.S.E. stands for *Adaptive Situational Exercise* – a term I created to describe what's below.

A.S.E. Training™ is where you use your environment to transform it to an exercise playground. For example, when waiting at the photocopier, you could do some dips against a bench (I used to do this at my corporate job). You could do some chin ups/pull ups on the horizontal handrail on the train (and yes, I do this on occasion too – as do my nieces). Doing bicep curls with your shopping bags on the way back home, or to the car. I do this quite often and it's amazing the workout you can get, especially as you must learn to stabilise your core while walking. And be sure to swap the hands you carry the bags in, as they will be different weights. I normally do about 30 – 40 reps and swap sides. *A.S.E. Training*™ is about adapting the things that you have around you to train with.

The gains for you will be massive.

N.E.A.T.

N.E.A.T. stands for non-exercise activity thermogenesis. It's something else that we can use to our advantage when thinking about movement, health, and exercise. N.E.A.T. is about the energy expenditure that you use when doing mundane and routine tasks. For example, standing or even fidgeting. By using a standing desk, you will activate N.E.A.T. and burn more calories as well as utilising different muscles to sitting. N.E.A.T. is a sub-set (in my model) for '*Integrative*' exercise, as things like walking can count as part of N.E.A.T.

The point of N.E.A.T. really is this – ***everything counts***. That means don't discard your ironing, cleaning, gardening, or playing with your kids. The more active you can be, and the more non-exercise activity thermogenesis you can 'integrate', the better.

Some suggestions to bring more N.E.A.T. into your life:

- Use a standing desk. Standing for just 30 minutes instead of sitting can reduce heart attack risk[352].
- Walk, or pace up and down, when on the phone.
- Iron, cleaning, gardening, and other housework all count.
- Raise the heels while seated activating the muscles in the lower leg.
- When queuing, alternate standing on one leg, and on tip toes.
- Use a stability ball (Swiss ball/gym ball) to sit on when at the desk.

There are countless other ways to activate N.E.A.T. so get creative. The thing is just to take advantage of our body's need to burn energy doing anything involving movement.

Five-A-Day Exercises

Many of us are short on time and sometimes feel like we don't have the time to exercise or get to the gym. As I have mentioned, you could incorporate Integrative movement into the day, *A.S.E. Training*™ or something I call Five-A-Day Exercises. The government recommends 5-a-day when it comes to fruit and vegetables, so this is my extension of that idea.

I developed several five-minute workouts which can be done first thing in the morning if you are pressed for time, or during your five-minute active breaks throughout the day. Each sequence has only five exercises in them and lasts for only five minutes. You perform each exercise for 30 seconds only and then move onto the next, so you cycle through twice.

If you only have five minutes you can get some movement into the body regardless of time. If you have ten minutes, then you can stack another Five-a-Day exercise set on top. None of them require any equipment. If you stacked all of them one after the other, it would take you 45 minutes – assuming no transition time between series – based on the nine developed so far.

The sequences are Mobility Series, Cardio Series, Foundation Series, Core Series, Stretch Series, At-The-Desk Series, Balance Series, Strength Series, Qigong Series.

For a video description of how to do each exercise, visit: **https://thethoughtgym.com/supervitality**.

Five-A-Day Exercises

Each exercise is performed for 30 seconds, and cycle through all five twice.

Mobility Series	Cardio Series	Foundation Series
1. Shoulder Rolls (round one), Windmill Arms (round two)	1. Jumping Jacks	1. Air Squats
	2. Mountain Climbers	2. Press Ups
2. Hip Rotations	3. Butt Kicks	3. Lunges
3. Knee Circles	4. Burpees	4. Straight Arm Circles
4. Side Lunges	5. High Knees	5. Back Extension
5. Cat-Cow Spinal Mobility		

A - ACTIVITY

Core Series	Strength Series	Stretch Series
1. Plank 2. Side Plank 3. Up/Down Plank (hands to forearms) 4. Back Extension from Tabletop or Plank position (extending opposite arm and leg away) 5. Leg Raises (double leg or single as ability allows)	1. SLOW Push Ups (5 seconds up, 5 seconds down) 2. Single Leg (Pistol) Squats 3. 90 Degree Squat (Wall squat, if wall available) 4. Jumping Squats 5. V-Sit Ups	1. Down Dog 2. Hip Flexor Stretch 3. Rag Doll (forward fold) 4. Standing Back Bend 5. Side Bend
At-The-Desk Series	**Balance Series**	**Qigong Series**
1. Seated Pigeon 2. Seated Twist 3. Seated Chest Stretch 4. Upper Back Stretch 5. Elbow Lat Stretch	1. Tree Pose 2. Dancers Pose 3. Standing Bent Knee Twist 4. Warrior Three 5. Half Moon	1. Spinal Rolls 2. Helicopter Arms 3. Corkscrew 4. Drunk Skier 5. Grouping Breath

Quick summary about movement and becoming superhuman...

1. 'Integrative' movement enables you to integrate movement into your daily activities without taking up any extra time.

2. Part of 'integrative' movement is *A.S.E. Training*™ and N.E.A.T. and this means that you can quickly rack up the hours of movement that you need each day.

3. We are recommended 5-a-day when it comes to fruit and vegetable intake, and you can adopt the 5-a-day approach to spending five minutes a day doing five simple exercises designed to get you moving and grooving.

Action plan for becoming superhuman...

1. Think about how you can integrate more movement into your life. Write down three ways to do so. Be that traditional 'integrative' approaches, *A.S.E. Training*™ or taking advantage of N.E.A.T. philosophies.

2. Commit to doing one of the three ways you determined for the next ten days.

3. Head to **https://thethoughtgym.com/supervitality** and review the 5-a-day exercises. Better still, work-out along with one of the routines right now.

3.3 Posture

Don't be no slouch…

"Posture for combat is so vital."

- Conor McGregor

A brief word about posture. While we might not be getting ready for combat in the MMA octagon ring like Conor McGregor, we are still entering the arena of life. And some might argue that's a tougher challenge. And many of us have terrible posture that is the result of decades of doing things that negatively affect us. Sitting down on chairs, couches and in cars. Wearing shoes even that restrict the natural free-flowing movement of our feet. And, if you wear heels (even men's shoes with heals) they will alter the way you walk and shorten your Achilles tendon.

It's beyond my expertise to give specific advice on posture and alignment, so all I would really say is that it's worth getting some professional assessments done. Many people I observe walking, walk with their feet turned out. A bit like duck feet. This can lead to multiple structural issues. People walk around with hunchbacks, the result of hours of looking down at screens. In fact, part of what got me committed to a regular yoga practice, were neck issues. Then when I would see older people on the street hunched over, it became a visual reminder of what I was looking to avoid.

Some things to consider would be to

- Get a workplace **assessment** for your computer set-up. If you work from home, then at the very least, research into the optimal set-up of your equipment. Working from cafés is terrible for most people as they hunch over their laptops. I have a portable laptop riser, separate mouse, and keyboard that I pack into my backpack and use when I'm working away from home and going to be working for longer than just a few minutes. Not ideal in cafés, I'll admit, so I tend to save that set-up for co-working spaces I visit.

- Visit an **osteopath, physiotherapist, Egoscue practitioner** or other body and movement specialist who can properly assess your posture and gait. They can then give you specific corrective exercises to address any imbalances.
- Consider investigating **Pilates, yoga, Foundation Training,** or the **Alexander Technique** which can all help with posture[*].
- A rule of thumb would be to make sure that you are holding **no tension in your neck, shoulders, or jaw.** Sometimes we clench our teeth when stressed or focussed. Also sit, stand, or move in a way that allows diaphragmatic breathing. If you can do that, then you are on your way.
- Spend as much time as possible being **barefoot.** Certainly, in your own home. It surprises me that some people wear shoes in the house. When you are wearing footwear, my recommendation is to purchase minimalist shoes, such as Vivobarefoot footwear, which do their best to keep you close to a natural foot movement pattern.
- Learn to **squat** again – as you did effortlessly as a child. Spend time sitting on the floor too. When we start to get back into more natural movement patterns our posture will also improve.

The problem is that many people who work out (especially with weights) or take up things like running, are loading their body with impact and weight under bad foundations. And hence, they increase their risk of injury. We all know that if you keep building storey upon storey onto a skyscraper with weak foundations, that it's only a matter of time before the cracks begin to show and the whole thing comes tumbling down.

I am by no means perfect regarding my posture. I have been working for many years to work on how my body moves to help minimise the risk of injury or other problems. It's a continuous process, for sure, and I come unstuck from time to time. There are things beyond our control and despite our best effort's life will still hurl things at us. Like with all the teaching in this book, stack the cards in your favour as much as possible and you'll be better able to deal with the issues when they inevitably appear.

---

[*] There are many body optimisation practitioners, so I won't mention them all here but as a starting point you could look also at The Bowen Technique, Rolfing and IDDT (Intervertebral Differential Dynamics Therapy).

At the very least, when sitting or standing, allow for space for diaphragmatic breathing to take place. That means no hunching over restricting the belly breathing we talked about in chapter 2.1.

Workplace Set-Up

Below are some ideas for you to set up your environment to have better posture, move more and have a bit of a workout too. Some will be dependent on how much control you have over your working space. Others are more subtle and easier to implement.

Standing Desk

A few years ago, I bought a standing desk. This sits on top of my normal desk and has quick and responsive levers either side that allow me to vary the height of the desk. In fact, I'm typing using that desk now. I am therefore sometimes sitting and sometimes standing. The brand I have is Ergotron which are expensive but well built. Another popular brand is Varidesk. Do some research. If I were to buy a brand-new desk now, I would probably buy a desk that is dedicated variable desk (as opposed to placing a unit on top of an existing desk like I do now). The reason is that the one I have, has two levels (so the monitor is higher than the keyboard). Fine for working on the computer but not well set up when I want to write. That said, I think the later models of Ergotron sit flusher with the desk.

Treadmill Under the Desk

I've yet to invest in a walking treadmill under the desk – but I will. There are specifically made treadmills for under the desk, or you could adapt others. I have yet to do much research into the best variety, but it's an option to use for some work that maybe doesn't involve a lot of typing. For example, meetings, interviews, research etc.

Balance Board

A balance board, like a BOSU balance board, or Indo board could be used by your desk too. These will help you work those subtle core muscles and improve your balance while on it. And in turn your posture. Of course, you'd need a standing desk first.

A - ACTIVITY

Golf Ball or Lacrosse Ball

When I had plantar fasciitis (pain underneath the foot) many years ago, I used to keep a golf ball in my drawer at the London Stock Exchange. I would slip my shoes off[†] and roll a golf ball under my foot. A lacrosse ball also works well. This action can help all the way up the leg – not just releasing tension under the foot which many people have. I still use a ball now – although primarily, I use a massage ball with spikes and have it under my bathroom sink and massage my foot while brushing my teeth.

Pull Up Bar

I have a pull up bar in the doorway to my home office. Throughout the day, I'll do a single pull-up (or chin up, reversing the grip) as I pass under it. This allows me to get some strength practice in, move my body differently, or maybe just release back tension if I just hang from the bar for 20-40 seconds.

Grip Strengthening Device

When I'm on a call, I often just pick up my grip strengthening device which sits by my desk. It's also good as a distraction when feeling a little bit agitated. Grip strength is associated with cardiovascular, respiratory, and cancer outcomes and all-cause mortality, as reported in the British Medical Journal[353]. The researchers conclude that:

"Grip strength is strongly and inversely associated with all-cause mortality and incidence of and mortality from cardiovascular disease, respiratory disease, chronic obstructive pulmonary disease, all cancer, and subtypes of cancer, including colorectal, lung, and breast cancer, with associations being modestly stronger in the younger age groups. Our results show that adding handgrip strength to an existing office-based risk score improves the prediction ability for all-cause mortality and incidence of and mortality from cardiovascular disease and that muscle weakness (using previously defined grip strength cut-offs) is associated with poorer health outcomes."

[†] Truth be told, my shoes would already be off as I always had my shoes off when at my desk in the office. A condition of me buying shoes was, and generally still is, that I can slip them on and off easily and subtly.

Yoga Swing/Trapeze

A yoga trapeze is used for aerial yoga and allows you to essentially hang out and swing in the air. It's very relaxing if you just swing in it, but you can use it to expand your chest, by performing a supported backbend, hang from it and create traction in your spine, opening the vertebrae. Stretch your hamstrings and whatever else the imagination allows. You'll need a space to hang it from of course, but if you have a pull up bar, then you are all set. I bought one back in 2020 and it's a go-to activity for all my nieces when they visit.

Dictation Software

I've yet to start with dictation software, as I do find it easier to write my thoughts down for articles and books. However, some people swear by it, and it can be a good use of time to walk (on your treadmill, or better still, outdoors) and dictate what you want to into the software. Software that has been recommended to me (but I have not used) is called Dragon. I believe they have smartphone versions as well as desktop. It seems to be quite a financial investment, however that's all relative to the time you might save, or money saved in secretarial costs if you currently have something like that in place.

Deskside Stretching

Just performing some subtle stretching at the desk will do wonders for your body. Even in a busy office environment you can perform some that no one will even notice. Some I used to do when working at the London Stock Exchange and Sainsburys were:

Seated Pigeon

For this, when at your desk, place one ankle on top of the opposite knee, and allow the knee from the raised leg to lower out to the side so that your shin is parallel to the floor. You can then still have your entire lower half of your body under the desk. Visit **https://thethoughtgym.com/supervitality** for a demonstration.

Seated Twist

Whenever someone behind me asked me a question, I used it as an opportunity to practice this one. Essentially, you are keeping your lower body facing forward to your computer, then just rotating at your torso to look behind you and respond to the person you are talking to. Instead of rotating the entire swivel chair.

Rebounder

The last one I'll mention is probably my most favourite piece of exercise equipment that I own. It's called a rebounder. Think of it as a mini trampoline. The model I have utilises bungee cords rather than springs. I have tested a few rebounders, and bungee cords allow a gentler bounce and more importantly are practically silent. Especially when compared to springs. You must replace the bungee cords every 2-3 years so there are some ongoing costs. I particularly use and recommend the Bellicon brand. Again, an investment but I think with some things it's just worth it. And this is one of those occasions.

Why rebound though? It's a gentle, yet moderate-to-vigorous, form of exercise. I've used a rebounder most mornings since 2011. I often also use it for a couple of minutes when I'm working during the day. There are many reasons why I like rebounding. Good for balance, core strength, easy on the joints, easy to exercise even when you don't feel like it and it's fun. In addition, the American Council on Exercise found that bouncing on a mini trampoline for less than 20 minutes is just as good for you as running but feels better and is a lot more fun[354]. NASA has studied trampoline training for astronauts and found it to be just as effective as running, with no significant difference in maximal heart rate, maximal oxygen uptake, or energy expenditure[355].

Quick summary about posture and becoming superhuman...

1. Good posture when sitting, walking, running, and doing any activity is a vital addition.

2. Our modern-day conveniences have meant that a lot of the natural body posturing we knew has been eroded away.

3. There are ways to mitigate damage using workplace workstation assessments and using the advice of trained professionals like physiotherapists and osteopathists.

Action plan for becoming superhuman...

1. Book an appointment with an expert in postural analysis and ask if they can create a plan for you.

2. Look into joining a local class in yoga, Pilates, or the Alexander Technique.

3. At a minimum, consider how your posture supports diaphragmatic breathing.

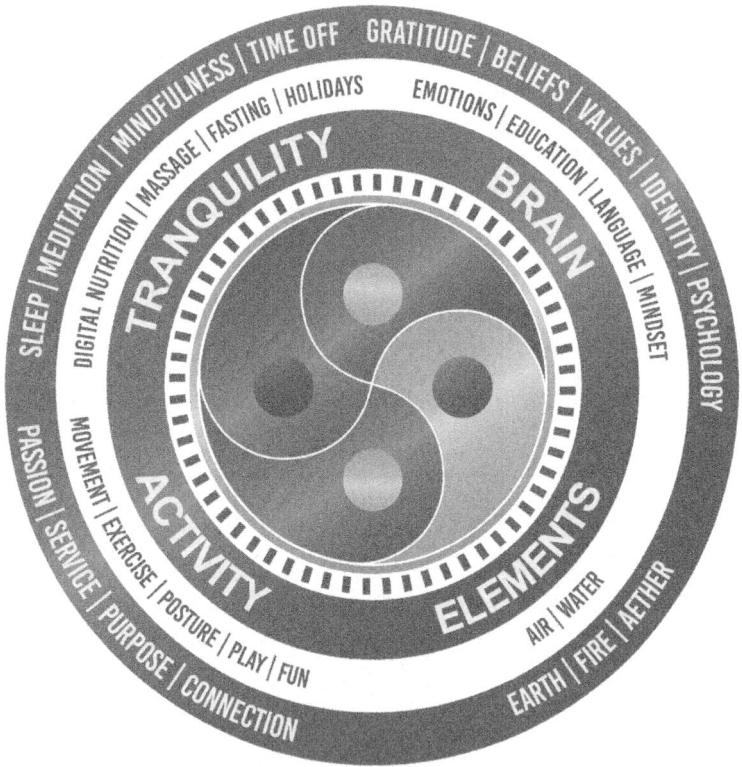

3.4 What I Do

Keeping busy…

"My mission in life is not merely to survive, but to thrive; and to do so with some passion, some compassion, some humour, and some style."

- Maya Angelou

ACTIVITY is all about the things that you do in a day. Not just exercise, movement or how you stand or sit. It's about whether you have passion in your life, fun, whether you laugh and volunteer your time in service to others and causes greater than yourself. Do you have strong social connections and relationships and whether you are driven by a greater purpose in life? What are your habits and routines like? All are important for health, vitality, energy and unlocking your inner superhuman.

PSPC

The following four criteria are what I call PSPC. Like many of the teachings in this book, the realisation that these things were important to health, vitality and energy came to me intuitively. I simply thought to myself – "when I do x, y or z, does that make me feel more energised?" I realised that these four things were important. Later I found out that others had reached similar conclusions or were researching the effect of these ideas too.

Passion

Have you ever met anyone who has so much passion for what they do that they have the energy of a 5-year-old? They can get by on very little sleep, even eat poorly, and skip exercising, and yet still have more energy than you. That's the passion fuelling them. The trouble is, that at some point, if the other

267

components of *The Leadership BEAT Model*™ aren't in place, things will unravel for that person.

Think about when you feel passionate about something. Do you have more energy? I'm betting yes. I might not have any studies to back up what I'm saying here about having passion creating energy, but do I really need to? I think it's self-evident.

You might be reading this and think that you are not passionate about the work that you do though. And that's a big chunk of your life. So, what do you do? Well, for one, I'm not telling you to leave your current job and follow your passion. You might do, but that's up to you. What I'm saying is find something in life to be passionate about. It might be your children, nieces, and nephews. It might be travelling or creating art. It could be exercising or doing stand-up comedy in the evenings*.

It might even be that although you don't have passion for your job, you might find areas within it to be passionate about. I know that I wasn't passionate about working in Service Transition when at Sainsbury's. I did, however, have immense gratitude about what it was allowing me to do outside of work. I also enjoyed creating new processes, templates and other solutions as part of my role. Whether that was an email template to make my colleague's work easier and quicker, improving on the technology roll-out plan or leading meetings and engaging with my colleagues. It might not have been my main source of passion in my life, but I decided to find some level of passion in elements of my role.

It might be that you are an entrepreneur and are passionate about your product, which is great. It's also easy to have passion for your product if you think it's really going to help people, and I'd offer something to think about. Look to have passion *for the process*, not just the *product*. Whenever we do anything in life and strive towards a goal, we must do lots of little things that might be mundane, boring, repetitive and so on. If you don't create some passion for the process, it will be harder. Imagine you are passionate about achieving an Olympic medal. The amount of training that you must go through, which is often repetitive and often mundane, is immense. If all your hopes and sights are set on the one achievement four years from now, all your passion is there,

---

* I did venture onto the London stand-up comedy circuit for a very brief period in 2012, performing seven gigs. Just 5-minute showcases, but a good experience. I wasn't very passionate about it, hence only a short-lived career.

and you don't achieve it. Then what? Even when you do, then what? You will have to find something else, and something else and on and on. That's not to say don't have goals – big audacious goals. It's to say that I invite you to also look at putting passion into the process, not just the product.

What can you be passionate about in life?

Service

Have you ever had very little sleep, but the next day still had lots of energy because you were getting up early to work in a soup kitchen or volunteer to deliver food hampers[†]? Volunteering for a cause bigger than yourself can give you energy when you might not have had it. Also, if you are focussed on your own problems in life and want a strategy for getting out of your own way, then focus on what you can do for other people. It's a great way to get you out of a poor headspace you might be in.

> *"The best way to find yourself is to lose yourself in the service of others."*
>
> *– Mahatma Gandhi*

Furthermore, a May 2012 study by the Royal Voluntary Service (formerly the WRVS) found that volunteering in later life decreased depression and social isolation. It was also found to boost quality of life and life satisfaction[356].

Volunteering can help you build new social connections (see the Connection section below for why that's important) and improve your family relationships according to a study comparing volunteers with non-volunteers[357]. Perhaps because caring for others carried over into their personal relationships. I certainly know that when I volunteer to do something for those less fortunate than me, it can give me a real sense of gratitude. And we already covered how important gratitude is for health.

[†] Each year in fact, thousands of people take part in Basket Brigade which delivers food hampers to those families in need at Christmas (or Thanksgiving in the USA). It's something I first started doing in 2010 as part of the UK's leading personal development community – The YES Group. It's really rewarding. People come from all over the UK to help, and there are now Basket Brigades all over the UK (and worldwide).

A - ACTIVITY

When listening to one of my favourite podcasts (The Model Health Show)[‡] the host – Shawn Stephenson highlighted[358]:

"One study that was done on older individuals who volunteered for at least 200 hours a year, were found to decrease their risk of hypertension by 40%. Think about that – they decreased their risk of hypertension by 40% from volunteering. That's incredible. Another study found that activities regarding service were found to improve health in ways that can lengthen your lifespan. Volunteers showed an improved ability to manage stress and stave off disease as well as reduce rates of depression, and an increased sense of life satisfaction when they were performing charitable activities on a regular basis."

Stephenson then goes on to say that:

"A study published in the Journal of Behavioural Medicine had researchers conducting a series of FMRI neuroimaging tests to explore the neuro-mechanisms of how specific brain areas were affected by giving versus receiving social support.

They found that giving ultimately had greater brain benefits than receiving. Now isn't this interesting that our brains are actually wired to be rewarded more for generosity, and for giving, and for selflessness than for meanness and selfishness?"

And of course, more and more studies are showing similar effects[356,359-364]. Which is not at all surprising when you think about it intuitively. We have only survived and thrived on this planet through cooperation and part of that is helping and supporting others. Also, if you can provide targeted social support to other people in need, then this activates regions of the brain involved in parental care which may help us understand the positive health effects of social ties, reports a study in Psychosomatic Medicine: Journal of Biobehavioural Medicine, the official journal of the American Psychosomatic Society[363]. By comparison, providing untargeted support such as giving to charity does not have the same neurobiological effects.

[‡] For a list of several other podcasts, I enjoy listening too, head to the appendices section at the end of the book.

Purpose

Purpose doesn't have to mean a life's purpose, as such. A life purpose can change over time as well, and so it isn't a static thing throughout your life. At least not for all. For some people it might be that their life's purpose is the same and that is to make people happy. Or make a positive contribution to the world. Or end world hunger. For you, it might be something totally different and ever-changing. When you were younger it might have been to save the world, or just to finish your degree. During your prime working years, it might be to raise the best family you can and be the best husband/father/wife/mother you can be. When you retire, your purpose might be to educate and entertain your grandchildren. If we go through life without a sense of purpose, then we can easily become de-motivated and lack energy.

Again, this came intuitively to me, but it is interesting to note that feeling a lack of purpose in life has been linked to conditions like depression[365], chronic fatigue syndrome and even longevity and healthspan[366].

Researchers from University of Michigan Schools of Public Health discovered that people with a purpose not only live a longer and healthier life than those who believe their life is pointless, but they are less likely to suffer from a chronic health problem, like cancer or heart disease as well as keeping inflammation at bay. The study, published in The Journal of the American Medical Association, revealed that people who didn't have a strong life purpose, which was defined as a self-organizing life aim that stimulates goals, they were more likely to die than those who did and specifically more likely to die of cardiovascular diseases. The study included nearly 7000 adults between the ages of 51 and 61 and found that people without a strong life purpose were more than twice as likely to die over the course of the four year study period compared to those who had one[367].

Do you have a purpose in your life? Even if it's a small purpose? We need a reason to get up each day beyond going to work and paying the bills. If you haven't got something that calls out to you that is greater than yourself, I suggest that you look to create a purpose. It's not about discovering or uncovering your purpose, but more that you can decide and create what purpose you want to have for yourself.

The Japanese have a word, not just for purpose, but more for a sense of, or reason, for being. They call it *Ikigai*, and it's sometimes thought of as the intersection between your values in life, what you are good at and what you love doing. Or sometimes the intersection between what you are good at, what you enjoy/love, what you can get paid for and what the world needs.

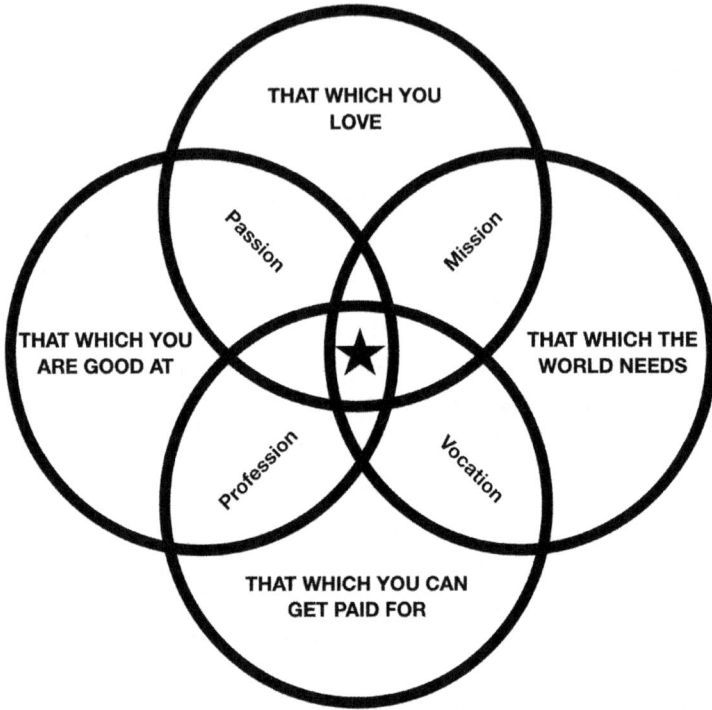

Figure 16 - Ikigai (Sense of Being)

How to find your life purpose? Isn't that the eternal question? Well, maybe you don't find it at all. Maybe you uncover it. You do different things, and you let it become clearer. What do I think my life purpose is? Or the purpose of life in general. I think it's simply this.

To experience life. And to love and serve others.

Connection

Connection with other people – relationships - might be the biggest indicator of longevity and healthspan[§] that there is. A Harvard study, the Grant Study, is the longest study on health and relationships spanning over 80 years[368**]. It can be summarised quite succinctly into its three main findings, which were that:

1. **Social connections are good for us.** Those who were in social isolation were less happy, their health declined earlier, their brain function declined earlier, and they lived shorter lives.
2. **The *quality* of those connections is important.** Those in good relationships at aged 50 were the healthiest at aged 80. Despite any negative physical markers.
3. **Social connections help protect the brain** from decline.

I also believe that real relationships, where we meet in person, and not just online, are important. Sure, virtual connections can offer some level of support and common interests, but having live connections will always be better, I believe.

[§] Healthspan, as opposed to lifespan, is more useful as we want to add *healthy* years to our lives and not just add years, which would be lifespan. I.e., living longer but being in poor health would be lifespan. Living long *and* strong would be healthspan.
[**] One of the Grant Study's original participants was future President, John F. Kennedy.

A - ACTIVITY

Connection is not just about emotional connections, but also physical touch. We all need to feel the physical touch of other people. Esteemed family therapist Virginia Satir is purported to have said that we need four hugs a day for survival, eight hugs for maintenance and twelve for growth. A recent study from the University of Colorado found that holding hands with a significant other can dramatically reduce physical pain too[369].

And research from the University of North Carolina found that hugs are remarkable at boosting immune system function. They found that a good hug stimulates the thymus gland which regulates and balances the body's production of white blood cells, your immune cells. Which keeps you healthy and disease-free. And they also found that before public speaking, a long hug reduced a person's blood pressure and kept their heart rate lower than those who had no contact[370].

As babies we needed physical touch in order to be well, grow and develop[371]. There is a story†† of an orphanage where the young babies being looked after were not held by the nurses looking after them. All except one. The last baby in the row that the nurse would hold because she was the last one and she had time to hold her. Compared to the other children this child got sick a lot less and was healthier than the others. This is easy to understand as even randomised controlled trials involving children either in orphanages or foster care show a marked reduction in IQ for those in orphanages[372]. Touch is vital for new babies and without love, touch and affection, babies simply don't grow and develop strong immune systems[373].

Even for adults, touch can slow down our heart rate, lower blood pressure, reduce levels of cortisol (often considered the stress hormone) and improve our immunity. It stimulates the release of serotonin, commonly known as the 'feel-good chemical' and nourishes emotional connections[374].

Connection isn't just about physical touch, but emotional connection too. Compassion for others. In one study of cancer patients, researchers found that patients lived longer if the vagus nerve was stimulated – which it can be done though meditation, yoga and practicing compassion and gratitude. Survival times were four times higher in people with high vagus activity[375].

Something that I found difficult as I started down this personal development and health journey was my existing friendships. I have had friends for many

---

†† This might be an old fable by now, but I believe there is truth in it all the same.

274

years. Since I was six years old. In fact, it was the one thing that I had *not* quit. Then I realised that we were starting to move in different directions. We had different interests, talked about different things. I struggled because I wanted them to come on my journey with me, but that wasn't their role. I shouldn't have expected that. What I came to understand is that there are different levels of friendships and that there might be an ebb and flow between them. What I think of as three levels of friendships:

Five-Minute Friends: These are friends that you are happy to chat to when you see them, and engage in a coffee chat, or over a drink for part of the evening, but there's not a huge amount of depth to it. You still like these people, but you don't hang out too often or depend on them for much.

Five-Hour Friends: These are people that you could spend the evening with, or the day with. You'd call them up to hang out, go to the cinema, have dinner with and much more.

Five-Day Friends: These are friends you'd spend more time with. Have deeper conversations. You depend on them. Go camping with, on holiday, celebrate important milestones with.

It's not an exact analogy but you get the picture. What I accepted was that some of my Five-Day Friends did transition to Five-Hour Friends and even Five-Minute Friends. And some went in the opposite direction. And both are okay.

Malcolm Gladwell, in an article in *The New York Times*[376] (and also in his best-selling book, *Outliers*) describes the town of Roseto, Pennsylvania. This is where over the years, starting in the late 19th century, many residents from Roseto, Italy emigrated to. Roseto was its own tiny self-sufficient town. As it would have remained were it not for a young physician, called Stewart Wolf, who spent summers in a house not too far from Roseto. After being invited to give a talk at a local medical society in the 1950's, Wolf was having a drink and a chat with one of the local doctors. The local doctor explained to Wolf how he rarely found anyone from Roseto under the age of sixty-five with heart disease. This was before current medications were prevalent and when heart attacks were a leading cause of death in men under the age of sixty-five.

After Wolf undertook some investigation, he found that people in Roseto, not only had significantly less heart disease than normal, but also died from any cause at 30-35% lower rates than expected. They were mainly dying from old age. Originally Wolf thought it was to do with diet but eventually ruled that out. Then Wolf thought it might be genetics. However, when comparing to other people from Roseto, Italy who moved elsewhere in the country, the Rosetans in other parts of the US followed the national trend for heart disease, heart attacks and deaths.

In the end, Wolf and researchers observed, and concluded, that it was the tight societal bonds that was the determining factor. Rosetans had strong communal bonds, several generations of families living together, everyone knew each other and would help one another. After presenting his findings and being met with scepticism, times moved on and the townsfolks children started moving further away. Life changed for the small town, as the pace of American life changed, and eventually, the health benefits that had been seen eroded and fell into line with the rest of the nation. Still this story serves as a great reminder about how important social connections are for our health.

The opposite of connection - loneliness, which people can feel even when surrounded by people, is a risk factor for poor health. One of the reasons loneliness is so bad for us is because it makes it harder for us to control our habits and behaviour. A survey by the Mental Health Foundation found that 48% of us believe people are getting lonelier in general[377]. Selected findings from the report, by the Mental Health Foundation - The Lonely Society – show:

- **Loneliness affects many of us at one time or another: only 22% of us never feel lonely and one in ten of us (11%) say we feel lonely often.** The same number (10%) don't have company when they want it. A quarter of us (24%) worry about feeling lonely, this is more commonly felt by those aged 18-34 (36%, compared to 17% of those over 55).
- **Four in ten of us (42%) have felt depressed because we felt alone.** This is higher among women (47%, compared to 36% men), and higher among those aged 18-34 (53%, compared to 32% of those over 55).
- **A third of us (37%) have a close friend or family member who we think is very lonely.** This is higher among women (41%, compared to 33% men) and people aged 18-34 (45%, compared to 31% of those over 55).
- **Over half of us (57%) who have experienced depression or anxiety isolated ourselves from friends and family.**

With the percentage of households occupied by one person more than doubling from 6% in 1972 to 12% in 2008[378], and showing no signs of abating, loneliness is not going anywhere. And the coronavirus pandemic introducing social distancing, working from home, and staying at home merely exacerbated the problem.

Good news though if you are married. Well, happily married anyway. A happy marriage is known to lower blood pressure. In 2007 the Focus on Families report by the Office of National Statistics showed that married people of both sexes have better health[379].

The connection piece, in addition to physical and emotional connections to others, is also about having a connection to oneself. That might sound weird, but how well do you really know yourself? How much time have you spent building a strong connection with yourself?

Many people are constantly distracted, even to the point that from the moment they wake up in the morning, the radio or music will start playing. I get it. I used to do the same thing and didn't think anything of it to have noise around me all day from the moment I woke up. And then as soon as I'd enter the house, I'd turn on the radio or TV to have 'company'. I slowly had that habit recede (via the influence of an ex-girlfriend) and didn't even notice it happening. It's not to say those things are bad. It's just to illustrate that often people struggle to sit with themselves. We can't even be bored anymore, because we can always get out our smartphone and look up something. I think being able to stare out of a train window and look at the countryside is a good thing. As is simply sitting and watching waves crash against a rock. As is merely spending time in a queue, being bored. Our brains these days don't even have to think too much, as we can look up the answer in minutes on our smartphones. All this distraction has led us further and further away from introspection. I'm not so sure Leonardo Da Vinci would have been such a prolific inventor if he had had access to a smartphone and social media!

Take heed from the Ancient Greek aphorism and "know thyself". And as the Ancient Greek philosopher, Socrates once said:

"The unexamined life is not worth living."

- Socrates

A - ACTIVITY
Play, Fun & Laughter

It is also important to have fun in life. To laugh every day. Play like you're still a child. As George Bernard Shaw once said:

"We don't stop playing because we grow old; We grow old because we stop playing."

– George Bernard Shaw

In 1979, Norman Cousins, the late American political journalist, author, professor, and world peace advocate, wrote a piece titled *Anatomy of an Illness (As Perceived by the Patient)* in The New England Journal of Medicine[380]. Cousins chronicled his remarkable recovery from a severe and life-threatening disease of the connective tissue called degenerative collagen illness. And his cure – a powerful drug called laughter[‡‡]. He would watch hours of side-ripping laugh-out-loud comedy and ask nurses to read to him comedic newspaper columns from E.B. White and Max Eastman.

It is commonly accepted that laughter produces *psychological* benefits, such as improving depression, anxiety, and stress[381-383].

What about physiological effects? Well, the research[384] is encouraging even if not complete[§§]. And besides, do you really think it will do any harm to laugh more?

Play improves memory and stimulates the growth of the cerebral cortex. Play and exploration triggers the secretion of BDNF (Brain Derived Neurotropic Factor) – needed for growth and differentiation of your brain neurons and synapses i.e., the brain wiring. BDNF also protects your neurons (brain cells)[385].

I mentioned it earlier, but *The Leadership BEAT Model*™ isn't about being perfect with every aspect of it. I certainly don't have every area nailed. I certainly could improve in several areas. For example, getting outside enough,

---

[‡‡] Of course, he didn't attribute his recovery solely to laughter, and recognised that the doctors play half the role, but the patient must play their part too.

[§§] Of course, whenever you read academic papers it's hard to pin a researcher down to put their 'stake in the ground' as it were. They usually will conclude that further research is needed.

getting into nature and the connection piece. Another area I feel is lacking for me is laughter and fun. It's not something I find myself doing regularly enough. Which is why I love spending time with my nieces because I always get to play, laugh, and have fun with them. In the past, I remember laughing every day when I was in one relationship, which was certainly great for me. If I don't find the opportunity to laugh with company, I will watch a comedy special on TV instead. Of course, there are also laughter classes like laughter yoga that you can attend now too.

I also think that although I do things I enjoy and even have a 'play' fund set up in my bank account, which is just for money I must spend each month on fun things, I don't think I get enough 'fun' in sometimes. I, like many, am driven and have a passion to succeed and work hard to achieve this end. And I lose sight of doing things just for pure fun.

The beauty of *The Leadership BEAT Model*™ is that it is a diagnostic tool. I can look at the different parts of it, detailed in this book, and recognise where I need to focus. Where am I 'off BEAT'? It might be that sometimes to develop one area; other areas will temporarily be neglected. That's fine and it might be that you rotate through different areas until you find the right balance for you at this stage of your life.

Quick summary about what you do and becoming superhuman...

1. It's important to have passion in your life, offer yourself in service to others or a cause greater than yourself and uncover a purpose for yourself. Strong social connections to others, both emotionally and physically along with a strong connection to self are of paramount importance.

2. It's important to have fun in life. Do things that you enjoy and allow you to play again. Laughing regularly is great for your health.

3. Consciously designing your life to include PSPC and laughter, play & fun will ensure that you maximise your opportunity to becoming your superhuman self.

Action plan for becoming superhuman...

1. Get clear on what your passions are. Take an inventory of what you can lose time doing. What websites, podcasts, TV shows, books and magazines can grab your attention for hours?

2. Look into some volunteering opportunities. This could be as simple as arriving early to a regular meeting that you might go to (e.g., PTA meeting) and setting up the chairs. You could sign up for the Red Cross, or volunteer at a shelter a couple of times a year, or mentor someone.

3. Re-watch a 'laugh-out-loud' funny movie, stand-up special or go to a live comedy show.

3.5 Rituals

Just do it, do it, do it…

---

*"We are what we repeatedly do. Excellence then, is
not an act but a habit."*

- Aristotle

Unconscious Mind

As you saw in Part 1 - BRAIN, the mind is super powerful and in control of much of what we do. We are creatures of habit, and these habits can either help or hinder us. Many of the actions that we do, we repeatedly do. In other words, they form part of our routine. Be that brushing our teeth, putting on our underwear or picking up the paper and a coffee in the morning. Most people have routines built in organically over time without even realising it. Unconsciously. It's time to take a little be more conscious awareness back into your life. If you live your live just at the whims of nature and whatever happens, then you'll be missing out on a great opportunity to surge forward.

When I was studying high performing people, one thing came up repeatedly. The benefit of having morning routines, or rituals. Creating empowering routines at certain points in the day set up these high performers for success. I had a morning routine, of course. I had just never taken an active part in designing it. I used to wake up to a radio alarm clock with the news playing, get up and go to the bathroom, shower, get dressed and eat breakfast in a rush before heading out the door to work.

My evening routine was even simpler. Watch television, then brush my teeth before turning off the light, jumping into bed, and then *trying* to sleep. I say 'trying', as it often took me up to 45 minutes to fall asleep. That was until I started implementing the strategies that I will share with you in chapter 4.1 on sleep.

A - ACTIVITY

And then, when I kept hearing about instilling morning and evening routines from more and more people I respected, I thought about it more carefully.

Routine versus Rituals

What's the difference between routines and rituals? Well, in my mind, a routine is something that is done repeatedly but may have no real meaning behind it. Or intention. When you create a ritual, you may be doing the same thing but the meaning you put behind it differs. For example, the late spiritual teacher Wayne Dyer used to think of two things that he was grateful for first thing in the morning when each of his feet touched the floor.

If you start assigning meaning and specific intentions to what you do, then they become a ritual. You're going to do these things anyway. Shower, make a cup of tea, do the dishes. So, you could create something more from them. When I do the dishes, I use it as an opportunity to practise some mindfulness. My morning routine (now I have actively instilled one), is a ritual to getting my body mentally and physically prepared for the day.

We can't always control what happens during the day. Too many other variables are present. The two times of the day that we can largely control, are at the beginning and end of the day. I strongly encourage you to 'bookend' your days by instilling a morning and evening routine that sets you up for the period that will follow. I go into detail below on my morning routine as well as evening routine, together with some rituals I implement during the day.

Morning Rituals

My morning rituals are quite elaborate now, but they started off being simple. I didn't do all of what's listed below from day one. It took years, and it's always evolving. Am I super strict with this and do it every day regardless? No. Some things I skip depending on whether there isn't sufficient time, or I just want a break. ***Flexibility within the framework***. Just so you have an idea though, here's my *ideal* morning ritual.

5.50 - 6.00*am	Wake up to a gradual 'sunrise' light alarm clock.
6.00 – 6.15am	Go to the bathroom, read a chapter from Og Mandino's book – *The Greatest Salesman in the*

---

* Timings might vary and be delayed if I feel I need to get up later for a specific reason.

World. Say morning incantation[†]. Brush teeth while rolling massage ball under my feet for a minute each side.

6.15 – 6.30am — Go to the kitchen and prepare (chop and soak) vegetables for later. Drink 400ml of warm water (1/3 hot, 2/3 cold). Prepare a second 400ml hot water (sometimes with Shilajit).

6.30 – 6.45am — Meditate (in front of a red light/near infrared light box). Usually with a 15-minute guided meditation[‡].

6.45 – 7.15am — Rebounding[§] (and other mobility exercises) while listening to some uplifting music or motivational speeches on my mp3 Sony Walkman headphones[**]. Use both a daylight (S.A.D.) lamp and my red light/near infrared lamps shining light on me while exercising. Review images and words relating to my primary life goals while rebounding[††].

7.15 – 8.15am — Do some more focussed exercise. Either yoga, Boxing HIIT training at home or a class in the gym. Sometimes a swim, sauna[‡‡][386] and /or steam.

[†] This was designed many years ago using the process described in the *Identity* chapter from my first book – *The Thought Gym*®.

[‡] I'm currently quite into Esther and Abraham Hicks' *Getting into the Vortex* Meditations. They are 15 minutes long and have a 4-beat rhythm that's easy to regulate breathing to.

[§] Rebounding is jumping up and down on a rebounder. A rebounder is a mini trampoline. It can be either with springs or bungee cords (as I have). For more on the benefits to rebounding, head to **https://thethoughtgym.com/supervitality** and watch the video I have on there.

[**] These have a built in 4GB storage, so I don't need to have Bluetooth enabled, which I'm not a fan of having directly against my head.

[††] I've set up a Keynote/PowerPoint presentation with my goals (words and images) on different slides that cycle through automatically and lasts about 15 minutes.

[‡‡] Sauna's have been shown to help protect against heart disease, lung problems, mental health disorders, boost immune and cardiovascular function.

A - ACTIVITY

8.15 – 8.30am	Shower[§§387]. Dry myself using just my hands to vigorously wipe away excess water[***], while performing breathing exercises and clearing the room of steam at the same time.
8.30 – 9.00am	Blend and juice my daily veg smoothie and juice while listening to an educational podcast. Often, I perform 'oil pulling' with coconut oil simultaneously[†††].
9.00am	Ready to work. Write in *The Super Journal*[‡‡‡], do my morning gratitude and prepare for the day.

Some days I need to leave the house at 7am or before, and so I might skip much of this. Or condense activities. Other times I might only have time for either a meditation or rebounding and I decide which is more important that day for me. Or I don't meditate and do a structured breathing routine instead like a Wim Hof Breathing session. If I'm getting on the train, I might do the rebounding at home and the meditation can be done on the train. If I'm cycling somewhere, I might meditate, and my exercise comes from the cycling. If I'm feeling tired or just not up for it (or it's sunny) I might just go for a walk in the park nearby. It's flexible. The above schedule is my *ideal* daily set of rituals. Remember though – ***flexibility within the framework***.

The key is having a baseline that you can have in place, but that you are not so caught up with that you can't alter it. You might meditate for five minutes. Move for five minutes and prepare juices and smoothies the day before (as I sometimes do for early starts). This means the vegetables are cut and soaking in the fridge. All the ingredients for the smoothie are prepared in a container,

---

[§§] Having cold showers, or contrast showers – alternating between warm and cold, ending with 30 seconds of cold is great for the body. Invigorating, but also boosting of the immune system and building the body's resilience and the minds ability to successfully manage the fight or flight (sympathetic nervous) system response.

[***] Yes, I know this sounds weird, but I got into the habit a few years back and it's a bit like a Qigong exercise which helps stimulate energy flow around the body. I love doing it!

[†††] Oil pulling (or swishing) involves putting a bit of coconut oil in the mouth and passing it through the teeth and swishing around the mouth. Coconut oil is anti-bacterial and anti-microbial and can be a good way to keep teeth healthy. There is some controversy as to whether this works any better than mouthwash or just saliva, but in any case, I'm using coconut oil for my smoothies, and some remains on the spoon, so I might as well do it. I still brush my teeth though.

[‡‡‡] This is a daily planner to help me stay focussed and on target towards my goals. I designed it for my personal use, but others like it so it's available at **www.TheSuperJournal.com**.

so I don't have to fiddle about with lots of different items. It significantly speeds up the process. Sometimes I might just make it the morning before and save half of it. Sure, they might not taste quite as nice, but I upgraded my juicer to allow the juice to taste a bit fresher. And then I spice up my smoothie with additional banana and lemon the morning.

If I were to be rigid, it would mean that sometimes I would have to get up at 4am just to get everything done in time. I'm not quite ready for that! Although in the past I did attempt something similar. The earliest I am willing to get up is 5.30-6am, unless necessary for a flight or train. In the future, that might become earlier. I used to think that anyone getting up before 7.30am was crazy and that it was impossible for me, but that changed, so who knows?

Of course, I don't suggest going from no morning ritual to this level of ritual. Or ever doing so much. You might be able to incorporate a lighter morning ritual? It could be drinking a large glass of water and moving a little. Spending some time in quiet reflection and focussing on your breathing for a minute.

In fact, what I aim to do as a minimum is think BMW. If you want to be a high-performance person, think about a high-performance car, like a BMW. In fact, think:

B.M.W.

B - Breathing

We've spoken at length about breathing so you shouldn't need convincing on this. It's a great way to stimulate the body in the morning, and ready the mind. This could be as part of a meditation, or it could be energising breaths. I often just do my breathing while in the shower and drying off.

M - Movement

Again, we've already covered the importance of movement, but first thing in the morning we want to jump-start the system. This will stimulate the movement of the lymph fluid within the body[§§§]. Along with deep diaphragmatic breathing, the only other way to move the lymph fluid, is with movement. You will also benefit from stretching out the body after a night lying down in bed. You might like to do one or two sets of the five-a-day exercises described in the movement chapter. Again, this could be done in the

---

[§§§] The lymph system (lymphatic fluid) is the body's natural sewage system.

bathroom before other people take your time away. Some squats going as low as the toilet seat is a great guide. Then some push ups against the wall or bathtub. Maybe some dips too. Just do 20 of each and you'll feel you've worked out a little.

W - Water

Another thing we've already covered and is critical, is water. Up to a litre of water can be lost overnight – just through breathing. Not to mention how much we might lose through sweat. When I first moved into my old flat, I didn't have a bed. Just a mattress on the floor[****]. And when I finally moved the mattress to put it on a bed frame after a few weeks, I noticed that the wooden floor and underside of the mattress had a black mark on it. I realised that it was from the sweat. There wasn't any circulation to evaporate it off. That's what we're losing each night.

This means, when we wake up, we are likely 1 – 2 litres in deficit[††††]. We should therefore look to consume a large glass of water immediately upon waking. What Shawn Stephenson on The Model Health Show Podcast calls taking an "inner bath". We take an outer bath each morning, so let's introduce an inner bath. I always say to people that the first thing you should be reaching for in the morning is either a large glass of water, or your significant other. Sadly, for most people, the first thing they reach for is their smartphone. When you drink 500 ml of water first thing in the morning, it boosts your metabolism by 30%, allows your body to detoxify, it relaxes the upper body when passing through the thoracic cavity and allows your body to release a little bit of dopamine, giving you a euphoric feeling[388].

So, your morning ritual could simply be B.M.W. Something you can do anywhere, and indeed any time you need more energy.

Daytime Rituals

During the day we are at the mercy of external events and people. Working in an office environment or at any job with other people involved, you are going to encounter factors beyond your control. It's not going to be easy to instil

---

[****] I also didn't have a kitchen so had to eat out a lot or cook everything on a microwave/compact oven and do my dishes in the bath. I also didn't have heating one winter which wasn't any fun.
[††††] Of course, if you breathe only in and out of your nose overnight, then you will lose less water than someone breathing in and out of their mouth, as discussed in the water chapter.

rituals that happen daily, but we can look to implement some flexible rituals. These can help create a bit of balance. I suspect that you already have some rituals for the day. It might be a mid-morning smoke, or pre-work latte. It might be a pint of beer at lunchtime or a biscuit (or three) around 3pm? The key here is to develop rituals that you feel will serve you *positively* in some way. It might even be that the examples I just mentioned do serve you positively – that's up to you, obviously.

Here are some that I put in place to help me and could give you some ideas.

- Doing one or two pull ups each time I walk through my office doorway[‡‡‡‡].
- Going for a walk in the park or local ecology nature reserve whenever the sun is out.
- Moving my body at least once every hour.
- Thinking and practicing the B.M.W. approach described above regularly throughout the day.

Something I've been looking to implement recently is to ensure that I treat each day as the G.I.F.T. that it is (corny, I know). By that I mean:

- **G – Gratitude.** Do I spend some time in gratitude during the day? Typically, this is in the morning with filling in The Super Journal, and at the end of the day (see evening routine). I often find time to pause throughout the day and find gratitude in simple moments. Right now I am on a train back to London from delivering a workshop in Bristol and I have immense gratitude for the train for being on time, spacious, finding a space to sit comfortably and work, being able to get back to London in 1 hour and 20 minutes, the group that I taught today, the fact the train journey this morning was smooth and on time, being able to see the countryside as I travel and not having to be stuck in a car.
- **I – Inspire** (others or be inspired yourself). Have I done something today that can help inspire other people? It might be an Instagram or Facebook post? It might be offering sincere appreciation to someone.

---

‡‡‡‡ I have a pull-up bar in my doorway, of course.

It might be sending a nice text or having a great conversation with an old friend or total stranger. Or in my case today, helping build the confidence of, and inspire, teenagers to become their best versions and go for their dreams. You could also do well to be inspired each day too. That might be by watching inspirational videos or listening to podcasts and audios. Or meeting up with people who inspire you.

- **F – Forgive** (self and others). We will look at forgiveness in the TRANQUILITY section in more detail. But often we need to let things go each day. It might be the long queue at the coffee shop or forgiving that rude driver for cutting you up. It might be forgiving yourself for not getting up at 6am or watching that extra episode on Netflix. None of us are perfect. So, let's stop giving ourselves and others such a hard time. Learn to forgive more. I don't normally like to eat too late, but immense days recently and teaching physical movement in the evening last night meant that I didn't eat until 10pm and then I went to bed immediately afterwards. Not ideal for me, but I'm not beating myself up about it. I made the best choice at the time.

- **T – Touch.** We mentioned in the PSPC section (chapter 3.4) how important touch with others is for feeling good, and how touching the earth (chapter 2.3) is also important. If you live alone that might not always be easy, but you might have a pet or be able to stroke cats and dogs when you see them (assuming they seem friendly and approachable). It might be that you put your bare feet on the ground or place your hand on a tree. And yes, I know this sounds like you might look like a tree-hugger, but doesn't it feel nice to connect with nature? Some exercises or sports you could choose might be those that involve others – Acro-Yoga, dancing or even Brazilian Ju-Jitsu or wrestling?

Each day is a gift, so why not give yourself a G.I.F.T. each day too? Something that will bring us improved health and happiness.

Evening Ritual

Again, my evening rituals might vary from the ideal below, but the key here is to have at least some kind of ritual that gets you set up for a great night's sleep. While at the same time remembering *flexibility within the framework.*

7.00 – 8.00pm	Start to limit blue light exposure. The timing of this depends on the time of the year, and whether I am out of the house. In winter it's earlier and in summer it tends to be later. I put on blue light blocking glasses and dim the lights. Apps like f.lux (for laptops) and Twilight (for Android phones) start to activate. Write in my family's WhatsApp group three things I'm grateful for[§§§§].
9.00 – 9.30pm	*Nein, after nine.* I put my mobile phone into airplane mode. Close my laptop and stop working. Turn off WiFi router. Fill in the final part of *The Super Journal* (if I haven't already done it). I turn any watch faces away from me[*****].
9.30 – 10.15pm	Get things ready for the next day. Do the washing up, read a book or run a bath. Brush teeth while rolling a massage ball under my feet to relieve tension. Write in my gratitude log[†††††] and spray magnesium over me.
10.15 – 10.30pm	Evening meditation (or if I'm feeling a bit lazy and want to lie down, I put on a guided hypnosis, guided breathwork session or yoga nidra[‡‡‡‡‡]).
10.30pm	Go to sleep[§§§§§].

[§§§§] Since 2019 several members of my family, at my suggestion, have been sharing with everyone three things we're grateful for.

[*****] I don't have clocks in my house, instead I prop up a wristwatch on my kitchen shelf.

[†††††] I've been keeping a gratitude journal since 2011. On one side of the page, I write three things I'm grateful for in my life (small or large) and then on the other side of the page, I write three future gratitude's, as if I already have them. See chapter 1.8 for more on this practice.

[‡‡‡‡‡] Yoga Nidra is a lying down yoga where you do progressive observations of parts of your body. You're not actually supposed to fall asleep, but I always do. And that's why I like it.

[§§§§§] Truth be told, the timings are all approximate as I rarely know the time after 9pm when I remove all time-telling devices. I've been using an Oura ring since 2019 (a wearable sleep tracker) so the following day I do get to find out when I went to sleep. It's usually between 10.30 and 11.15pm.

A - ACTIVITY

I wouldn't usually watch programmes in the evening on TV or the internet during the week, but often on a weekend I will. I still aim to have the lights low and wear blue light blocking glasses. I also have an app called *f.lux* (which removes the blue light) installed on the computer that sits under my television, so it dims the screen out. You do get used to it, and if it's too dark to properly watch a program, then I turn it off. I would still wear the blue blocking glasses though.

Regardless, if I do watch programmes into the evening (weekday or weekend) I still aim to allow myself 45 mins from the end of the show, to turning in for the night. This includes brushing my teeth, meditation and writing in my gratitude log along with anything else I can put in there like emptying the dishwasher to allow some time for my brain to relax from the stimulus of the programmes. I notice that on the days when I don't give myself plenty of time between switching off the TV and going to bed, I then struggle to switch off and sleep.

The Super Journal

If you are an entrepreneur, solopreneur, or freelancer, then you'll know how time can escape you during the day. And if you run your own company or work for others, I'm betting you can appreciate that too. Sometimes the end of the day comes, and you think to yourself, "What have I actually done today?", "Where did my time go today?"

It might be that you have certain goals in business and life, but other things seem to get in the way. Life just intervenes. Or as I like to think of life sometimes. L.I.F.E. = Little Inconsequential Futile Events. *Think about it. How often do we spend our time doing things that don't really propel us forwards?* I'm not saying that everything we do, for every minute of the day needs to have an agenda around it. What I am saying is, that it's my experience, and the experience of many of the people I coach, train, and speak to, that they leave the day feeling unsatisfied with what they've accomplished, or not even knowing what it is.

I tried many different systems to remedy this, and, in the end, I decided to create my own. A system which fused together different ideas and principles I have learnt from others. It started off as a productivity pad in 2016, and then I added pieces to it and created a journal with it in 2017. For all of 2017 it was just me using it. I created a long pdf file and uploaded it to a self-publishing company. And then I would order copies for myself.

As people started seeing me use it (what I started to call *The Super Journal*), more people would ask me about it. As a result, I decided to enhance it, give some instructions on how to use it and make it functional for a few more people.

We all think differently, so it might not be for everyone, as it's designed for my brain, however I'm willing to bet that there are quite a few people out there who would benefit from a more structured approach to their day. A system that will help them achieve their primary goals in life and keep track of the important (and not so important) tasks, freeing up their minds to focus on other things.

The journal includes things like daily gratitude, what would make the day great, who do you need to reach out to and who are you waiting on information from to move things forward. A daily reflection on what went well, how you could improve and what you learnt. As well as inspirational quotes, free space for notes and an 8am – 8pm timetable in 30-minute segments to keep track of your day. There are also weekly and monthly planning and review pages to get you clear on your week and month ahead.

It really has been transformative to my work, productivity, and results. As well as helping me reduce my stress and keep a journal of my life.

Some examples of the main pages follow. For more information and to order yourself a copy (each book lasts three months), visit **www.thesuperjournal.com**.

MONDAY ____ / ____ / 20____

🙏 TODAY, I'M GRATEFUL FOR...

😊 TODAY WOULD BE A GREAT DAY IF...

🎯 [1] MY ONE THING FOR THE YEAR

Things to be aware of for my ONE thing (not necessarily actionable)

● ● ● ●

🎯 [2] SECONDARY GOAL 🎯 [3] TERTIARY GOAL

Things to be aware of for my additional goals (not necessarily actionable)

● _____ ● _____
● _____ ● _____

ONE THING FOR THE MONTH	ONE THING FOR THE WEEK	ONE THING FOR THE DAY

👥 Awaiting input from the following people 👥 Reach out to the following people

☐	☐	☐	☐
☐	☐	☐	☐
☐	☐	☐	☐
☐	☐	☐	☐

📝 TODAY'S TASK LIST
(To be completed after ONE thing for the DAY achieved. Refer to Weekly Task List, if needed.)
Prioritise each task (A - Action , B - Beneficial , C - Consider , D - Delegate , E - Eliminate)

☐	☐
☐	☐
☐	☐
☐	☐
☐	☐

Figure 17 - Sample Pages taken from The Super Journal

TIMETABLE

08.00 - 08.30 ....
08.30 - 09.00 ....
09.00 - 09.30 ....
09.30 - 10.00 ....
10.00 - 10.30 ....
10.30 - 11.00 ....
11.00 - 11.30 ....
11.30 - 12.00 ....
12.00 - 12.30 ....
12.30 - 13.00 ....
13.00 - 13.30 ....
13.30 - 14.00 ....
14.00 - 14.30 ....
14.30 - 15.00 ....
15.00 - 15.30 ....
15.30 - 16.00 ....
16.00 - 16.30 ....
16.30 - 17.00 ....
17.00 - 17.30 ....
17.30 - 18.00 ....
18.00 - 18.30 ....
18.30 - 19.00 ....
19.00 - 19.30 ....
19.30 - 20.00 ....

"WE ARE WHAT WE REPEATEDLY DO. EXCELLENCE, THEN, IS NOT AN ACT, BUT A HABIT."

ARISTOTLE

GENERAL NOTES...

WHAT WENT WELL ABOUT TODAY WAS...

WHAT I LEARNT TODAY WAS...

HOW I COULD IMPROVE ON TODAY'S PERFORMANCE WOULD BE...

END OF DAY CHECKLIST

WEEKLY TASK LIST REFERRED TO ☐   UPDATED THE WEEKLY HABIT TABLE ☐   PLANNER FILLED IN FOR NEXT WORKING DAY ☐

37

Figure 18 - Sample Pages from The Super Journal

A - ACTIVITY
Choices in Advance (C.I.A.)

It's claimed that each day the average person makes an estimated 35,000 decisions, although I've seen estimates up to 90,000[******]. That's exhausting. Each time your brain is occupied deciding, it means something else must get bumped. Thinking is energy consuming work. Although your brain weighs about 2% of your body mass, it uses 20% of your energy needs when the body is at rest[389]. Each time you decide, you use up energy. Glucose – your brain fuel. It can wear you out and make you tired.

Ever wondered why it was that Steve Jobs wore the same clothes repeatedly? Or even Mark Zuckerberg when his 'uniform' used to be a grey t-shirt and jeans[++++++]? Many successful people I have investigated, adopt similar principles. Not necessarily with clothes. Some aspect of their lives. Many aspects in fact. They choose in advance what they are going to wear, eat or whatever it is. They eliminate as many decisions as possible, so they can focus on the main decisions they need to make. The crucial ones for running multi-billion-dollar companies. It's not just businesspeople, of course. I heard an interview once with the author Neil Strauss, being interviewed by Tim Ferriss, who said that when he's writing he has the same lunch delivered each day. Every Monday he'll have the same meal. Every Tuesday, the same meal (but different from Mondays). Likewise for Wednesday, Thursday, and Friday. He doesn't want to lose brain processing power deciding each day on lunch, when he has more important things to be deciding. Like how to create a compelling chapter.

That's one reason to call in the C.I.A. – *Choices in Advance*. We often ritualise (or have routine) in our lives, and these can most definitely serve us. Making choices in advance can free us up to make real choices when we need to. And we won't be depleted.

Another reason for C.I.A. is that when you make choices in advance, studies show you are more likely to follow through. In one such study, people were divided into three groups[390].

[******] The exact number isn't important, suffice it to say that we make a lot of small decisions each day.
[++++++] And Zucks took inspiration from occasional mentor Steve Jobs on this.

Group 1 was the control group. They were asked to keep track of how frequently they exercised over the next two weeks. Before they left, each person was asked to read the opening three paragraphs of an unrelated novel.

Group 2 was the motivation group. They were also asked to keep track of how frequently they exercised over the next two weeks. Then, each person was asked to read a pamphlet on the benefits of exercise for reducing the risk of heart disease. Participants in Group 2 were also told, "Most young adults who have stuck to a regular exercise program have found it to be very effective in reducing their chances of developing coronary heart disease." The goal of these actions was to motivate Group 2 to exercise regularly.

Group 3 was the intention group. After being told to track their exercise, they also read the motivational pamphlet and got the same speech as Group 2. This was done to ensure that Group 2 and Group 3 were equally motivated. Group 3 were then also asked to schedule in advance when they would exercise over the coming weeks.

The results were interesting. In Group 1, 38% exercised, in group 2 it was only 35% but in group 3 it was 91%. Hundreds of other studies show similar trends. Making the choice in advance is strongest when it's specific. Rather than saying that you plan to exercise twice next week, it's stronger when you say that you will exercise twice a week but state on which exact days that will be. It becomes stronger still when you say something specific, such as you will exercise on Tuesday from 10am – 11am after your morning team meeting, and then again from 1pm – 2pm on Thursday before the board meeting.

Anchoring Rituals

You could also 'anchor' a new ritual onto a previously existing one. For example, you shower each day. Well, once you've finished your shower, you could create a new ritual of doing a few push-ups. Perhaps starting with a comfortable number, near the limit of as many as you can do – even if it's just one. That's exactly what I used to do when I wanted to get into the ritual of doing daily push-ups. Each day after the shower I would do a few. Starting at ten and building up by two each week.

A - ACTIVITY

Pretty soon, as soon as I would step out of the shower into that space, the brain would associate doing push-ups and it became automated.

Keystone Rituals

As mentioned in chapter 1.1 we can also have keystone habits or rituals. Some rituals can snowball into other rituals or activities you do. For example, you might realise that you have a routine that only takes place when you leave the office with a certain colleague. You notice that you end up visiting a bar on the way home. This might then lead to eating late or poorly and going to bed late. Then you don't fancy the morning workout, or you get up too late to do your morning ritual to set you up for a great day. Or you are not as productive as you would wish. All this stemming from the one action of leaving the office at the same time with this friend. When you identify the keystone rituals in your life, you can then change many of the downstream ones easily. You leave slightly earlier or later than the colleague who tempts you. And then you cook at home, go to be early, wake up fresh and the next day is a day of super productivity.

Quick summary about rituals and becoming superhuman...

1. We are creatures dictated by our unconscious mind and already have many routines in place. These are instilled unconsciously in most cases. If you want to maximise your performance instilling some conscious rituals will be a good idea. The difference between a routine and a ritual can be in the intention and mindset behind the ritual.

2. We often can't control what happens to us during the day, but at the beginning of the day and end of the day it's a different story. Design some rituals for the morning and evening to set you up for a dynamic day and successful sleep.

3. Making choices all the time can be exhausting. Eliminate mundane or routine choices by employing a C.I.A. approach. This will free up more brain capacity for the important decisions. It will also make you more likely to follow through on choices when they are made in advance.

Action plan for becoming superhuman...

1. Create a light morning ritual for yourself. Start with thinking about B.M.W. and adapt from there.

2. Look at where you can make use of the C.I.A. approach in your week. Which choices can you make in advance to reduce brain drain?

3. Anchor a new ritual to an existing ritual to make it easier to adopt. Review any keystone rituals you might have. Do they help or hinder you?

TRANQUILITY

Part 4: TRANQUILITY

Finding calm in the storm…

---

*"Tranquility is a choice. So is anxiety. The entire
world around us may be in turmoil. But if we want to
be peaceful within. We can."*

- Anonymous

Most people when they talk about health & fitness, think in terms of diet and exercise. Some people might even include sleep. Rest. That's not the end of the story though. TRANQUILITY is more than sleep. Or resting more. It's about finding tranquility in your life in all areas. Physically, emotionally, mentally, and spiritually.

If you picked up this book you might be someone who's seeking to be the highest performer they can be. An achiever, or maybe you're an 'A-type' personality.

You might have lofty goals, be responsible for large numbers of people or manage a huge budget. You might have a noble world vision and want to change the world for the best. You're a change-maker. And the chances are, that you might not give this part of your life the attention it deserves.

You might give your maximum effort to others. Or causes. Your work. Your sport. Your goals. We are humans though. And even though we are *becoming* superhuman, that does not mean that we do not need to rest. That we do not need to find time to be tranquil. To slow things down. Pause. Stop.

If we don't look after ourselves, we can't fulfil our greater mission. Most people are familiar with the airplane safety briefing instructions. When they do the safety demonstration before a flight takes off, they always instruct you to put your own oxygen mask on first. Before helping other people. If you

VITALITY

don't look after yourself first, then you cannot be able to help others on the flight – or in this case, life. I know that this can be counter-intuitive for parents. Most parents will do anything for their children. Often putting their children above their own needs. At what cost though? Can you really be all you can be for your children or other dependants when you are not operating on all cylinders? I know that at times your needs might have to take a back seat. That's okay. Just be mindful of the fact that if your own 'cup' is empty, there will be nothing to give others.

TRANQUILITY is about how we rest, recuperate, regenerate, repair, rejuvenate and restore ourselves. In this section we'll explore a few of the strategies that have worked for many people - me included – and that you might find useful. Like everything in this book, take what you need from it. Rather than getting overwhelmed with trying everything or thinking something isn't for you and then 'throwing the baby out with the bathwater'.

4.1 Sleep

To sleep - perchance to dream...

---

*"I love sleep. My life has the tendency to fall apart
when I'm awake, you know?"*

- Ernest Hemingway

Sleep. Often thought of as the third pillar in the healthy body-mind, along with diet and exercise. Often, it's overlooked or not taken as seriously. Even though you will be less productive, more susceptible to illness and might even cause accidents from operating cars or machinery while being sleep deprived. I know too, that if you are a new parent then there are certainly extra considerations and certainly the quantity of sleep may well suffer. The good news is though that there are ways though to optimise the *quality*, even if your *quantity* suffers. Perhaps taking alternate nights with your partner in getting up, if that's possible, so you get a full night's sleep every other night. Even if you are a new parent, with a 3-month-old screaming all night, there will be plenty in this chapter to help you with your sleep.

Why we need sleep

So why do we need to sleep anyway? Obviously, we get tired if we don't, but beyond that? Here are just a few reasons for sleeping. Sleeping:

- Fortifies the immune system.
- Balance hormones.
- Boosts the metabolism.

301

- Increases physical energy.
- Improves the brain function.
- Contributes to the growth of skeletal and muscular functions.
- Organises memories and help store information.

Research in Brief

- Daytime naps of 20 minutes can offer memory consolidation advantage as long as have enough NREM sleep[391].
- After being awake for 19 hours, sleep deprived people are as cognitively impaired as those that are legally drunk[391].
- Less than 5 hours sleep, and risk of car crash increases 300%[391].
- If you have 4 hours sleep, you are 11.5 times more likely to be in crash[391].
- After 10 days of just 7 hours of sleep, the brain is as dysfunctional as going 24 hours without sleep[391].
- 60% amplification in emotional reactivity of amygdala in sleepdeprived[391].
- Lack of sleep increases chance of injury in sportspeople[392].
- Sleep improves motor skills of junior, amateur, and elite athletes across sports as diverse as tennis, basketball, football, soccer, and rowing[393].

I've delivered sleep workshops to thousands of people over the years and found that when I ask who wakes up regularly feeling tired, I find it's around 60 per cent. And the topic of sleep always gets a lot of interest from people. My sleep improvement videos are also the most popular on my YouTube channel, which you can access for free via the 'Sleep Playlist' at **youtube.com/thethoughtgym.**

If, like me, you like working out, understand that you are only building your body when you sleep. Not in the gym. In the gym, when you are working out, you are breaking down your body. That's why most professional athletes who are really excelling in their field, sleep so much. They are breaking their bodies down to such an extent that they need to rebuild it. Human growth hormone that is needed for this process happens mostly overnight[394].

And when it comes to the brain too, there is a system called the glymphatic system. It's a bit like the lymphatic system mentioned earlier in this book. The sewage system for the body, but in this case it's for the brain. And it predominately works overnight when you are sleeping[395]. Not when you are awake.

Consequences of lack of sleep

What happens when we don't sleep enough? Among some of the problems linked to a lack of sleep are[391]:

- Type-2 diabetes
- Heart disease
- Cancer
- Memory loss
- Depression
- Obesity
- Alzheimer's

One thing that might scare you into action is that when examined, those people getting less than six hours of sleep per night were 13% more likely to die from all-cause mortality than those getting 7-9 hrs. And still, those getting 6-7 hrs were 7% more likely[391]. That's significant.

Just 24 hours of sleep deprivation caused a 6% reduction in glucose (your brain's preferred and primary fuel source) reaching the brain[396]. Moreover, the parietal lobe and prefrontal cortex (the executive function of the brain – the part that is needed for decision, logic, and human specific functions) had a 12 – 14% reduction[396]. Which might explain the following experiment.

In an experiment with sleep deprived surgeons (not at all unusual), the surgeons were found to take 14% longer completing tasks while making 20% more errors[396]. Think about it this way. *Do you want to spend longer at work, making more mistakes in your work, so you can spend longer still in correcting them?* Prioritise your sleep.

It's also worth noting that when you have poor sleep your hormones are affected. Specifically, in my talks about sleep, I talk about ghrelin and leptin. Ghrelin is the hunger hormone. Having more of it, makes you feel hungrier. Leptin is the satiety hormone and helps you know when to feel full and satisfied.

When you have poor sleep, go to bed late or have otherwise disrupted sleep, then the amount of ghrelin will increase, and leptin decrease. Not a good thing.

T - TRANQUILITY

To remember which way round it is, I like to think of it like this. 'Ghrelin the Gremlin' and 'Leptin the Leprechaun'. If you've seen the 1980's movie *Gremlins*, you'll know that the cute little Mogwai shouldn't be fed after midnight, or he will turn into a Gremlin[*]. It's a fun way for me to remember that Ghrelin the Gremlin isn't something we want, but Leptin the Leprechaun is[†].

Circadian Rhythm

It's worth knowing something basic about our bodies. We have what's called a circadian rhythm. It's a 24-hour clock cycle. In fact, it's 24.18 hours[397‡], but using external stimuli, we re-set it each day. Light plays a vital role in this reset. Our circadian rhythms are largely determined by our light exposure and too little light in the early parts of the day, or too much artificial light at the end of the day, will negatively impact our circadian clock and ability to sleep optimally. The circadian rhythm we all have also means that at certain points of the day our body is better suited for certain things. See the diagram below.

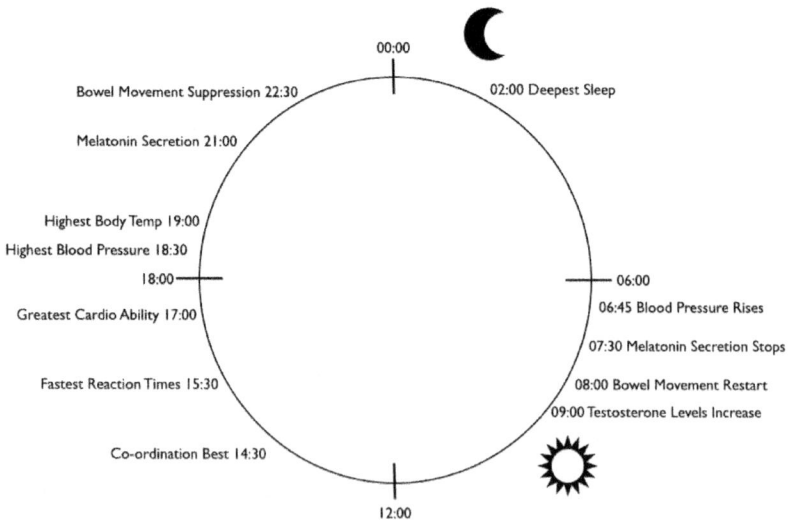

Figure 19 - The 24-hr Body Clock and Functions

---

[*] And when you spill water over them, they multiply.
[†] Leprechauns are harmless, right? They are at the end of rainbows along with a pot of gold!
[‡] Give or take. It can vary a little from this, person to person.

When we sleep, we move through different stages of sleep. There are five stages[§].

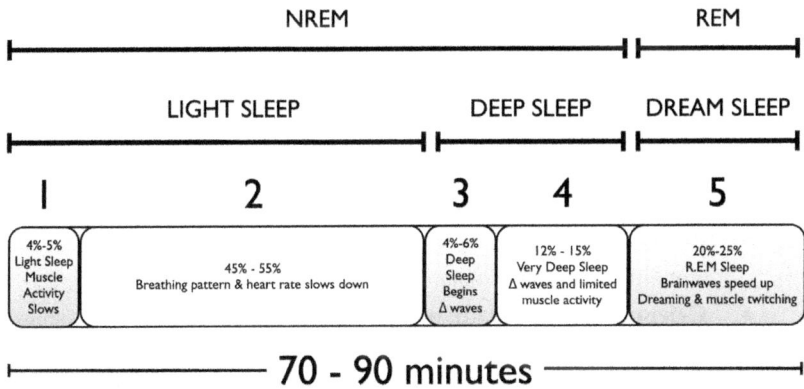

Figure 20 - Sleep Stages

In a typical person this is around 90 minutes. It could be between 70 – 100 minutes and even as low as 60 minutes, but it's safe to assume 90 minutes. If we wake up in deep sleep, then we feel groggier, and it takes us longer to wake than if we are woken during our light sleep stages.

The Gut-Sleep Connection

When I started changing my diet back in 2011, I noticed that it improved my sleep. As mentioned, light plays a pivotal role in our sleeping patterns, and it also affects a powerful neurotransmitter called serotonin. Often associated with feelings of happiness and wellbeing, serotonin is vital for regulating our internal body clock. Serotonin is also the building block for the 'sleep' hormone melatonin. With most of your serotonin located in your gastrointestinal tract – gut[398]. Serotonin is influenced by your diet, as well as activity levels and the amount of natural sunlight you get. The gut is a mass of neural tissue – filled with 30 types of neurotransmitters (just like in the brain)[399]. And the gut has been found to contain 400 times more melatonin that the pineal gland in your brain[400].

Now, in terms of foods to help with sleep. Well, the *PANLO 80/20* approach for a start. Eliminating processed foods. Eliminate sugar if you can – at least

---

[§] Sometimes you might see reference to three stages – light, deep and dream. Or even two stages. REM and NREM - Rapid Eye Movement (REM) and Non-REM.

after 4pm seems to work for me in terms of sleep quality. Plenty of vegetables and then incorporating the following:

- **Selenium** (Brazil nuts, sunflower seeds, cremini mushrooms, beef, oysters, chicken)
- **Vitamin C** (camu camu berry, amla berry, acerola cherry, bell peppers, green leafy vegetables, kiwi fruit, strawberries and citrus fruits)
- **Tryptophan** (sweet potatoes, chia seeds, hemp seeds, bananas, almonds, leafy greens, turkey, chicken, eggs)
- **Potassium** (leafy greens, potatoes, dulse, avocados, broccoli, cremini mushrooms, bananas)
- **Calcium** (kale, collard greens, mustard greens, sea vegetables, sesame seeds)
- **Vitamin D** (sunshine, shiitake mushrooms, swordfish, salmon, tuna, mackerel)
- **Omega-3 fats** (chia seeds, pumpkin seeds, hemp seeds, flax seeds, walnuts, halibut, salmon)
- **Melatonin** (tart cherries, walnuts, root ginger, asparagus – and foods that boost melatonin like pineapples, tomatoes, bananas, and oranges)
- **Vitamin B6** (bananas, cashew nuts, peanut butter, almonds, avocados, fish, tomatoes, spinach, sweet potatoes, sea vegetables and eggs)
- **Probiotics** (sauerkraut, kimchi, pickles, miso, yoghurt (including non-dairy), kefir, kombucha tea
- **Magnesium** (green leafy vegetables, pumpkin seeds, sesame seeds, Brazil nuts, spirulina)[**]

========

SLEEP STEALERS

Let's look at what is causing poor sleep. Whether that is the time it takes to fall asleep, staying asleep or waking up feeling tired. Then we'll look at some sleep strategies.

[**] We'll cover magnesium in more detail later, as the best way is really to supplement.

Unnatural Lives

The first thing to acknowledge is that for most people living in the industrialised world, we are so far removed from our natural patterns it's laughable. Or at least, it would be if it weren't so tragic. We should be rising with natural sunlight, going to bed when it gets dark, perhaps having naps during the day. We may even have been polyphasic sleepers once upon a time, which means sleeping not just in one large chunk, but in a large chunk and one or two smaller sessions[401]. We should be sleeping more in the winter, and less in the summer. We should be living outside more and not under artificial lights. We should also be moving more, eating real food and everything else that is now slowly eroding. This is a major part of our sleep issues. Let's investigate these further.

1. Blue Light

The Issues

This is getting more and more attention now. The blue light emitted from our devices is hindering our sleep. Blue light isn't bad. It depends on when we are exposed to it. All light has various wavelengths (colours) within it. Daylight has a spectrum within it, but we really need the blue light at the beginning of the day (and during the day) to signal our body that we should be awake. The blue light in the morning will raise cortisol (often seen as the stress hormone, but so much more) which is needed to wake us up.

Thanks to Thomas Edison, towards the end of the 19th century, we started to use artificial lights. This meant that people could work later, socialise later and do so under light that our bodies hadn't adapted to. Moonlight, candlelight, and firelight has been part of human evolution. Artificial light hasn't. We haven't adapted to it. In a couple of hundred thousand years that might change, but for now - no.

In addition, artificial lighting could be an unsuspected cause of 'diseases of ageing', such as osteoporosis and muscle loss according to one study. Countless studies are showing we evolved to require periods of darkness (common sense dictates that too). In this one study, from Leiden University Medical Centre in the Netherlands, they exposed mice to constant light for 24 weeks. The mice's usual circadian patterns were affected by 70 per cent, and their bones showed signs of deterioration, and triggered a proinflammatory state, that is normally seen when exposed to pathogens. Symptoms disappeared after two weeks of normal day/night cycles[402].

And while artificial lights are part of the problem, what's becoming more of an issue are the devices that are being used continuously. Previously it was simply lights and the television. Now it's laptops, smartphones, and tablets. These have a strong blue light presence (and held closer to you) and they are, likely, impacting your sleep.

One study found that two hours of iPad use in the evening was enough to suppress melatonin by 23%[391], although other studies have suggested that possibly this could be offset by getting ample blue light during the day[403]. Melatonin is naturally secreted by the body (as part of the circadian cycle) around 9 – 11pm to help us get to sleep. Not only is melatonin important for sleep but also to help keep you looking youthful[404], it helps promote brown fat[405] (a good kind of fat that helps you lose or maintain your weight) and is thought to assist in keeping cancer away[406]. And many people are effectively removing one quarter of their supply of melatonin.

The Solutions

When we are talking about reducing our impact from blue light there are a few practical solutions that I use.

Ambient Light

If you can limit this by using dimmer switches, which although won't remove the blue light, will create a nice calming night-time atmosphere for you. You might switch off main overhead lights and just use side lights? Even better, use candles (if you are comfortable with using them in the home[††]).

Blue Blockers

Every day since 2015 when I'm at home, and even when I'm away at lot of the time, I use blue light blocking sunglasses. Yes. I wear sunglasses at night. Part crazy, part pop star! These are specially designed to filter out the blue light. I still have my lights on low, or use side lights only, and I don't ever turn those lights on until I have my

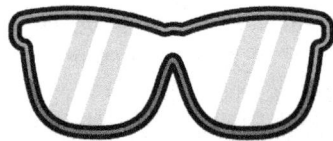

[††] And an obvious fire safety warning here.

blue-blocking sunglasses on. I know it sounds crazy, but if there is one thing that can really affect my sleep quality, it's whether I wear them or not. Sometimes if I'm away, or I have guests over in the evening, then I might not wear them. I do, however, notice the difference in my sleep. I recommend getting 'wrap-around' versions so that minimal light enters the eye from the side. They really have made a massive difference to me and, I would suggest everyone to own a pair. I sometimes even have them on me when I'm out in the evening to wear on the train ride home to get myself ready. I live in London, so no-one really cares, or finds it that unusual, to wear sunglasses at odd times or in odd places! There is even evidence to suggest that all the artificial light that we are exposed to is contributing to the 'diseases of ageing'[402].

Devices

When using my devices at night, I use software that removes the blue light automatically. You tell it what time you wake up in the mornings, and where you are on Earth (although it can figure that out usually) and you just set and forget it. For laptops I recommend using a free piece of software called f.lux. You can download it for Mac and PC from justgetflux.com. On my Android smartphone I use Twilight. Unfortunately for iPhones I think you are limited because of how their app store works with third party apps controlling phone functions, but Apple have built in Nightshift to their operating systems. I don't have much experience with Nightshift so can't say if it really blocks blue light or just dims the screen and how much you can control it. It's bound to be better than nothing though.

Even with f.lux and Twilight installed on my devices I still use the blue-blocking glasses in tandem with the software solutions and low lights. Controlling my light exposure in the evening is the number one thing I would suggest helping with a great night of sleep.

2. Electronics

The Issues

These days our devices are practically extensions of our own body. Almost like an additional limb. We are addicted to them. Quite literally in most cases. I was walking along the beach in Crete the other day thinking about this concept – having a device as a limb – when I saw a young lady walking down the beach for a sunset stroll, her feet skirting the water's edge. She was

309

wearing just a bikini and nothing else. And yet, in her hand, whilst walking along this gorgeous beach with this serene sunset was her mobile phone. Sometimes looking down to check it, sometimes interrupting the moment to take a selfie. Presumably posting it. Have I ever done this? Yes, of course. And I'm judging this lady on one experience. It might be that it's one experience in ten and the other nine she is just enjoying the moment. I hope so. I know that although I am sometimes guilty of interrupting these moments with a snap, often I take these moments with no mobile phone or camera in sight.

Even when we limit the blue light coming from our devices – be that phones, tablets, computers, or TV's, they still do something quite detrimental to our sleep. They activate our brains when they should be winding down.

What you put into your head last thing at night is important. If you are highly stimulated from watching a movie or the latest Netflix boxset binge, it will affect you. If you watch the news just before bed, it will affect you. If you check your Instagram or Facebook newsfeed and compare yourself positively or negatively to others, it will affect you. Make no mistake in that.

Most people I speak with are plugged-in to the wider world from the moment they wake up, until the moment they turn in for bed. And they wonder why they have all these racing thoughts. It's not rocket science. Entertain the idea of a screen curfew.

The Solution

I will be the first to admit that I might not adhere to this 100% of the time, but the times when I don't, I can tell you that I don't sleep as well. Here's my philosophy, and you would have seen it mentioned before in the chapter on rituals (chapter 3.5).

Nein, after nine.

Nein, as in 'no' (in German). After 9pm. The time is arbitrary, but I would say it should be 90 minutes before your planned fall asleep time. If you prefer, this could be *Nein, for Ninety* instead. Eliminate tech and distractions for 90 minutes before bed, ninety minutes on waking and 90 minutes during

the day. If you go to bed at 11.30pm, it might be that your phrase is "turn off at ten". I like phrases that have a bit of alliteration in them as it seems nice to say. And I remember them a bit more. Nein, after nine has become a staple for me. So, at 9pm I normally make sure I close my laptop, put my phone in airplane mode and do something non-tech related. Sure, I do sometimes watch TV, which doesn't help for the reasons of brain stimulation I mentioned, but I'm not perfect. When I am veering more to perfection, I would read a book or do the washing up and run a bath and listen to some chill-out music. I sleep much better those nights.

I know you might be reading this and think that it would be impossible to do *nein, after nine.* How can you put your phone into airplane mode. What if someone needs to get hold of you. *Really? How many times over the last year has there been a genuine emergency when you really needed to be contacted?* And besides, if you have a landline and the person is important to you, give them that number. Think back to when you might have had an 'emergency'? Firstly, was it a genuine emergency? And secondly, was there something you could do about then and there? Remember, there *were* emergencies before mobile phones, and we found solutions.

I remember only three times when I had a genuine emergency and didn't take a call. One was in 2011. It was before 9pm too, but I was eating dinner and decided not to pick up. It was my best friend's fiancé calling. And she kept calling, so I called back after the third or fourth missed call.

He had suffered a heart attack. He was 33 years old. He was alive and had been rushed to the best hospital in London for heart care. He was (and still is) a doctor, so was self-diagnosing to the paramedics. Luckily, they didn't take him to the local hospital which was only two minutes away (as perhaps he wouldn't be here now – it's not a good hospital). It was a truly tragic experience. There was also absolutely nothing I could have done at that moment. I got the message from his fiancé and called the hospital straight away and was able to talk to him. I visited him first thing the next day and again in the afternoon and evening.

Another time was in 2005. I was on nightshifts at the London Stock Exchange. It was about 9pm and I was just getting up to eat and head off. During my sleep my phone was off when a good friend of mine had tried calling. He left a voicemail though and told me to call him back urgently. We had just received word that one of our best friends – someone I'd known since I was six years old and still hung out with often – had tragically died. Initially we

311

were told that it was a motorcycle accident. The following week, his parents shared the true and tragic circumstances of his death, as they understood them. Suicide.

The third and most recent time was Christmas Eve, 2023. My phone was on, but on silent. I was using it to hotspot the internet, as the place I was staying didn't have Wi-Fi, and I was doing a yoga class on YouTube. When I finished my class 20 minutes later, I saw missed calls from my mum and younger sister — messages about an emergency with Dad.

I immediately called my mum, who was desperately trying to give my dad CPR (Cardiopulmonary Resuscitation) while at the same time using his phone to take instructions from the emergency services.

I won't go into too much more detail here, but tragically, my father died.

Could I have changed anything by picking up the phone earlier? Could I have comforted my mum more, or given her better instructions that might have saved his life?

It's a question I sometimes ask myself, but ultimately, I've concluded that it wouldn't have changed the tragic outcome.

That day was devastating to us all — especially for my mum, who had been married to my dad for over 52 years (and together even longer).

All three events were life-changing for those involved and tragic. Would I have been able to do anything knowing earlier? Probably not. That's not to say that's always the case. It's just to say that I really can only think of three times where there was something like that going on. Perhaps you being on the end of the phone is going to help save someone's life, but can we really be reachable 24 hours a day, 7 days a week, 365 days a year without fail?

I'm not here to say that you should ignore all your loved ones and not be there for them. Just think about whether you really need to be contactable 24/7.

You might find a time when you are on the underground (subway) and you don't have signal. People can't get hold of you then. We can't live being always contactable. We never used to be reachable in this way. It's different if you are on-call for your job. I have done this role, and I could never sleep as well knowing the phone *could* ring. It's different if you have a loved one ill at the hospital as my mum did with my grandmother. As she could take a call at 3am and be by my gran's side in under five minutes. And she frequently was there. Including the night that my grandmother passed away.

Realistically speaking though. These are not daily occurrences. Your sleep is though. I share this with you so that you can, if you need it, have the permission to switch off your mobile phone. Give your landline number (or spare mobile) out for real emergencies. Following my father's passing, I do have a second phone, especially as landlines are becoming obsolete in many homes. The spare phone is always on, and only three people have that number though.

I hope that all makes sense. And I know I get a lot of push back from people on this idea. So, it's up to you. You might like to test it out for a few weeks and see how it works for you.

3. Drinks

Alcohol - The Issue

We've mentioned alcohol before in the section all about food, but because some people use it to get to sleep, I must mention it here too. While alcohol might help you fall asleep, study after study shows that the *quality* of sleep will suffer[391]. And not just because you might get up for the toilet. Yes, alcohol will also dehydrate you, but more importantly it affects the deep sleep you get and is more akin to a sedative than a sleep promotor. As Matthew Walker, sleep researcher and author of hugely popular book, Why We Sleep, often says: "sedation is not sleep."[391]

Alcohol - The Solution

I assume that the solution for you isn't to stop drinking. Although that is one solution, and probably the best one. Here is how you might drink and have your sleep less affected. A general rule of thumb would be to *allow one hour to pass for each alcoholic drink unit you have.* If you have dinner from 7pm – 8pm and you have two glasses of wine in that time, i.e., you finish drinking by 8pm, then by 10pm – if that's your bedtime, you should be okay. If, on the other hand, you are out and drinking until 11pm, the likelihood is that you would have had two or three drinks. You wouldn't be giving yourself enough time. Perhaps intersperse the drinks with water and take your time in drinking them if you are at a work function and feel obligated. Your first drink could be a vodka and soda, and then, the rest of the night they are all just soda with ice and lemon. No-one will be any the wiser. Or say that you're "in training" so are not drinking. People usually give you a pass on that one and don't press too hard. If they ask what you are training for – the answer I often give (and you can borrow) is… "life."

Caffeine - The Issue

Many people simply must have caffeine to function in the morning. When I decided to experiment dropping caffeine in 2011, it was because I recognised in myself that if I needed a dose of caffeine to get me going in the morning, then something was wrong elsewhere.

And while caffeine has its perks[‡‡], it can also be a major problem when it comes to sleep. Caffeine is one of these substances that people can build a tolerance to, so they need more and more of it to have similar effects.

Here's the rub when it comes to caffeine and what you need to know. Caffeine affects something called adenosine. Adenosine is a central nervous system neuromodulator. A simple way to think of this is that when we are up during the day our brains produce neural waste by-products because of activity in the brain. This is called adenosine. The adenosine would normally bind to certain receptor sites to allow neural activity to slow down. The interesting thing is this. Caffeine also fits into the receptor sites. As you consume caffeine, the caffeine will bind to the receptor sites tricking your body into thinking that it isn't tired, even though there is still all this by-product (adenosine) waiting to get in. And then more and more of it is produced with nowhere to go.

Am I telling you to give up caffeine? No. I'm also not telling you to start drinking it if you don't currently drink it. What I would say is understand the following. Caffeine has a half-life of between 3 – 8 hrs. This depends on the source of caffeine, how it's brewed, the type of bean and your own body. That means that it could take eight hours for half the amount of caffeine to be released from your system. The average cup of coffee might contain about 100 mg. That means that if you only have one cup of coffee the entire day, and that's at 2pm, there could still be 50 mg of caffeine in your system at 10pm. Or another way to look at it is like this. It's equivalent to drinking half a cup of coffee at 10pm at night – just before going to bed.

[‡‡] Used sparingly and with intelligence and intention, caffeine can be a performance enhancer that many professional sportspeople use. Used every day, three times a day, however, is another matter.

The reality is, that most people might drink two or three cups a day. They might drink into the afternoon. They might buy fancy coffees with even more caffeine in them (not to mention sugar too). Personally, I think it's best avoided, but if not, then here's a potential solution.

Caffeine - The Solution

Other than not to drink it then, or save it for times when you really want to perform athletically? Simple. Give yourself a *caffeine curfew*. Decide on how much you will drink a day and by which time you'll finish. I would suggest no later than 2pm, although 12pm would be even better. Switch to decaf in the afternoon (although this still has around 3 mg of caffeine in an average cup). Better still, drink herbal tea in the afternoon instead. You will still get that feeling of a hot drink without any of the caffeine. Note that green tea, jasmine tea (depending on whether it's pure jasmine flower tea or had the flower dry on top of black tea), matcha (a concentrated form of green tea) all have caffeine in them. They are not a definite 'no-go'. Green tea and matcha are considered health promoting[407]. Perhaps have them before 12pm though? And if you are reliant on caffeine to start your day then it's likely that there are other issues elsewhere that need addressing.

4. Weight

The Issue

I think most people are aware that if they are not an appropriate weight for their frame then they are likely to be at greater risk for a whole host of health issues. That should be a no-brainer.

Being an unhealthy weight can affect your sleep though. A study from Deakin University in Australia examined the cortisol (stress hormone) levels of participants after meals. What they noted was that in healthy weight people, after meals their cortisol levels increased by 5%. In overweight people, however, their cortisol levels increased by 51%[396]. You might remember that cortisol is not a bad hormone to have…in the morning. It will naturally rise to get you going. At night however, it's a different story. We need to reduce it. Anything that raises our cortisol levels is likely to affect our sleep. And as most people eat at night for dinner, it means that cortisol levels for overweight people will increase more than those of a healthy weight.

Additionally, if you are overweight, then you are more likely to suffer from sleep apnoea[408]. That is, the breath pausing for extended periods of time

315

overnight. In addition, it's often the case that a significantly overweight person will have hypertension which will cause more stress on the system[409].

The Solution

No easy way to say this, but if this is you, you must get your weight under control. The good news is that if you follow the advice in this book, that will happen. Eating real food, the *PANLO 80/20* approach, moving more, managing your stress and everything else in this book will help you reach your natural 'set point' for what weight range you should be in.

5.   Stress

The Issue

If there's one thing that is guaranteed to impact your sleep, it's stress. This can come in many forms and sizes. The mind might be racing about having to get up earlier than usual, or a presentation that needs to get done. It might be a difficult conversation that needs to happen, or that has happened. It might be noise pollution or light pollution causing stress. This rise in cortisol should be avoided when going to sleep.

The Solution

Depending on the cause of the stress, the solution will be different. If you are stressed because of financial worries, then it is unlikely to resolve until you make headway in resolving them. Here is some general advice. Focus on what you can control *in the moment*. Likely that isn't going to be too much. If there are thoughts circulating, write them down. Keep a book and pen by your bed so you can get them out of your head and onto paper.

I've already mentioned it but give yourself 90 minutes to unwind before bed. No news or stimuli. Find ways to relax. Music, a long bath, meditation, gentle yoga, hypnosis audios, Emotional Freedom Technique (EFT - also known as Tapping), massage, light stretching, focussed breathing.

Recognise what you can control in the situation and create a plan of action. You can't control most things, so why worry about that? This is one of my favourite quotes from the Dalai Lama.

> *"If a problem is fixable, if a situation is such that you can do something about it, then there is no need to worry. If it's not fixable, then there is no help in worrying. There is no benefit in worrying whatsoever."*
>
> *– Dalai Lama*

Or how I normally say it is like this:

> *"If there's something you're worried about, and there's something you can do about it – why worry? If there's something you're worried about, and there's nothing you can do about it – why worry? Either way, why worry?"*

Of course, if you suffer from chronic stress about something, you will need to address the root cause. Face the cause of the stress. That will be the only real remedy.

If you are struggling to get to sleep on account of stress, and writing things down hasn't helped, and you've been lying there for longer than 15 minutes or so, I would encourage you to get up. The longer you lie there, the stronger will become the association with not sleeping in bed. Better to get up, move a little and then try again later.

6. Exercise

The Issue

Exercise is great for you. When done appropriately for your ability. In terms of sleep, when done at the appropriate time of day. Granted, there are many factors that will dictate when you can exercise. From work commitments, family commitments, leisure commitments, cost, and other considerations. However, assuming that you can exercise whenever you like during the day, when would be the best time to exercise when it comes to sleeping?

Depending on the type of exercise and your goals, along with your body chemistry, different types of exercise will be most beneficial at different times of day. Research is a bit mixed for optimal times although some suggesting that strength and flexibility training is best done in the late afternoon. However, working out in the morning can be better to create more consistency as it's less likely that 'l.i.f.e.'[§§] gets in the way and stops your afternoon workout. Plus, you can work out in fasted states which personally I find to be more beneficial in terms of the effort I can put in, my mobility and more.

In terms of sleep though, if you work out a couple of hours before bed, your body temperature may become elevated depending on the intensity and type of exercise. Your body temperature needs to lower when it's time to sleep, so this could cause problems. In addition, intense exercise will raise your cortisol levels (stress hormones). Cortisol needs to be lower in the evening and higher in the morning.

A study from Appalachian State University[410] found that morning workouts are ideal if you want to sleep better. The researchers tracked the sleep patterns of participants at 7am, 1pm and 7pm. What they found was that 7am exercisers slept longer and deeper than the other two groups. In some cases, the morning exercisers had up to 75% more time in the restorative deep sleep stages.

Of course, if you leave for work at 6am, working out at 4am or 3am might not be the best thing either. Your body (circadian clock) is still in night-time hormone mode, although time of year (light) might affect this. It might be to adapt to an active commute instead. Or agreeing to a 2-hour lunch instead of one. Many employed people are contracted to work 9am – 5.30pm. At least, I was in many of my jobs. And yet people often arrive at work at 8 or 8.30am and then leave at 6, 7 or 8pm (or later). Personally, I would be happy to be contracted to work 9am – 5.30pm but start at 8.30am and work until 6pm with 2 hours off at lunch. Giving ample time for a workout, travel there and back, changing and eating. This will naturally depend on your relationship with your boss, the culture of the company and your reputation as an employee. It's worth considering though.

If you do work out in the evening (as I did several years ago), recognise that it could take five or six hours for your core temperature to drop down, and your cortisol levels.

[§§] L.I.F.E. = Little Inconsequential Futile Events

The Solution

Assuming that you can dictate when you exercise, do it earlier in the day. Now, my main exercise period is in the middle of the day, but I still do some rebounding, mobility and stretching in the morning. Occasionally, I will exercise in the evening if I've been presenting during the day. If I've just done an hour of Thai boxing, I tend to follow it up with an hour of yoga to down-regulate my 'stress' levels.

If you exercise in the evening, consider doing less 'stressful' exercises at that time. Or finish your shower with a cold shower and create a cooling environment. Practising some deep diaphragmatic breathing can help lower your cortisol levels as well.

Also, it might be worth re-examining your schedule and see if you can change things up a little. I was never a morning exerciser and then in 2009, I recognised that I wanted my evening's back and that I wouldn't have to change too much to exercise in the morning. So, I went back to that question of asking "how". How can I arrange things, so I can exercise in the morning? For me, the answer was to join group classes. Even to this day I find it more challenging to exercise to my full potential in the morning if I am just left to my own devices.

=========

SLEEP STRATEGIES

1. Morning Light

A good night's sleep starts the moment you wake up. We need light as an external indicator for our body to reset to a 24-hr circadian rhythm. Ideally get some natural sunlight for 15 – 20 minutes between 6am – 8.30am (without sunglasses or contact lenses). This will be dependent on where you are on the planet and the season that you're in. This is one that I struggle to achieve most days. In the summer, it's okay for me. I'll take a walk round the park first thing or open a window and get direct sunlight on me while I do a morning meditation. The challenge I have is working from home and with such an extensive morning ritual, I can often find that I don't even leave the house until 11am or later.

T - TRANQUILITY

Light Boxes

I mentioned it earlier, but in the winter of 2017, I got an S.A.D. light box[***]. These are very high lux[†††] lights. 10,000 lux in my case. They have been shown to be beneficial for mood in those people that suffer from the winter blues[411]. I recognised the importance of light from an intuitive standpoint when developing *The Leadership BEAT Model*[™]. And I have since seen growing evidence supporting the idea of needing light for optimal health, vitality, and energy. Hence it forms part of the ELEMENTS section - Fire.

I've used high lux light over many winters and can say that, subjectively, I've noticed a massive difference. I have increased alertness and energy in the mornings and sleep better. Of course, this is just a singular (n=1) experiment, but my experience echoes that of others.

I really recommend investigating these lights and consider buying one. Just having them on for 15 minutes while getting ready, exercising, eating breakfast or whatever you end up doing first thing in the morning, will help your circadian clock reset. If you walk to work, or cycle and are outside with the light for at least 15 – 20 minutes then you might be okay as you are. Even if it's a grey day. A bright sunny day could be 111,000 lux, but even a cloudy day is around 2,000 lux. Normal daylight could be considered around 10,000 lux but most offices are lit at around 250 lux, or thereabouts.

The bottom line is that we need light. And to re-set our body clocks and ensure we produce melatonin in the evening, we want to aim to get 15 – 20 minutes first thing in the morning. Waking up with a dawn simulation is also something to consider. By dawn simulation, I mean a daylight alarm clock. One that gradually wakes you up by simulating dawn with a bulb which gets brighter over 30 minutes. Those participants in one study published in the European Journal of Applied Physiology, reported better sleep quality. Ratings of alertness, cognitive performance, reaction time and physical exertion on a self-paced cycling protocol also increased[412].

[***] S.A.D. – Seasonal Affective Disorder
[†††] Lux is a measure of the number of lumens falling per square metre. I.e., 10,000 lux means that 10,000 lumens of light will be concentrated in an area of 1 m². A lumen is a measure of the total quantity of visible light emitted by a source.

2. Sleep Routine

Have you ever had young children? Or been around them? If you are a parent then you might recall that when you were putting your young children to bed, you didn't just pop them in bed, turn off the lights and say, "see you in the morning".

You would have bathed them, read them a story, dimmed the lights, and got them to chill out as much as possible. *And then what do a lot of adults do as their routine?* Have a glass of wine, have bright lights on, watch the 10 o'clock news (and all the 'joyful' night-time stories that might give you), look at their smartphones, check social media and then do their teeth, check their phones once again, turn the lights off – just one more check of the phone and then say... "Damn it, I can't seem to fall asleep!"

I would encourage you to adopt some form of night-time routine. No matter how short. As I mentioned before, if you can start 90 minutes before bed, even better. *What would you do for 90 minutes though?* Read a traditional book, talk to your other half, plan the following day, tidy up the house, do the dishes, empty the dishwasher, have a bath, listen to music. I don't know – *what did people do before becoming glued to TVs and devices?*

Even if you can't do 90 minutes (I don't always, either). Aim for 30 minutes. This can include time getting ready for bed. Dim the lights, do your teeth, write in your journal or gratitude log. Meditate or listen to some hypnosis audios.

I've detailed my evening routine in chapter 3.5 on rituals so you can use that as a starting point, look up other ones online and create something that works for you.

The key is to prepare for bed, rather than just jumping straight in. You may benefit from setting an alarm for bed to go to sleep, rather than waking up.

3. Magnesium Baths

I mentioned (in chapter 2.3) that magnesium is a mineral that we all need. And many people are deficient in it[413]. I use a magnesium spray each evening just before I climb into bed. It's great in aiding sleep, releasing tense muscles (and treating delayed onset muscle soreness – DOMS) and 600+ beneficial processes that it does for the body[227,414].

When time allows, or if I get up late that morning, and think that I won't sleep easily, or I'm injured, nothing beats a long soak in a bath with Epsom salts. Epsom salts are the same thing as magnesium salts or flakes. All you need do is pour a cup's worth of Epsom salts into a nice warm bath. Have the bathroom lit via candlelight and put on the most relaxing music you have.

I will warn you; you might end up feeling *really* tired. It's a good idea to do all the things you need to do prior to bed, *before* stepping into the bath. I brush my teeth, prep my bag, write in my gratitude log - all before getting in the bath. Usually when I get out of the bath, I'm so drowsy that I just climb into bed and fall straight asleep. I won't be inclined to meditate – perhaps a hypnosis audio track instead, so I can just lie down and drift off.

I found the first Epsom salt bath I ever took, to be the most powerful one. Perhaps as it was my first? I think the same dangers of failing asleep apply here – even more so, so go easy to begin with. If you feel comfortable, leave the door open (or unlocked) so someone can come and check on you. It's just worth a word of warning, as they can be very powerful.

4. Hide the Time

As part of the *'Nein, after nine'* approach I adopt – mentioned earlier in the electronics section of this chapter - I also hide the time at 9pm. Why? Well, what's the last thing (or one of the last things) that people do before turning in? Check the time. And then what. They say to themselves: "Oh, I've got to be up in six hours." Or: "I really shouldn't have watched that last episode of Game of Thrones. Now I've only got five hours of sleep left." Or whatever variation it is. The fact is, it's done now. There's nothing you can do. If you go to bed later than you really want, it's likely that there's a little cortisol hit that you will receive when you find out the time. If you are doing a 90-minute wind-down or similar, then you know that at 9pm (for example) you should start to wrap things up. This might be the time that your bedtime alarm is set for. On some phones you can even automatically turn the screen to greyscale or amber. Having it in greyscale makes apps seem less appealing, and amber, or removal of the blue light, will help with sleep too. Currently my phone automatically goes to grey at 9pm (until 9am, or first alarm), and I have an app called Twilight installed to remove the blue light from about 7pm.

Knowing the time typically stresses most people out. Even if they don't realise it. I don't have any clocks in my house for this reason. I have a small wristwatch that rests on its side in my kitchen and at 9pm I turn it to face away from me. If I'm on the computer late or using the TV to watch something, I still don't see the time. I trained myself not to look at it. If I need to check my phone – for example to play some meditation music, or ensure alarms are set, then I use a small piece of tape to cover the corner of the phone with the time on it, so I don't accidentally see the time. If I have no tape (which is usually stuck onto the phone cover during the day) then I quite literally put my finger over the notification bar at the top, so I don't see the time.

I'm strict about this. Even when I'm out at an event, and I *know* that it is late because the event itself didn't finish until 10.30pm. I do my best to ignore the time at the station platform and in my head at least, it's still 10.30pm. Though it might be midnight.

So, the truth is that I don't know exactly *when* I go to bed[‡‡‡]. I estimate that most days it's around 10.30pm. It could sometimes be as late as 11.30pm or 12am. Or as early as 10pm. Either way, there's no need to know. I will be

---

[‡‡‡] In March 2019, I bought an Oura ring (a sleep tracking device), so now the next morning I can see more accurately when I went to bed.

getting up at the same time. If it comes to 6am and I'm really feeling I need more sleep, I sleep in. Normally I'll wake after one more 90-minute cycle at 7.30am and then get up. That could be the case whether I went to bed at 10.30pm or 12am. It really depends on how my body is feeling that day.

Ideally, we would get up at the same time each day (including weekends) and go to bed at similar times. If you had to choose one, then it's more important to have a fixed wake up time[415], and this is often the least flexible thing to move anyway.

This might sound crazy to you but give it a try for a week. See what difference it makes. You may find that you naturally want to get to bed earlier. Sometimes we just think we should go to bed at a certain time. What we really should be doing is living in harmony with our biology. Sleeping longer in the winter, less in the summer. Rising with the sun, winding down with the sun. Virtually no-one does this now, of course. To our detriment. If we can at least make strides in the right direction, even if we don't ever get back there, that's all we can really do.

5. No News

I also strongly encourage you to avoid the news before bed. Just before going to bed is not when you want to hear about the worst news of the world. Your sub-conscious mind is most susceptible just before going to bed (and immediately upon waking). The last thing you want just before going to bed, or waking up for that matter, is exposure to the news. If you must get the news in, I suggest getting it in, in the middle of the day. Perhaps curating the news for things that interest you or are relevant to your life or business. I personally haven't watched the news since 2011. I still check in three or four times a week online, but I don't watch it. Sure, I might get snippets here and there when waiting in a public space, but the key is not to turn on the radio or television and sit there watching it just before bed (or upon waking up).

I tell my audiences how your sub-conscious mind is a bit like a five-year-old. It can take things personally and get scared quite easily. *Would you allow a stranger to come into your living room at night and whisper into your 5-year-old son or daughter's ear about all the bad things in the world and then send*

324

them off to bed? I wouldn't have thought so. So why would you do it to yourself?

Trust me, you'll be better off without it. If you must get the news, do it, but not first or last thing in the day. Not 15 times a day either!

6. Meditation & Breathing

We'll explore meditation later in this section but adding some form of meditation practice to your day can help you with your sleep. Even if you do it in the morning. I personally started meditating at night (later I went to both morning and night on most days). What I found when I started meditating at night, just before bed, was that I was able to get to sleep quicker and I found my sleep felt deeper. Check out the simple techniques for meditation later in this part of the book on TRANQUILITY.

Even if you don't meditate, performing some simple breathing techniques can help. Taking deep breaths into the belly, and out again, especially if you exhale double the time of the inhale. This can stimulate your parasympathetic nervous system (rest & digest). This will reduce blood pressure, cortisol levels and heart rate and help you relax before bed[416,417]. There were some simple and effective techniques described in chapter 2.1 (Air) that I recommend you revisit.

Another breathing technique that I like before bed to calm the nervous system down is alternate nostril breathing[418]. The simple technique goes like this:

1. Cover one nostril with your thumb.
2. Breathe in through the open nostril.
3. Cover that nostril (with the ring finger of the same hand).
4. Release the thumb.
5. Breathe out through the (newly) open nostril.
6. Breathe in through the same nostril.
7. Re-cover the nostril with the thumb.
8. Release the ring finger covered nostril.
9. Breathe out through (newly) opened nostril.
10. Breathe in again through the same nostril.

Keep repeating that process for a few minutes. Five minutes or more is a good amount of time. It can be a great technique for calming down before bed[§§§].

Alternate nostril breathing has also been shown to affect either your sympathetic (fight/flight/freeze) nervous system or your parasympathetic (rest & digest) nervous system depending on which nostril you inhale through. Breathing through the right nostril activates heat and energy in the body in terms of the sympathetic nervous system. Breathing through the left, activates the parasympathetic nervous system[419].

7. Golden Hours

Something to be aware of is that the hours between 10pm – 2am are prime sleeping real estate. Exact timings might vary depending on the time of year and distance from equator. They say an hour before midnight is worth two after. And they're right. At least reviewing over six years of my sleep data suggests this is correct. Our body clocks work on the natural light/dark cycle and our melatonin (the sleep hormone in essence) will reach its peak a few hours after sunset. Typically, between 9pm – 11pm. Later for teenagers though[420]. As this happens, some deep restorative and repair processes will start in your body. If you're not heading to sleep, you might find that you receive a "second wind" and have energy again, when earlier you were tired. All that restorative energy is being wasted in keeping you up, rather than repairing you.

If you are currently aware of your sleep time and it's quite late, then start scaling it back by 15 minutes a week until you're closer to 10pm. You might also have to adjust your wake time (moving that back) to ensure you're tired enough by the evening. Of course, if your wake time is already 6am but you are going to bed at 12am or 1am, then you'll still need to keep the same wake time, and you may well find that you needed that extra sleep all along.

[§§§] As a side note, this technique is purported to increase the thickness between the connections from the left hemisphere of the brain to the right. The basal ganglia. I've never been able to corroborate this with any science-backed research so am not stating it as fact but thought it interesting. Especially, as when researchers investigated Einstein's brain to find out what made him so smart, they noticed something peculiar. His brain wasn't larger, nor did it have more connections than you might expect. What was unique though was the thickness and strength of the basal ganglia joining both hemispheres. That was (possibly) why he was able to be both quite logical and creative at the same time and re-define how we view the universe and laws of nature.

You might be thinking to yourself that if you go to bed that early then you won't have time to do much of anything in the evening. Maybe? Or take an inventory of where that time is going? You might find that watching TV can wait until the weekend. The 30 minutes of social media can wait until lunchtime the next day. Or whatever else it is. Let's say that you come home at 9pm, and by the time you eat and sit down it's 10pm. You want to watch a little TV and then go to bed. Does that 'little' TV mean 20 minutes, or does it end up being an hour? Can you do something else to unwind? Knowing that watching TV or using the internet will stimulate your brain and not prepare it well for bed.

I know it's challenging. I find it challenging too. Sometimes I'm better at these principles than at other times. This book is about giving you options though. Tools for your toolbelt. It's up to *you*, which ones you choose to use.

========

Owls and Larks

There are of course differences among people. Some are naturally 'larks' and like to get up early. Some are 'owls' and do their best work later in the evening. Most of us are somewhere in between. I suspect though, that even if you are an owl, you are being kept up later because of modern life. Whereas if we all lived in harmony with our natural rhythms it might be that the larks would be asleep by 9pm whereas the owls by 11pm. Not necessarily 2am, 3am or later. If you were on an island, or camping in the countryside, with no phone or distractions and you were able to go to bed when tired and wake up when refreshed, would it be the same?

In fact, Dr Michael Breus, the author of *The Power of When*, categorises four groups. Bears, Wolfs, Lions and Dolphins. With 50% of the population matching Bears – people with traditional sleeping patterns, and who feel more productive mid-morning. Wolfs (night owls) are about 15-20% of people, and most productive in the late afternoon and evening. Lions are early birds and account for 15-20% of people. Their peak productivity is morning until noon. Finally, Dolphins, who are light sleepers, and their productivity is best mid-morning to afternoon. About 10% of people fit into this category. According to Dr Breus, the category you fall into is dictated by your genetics so you might not have a choice in the matter really. I think many people are kidding themselves that they are natural late sleepers, when they then walk around tired all day long. Something doesn't seem right there?

N.A.P.'s – Non-Activity Periods

It could be a recent phenomenon to sleep in one big chunk[421]. And in some countries, like Spain, Italy, Greece and others, the idea of a siesta is still very much present. Although for how long, I don't know****? There seems to be evidence from historic notes[422] and looking at modern day hunter-gatherers that sleeping in two chunks – bi-phasic sleeping might have been the norm. Some suggest it might have been polyphasic with a main portion at night but then one or two smaller ones in the afternoon and early evening. The advent of street lighting (from candles) in the 17th century seems to have meant more night-time activities and less of the historical sleeping patterns.

Whatever it once was is interesting, but not necessarily important to me. The fact will be yours to determine. Do you feel good with a short sleep at some point during the day or early evening?

Some companies are seeing the benefit in providing places for employees to sleep or take some rest in the working day. A short N.A.P. – non-activity period, as I call it, can increase focus, creativity, productivity, and mood for the rest of the day[423]. And more besides. These N.A.P.'s don't have to be sleep. If you're able to, then great. A 20 – 30-minute sleep is great. If you can get a full 90-minute cycle - even better. If you wake somewhere in-between you might feel quite groggy on waking, although that will pass. It's usually recommended to get a short 20-minute sleep which will give you great benefits but not feel too groggy.

Other alternatives included within the idea of N.A.P.'s, is anything that chills you out. It could be lying down but not sleeping. It could be a bit of meditation or focussed breathing. Some guided hypnosis, yoga nidra or a walk in the park. Whatever will recharge you a little.

If your work permits you, try to experiment with N.A.P.'s. I don't often feel the need to sleep unless I've been presenting all day and then must work in the evening too. Or if I've gotten up early to teach, and haven't had the best night's sleep, then I'll sneak in a quick 30 minutes at some point if I can. I find however, that if I am to sleep, then it's best to do it before 3pm. Anything later and I find it more challenging to fall asleep at my usual time. In the case when I do sleep later – say at 5pm for 30 minutes, then I might employ the

---

**** It seems to be a dwindling practice to have a siesta even in those countries now too. Especially among young professionals.

above strategy of a magnesium (Epsom) salt bath to jumpstart my sleepiness that evening.

========

WAKING STRATEGIES

As reluctant as we sometimes are to go to bed in the evenings, we might be doubly reluctant to wake up the next day. Perhaps on account of going to bed too late, or not getting a decent sleep in? Here are some simple strategies that I have employed (or still employ) to help me wake up on time and not snooze[††††]. At least not too often![‡‡‡‡]

1. Opportunity Clock Placement

The late great motivational speaker, Zig Ziglar, liked to call alarm clocks, 'opportunity' clocks. And I quite like that too. 'Alarm' clock sounds quite dramatic, doesn't it? When we think of alarm – it's about stress, right? Whereas a new day is coming when we wake and it's a new opportunity to do something great in the world.

A simple strategy I still use is to have my opportunity clock away from my bed. So that I must get up if I don't want to continue hearing the sound. In fact, I saw on a crowdfunding site a while back, a new 'opportunity' clock that will only turn off when you stand on a special mat for 30 seconds. The idea here is to force you to get up out of bed and not snooze.

2. Opportunity Clock Music

We now have a benefit that we didn't have in the 1980's. We can *choose* the kind of music or sounds we wake up to. It doesn't have to be a buzzing sound or the radio. We can wake up to classical music, a motivational speech, a dance number or one of my favourites right now – *Come Alive* from *The Greatest Showman* soundtrack. You can have different soundtracks for different times of the year, or even time of the day. I sometimes have a morning alarm to remind me to leave the house too. And you don't need to use your mobile phone for this either. Some alarm/opportunity clocks have

---

[††††] When we snooze, we do ourselves a disservice as we enter back into fragmented sleep usually.
[‡‡‡‡] It should also be said, that if you can wake up on time without an 'alarm' clock, then even better. That's ideally how it should be. It will generally mean you've rested enough.

ability to add an SD card with your own mp3 music on, or like me, you might choose to have a separate phone loaded with music.

3. Voices

We all hear voices in our heads (no, you're not crazy). They tell us things like "just stay five more minutes in bed. Come on, you deserve it." Or "if we skip breakfast and don't bother washing our hair then we can get an extra 45 minutes in bed." Or "you don't need to bother with the gym this morning, just skip lunch to compensate."

Or something similar.

The thing is, when we recognise and acknowledge that these things will come up for us, we can do something about them. Especially as the excuses tend to be very similar day-to-day. We can create a new statement, and new voice in our head that counteracts that other voice.

Recognise the next time that voice appears – *where does it seem to come from? Is in inside your head, or does it appear from outside? From the left, or right? Front or back? Is it your voice? Or someone else's?*

If you find that the voice is coming from the right, 'instil' a voice that comes from the left. A voice of you in your best most motivating way. Or the sound of someone famous. Like Dwayne "The Rock" Johnson. *Do you know what he sounds like? Can you hear his voice in your head now?*

This is a little technique adapted from the idea of sub-modalities from Neuro Linguistic Programming (NLP). A modality is a main way of experiencing the world though one of the five senses (or modes) – visual, auditory, kinaesthetic, olfactory, and gustatory. A *sub*-modality is a more specific subset. For example, pitch, loudness, and distance away from you could be sub-modalities of an auditory modality.

By moving that voice further away, or turning down the volume dial on it, it can reduce its power. Also introducing a new empowering voice supporting you, for example from a celebrity you admire, can change how your inner voice comes across to you. There's a video on the "Sleep Solutions" playlist on my YouTube channel that talks about this. Head to **https://thethoughtgym.com/supervitality** for more.

4. Visualisation

Normally when we go to bed and think about getting up in the morning, or when we just think about waking up, we can picture something in our head. It might be the struggle of getting up in the morning, checking our phone or something else. The point is, that we have created a picture in our head. To use visualisation for our benefit though we could deliberately visualise the kind of morning we do want when waking up.

Take some time (1-2 minutes) just before going to bed to sit on your bed and just see yourself waking up the next morning. See yourself waking up two minutes before your alarm clock. Waking full of energy and getting straight out of bed. Ignoring snooze, ignoring the phone and going straight into your morning routine.

Continuing to do that day after day, will eventually result in that being how you wake up. For some people, it happens the first time they visualise it, so get visualising!

=========

Sleeping in Cycles

You've no doubt heard that you need eight hours of sleep a night. Strictly speaking, that's not exactly true (it depends on the individual and other factors). However, almost every adult needs somewhere between seven and nine hours a night. With significant, and serious, consequences for getting less than that[391].

We also sleep in cycles of roughly 90 minutes. The way that elite sports coach Nick Littlehales gets his athletes to think of sleep is in terms of cycles per week, rather than hours per night. For example, for me personally, I feel I operate best on 7.5 hours of sleep a night, or five cycles. This amounts to 35 cycles per week.

These five cycles need not be all in one overnight section but can be in the day as well. Littlehales does suggest, and I feel it to be true as well, that a daytime cycle can be shorter than 90 minutes and still get the benefits. For example, you might have four cycles overnight but have had a 30-minute cycle (equivalent to the 90-minute overnight one) during the day. It also allows for cycles to be thought of in terms how many you get per week, he suggests. So that if you do get only three or four one night, you catch up later in the week with more cycles. In practice, I'm not sure how well this works for me beyond a night or two, but it's an interesting approach that can help relieve the stress of missing a cycle here or there.

Here's another key thing with sleeping in cycles, according to Littlehales. If you miss your entry point, then you must jump into bed on the next one. For example, most people will have a set wake up time (at least during the week, and as the body needs consistency it's best to maintain it at the weekend too). Let's say that's 6am. If you have typical 90-minute cycles, and you require five cycles per night, it means being asleep by 10.30pm. If you come home at 11pm, then this approach, from Littlehales, requires that you remain up until 12am, missing one complete cycle and jumping in later.

This doesn't really work for me, because I follow a 'nein, after nine' philosophy and hide the time after 9pm most nights. I think it can make sense, but how easy is it to come in at 12.05 having missed two entry points and staying up until 1.30am on a weeknight and then getting up at 6am. I for one, wouldn't even know the time in that scenario, so would just go to bed when I get in.

Still, I wanted to include this idea of counting cycles as another option for you, as a busy person, to use in your sleep toolbox.

==========

SUPPLEMENTS

What about supplements when it comes to improving sleep? Yes, they can help, but I believe that they should be a supplement only. By that I mean, that you've done everything else right in terms of screen time, lights, stress management, alcohol, and everything else we explore in this chapter.

I don't think that they work particularly well if you're not doing the other things right.

That being said, let's look at a few.

1.   Magnesium

I mentioned magnesium above when it was about baths, but I do like magnesium as a supplement too. I use it every night by way of a spray that I put on topically. Typically, 10-20 sprays. It's great as a muscle relaxant and helping with sleep, and I've been using it each night since 2013. Many people are deficient in this all-important mineral and so supplementation should be something that you consider.

2. Camomile

Often taken as a tea, this daisy-like plant (herb) can be a great cup of something hot before bed. I just wouldn't take camomile when you want to be alert. I do sometimes take it in the middle of the day to relax a little though.

3. Valerian Root

Valerian root is an herb native to Europe and parts of Asia and grows in North America. I often take a 'bedtime' tea from a tea company that is a blend of different herbs for inducing sleep, which includes valerian root. It contains fennel, chamomile flowers, peppermint, cardamom, lemon balm, lemon grass, valerian root, sage, lavender flowers, nutmeg. I find it's helpful for relaxing prior to sleep. I do tend to re-use the bag a few times the same evening, so I get the most out of it.

4. Ashwagandha

Ashwagandha is a herb which is classed as an adaptogen (which means it helps the body's adrenal system regulate hormones and helps the body cope with stress). It supports healthy sleep by rejuvenating the body and addressing stress related exhaustion. I like drinking an Ashwagandha and turmeric tea.

5. Kava

When I left university in 1999, I went travelling for over two years before coming back to London and seeing my family again. On my travels in 2001, I went to the South Pacific Island of Fiji, where I took part in a Kava ceremony. Kava (or Kava-Kava as I knew it), is a crop of the Western Pacific. It means 'bitter' in Tongan. The roots are brewed to make a very sedative drink. I didn't realise this at the time, as we all took part in the ceremony. We were all seated or lying down in a big circle, taking it in turns to drink from the Kava bowl§§§§. I did find myself getting incredibly tired and retreating to my bungalow next door.

---

§§§§ And coincidentally, my family had the exact same style of bowl at home for many years prior to this, which we use as a fruit bowl.

I've not had it since, but if you need something to help induce sleep, this could be it (minus the ceremony). And even long-term use doesn't seem to show a decrease in cognitive function, just mentally relaxed like having a glass of wine (but mentally clear)[424].

As with everything in this book though, do not construe this as medical advice, and there may be some side effects or negative consequences to taking Kava (or any herbal supplement), so do further research if this interests you. I am just highlighting some of the solutions out there for you.

6. Melatonin

I don't personally recommend relying on this long term. Still, worth putting in here as I'm often asked about it, and you might want to explore it. Exogenous melatonin means taking in something the body should be producing on its own – in this case melatonin – and then putting it into you. It's not to be taken lightly and from what I've learnt about it, although taking it might not stop your body producing melatonin, it does apparently reduce the body's ability to use the melatonin it does produce. I think the evidence is a bit contradictory in this area, but at the end of the day, it's not what the body is expecting.

Short-term use to reset the body clock (when crossing multiple time-zones, which is the only time that I've used it, and only for the first couple of nights) might be an option to get you back to local time. However, I would first start doing things such as setting your clock to the destination time as soon as getting on the plane, get into the destination routine on the flight, getting natural light when you arrive, grounding yourself, eating when it's the local time to, staying up if arriving in the morning and it's really your evening, or not even adjusting at all if you are going home again in a day or two. And according to Matthew Walker, author of *Why We Sleep*, unless you are in your senior years of life, the efficacy of habitual melatonin use is coming from the placebo***** effect rather than the actual substance[391].

———————

***** The placebo effect (in medicine) is when an inert substance is taken (or one showing no objective effect) but the patient still derives the reported benefits purely down to their mind and the belief that it is doing them some good.

Bedroom

We also need to have a word about your actual sleep environment. The key point I'd like to make here is that the room that you sleep in should only be used for sleep, and...sex. That's about it. That means that you shouldn't do work in there, you shouldn't eat or watch TV. No arguments with your other half. Nothing but sleep and sex. Why? Otherwise, you may get mixed associations with that room. The bedroom should be a sleep sanctuary for you and nothing else.

Building on from the idea of your bedroom being a sleep sanctuary, it also makes sense to remove clutter and untidiness from your bedroom. When you sleep, you want to be able to create a clear and uncluttered mind. Not as easy to do if you are surrounded by clutter yourself.

Basic Sleep Hygiene Tips

There are several things that you can do to improve your sleep - basic sleep hygiene and here are some for you to consider:

1. **Sleep and Wake Time:** Your body needs to have a regular sleep and wake time to keep the circadian rhythm in check. Ideally wake up the same time every day (even on weekends) and if possible, go to bed at the same time. Irregular sleep patterns cause bacterial dysbiosis in the gut, that can lead to metabolic disorders[425].

2. **Dark Space:** Create as dark a space as possible. Our bodies are reset by the light/dark cycle so use this to your advantage. Install black-out blinds or curtains and consider eliminating all the light that gets around the edges too. Consider using a sleep mask when you are not able to black-out the room. Realise though that sleeping with a sleep mask does not prevent photoreceptors on the rest of your body from being triggered, although the eyes are the most sensitive area. Also note that sleeping with a sleep mask might produce more 'sleep' in your eyes in the morning, due to lack of air circulation. I slept with something covering my eyes for over 20 years and always suffered with 'sleep' in the eye, never putting the two things together. When I weened myself off using a sleep 'mask'[†††††] the 'sleep' accumulation started to disappear too.

[†††††] Most of the time I used a t-shirt to cover my eyes, rather than a purpose-built eye mask.

335

3. **Go to Bed Alarm:** Set an alarm to signal the time you should start going to bed. This is like waking up, but in this case, it's designed to get you start getting ready for bed. This might tie in with the *'nein, after nine'* philosophy?

4. **Chill-Out Routine:** Create an evening chill-out routine that you can do when your bedtime alarm goes off. This can include things like reading a book, getting your bag ready, tidying up, washing up, chatting with people you live with, running a (magnesium) bath, doing some light stretching or restorative yoga, meditation, hypnosis or focussed breathing techniques.

5. **Electronic Exit:** Turn off all electronic stimuli before bed. Ideally 90 minutes, but a minimum of 30 minutes. *'Nein, after nine'*, or *'Nein, for ninety.'*

6. **Eliminate Distractions:** Anything that isn't there to promote sleep, remove from your bedroom. This includes televisions, mobile phones, other gadgets and tech, work papers and more.

7. **No Time:** Avoid looking at the time past a certain hour in the evening – say at the beginning of your evening routine, which might be a full 90 minutes before bed. E.g., if aiming to be asleep by 10.30pm, avoid looking at the time after 9pm. *'Nein, after nine'*. I personally don't have any clocks in the house and use a wristwatch on a shelf that I turn to face away from me at 9pm. I also turn off the clocks on my laptop and PC around that time (if I am using them), so I don't inadvertently look at the time. When I use my phone after 9pm, I cover the notification bar with my finger or piece of black tape I have stuck to my phone cover.

8. **Magnesium:** Either run a magnesium (Epsom) salt bath and/or spray magnesium spray onto you topically (directly onto the skin). This mineral, which is needed for over 600 enzymatic reactions in the body[227,414], also helps to relax muscles, ease tension, and induce sleep.

9. **Silent Night:** Aim to sleep in as much a quiet environment as possible, as any noise can affect sleep negatively. If you can, keep the windows double-glazed and closed if you hear street traffic. Consider the use of ear plugs too.

10. **Listen Up:** Consider using sound to your advantage though. In contrast to random noise which you can't predict and affects your sleep negatively, sounds that are sleep inducing for many people could be white noise, meditative sounds or yoga music tracks. Also using hypnosis audios (provided they don't bring you out of the hypnosis at the end) can also be used for sleeping. I sometimes use meditation sounds and sometimes a hypnosis audio (which I have edited to remove the last 30 seconds which takes people out of the trance. That way I can just drift straight off to sleep).

11. **Room Temperature:** Keep the room cooler than you would normally have. Our body temperature drops overnight, and we need a cooler room to sleep in. Around 16 - 18 degrees Celsius (or 60 - 65 Fahrenheit) is recommended, but even around 20 is good for me. You want it to feel like you can't wait to jump under the covers.

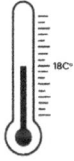

12. **Eating Time:** Give yourself ample time from your last meal to going to bed, if possible. The average eating time for dinner has gotten later from 5pm to 8pm in the UK in recent decades[391]. Ideally you shouldn't go to bed too hungry or too full. Your body clock also starts its night-time shut down processes in the early evening, so eating earlier will be better. For example, it's recently been discovered that all cells in the body have their own body clock, and the liver starts to shut down around 6pm[426]. Aim for three hours from finishing your meal to hitting the sack. Going to bed at 10.30pm, you want to finish by 7.30pm. Of course, this will be highly individualised and dependant on whether you are practicing intermittent fasting, exercising, or working at night and many other factors.

13. **Writing:** Consider keeping a journal or writing pad near the bed. You can do a traditional journal where you write down thoughts about the day and reflections about what happened. You can also use it to write down whatever is floating around in your head late at night keeping you awake. Problems, ideas – whatever. Getting it out of your head and on to paper will help free up space in your head and give you the comfort that you won't forget about the idea you have. Or if it's a problem (or several) you are musing over, by writing them down it can often help gain clarity. Or to see that the problem isn't so big or find the next step in the solution. Also, consider writing out

your next day's "to-do" list the night before, or as the last thing you do in the working day.

14. **Massage:** If you're able to convince someone to do so, a nice massage or foot rub before bed can help the slumber to arrive sooner. Of course, you might have to reciprocate another night!

15. **Covers:** Make sure that your bedding is appropriate for the season you're in. In the winter you might want a heavier tog rating duvet (or more blankets), and in the summer it might be a lighter tog or just a sleeping sheet. I have a gravity blanket (also known as a weighted blanket) that is 9kg. Originally gravity blankets were developed to help autistic children, but I, and others, have found benefit in using them for better sleep. I love my gravity blanket and don't (objectively) sleep nearly as well as when I don't have it.

16. **Pillows:** I've experimented many times over the years with pillows. It's worth spending time getting one that makes you feel comfortable. Ideally the pillow should allow (when you are lying on your side on the mattress) for your neck and spine to stay level. Don't be fooled by all these orthopaedic expensive ones, just trial and experimentation will tell you.

17. **Mattress:** We spend a third of our lives on our mattresses, yet many people often spend more time deciding on clothes, cars, and other consumables rather than getting the best mattress for them. Again, just because something says orthopaedic on it, doesn't make it good. And again, a mattress that allows your spine to stay neutral when on your side is going to be best according to Nick Littlehales, author of *Sleep*. What I would watch out for is whether the mattress has nasty components in it like formaldehyde (which many, if not most mattresses have), as it is highly toxic systemic poison that is absorbed well by inhalation, and can cause irritations of the throat, lungs, eyes, and ears. Unfortunately, there are many components that go into mattresses that can cause 'off-gassing' including toxic flame retardants and more. See if you can get a complete list of what is made to make up your mattress and spend a bit of time researching (much harder than you might think actually). It might be time consuming, but likelihood is that you will only need to do it once every ten years.

18. **Exercise Regularly:** Studies show that exercising can help with sleep and experientially I'm sure that you already know this. It does matter at what time you exercise though, so earlier in the day will be

better, followed by mid-day/mid-afternoon. Late into the evening is not best for intense workouts but something more restorative will be fine. Of course, if it's a case of evening or nothing, it is better to go for evening exercise and give time for the body to cool down and cortisol to drop. Perhaps including something like meditation in the evening will help reduce your cortisol levels too.

19. **Avoid Alcohol:** It might help you fall asleep, but really, it's a sedative. You'll not get proper sleep; you'll have less REM sleep, and it will be more fragmented. Avoid it if possible and give yourself at least one hour per unit drunk, if you chose to drink it.

20. **No Smoking or Nicotine:** Nicotine is a known stimulant, and smokers tend to sleep lighter and wake up earlier due to nicotine withdrawal. If you are reading this book and looking to unlock your inner superhuman, then I really shouldn't need to convince you of this one. If you are a smoker though, check out resources like Allan Carr's *Easy Way to Stop Smoking* (books and courses), consider going to a hypnotherapist or other therapist for help. For example, a therapist experienced in Cognitive Behavioural Therapist (CBT), Neuro Linguistic Programming (NLP) or Emotional Freedom Technique (EFT) could be a good start.

21. **Caffeine Curfew:** Decide upon a caffeine curfew, say 2pm, after which you won't have any caffeine. Remember that decaffeinated drinks also still have caffeine in them (albeit small amounts).

22. **Sheets:** Invest in some quality sheets. They do make a difference. I used to have Egyptian cotton (get the best thread you can), but now I use bamboo sheets and/or grounding sheets. They are amazing[‡‡‡‡‡].

23. **Blue Light:** Minimise night-time lighting and if you can use devices that block out blue light such as f.lux, Twilight, Nightshift, and blue-blocking sunglasses. Use candles (if you are happy to) or dim low-level lights. If you can buy any lights that automatically have blue light stripped from them, then purchase those for the evenings.

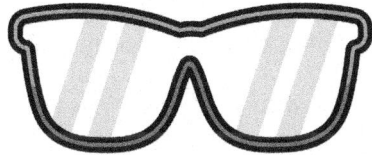

[‡‡‡‡‡] I only use the bamboo sheet for a duvet cover, as my base sheet is a special 'grounding' sheet. Check the chapter on 'Earth' for information on 'grounding'.

24. **Morning Light:** Get yourself exposed to light first thing in the morning for 20 – 30 minutes (consider using an S.A.D. lamp – especially in the winter). Aim to get another 30 minutes during the day too. Exposure to sunlight is a key component of sleeping well and good sleep hygiene.

25. **Breathing Technique:** Spend some time before going to bed doing some releasing breaths described in chapter 2.1 (Air).

Quick summary about sleep and becoming superhuman...

1. Sleep is the foundation on which other aspects of health are built, and we're getting less of it and worse quality now. A lack of sleep is associated with countless health issues and affects every part of our body.

2. Although we live un-natural lives, away from our biological rhythms and evolution, there are things we can do to minimise the negative effects of this kind of living. From light management and stress management to supplementation, exercise, and good sleep hygiene practices.

3. Everyone (except for 1 in 12,000 people[§§§§§]) needs between seven and nine hours of sleep over a 24-hour period. Alternatively, 35 cycles per week is another way to view sleep requirements. Most overnight sleep cycles are 90-minutes long and we have three main stages of sleep – light, deep and REM. Sleep prior to midnight is super crucial.

Action plan for becoming superhuman...

1. Make sleep a priority in your life starting tonight. Go to bed 30 minutes earlier tonight than you normally would.

2. Decide on one sleep hygiene tip that you can implement this week and commit to it for the next ten days.

3. Create a simple sleep routine for yourself. Slowly start adding more of the sleep tips over the next month

---

[§§§§§] According to sleep scientist Matthew Walker, in his book *Why We Sleep*, 1 in 12,000 people have the BSBB variant gene which means they can still thrive on less than seven hours sleep. To put it in context though, you are just as likely to be hit by lightning in your lifetime as to carry that gene.

4.2 Meditation

Meditation, not medication…

"Half an hour's meditation each day is essential, except when you are busy. Then a full hour is needed."

- Saint Francis de Sales

Meditation. It's been getting a lot of press the last few years. And rightly so. This ancient practice has only recently (in the last 50 years or so) been adopted and examined by people in the West in any large numbers. And compared to today the last five or ten years it's really exploded. No longer do executives and other professionals 'hide' their meditation practice. There are apps worth hundreds of millions of dollars teaching meditation. It seems that everyone is now at it. It's not a panacea of course, but there are many reported benefits to practicing meditation. Even for just a few minutes a day.

Health Benefits to Meditation

The health benefits to meditation include, but are not limited to:

- Decreased blood pressure[427].
- Reduced cortisol levels[427].
- Boosts the immune system[428].
- Reduces chronic inflammation[429].
- Improving anxiety[429].
- Helping with asthma[430].
- Combatting depression[431].
- Helping with heart disease[432].
- Reducing pain[433].
- Releasing tension headaches[434].
- Helping with reducing cancer effects[435].

- Increasing self-awareness[436].
- Improved attention and psychological well-being[437].
- Improving emotional processing[438].
- Increasing patience and tolerance[439].
- Increasing telomere[*] length and potentially increasing your life[440†].
- Reduce 'mental fuzziness' or 'chemo brain' in cancer patients[441].
- Increases neuroplasticity[‡] in the brain[442].

What is Meditation?

In the spirit of keeping things simple, meditation is effectively a practice whereby you train your attention onto one thing and set aside a specific time to do it. There is lots of varying descriptions of what meditation is and what mindfulness is. Meditation is a tool that can be used to access a state of extreme rejuvenation and calm. It's not sleeping, dreaming or being awake. It's a higher (and different) level of consciousness[§].

Yes, meditation (at least how I consider it) is a form of mindfulness (see next chapter for more on mindfulness). Some people consider doing activities meditation, like running or swimming. I would usually put that more in the mindfulness camp. Mindfulness is paying attention to what's happening in the present moment and can be anything from when you are buttoning your shirt or washing the dishes to sitting and focussing on your breath or sensations in the body. Mindfulness can also be done while doing other things (e.g., the

---

[*] Telomeres are protective caps as the end of your chromosomes. Like aglets at the end of shoelaces to stop them fraying. Each time a cell divides (as is normal) the telomeres get shorter. Telomerase is an enzyme used to build telomers and is produced when meditating regularly. Studies have shown that telomere length can increase, not simply decrease, as previously thought.

[†] Telomeres are one indication of ageing. There is a difference between someone's chronological age (i.e., how many years since they were born) and biological age (i.e., how old someone is biologically. E.g., if that person had total amnesia and no-one knew who they were, and someone was to assess their age). Biological ageing can be determined by a multitude of methods, including, but not limited to, telomere length, mitochondrial health, DNA methylation, reaction time, skin elasticity, bone strength, bone density, face

pigmentation, flexibility, body composition, aerobic capacity, blood glucose control, blood pressure, blood lipids, strength and muscle mass, cardiorespiratory fitness, as well as other biomarkers like c-reactive protein (CRP), total cholesterol, albumin, creatinine, hba1c (your average blood sugar), alkaline phosphatase, and urea nitrogen. So, your 'age' might be different from the one indicated on your passport. Perhaps insurance companies will be assessing you on your biological age, and not chronological age in future.

[‡] Neuroplasticity is the brain's ability to adapt and change – forming new neural pathways.

[§] And let's not even get into what consciousness is. Experts have written a plethora of books on consciousness and still not been able to accurately explain what it is.

dishes), or you can set aside time and practice a specific type of mindfulness (e.g., going through all your senses and observing what you can within each sense).

For me, I don't know if I consider activities a real form of meditation as you will inevitably need to focus on different things. For example, when running, yes, you might get into a meditative state, but you still need to be aware of traffic, the surface of the ground beneath you and so on. However, I'm not precious about this, as it's just semantics really. For what I describe in this chapter though, I am considering meditation a sub-set form of mindfulness whereby there is a singular focus on something like the breath, a mantra (short phrase you repeat), external object (such as candle) or internal focus (such as body sensations).

So, in short, meditation is any practice where you bring your attention to a singular point and keep coming back to that point when your mind wanders. It's something you set aside a specific time to do, and it can allow you to access different levels of consciousness and put your brain waves into a state that is not waking, sleeping, or dreaming.

MYTHS OF MEDITATION

There are many common misconceptions about meditation. Some of them are that:

1. One must sit cross-legged or in lotus position.
2. One must have no thoughts enter your mind.
3. One must sit for 20 minutes, or an hour.
4. One must do it every day or not at all.
5. It is for everyone.
6. It's about burying your head in the sand and avoiding life.
7. It's just for hippies.

Let's address each of these myths.

1.   You must sit cross-legged or in lotus position

You do not need to sit on a special cushion or in a special position. Any comfortable position will do, even if that means in a chair. That is totally fine. The only soft requirement is that your spine is straight, and you are upright. So that means you can sit in lotus if you wish, or cross legged, or in a chair or kneel. What about lying down?

Lying down is not necessarily encouraged for a couple of reasons really. Firstly, you'll be more likely to fall asleep and secondly, it's believed that the flow of energy in the body works best when the spine is upright. I will say something about this though. I sometimes do meditate this way. It can still serve to relax you, get you to focus and I don't see anything wrong with this if what you're looking for is to just chill out, or to fall asleep anyway – such as just before bed. Knock your socks off.

If you can get into the habit of sitting upright though, it's a good practice to get into. You can support your spine against a chair or wall as you get used to it.

2. You must have no thoughts enter your mind

People often tell me that they can't meditate because their minds are too busy. Well, that's the reason to get into it in the first place. The goal is *not* to have no thoughts. That's impossible. The goal is just really to notice these thoughts as they come into your mind, and then allow them to pass out again. Gradually you will increase the space between these thoughts from a couple of milliseconds to a few more milliseconds, and one day even a second or two. Even longer, perhaps.

When the thoughts come in, just imagine that they are like clouds in the sky passing by the screen of your mind. The key is not to get fixated on them, but just to bring your awareness back to something else. Whatever your 'anchor' is. Be that your breath, a candle, a mantra, or something else.

3. You must sit for 20 minutes, or an hour

Some meditation practices, for example Transcendental Meditation, do suggest sitting for two 20-minute periods each day. But you don't have to do that. There are many ways to meditate. When I started, I started without any guidance and simply spent a few seconds on it. Yes, just a few seconds. Before I went to bed I would sit on the pillow and count my breath (in my head) and when breathing in say "one" and then breathing out say "two", and so on until I hit the number ten. I did that for a few weeks and then went to the number 20. Eventually I set a timer for a few minutes. After about six months I went up to 15 minutes just before bed. Now I aim for 15 minutes first thing, and last thing each day.

4. You must do it every day or not at all

I don't always get around to it. Some days I do one session, or even no sessions. Yes, it's better to have a regular practice but something is better than nothing. You can even just go inside yourself (i.e., meditate) when on the underground/train, or even in the lift (elevator). I do these micro-meditations quite often in lifts. Don't get caught up with dogma and purists who say you should do it this way or that way. Yes, there are best practices, but some practice is better than no practice.

5. It's for Everyone, or is it?

I do believe that most people will benefit from meditation. However, some styles of meditation might not be appropriate for some people. If you suffer from schizophrenia for example, focusing on each body part as you scan your body (a type of meditation practice), might leave you worse off. I personally don't know anyone who has had a worse time by meditating but I believe that for a tiny percentage of the population, meditation isn't for them.

6. It's all about burying your head in the sand and avoiding life

If you think that, then you're a bit like my mother! She thinks that but I'm hoping this chapter will change her mind. In fact, meditation brings greater calm and clarity to challenges that you face so you can address them intelligently and with a balanced view. It's not in any way about avoiding your issues. Meditation helps build your resilience and allows you to deal with what life throws at you in a more robust way.

It might be that by meditating you don't get drawn into trivialities and gossip or drama, and so perhaps to some people that is ignoring issues and burying your head in the sand. Well, if that's the case, then so be it.

7. It's Just for Hippies

The 'hippy' generation of the 1960's, and spearheaded by *The Beatles*, made the West more aware of meditation, but you don't have to have long hair, be fighting for a cause or live in a cave to meditate. Many top-level CEOs meditate. Phil Jackson, one of the most successful basketball coaches in history winning six NBA Championship rings with the Chicago Bulls and five with the Los Angeles Lakers, is an avid Zen meditation practitioner and even introduced it to superstar NBA players like Michael Jordan, Kobe Bryant,

Scottie Pippen, and Dennis Rodman. If you think of hippies, you don't really think of 6'6'' macho basketball players earning millions of dollars, do you?

=========

HOW TO ACTUALLY MEDITATE

Anchors

A common approach to many types of meditation is to use an anchor, to bring your attention back when it starts to wander. Which it will. A lot. There are many things that can anchor you. Some of which I list below.

1. The Breath

This one is great as it's always with you. You can focus on many different aspects of the breath. From noticing the temperature as it enters the nostrils and out again (remember we want to breathe in through the nose and not through the mouth as we talked about in chapter 2.1). You may notice that the temperature is warmer on the way out than on the way in.

Another way to focus on the breath is just to notice as it comes in and out of the 'belly'. Notice the rise and fall of the belly. I often just assign a word, or two, to the inhale and exhale. Some of the common ones I use are:

Inhale	Exhale
One	*Two*
Three	*Four*
Re-	*lease*
Re-	*lax*
Let	*go*
I'm	*safe*

Any two words or syllables will do. You could also (as I did when I first started) count to ten. Each in and out breath being one number, and then repeating. I found that my mind starts to wander way before getting to the number ten though. Hence now only going to the number four.

This way of assigning words is sometimes called having a 'mantra'.

2. Mantras

A mantra[**] is just a word or phrase that is repeated. Just in your head – not out loud. At least not usually. This helps keep your focus on the phase or intention you want to set, but also the neural pathways in your brain which associate with that phrase will still be activated – whether you say it out loud or not. As well, as it's believed by some, the phrases can create a specific vibration. I wouldn't get caught up on all that though.

I personally only use the kind of mantra's I mentioned above (like "re-lease"). I don't use longer sentences although you can. For example:

- "I am calm, relaxed and in control."
- "I am happy and grateful."
- "I can handle what life offers me."

Other mantras might merely be sounds or Sanskrit[††] words. It can be a good idea to use something like this instead of words in your native language as it can really take you away from it all.

Here are some Sanskrit mantras in case you want to explore using these.

Mantra	Pronunciation	Translation	Why Say It
Om	A-U-M	Said to be the primordial sound of the universe. It's birth sound.	OM is said to vibrate at 432 Hertz, which is the natural musical pitch of the Universe. The vibrational sound of the Om is said to unblock the throat chakra, which it's said can lead to better

[**] In Sanskrit, "man" translates to mind, and "tra" means to free from. Mantras are used as a tool to free the mind.
[††] Sanskrit being the ancient India language associated with yoga and other practices from the East, like meditation.

			communication with others.
Om śāntiḥ śāntiḥ śāntiḥ	A-U-M Shan tea Shan tea Shan tea	Om Peace Peace Peace	Who doesn't want a bit more peace in their lives?
Lokah Samastah Sukhino Bhavantu	Lo-car sama-star sook-ee-noo bar-van-two	May this world be established with a sense of well-being and happiness.	This is a general chant for wellbeing and happiness.
Sacchidānanda	Sat Chit Anan-da	Existence, Consciousness, Bliss	A description for the subjective experience of the ultimate, unchanging reality.
So Hum	So Hum	I am	I like this one to remind me that this is the one constant. Our true selves. For example, you might say I am *angry*, I am *happy*, I am *a mother*, I am a *CEO*, I am *hurt*, I am *hungry*. The one constant. The non-changing is the *I am.*

Ong Namo Guru Dev Namo	Ong namor gurou dev namor	I bow to all that is. I bow to the Devine Wisdom within myself.	Reminding ourselves that all the wisdom we really need is within us. I like to chant along to a recording I have of singers singing this.

3. Candle

Another nice way to keep your focus on a single place is to use a candle. If you've ever found yourself staring for hours into a camp bonfire, then you will appreciate that there is something hypnotic about looking at flames. Assuming no big bonfire about, not to mention the fire risks, using a candle can be just as hypnotic.

I sometimes do use a candle but find that I can get quite tired with it and my eyes begin to close and I fall asleep. Not wanting to create a fire hazard (especially since usually this is in my bedroom at night when I'm heading to bed) I don't use it often. An alternative – although not as effective in my experience – is using a video of a candle. This means however that technology is present in your meditations. Or you can purchase a fake candle that flickers, like they often use in yoga studios.

4. Sensations

One more anchor you could experiment with is sensations in your body. This could be one area, or you could do a form of 'body scan'. Focussing on a particular area, then moving sequentially through the body.

When I went on my Vipassana meditation retreat this was the practice. Vipassana is a 10-day silent meditation retreat, with centres around the world. It works on a donation basis. After you have completed the retreat, if you want to, you can effectively 'pay-it-forward' to someone else. Giving what you can afford and want to offer.

The retreat is tough. You aren't allowed any talking, communication devices of any kind (yes, that's a no to mobile phones). No paper or pen even. No exercise or leaving the venue. Not even any eye contact with other people. It's weird sharing a room with others and not making any eye contact.

The reason behind this, is so the experience is yours and not influenced by external factors. On the retreat (although it's hardly what I imagine when I think of the word retreat), you wake at 4am. Start meditating at 4.30am until 6.30am. Then you have breakfast break until 8am. From 8am – 9am there is a group meditation at which point you are not supposed to move at all for one whole hour. Yes, no scratching, itching or anything for one hour. Then more mediation from 9am-11am. Then lunch and more of the same in the afternoon. All being told, you have three one-hour segments a day when you aren't supposed to move or fidget at all. In total there's about twelve hours of mediation a day.

It is intense. But very rewarding, if you can learn some lessons from it. The three main things it taught me – experientially and not intellectually – were:

1. **Life is transient.** All things come and go. Just like the seasons. Pain, pleasure, happiness, sadness, broken bones, health, ill-health, relationships – even the universe. There is an impermanence to life and our fixation with wanting things to stay as they are, is the root of many of our problems. Whenever I'm going through bad times (and good) – I remember that *"This too shall pass."* It's my main guiding mantra in life.
2. **Be the observer.** Just notice things and don't get attached. Sometimes when meditating you might get a particular pleasant sensation but just observe it. Don't get attached. Developing a craving towards it. Likewise, when there are negative feelings or emotions, just observe them. Don't get attached and drawn in. The aversion to them. Craving and aversion. Attachment. Just notice.
3. **See things as they are, not as you want them to be.** This might be difficult to grasp, especially if you are looking at the world and wanting to see it better. It doesn't mean that you can't imagine a better world or make moves to make it better. What it means is to get real about the situation you are in. When you acknowledge the truth about the situation, and whether there's anything you can do about it, you become able to make the changes or make peace with the way things are.

I know that some of these lessons might make sense to you intellectually, but through the process of the many hours of vipassana, they become experientially embedded into your psyche – or at least they did for me. Sitting for an hour and then noticing an itchy nose within the first five minutes of your one-hour static meditation can be excruciating. Then you decide to just be the observer. Not avert the feeling. Just observe. And then you notice that it passes. It's not there forever. And you didn't have to move to scratch it either. For me, the third lesson came from the fact that I ended up sitting next to someone for the whole ten days (in the group sittings) who had a bad cough (and it was annoying). I had to see the situation as it was. I wanted it to be nice and silent, but it wasn't. Real life isn't silent either. It won't go exactly the way you want it to either. For me, that person was my lesson. I had to learn how to see the situation as it was and continue.

It was the hardest experience of my life – and I've climbed Mount Kilimanjaro, run a marathon, reached Everest Base Camp, competed in triathlons, obtained a first-class degree, bungy jumped and jumped out of a perfectly good plane – twice! And Vipassana was harder than all those things.

There are many books out there that will teach and talk about meditation in more detail. Also courses and classes that you can go on. I do advise these, of course. However, don't wait to attend a course or read a book before you get started. Find a YouTube video or download an app that will teach you the basics. I knew less than what I've described in this chapter before I started. I just kept hearing about it from lots of successful people. So, like I said above, I just found a place that I could be quiet, sit upright and focus on noticing my breath while counting. That's it. That's really all you need to do. Perhaps use one of the mantras given. Check out the different types of styles and teachers to know more and go deeper, but in the beginning don't over-complicate it. Keep It Solution Simple (K.I.S.S.).

Quick summary about meditation and becoming superhuman...

1. Meditation is a practice whereby we direct our focus towards one singular point. The idea is not to have no thoughts, but just to release the thoughts and not get attached to them.

2. Meditation is far from being 'woo-woo' but has been backed up by thousands of studies (not to mention thousands of years of people using it) on its efficacy. Everything from reducing blood pressure, pain, and stress to increasing focus, happiness, and performance.

3. Although meditation forms part of some religions, it is not a religious practice. You can meditate without any religious inclinations whatsoever. And you don't need to sit cross legged in a cave or go to yoga either!

Action plan for becoming superhuman...

1. If you don't currently have a meditation practice, then simply start. Commit the next ten days to a practice of sitting comfortably, closing your eyes, and counting your breaths in and out. Inhale 1, exhale 2, inhale 3, exhale 4. Set a timer for a minute or two and simply start with this technique.

2. Consider looking into one of the many meditation apps or videos online and do a longer guided meditation.

3. Set aside two minutes in the middle of the working day to go somewhere quiet (a toilet cubicle is a good option) and do a mini meditation.

4.3 Mindfulness
Mindful, or mind full…

"What day is it?" asked Pooh.

"It's today," squeaked Piglet.

"My favourite day," said Pooh.

How does mindfulness differ from meditation and what is it all about? You may have heard about mindfulness and terms like MBSR (Mindfulness Based Stress Reduction). Mindfulness, in my view, is just present moment awareness. Meditation, again in my view, is a form of mindfulness. Some people might consider all sorts of activities meditation activities. Swimming, gardening, and walking for instance. I consider those more mindful practices when done with awareness to how you are functioning in the moment. Let's not get caught up on semantics though. If you want to blur the lines between the two, then that's fine. I do consider that in meditation it's a little more inwardly focussed – focussing on your breath, sensations or maybe some kind of visualisation. Yes, I did talk about the candle exercise, but really that candle is just hypnotising you into a relaxed and focussed state. Where mindfulness comes into play, is that you have awareness into activities that you are doing. And while you might do micro-meditations as I suggest, typically mindfulness can be short or long. Meditations are usually several minutes long.

What does all that mean? Many of us go through life very unconsciously. By that, I mean we are almost sleepwalking through the day. Not being aware of our emotions and often letting them run ragged.

Mindfulness practices are simply taking time to notice certain things about the activity you are doing. There are countless easy ways in which to start doing this. And the best bit is that you are doing the activities anyway, so it won't require any more time.

T - TRANQUILITY

Some of the reported proven benefits to mindfulness include reducing stress and anxiety, lowering blood pressure, becoming more resilient, enhanced emotional processing and coping regarding the effects of chronic illness and stress, improved self-efficacy and control, and a more differentiated picture of wellness in which stress and ailments play natural roles but still allow enjoyment of life as full and as rich[443].

Here are some ways in which you can start to incorporate more mindfulness to your life:

1. When **washing your hands** really pay attention to the process. The feel of the soap on your hands, the temperature of the water, how you move your hands over each other.

2. When **walking** down the street, just notice each step you take between a set of lamp posts (or other markers). You don't have to be mindful for your entire walk, but just part of it.

3. When you **brush your teeth**, just pay real close attention to the act, rather than thinking about work or whatever else usually would occupy your mind.

4. The next time you are stuck in traffic, rather than getting upset, **notice your breath** and count in and out up to 10. E.g., and-1, and-2, and-3. On each inhale you say "and" and on each exhale you say the number.

5. Look at the **palm of your hand** and just start to notice the lines, the bumps and then use the other hand to feel the texture of the hand.

6. Take a **barefoot walk** on the grass or sand and just notice the feeling beneath your feet.

7. Take one meal out a week where you are just **focussing on eating**. No phone, no conversation, no TV, no book. Nothing but chewing and noticing the food. Notice how the taste changes in the food as you chew more.

8. When you take a **sip of water** (which hopefully you'll be doing a lot now), just notice as the water goes down the throat. Is it cold or room temperature?

There are countless ways to incorporate mindfulness into your day. This is all well and good of course, but sometimes you might just forget. A good way to be more mindful is to introduce certain anchors or hooks to remind you.

One of the simple ways that I remember to be more patient, for example, is with my jacket zipper. I have this jacket that I really love – which is why I have had it for over 17 years. About nine years ago though the zipper broke.

Not entirely, just the bit that you hold on to. I could have, and probably should have, gotten it fixed sooner, but early on I decided to use it as a teaching tool for me. You see, it became a bit more intricate to operate. It took more time as I carefully had to perform the act of zipping and unzipping. If I was stressed, or tried to rush it, not only wouldn't it work, but (and this happened a few times) the zipper would get stuck and take me even more time to sort out. The reason I kept it as it is, is that it reminded me to be more patient. I kept it 'broken' for over six years before I got it fixed and now that sense of patience has been embedded into me when zipping up the jacket – even with the zipper fixed!

What reminders can you use? Each time you walk under a certain doorway perhaps taking a mindful moment. Or setting an alert on your phone. When I brush my teeth now, I use it as an opportunity to roll a foot-tension-releasing ball under my foot. I then get to notice the sensations underneath my foot while at the same time releasing tension along the foot and even leg.

The Power of the Pause

When I attended a *Practical Philosophy* course in London a few years ago, many of the ideas and concepts were already familiar to me, but one thing that I did really like and take away was this idea of the 'pause'. Usually in our day, we rush from one thing to another, never really stopping. It's like reading a book that has no full stops or commas in it. The idea of a 'pause' is simple. Instead of moving between activities, for example, going from outside your house, into your house, you simply stop, pause for a second, and then go through the door. Of course, you might already think you are pausing as you fiddle with your keys. The idea is that this is a conscious pause. Taking a breath. It need only last one second. Maybe two, but no more than that is necessary.

You might pause each time you exit the bathroom, or as you enter the lift (elevator). It can be as often as you like throughout the day. The idea is simply to punctuate different parts of your day. What starts to happen is you simply start to get more mindful as a result.

There are plenty of books explaining mindfulness, but really there's not much more to it than that. That's all you need to know to get started. Just take a couple of minutes out of your day to pay close attention to what you are doing. That could be breathing, or any other activity.

The Four-Count

Over the last few years, I've really been getting into counting…to four. Yes, there's something deeply hypnotic about focussing on a four-count. Perhaps that's why so many hit songs have a four-beat count in them. When I cycle, I often count with each peddle stroke "one, two, three, four." Or when I'm walking. Each step "one, two, three, four." It just brings me to a mindful place. I sometimes mix up the numbers with a four-count of a phrase. For example, I might use the following (especially if it's a tough cycle):

- "Get-ting strong-ger."
- "This is ease-sy."
- "Fast-ter, strong-ger."
- "Nice and ease-sy."

What this does, is it starts to re-enforce into my subconscious the commands I want it to pay attention to. Almost always, the cycle becomes easier, faster or I feel stronger. As we already mentioned, way back in the first section BRAIN, our inner dialogue is super important. When you learn to appreciate that you can in effect command it by clear instructions you become very powerful indeed.

MINDFULNESS EXERCISES

If you want some structured mindfulness exercises, there are plenty available to you. Below I've detailed a one of the ones that I sometimes get delegates to experience in my seminars.

54321 – Five Senses

1. **SEE**: Notice **five** things around you that you can see. Notice details in each object closely. View it as if it's the first time you've ever seen that object. Almost like you are an alien. In fact, for all these steps, come from the frame of mind that you are an alien visiting this planet for the first time, and have never witnessed these things before.
2. **FEEL**: Now pay attention to **four** things that you can feel. Your clothes on your body. Your foot in your shoe. Maybe the table, the

grass, the brickwork. Maybe it's a sensation in the body. Doesn't matter what it is. Just find four things you can feel.

3. **HEAR**: Now pay attention to **three** things you can hear. It might be the birds chirping. The sound of the air-conditioning, or the traffic. The sound of the wind or your own breath. Pay attention, and with curiosity about what you are hearing.

4. **SMELL**: Now focus on **two** things you can smell. Maybe it's someone's food, or perfume. A flower. A cup of tea. Whatever it is and is around you.

5. **TASTE**: Finally, focus on **one** thing that you can taste. Maybe it's your own saliva, or your toothpaste, or coffee still lingering in your mouth. Maybe you have some food, and you really chew it, taste it, experience it.

Again, you do all the above steps, taking as long as you need, and with the curiosity of a child or alien.

Raisin Exercise

This can be done with a raisin, grape or even chocolate. Anything really. You hold the food item in your hand – but don't eat it. Yet.

1. Start by looking at the item. Notice the shape, colour, size, any cracks, lines, and deviations. Notice anything you can visually. The colour comparison to your hand. And so on.

2. Then the smell. Take a sniff of it. What's it like? Close your eyes.

3. What about its texture. Squeeze it. Roll it. Play with it in your hand.

4. Finally put it in your mouth. But don't start to chew straight away. Allow it to sit there. Move it about. Are any taste sensations coming through. Only when ready, start to chew it. Has the taste changed?

The idea is that you take your time eating it. Imagine you are an alien or a child and has never seen this thing before. You're curious. Maybe even suspicious.

Mini Mindfulness Exercise

At any point in the day, and you remember this exercise, you simply – PAUSE.

1. Pause and stop what you are doing.

2. Bring your awareness to your breath.

3. Take six long deep diaphragmatic breaths.
4. Start to expand your awareness or consciousness outwards. Beyond your body and into the wider world.
5. Then just go about your day.

3-min Breathing Exercise

Take three minutes out of your day to follow either a two-part or four-part breathing pattern.

- For two-part breathing I usually like to say one of the following in my head:

  Re-lease; Let-go; Re-lax; All-good; I'm-strong; I'm-safe; Be-lieve

- For four-part breathing (i.e., counting to four in my head) I might say something like:

  One, two, three, four; I am pure soul; This is all good; I am fine now

You can also come up with your own versions.

Body Scan / Sensations Exercise

It is recommended you allow about 30 or 40 minutes to let yourself really investigate this practice. But if you don't have that much time, that's fine. You might want to lie down, although you can also do it sitting up.

1. Closing your eyes can be helpful to allow you to focus or, if you'd rather, you can always lower and half-close your eyes.

2. Bring awareness to the body breathing in and out, noticing touch and pressure where you connect to the seat or floor. Allow the time you need to experience and study each area of the body.

3. Intentionally breathe in and move your attention to whatever part of the body you want to explore. You might choose to do a systematic body scan beginning at the head or feet. Or you might choose to explore sensations randomly.

4. Sensations might include buzzing, or tingling, pressure, tightness or temperature, or anything else you notice. What if you don't notice any strong sensations or things feel neutral. Simply notice that, too.

There is no right or wrong way on how to feel. Just tune in to what's present for you and without judgement.

5. Be curious and open to what you are noticing, investigating the sensations as fully as possible. Then release the focus of attention and move to the next area to explore.

6. At some point, your attention will have shifted. You can't stop your attention from wandering. That's normal. However, with practice you can train it to stay for longer periods: practice makes progress.

7. Each time your attention wanders, simply notice it and without harsh words or judgement. Then direct your attention back to exploring sensations in the body. Keep cycling through body parts until you've completed exploring your entire body.

8. When you finish this exploration of your body's sensations, spend some time to widen your attention to feeling your entire body breathing.

9. Finally, open your eyes and continue with the rest of your day in a mindful way.

Quick summary about mindfulness and becoming superhuman...

1. Mindfulness doesn't have to be complicated, and you don't need to go on an eight-week certification course to get started. You can learn a lot from a course, for sure, but you don't need it.

2. Mindfulness is simply paying attention to what is happening in the moment. That could be noticing your body sensations, the wind on your face or just your breath.

3. Mindfulness carries with it many health and performance benefits including increased focus, lower blood pressure, reduced stress and anxiety and increased tolerance to pain[444].

Action plan for becoming superhuman...

1. Decide on something that you do each day anyway, that you can introduce a mindful practice to. That could be washing your hands, brushing your teeth, walking to pick up the newspaper or anything else.

2. Introduce a 'pause' into your day. Even if it's just one pause a day. Take a one second break between activities.

3. Take a walk into nature, or a local park without your mobile phone, music, or any distractions. Just notice the space around you. The grass, the trees, the birds and the ducks. Notice the people playing. Perhaps practising the 54321 Five Senses practice outlined above.

4.4 Fasting

The Fast and the Furious...

"I fast for greater mental and physical efficiency."

- Plato

Fasting. Part of having TRANQUILITY in life is giving yourself tranquility in your body too. Fasting gives the opportunity for you to take a 'pause' on your digestion. Think about it. Have you ever given your body time off from the labour-intensive process of digestion before? I remember when I was at Primary school, I must have been about nine or ten years old and there was a sponsored 24-hour fast. It was gruelling for me. It was also the first time I'd been a day without eating.

When you eat, a lot happens in your body. Depending on the kind of food you've eaten, blood glucose levels (sugar) will rise. Then your pancreas will secrete a hormone called insulin to regulate this rise in sugar. Insulin instructs the cells of your body to use glucose for fuel and your gut breaks down your food. Then your body will release hormones like leptin and cholecystokinin to signal that you are full.

In modern society there is food readily available, that it's rare for us to ever go to bed hungry. We also eat lots of highly processed carbohydrates which are easy to break down and can mess up your body's signal to tell you that you are full. Your body might struggle to keep up, and the pancreas might need to work overtime to produce enough insulin. Excess glucose that isn't being used will get stored as fat.

Pretty much the only time we might go without food is when we become sick and don't have the appetite. And that should tell us something too. Remember K.I.S.S.? Keep It Solution Simple. The body, at rest, uses a significant amount of energy simply to digest your food. Roughly 10% of your daily energy expenditure is used to digest food[445]. Even more at rest. And interestingly, when at rest, the brain which only weighs around 2% of the body, uses 20% of the body's energy needs[446]. When you take a break from eating, you allow (this is my theory) that energy to be diverted to other things, like healing. Certainly, I remember once having a bad finger injury from playing basketball. It had been about six or seven weeks without progress or healing. Then I went on a 5-day juice fast (consuming nothing but water, vegetable juices and herbal teas) and within five days the injury had healed. Coincidence? I tend to find similar things happen each time I've done an extended fast. And now I'm into double digits on the number of extended multi-day fasts I've completed.

OK, so what is fasting exactly?

What is Fasting?

Fasting is going an extended period without consuming foods or liquids that require the digestion process to commence. I say liquids too because consuming smoothies breaks a (pure) fast. As they have fibre, calories and require digestion still. Drinking a smoothie is like you eating the food but all the blender is doing, is a really good job of 'chewing' the food for you before you swallow. Of course, when you chew yourself, you also get all the digestive enzymes being released in the mouth.

Other experts may think that breaking a fast could include vegetable juices, and coffee. There are many different approaches to what constitutes being in a fasted state. I tend to think of it like above – i.e., if there is no digestion or calories consumed, then you're fasting. I do consider caffeinated drinks to interfere with fasting so I would say no to coffee, tea and green teas when fasting.

Studies show that water fasting can trigger something called autophagy – programmed cell death. Where old cells are broken down and eaten by the body, which can benefit people suffering from cancer, neurodegeneration and microbial infections[447]. As well as improving signs of ageing in the brain[448]. Medically supervised water only fasting has been shown to lower blood pressure in those with hypertension disease[449], and also lower blood levels of cholesterol and triglycerides as well as increase human growth hormone[450]. Short-term fasts of 48 hours were shown to protect cells in mice exposed to chemotherapy. However, the cancerous cells were *not* protected from the chemotherapy. Probably a good thing. With human patients who fasted having reported less fatigue, weakness or gastrointestinal side effects while undergoing chemotherapy[451].

I find that when I fast, I have increased energy, clearer and smoother skin, sharper mental clarity and more mental awareness about certain habits. For example, the habit of 'needing' to eat something while sitting down to watch a movie, or just because it's a certain time of day – even if I'm not hungry. I have also measured my weight, fat and muscle percentages and have never recorded any muscle mass loss. Quite the opposite usually. I do release* weight. Sometimes up to 5kg in five days of fasting. This normally comes back. The only time I've lost a vast amount of weight, and it hasn't come back after a fast, is if I also do a few colonic hydrotherapy sessions as well. This just tells me that I had something in my gut that I probably didn't need and was carrying around all this time.

And I also find that I don't have to adapt my life because I'm fasting. I don't need to take time off work, presenting or physical workouts. I do train lighter these days when fasting but have in the past completed intense workouts like Cross-Fit in fasted states and found myself to have amazing energy and endurance†.

Fasting or Detoxing?

Sometimes these phrases are inter-twined. And they can sometimes be the same thing. When you fast, your body will detox. It detoxes every day anyway. You just give it more of an opportunity to do so when the body doesn't have to also deal with digestion. You can however, detox while not fasting. You might be 'detoxing' from caffeine. Allowing your body to get rid of the dependence on caffeine. You might also detox from heavy metals that are accumulated in your body by a process of chelation and use specific chelates to achieve that. For example, coriander is a good natural chelator[452], as is something like bentonite clay[453]. A chelator removes toxins from the

---

* I prefer the word 'release' instead of the word 'lose' as think about it; when you lose something you usually aim to find it again. The subconscious mind is very suggestive, and so it might look for the weight it's lost. Releasing weight allows it to leave and not return.
† I didn't do this kind of physical exercise on my first five or six fasts though. I've now completed over a dozen extended day fasts consuming vegetable juices, and so have some level of experience over what I can and can't due during a fast. And recognising that each fast is different, so I never commit to anything strenuous ahead of time. Favouring listening to my body moment-by-moment instead.

body, assisting the body's natural systems. There are detox teas and other potions that will claim to detox the body. Some work, some don't. Although typically you would alter your diet when detoxing, it doesn't mean that you are fasting. So, fasting and detoxing are slightly different in my view. Some people say they are on a juice detox, when really, I think they mean they are on a juice fast – or maybe more accurately a juice feast. This is because you are not actually starving your body of nutrients. Quite the opposite, in fact. You are (most likely) feeding it more nutrients than it would normally get.

Types of Fasting

Again, there a quite a few ways of fasting so we won't cover all of them here, but here are a few that you might come across.

==

Warning and Disclaimer: Obviously you participate in any of these at your own discretion and I would strongly recommend (at least for the first couple of times) to do any fasting under expert supervision. People who should not fast are those under age 20, over 65 and never having done it before, pregnant and/or breastfeeding, on dialysis, if you are severely ill or have recently undergone an operation. Also, if you suffer from the following conditions, I wouldn't recommend fasting: Type-1 diabetes, thyroid hyperfunction, liver or renal dysfunction, cardiac disease, cancer, polyarthritis, gastric and intestinal ulcers, drug, and alcohol addiction, if you have eating disorders like anorexia, bulimia or binge eating, depression or emotional instability. If you are on medication, I suggest taking expert counsel and/or going to a fasting clinic.

==

The first couple of times I fasted for extended periods of time, it was on retreats. I recommend that to start with, as not only is there support and guidance, but you are also away from your normal day-to-day environment. Allowing you to focus on the fasting. My first fast was 7.5 days in Thailand in 2012. That fast included fibrous drinks such as psyllium husk (to keep you feeling full) and bentonite clay (for detoxification purposes), along with soups/broths and coconut water and juices. It also involved lots of massages, self-administered colonic irrigations (called colemas – or coffee enemas)[‡],

---

[†] An enema involves inserting a tube up the rectum and allowing water to enter and break up and release 'things' collected in your colon. Coffee enemas use coffee to stimulate movement. It's diluted with warm water though. Colonic hydrotherapy is slightly different – although similar – as you work with a practitioner, and they can get the water further in and also

steam rooms, swims, yoga, sleep, and relaxation. My second one in 2013, was very different as it was purely juices (no fibrous drinks) and using enemas – again!

Water Only

This is one I haven't done yet myself – well, at least not for more than 24 hours. This involves literally taking nothing but just water throughout the fasting period. Pretty extreme but I know people who have had good success with joint pain and other pains doing 10-day water fasts. I even once met someone who runs a water fasting retreat in Costa Rica so you can do it under supervision (which I'd recommend for sure unless you are an experienced faster). He told me a miraculous story about one participant who came to the centre with stage-4 testicular cancer and did a four-month water-only fast. Yes, you read that correctly. Four months! Before I heard that (and I've not personally verified it), I would have said you can only survive for maximum a couple of months on just water. Still, if true, it worked for him as there was no trace of the cancer afterwards. I also think he had quite a lot of energy (i.e., fat) in reserve to be able to do that. I don't think that the average person could last that long.

Dry Fasting

This type of fasting involves abstaining from everything. Food and water. I've not done it, don't recommend it and don't think there have been any long-term studies showing any benefits to this, although I could be wrong. In one short study it showed that fasting without hydration increased lipid (fat) levels[454]. However, I recently read about a woman who went to a supervised nine-day dry fast in Siberia and was able to cure her Lyme disease after trying everything else for several years[455]. I can't quite see how she was alive not drinking but apparently sleeping outside allowed for moisture to come into the body. Honestly though, I think this is for very few, if any, people to try. Remember that one should only ever consider this under expert consultation and supervision.

---

massage stubborn areas to release. If you're more curious on my experience of the colema, it's one of my most popular YouTube videos on my channel –
http://youtube.com/thethoughtgym. Don't worry, I spare people the actual process – just a before and after summary.

T - TRANQUILITY

Juice Fasting

This is the type of fasting that I am personally most familiar with. Essentially, it's where you don't consume any solid foods or things that require digestion – like smoothies[§]. I usually do between three and seven days of this type of fast. During that fasting time, I drink low-to-no sugar vegetable juices, water, non-caffeinated herbal teas, and that's pretty much it. It's more like a juice feast rather than fast, as I'm having tons of nutrients so I'm not really starving my body of most of what it needs.

Sometimes when I've gone for nine days or so, I have used the first two days and the last two days of the fast to also include smoothies. Thus, adjusting my stomach and mind for the main juice fast.

I usually notice that when I do a fast, it's more of a mental game than anything. I must go into it knowing I will complete it. It's surprising really, as when I do it, I can easily go a few days on nothing but juices. When I'm eating normally though, I sometimes get hangry (hungry and angry) from even the slightest delay in eating!

For me, this type of fasting a couple of times a year or more, is a good way to reset the body and spark some rejuvenation into the body. I don't think it's great though when people think that they can do this for a week and the other 51 weeks of the year they revert to destructive eating behaviours. It's like going on a week-long boot camp or yoga retreat and then not moving the rest of the time. Sure, it's a great way to feel good short-term but really, long term, it has little effect. It can, however, be a catalyst and provide motivation for longer lasting change and even (for me, this is often often) help heal minor physical complaints.

If you do consider this kind of fast, or any really, the ramp up and off time is also crucial. It would be a good idea to spend a week or two before the fast starting to eliminate items like sugar, processed food, gluten, meat, caffeine, alcohol, and dairy. This will allow the body to ease into it. Of course, if you are eating a *PANLO 80/20* approach and following the suggestions in this book, it won't be much of a stretch. And coming off it, start to ease back into the eating. Starting again with simple, plant-rich foods. I've not always

---

[§] Smoothies, unlike juices, contain the whole veg/fruit so you are getting the fibre too (soluble and insoluble fibre). Juices on the other hand, are effectively just the nutrient rich water from the veg/fruit without most of the fibre. So, in the cases of juices, you are not feeling so full, and your digestive system doesn't have to work really.

followed this myself and sometimes had big meals out to break the fast. Luckily, I've quite a robust digestive system, so no ill effects, but you might be different. So maybe sticking to salads when coming off it might be a good idea.

"Every fool can fast. Only a wise person knows how to break a fast"

– George Bernard Shaw

Intermittent Fasting

There are many ways to approach intermittent fasting. I'll just describe a couple here and what I tend to do and how I do it in case it's something that offers value to you.

In summary though, intermittent fasting is about limiting the times that you eat, rather than what you eat. It's nothing new, as this is how our ancestors would have eaten. When you think about it, why should we eat three square meals a day. Who says you should? Well, marketers of food products for one. Throughout history we would have evolved to feast when food was available and then cope with times of famine. This might have been feasting more in the summer to stockpile bodyfat for the winter. It might be that we ate, then went days with very little until the next big kill came in. We certainly weren't eating continuously. Which is how society is set up now. We don't have to move very far to get our food today. Food is energy (amongst other things), and we don't typically use up energy to get food anymore, so we just stockpile energy, never really using it.

When you practice intermittent fasting, you revert to a version of how we likely evolved to eat.

Benefits to Intermittent Fasting

Studies on intermittent fasting have been conducted for years on rats and mice and more recently with humans. Intermittent fasting has been proven to reduce oxidative damage and inflammation, boost energy and increase the protection of cells. It also appears to improve obesity, hypertension, asthma and rheumatoid arthritis**[456]. It may also reverse the worst effects of MS (multiple sclerosis) according to a multinational research team led by Valter Longo from the University of Southern California[457].

In animals, intermittent fasting has been shown to be beneficial against cancer, diabetes, heart disease and neurodegenerations, and was as effective as pharmaceutical drugs for reducing brain seizures and seizure-induced brain damage[458]. Performing as little as a 24-hour fast (in mice) was shown by MIT researchers to help regenerate stem cells in the intestines[459]. The gut is where most of our immune system emanates from, so if this research is also applicable to humans fasting can have profound effects on a person's health. Other research also corroborating the benefits of fasting for extended periods of time on the immune system[460].

According to Sonia Wisinger[461], a certified health and fasting coach, there are many overall benefits to fasting, including:

Health

- Mobilises the body's defence mechanisms.
- Cleanses the body.
- Gives the digestive organs a rest.
- Helps prevent chronic and acute disease.
- Reduces body fat.
- Supports the maintenance of a healthy body mass index (BMI).

Wellbeing

- Increases energy and vitality.
- Increases serotonin levels resulting in improved sleeping patterns.
- Quiets the body and mind.

Beauty

- Helps prevent signs of premature ageing.
- Clears away redness for sparkling eyes.
- Healthier hair and nails.

** As any condition with an '-itis' at the end it means inflammation, and intermittent fasting has been shown to reduce inflammation, it's no surprise to me that it helps with arthritis.

Lifestyle

- Increases inner strength and focus.
- Promotes better eating habits.
- Foster better impulse control.
- Restores the ability to eat moderately and sensibly.

5:2 Intermittent Fasting

This was the first type of intermittent fasting I heard about several years ago, although I've never tried it. In short, you fast on two non-consecutive days of the week when you eat less than 500 calories a day, and then on the other days you can eat normally. Essentially, this is a calorie-restricted diet. Unless you get it wrong, as many do, and really go overboard, on the five days that you are permitted to eat more than 500 calories. Another way people go wrong on this diet (in my view), is that they think that they can eat whatever they want on the other five days. Stick to healthy meals on all seven days and this can work nicely. A more extreme version might be to do 24-hr fasts on the two days and consume zero (rather than 500) calories. A study published in JAMA Internal Medicine by the American Medical Association[462] took a look at the effects of alternate day fasting versus calorie restriction in 100 obese adults. The participants were divided into two groups: an alternate-fasting group and a calorie restricting group. Over the course of one year, both groups lost weight, but the study couldn't find much of a difference in overall weight loss between the groups. So, in terms of losing fat and weight, intermittent fasting as a weight loss strategy is like calorie restriction. However, fasting could have all the additional benefits mentioned in this chapter, and for many people might be easier than restricting calories.

Fasting Mimicking Diet

This type of intermittent fasting is popularised by one of the leading researchers in the field of longevity and fasting, Dr Valter Longo. Essentially it mimics fasting while still eating. For five days every three months you effectively eat a calorie restricted diet. However, the proportions of fats, carbohydrates and proteins are important. Your body then thinks it's fasting when in fact it's not. I've personally never tried this but do have friends that enjoy it. I find that it's just simpler and easier for me to not eat for those five days and do a juice fast instead. Still, it's worth investigating the fasting mimicking diet for the specifics if you are interested in giving it a go. You can do it yourself, or they make it easier for you by sending you a kit with everything that you need for the five days[††].

8+16 Intermittent Fasting (Time Restricted Eating)

This type of intermittent fasting is the one I follow the closest. Essentially the way it works is to compress the eating window to eight hours. Allowing 16 hours of fasting time. So, you might eat breakfast at 10am, lunch at 1pm and dinner at 5pm to finish eating by 6pm. That gives you 16 hours until you eat again. A study done by the University of Illinois observed benefits in obese individuals who ate food between 10am and 6pm and did a water fast until 10am the next day. After three months, the participants instinctively reduced their daily calorie intake by 300 calories without counting them. As a result, they lost about 3% of their body weight[463]. Another study published in the Journal of Translational Medicine took 34 men and split them into two groups: an intermittent fasting group and a control group. Both groups then completed an eight-week long strength-training program. After eight weeks, both groups of men increased strength and muscle mass. However, the intermittent fasting group also found a decrease in body fat[464].

Ways to Practise Daily Intermittent (8+16) Fasting

I don't do intermittent fasting the way of 8+16. The way I like to look at it is just to have a 16-hour window from my last meal of the day to my first meal the next day. How is that any different?

I could, for example one day eat breakfast at 9am (usually that's a vegetable juice and smoothie), maybe have lunch after a mid-day workout, but then I might be invited out for dinner, so I end up eating at 9pm at night. Normally I would like a minimum of 12 hours between last meal and first meal, so 9am the next morning to eat would be okay, but if I wanted 16 hours I simply wouldn't eat again until 1pm the following day. I then might eat all the way up until 9pm, or stop at 6pm, if I wanted to tweak when I would break my fast the following day. So, some days I might eat in a 12-hour window, other times a 6-hour window. I prefer to finish my last meal at whatever time is socially convenient[‡‡] and then give a minimum 12 hours, often 16 hours, until breaking the fast.

[††] They market this under the ProLon name.
[‡‡] Truth be told, I prefer to finish eating by 6pm as I find it negatively affects my sleep the later, I eat. And 80% of the time I aim for this, allowing 20% flexibility.

When travelling (without my blender to make breakfast smoothies) I often skip breakfast and just eat lunch and dinner. The reason is that it's usually easier for me to find something decent to eat for lunch and dinner (and gives me more time to find a place) than what is typically served for breakfast. From a social standpoint also, when travelling, it's more likely that I would eat dinner out with friends.

That said, if lifestyle circumstances permit, I encourage finishing eating by 6pm. Biologically, each of our cells has a circadian rhythm and certain organs, like the liver and pancreas for example, will 'close up shop' for the night around then[§§][426]. If you eat dinner early, then you'll more likely want to sleep earlier, wake earlier, and get started on your day sooner. Of course, going to bed hungry can impact your sleep negatively too. This is because usually you will become more alert and focussed as evolutionarily speaking you would still be hunting for food, so you don't starve to death. So, you might find it troubling to fall asleep if you are too hungry[391]. You want the sweet spot where you've eaten enough to fall asleep but early enough that the body isn't working overnight or late into the evening to digest it.

Sometimes, if I eat a huge lunch I might even finish eating by 3pm. I find that I sleep well that those nights, and my heart-rate variability (HRV) is high[***]. Another study had participants finish their meal at 3pm and go on a 16-hour fast. They found improved insulin sensitivity, blood pressure, and oxidative stress even without weight loss in men with prediabetes[465]. Changing the time when eating dinner and breakfast was shown in another study to result in fat loss, even when the same foods were eaten. By eating breakfast 90 minutes later and dinner 90 minutes earlier, helped study participants to lose up to double the body fat as those sticking to normal mealtimes[466].

Another study showed that people with the most amount of body fat were consuming most of their calories closer to the time when the body starts preparing for sleep. The study did show that overweight versus normal weight people seemed to have had slightly different circadian rhythms and that the right amount of food spacing – time between meals – also played a part[467].

They suggested a four-hour gap between meals, so that might be something like breakfast at 10am, lunch at 2pm and dinner at 6pm, leaving a good few

---

[§§] For more on this, investigate chronobiology.
[***] HRV is a measure of health and is the beat-to-beat changes in your heart rate. A high HRV is generally considered a good thing.

hours before bed. This of course depends on bio-individuality of course, and the best thing is to experiment with timings for yourself. Social, exercise and professional circumstances all play a part in how manageable this is. Another study showed that people who ate their last meal before 9pm are, on average, 20 per cent less likely to develop breast or prostate cancer compared to those that ate after 10pm[468].

The best thing is to experiment and see what works for you. Have a framework in place but have *flexibility within the framework*. Like I already mentioned, for me it is easier to focus on the gap from the last meal of the day to first meal the next day, rather than an eating window. I also don't get too caught up in making it 16 hours every single day. I aim for minimum of 12 hours though but usually it's between 14 and 16 at least four or five days a week. And possibly an 18-22 hour fast once a week or fortnight.

There's also more and more research coming out on calorie restricted diets (eating around 30 per cent less each day) for helping with staying young biologically. Of course, these have mainly been done in mice, but it could be an interesting finding for humans too, if the results are transferable to humans. Meaning we can stay younger for longer by simply eating less[469-471].

I do remember watching a program profiling people having followed calorie restriction for a long time, but I seem to recall that they felt cold all the time. I'm not sure if that's the best approach for me. Still, most people simply eat too much anyway, so maybe it's something to consider?

Quick summary about fasting and becoming superhuman...

1. Fasting comes in many forms from extended fasts, water only, dry fasts, juice fasts and intermittent fasting. Fasting generally, when practised safely can have many benefits for the body and mind including healing, more energy, less brain fog, better self-control, and increased resilience.

2. Fasting is nothing new, and ancestrally speaking, we've become adapted to it. If we weren't, our ancestors would never have survived, and we wouldn't be here.

3. Today, the accessibility of food (not necessarily healthy food) is ubiquitous. We don't have to move to find it. We don't hunt or gather it. We store more energy (from food) than we need. We need to recondition ourselves to going without as much energy-dense (high calorific) food.

Action plan for becoming superhuman...

1. Make a note of when you stop eating today, and what time you start again tomorrow. Remember that even a coffee (especially if you use milk or cream) will count to breaking the fast if it has calories in it.

2. Start to introduce a 12-hour fasting window to your schedule. Do this by eating one hour earlier for dinner, and one hour later for breakfast, until you get to 12 hours.

3. When you have managed a 12-hour window, work up to a 14, then 16-hour window. If you want, you could even go to 18, 20 or 22-hours. Aim to do a 16-hour window 2-3 times per week, if not even more often, if possible.

4.5 Digital Nutrition and Dieting
The Connected Conundrum...

---

*"The difference between technology and slavery is that
slaves are fully aware that they are not free."*

– Nassim Nicholas Taleb

A Connected World

Today we live in an ever-connected world. The trouble is many of us are feeling more disconnected from each other than ever. The ability to be contactable 24/7 has left many people feeling obligated to be reachable. This has meant that for many people from the moment they wake up until the moment they go to bed there are tethered to the outside world.

The smartphone revolution has only served to exacerbate this issue. Even yesterday, I was walking along a beach in sunny Cyprus, and I felt quite sad as I witnessed all the people glued to their smartphones. Many just scrolling sites like Instagram to see other people's highlights. Or to post something of theirs to show the world that they are fulfilled and having a great time. I saw a couple who were both on their smartphones rather than engaging with each other. Parents checking out what's what online rather than playing with their children. Children who will probably never know what it's like to just sit and marvel at water splashing over the rocks, as they are too caught up in the latest happenings on social media.

Am I a luddite? Of course not. I also post to social media; I'm writing this on a laptop right now while looking at a gorgeous blue sea. I enjoy the trappings of new technology. I'm just doing my best to not be trapped *by* it. Are you using technology or is it using you? In most cases I observe, I would say that people are becoming a slave to technology.

T - TRANQUILITY

This chapter is all about how we can use technology to help, not hinder, us.

The problem with digital detoxing

You may have come across the term digital detoxing. Whereby a person will abstain from their smartphone (and other tech) completely for a day or more. Some people even go to retreats and have their phones taken from them. While this is a good practice to do periodically, it's a bit like when people go on food detoxes. They pay all this money to go to some fancy place in Thailand and juice and have yoga and colonics and who knows what else (and I've done them too so I'm really a big fan and not knocking them). What happens though the other 51 weeks of the year? Sure, a detox can open a window into what the world could look like to you, but if you revert to the way you were previously after it ends, did it really give you maximum benefit?

Far better to use technology wisely throughout the year. Just like eating well all 52 weeks of the year. You could, in addition, have a longer detox once or twice a year too. Just don't use the detox as the excuse to do things that don't serve you the rest of the time. That's why I like to talk about digital dieting and digital nutrition.

Digital dieting is about watching how much media you consume in this hyper-connected world. Digital nutrition is about watching the kind of things that you consume, not just the amount. I'll share some of my strategies below that you might like to adopt, or perhaps adapt, as you wish.

The Problem with Tech

You might not think that you have a problem with technology. That might be true. Or you might not think that technology is bad. You're right. Technology isn't bad. Just like a knife isn't bad. A knife is just a knife. It's how it is used that matters. A knife can be used to kill, or it can be used to contribute to making the most amazing meal. Technology in and of itself is just technology. It's neutral. Neither good nor bad. Our use of it dictates whether we might consider it good or bad. However, unlike a knife, a smartphone often *reaches out to us* to use it, unlike the knife where *we reach out* to use it.

Let's look at some numbers[472-474]:

- 61% of people are addicted to their devices.
- People spend two hours per day recovering from distractions.
- People visit on average 40 websites a day.

- People engage in 37 activities per hour.
- People change tasks every 2 minutes.
- The mind wanders around 47% of the time.
- Presenteeism (being at work but not really being at work) costs six times as much as absenteeism.
- Having awareness of one unread email in the inbox is equivalent to a 10-point IQ reduction.
- People spend 8 hours and 41 minutes looking at screens each day.
- The average person checks their smartphone 150 times a day.
- 80% of people admit to checking their smartphone first thing in the day.

What's more, being constantly connected means that we end up continuously in a state of fight or flight. Every email alert, notification and text creates a slight elevation in cortisol (our stress hormone). We are designed to have some spikes in cortisol and then act to disperse it. We encounter a tiger; we have a massive rush in cortisol and then we run away which releases all the built-up cortisol in the system. However, what we are now experiencing is constant low-level rises in cortisol with every 'beep' that comes our way.

Not only that but constantly being connected is eroding our ability to be present in the moment and focus on the task in hand. We also often now think that the 'grass is always greener on the other side of the fence'. I.e., other people are having better lives than us. Whereas the truth is that the grass is greener where you water it. I.e., put your attention and energy.

I have a friend (who shall remain anonymous) who I really struggled to be around in the past. Whenever we would meet it was like they weren't fully there. They would constantly be grabbing their phone or looking towards it and even when I did manage to get them not to have it out there on the table, I could tell their mind was anywhere but in the present conversation. I was even at the cinema with them once and they had to have it on till the last moment – even when the movie had started. This isn't a unique episode. We all know people like this. Maybe...*we* are people like that?

The truth is that most of us are not on-call 24/7. Yes, you may be a parent. But what did parents do before the arrival of mobile phones. Were there other ways. Of course, there were. I used to be on-call when I worked at the London Stock Exchange. I can tell you, that I never slept that well, as I was always thinking that I might get woken up. You end up sleeping with the phone on and close by – which isn't a good thing if you remember what we talked about with EMFs back in the chapter on Aether? Then I changed role and my last night being on-call was New Year's Eve. When it was midnight, I turned my phone off. It did have unintended consequences though. I decided, in my drunkenness[*], to leave the party I was at, and didn't tell my friend. My friend who was planning to stay at my flat with me. I awoke the next day to him knocking loudly on my front door. He had come around earlier, around 2am, but I'd been totally oblivious to his knocking. Of course, he couldn't phone me to find out whether I was in or what happened to me[†]. In the end, he had to go around the corner to my sister's flat and wait in their front garden for them to come home and sleep at theirs. So yes, that time there was a bit of an issue with having the phone off, but nobody died. It all worked out. Do you really need to have the phone always on and available? In an emergency can someone have a landline or alternative contact? Are there any other options? That's all I'm saying. Think about it and I think you'll find that there are alternatives.

Constantly being on technology can enslave us, create constant cortisol elevations, and make us less focussed and less present. It also has a more nefarious side, as mentioned in the list at the beginning of this section. Addiction.

Hooked on Dopamine

You might not be aware of this, but the best minds in the world are employed by smartphone app manufacturers and social media sites to make their applications 'stickier'[‡]. To get you to spend more time on their apps. They do this by taking advantage of some hormones that are secreted in our body. Namely dopamine. Often thought to be a pleasure hormone, it's recently been discovered to be in fact a *seeking* hormone. In that it creates a desire in us to seek out new experiences and then get a small opioid hit when we find what we are looking for. The challenge is this. The opioid reward is comparatively much smaller than the dopamine secretion and so we end up wanting to seek more to satisfy our craving, and thus, we can never be satisfied.

Dopamine thrives on unpredictability. That means that with each visit to Facebook you don't really know how many notifications you are likely to get,

---

[*] This was when drinking was a bit more common for me.

[†] I had no landline at the time.

[‡] I recommend watching the Netflix documentary *The Social Dilemma*.

or how many likes on Instagram, or how many emails you will be getting. This unpredictability feeds dopamine. It adds fuel to the fire. Interestingly, brain scan research shows that the brain has more activity when people are *anticipating* a reward rather than receiving one[475]. The dopamine release being stronger than the opioid release. Research on rats shows that if you destroy dopamine neurons, rats can walk, chew, and swallow, but will starve to death even when food is right next to them[476].

In short, the way that some technology is designed, either intentionally or unintentionally, is that it creates addicts out of all of us. I see this frequently. In other people yes, but also in me too. I have developed ways in which to manage it (see below), but I still get caught out more often than I'd like. We're living in what's called an *Attention Economy*. Your attention is valuable to companies. More attention means more advertising, more time spent in apps, more revenue. It's not just me saying this. There are former (and even current) high profile tech employees trying to warn people just how real this issue is. We don't want to throw out the baby with the bathwater. We still need technology. It's useful. Only if we use it right though. Unfortunately, most app designers are going to be given the remit of making their apps or products highly attention grabbing, therefore it's up to the individual in the first instance to manage technology, so one doesn't become a slave to it.

How to use tech

The first thing that we should understand is that we are supposed to be technology's master. Not the other way around. Most people, for example, use the smartphone in a totally slave-like way. They use it as an interruption tool. Allowing other people to dictate their schedule and interrupt their flow because of someone else's need to get in contact with them. That's why you'll usually find my phone on silent (if not in airplane mode). Does it mean I miss calls? Of course, it does. Why should I stop what I'm doing just because someone else wants a piece of me. Most the time it won't be a call anyway, but a text or other notification. Hardly ever, does the call/text even require my immediate attention. I'm not that important. I'll get back to the person on my schedule. And if that means we miss each other then I arrange a convenient time to call. Schedule a time to speak. Just like a meeting. If I'm expecting a call from someone – say I'm picking them up at the airport, or I'm waiting for the boiler repair person to call, then yes, I'll have the phone on and ringtone active. Most of the time though this isn't the case. And yes, on occasion this practice has cost me work and money due to lost opportunities. It's something

T - TRANQUILITY

I'm prepared to live with though for my own mental health.

Beating Technology

Whenever I deliver my Digital Dieting & Nutrition workshops, people always want to go straight to the apps that are going to help them with technology. However, the apps, while useful, are not the solution. At least, not at first. And they won't work unless you can put some other things in place first. In author Nir Eyal's excellent book *Indistractable* he explains that there are four stages that need to be in place for you to fully master technology (or other distractions) around you. The following are adapted from Eyal's work, although with my own frameworks, spin, and tweaks.

1. Mastering Your State and Emotions

The first thing to understand is that when you are bored, procrastinating or feeling in a low state or emotion, that's when you are likely to be sucked in by technology, or to some other distraction. You see, technology isn't the problem. For as long as there's been things to do, humans have had to deal with distraction. So, the first thing is you must learn how to master your emotions and state. Luckily, you already know how to if you have read chapter 1.6. It's the three things that I explained in that chapter that dictate how you feel at any given moment.

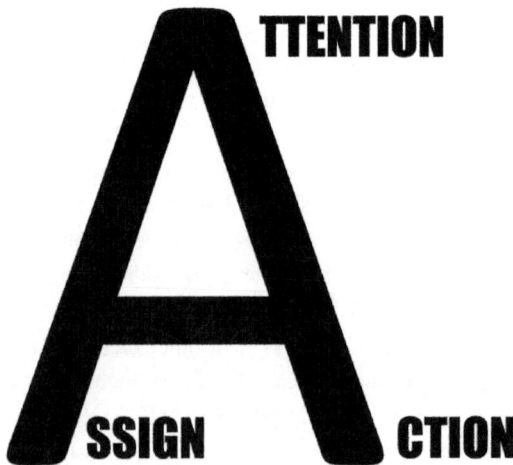

Figure 21 - The Three Things That Dictate Your Mood or State

2. Schedule and Plan Time

The second thing to understand is that when you are distracted (be that on technology or anywhere else), you must be distracted *from* something else, that you were planning to do. Often, when I ask to see people's plan for the day, what they are doing with their time, they don't have anything to show me. If you don't schedule in activities, then you aren't really being taken away from them with your tech. Because they were never there in the first place.

Studies show that when you schedule in what you want to do it is more likely to happen. Remember the study from chapter 3.5? The study[390] had volunteers divided into either a control group, or one of two intervention groups. Group 1 was the control group. They were asked to keep track of how frequently they exercised over the next two weeks. Before they left, each person was asked to read the opening three paragraphs of an unrelated novel. Group 2 was the motivation group. They were also asked to keep track of how frequently they exercised over the next two weeks. Then, each person was asked to read a pamphlet on the benefits of exercise for reducing the risk of heart disease. Participants in Group 2 were also told, "Most young adults who have stuck to a regular exercise program have found it to be very effective in reducing their chances of developing coronary heart disease." The goal of these actions was to motivate Group 2 to exercise regularly. Finally, there was Group 3. These subjects received the same presentation as the second group, which ensured that they had equal levels of motivation. However, they were also asked to formulate a plan for when and where they would exercise over the following week. Specifically, each member of the third group completed the following sentence: "During the next week, I will partake in at least 20 minutes of vigorous exercise on [DAY] at [TIME] in [PLACE]."

The results. By the end of the three-week study, exercise participation had decreased to 38% for Group 1, 35% for Group 2, but by the end of the three weeks still 91% of the third group were still engaging in exercise. This was the group that formulated a plan of exactly when and where they would exercise.

What am I saying then? In short. Plan your time. Schedule it in and it will be more likely to happen. Recall the idea of C.I.A. from chapter 3.5?

C.I.A. – Choices in Advance

And when it comes to scheduling, I would also say that it's important to schedule your values first. Not to schedule your 'to-do' list, as many people tend to do. Remember the values exercise from chapter 1.3? If you haven't done it, it's worth just thinking about what is important to you in life. So, if it's your health, family and adventure for example, schedule time in for those things *before* you put in your other commitments.

In addition, sync your calendar with any stakeholders that you might have. They might be people at work you report to, or report to you. Family members, friends and so on. Let them know more about how you plan your time. Perhaps even share protected versions of your calendar with them which shows when you are free to respond or be interrupted. If people are clear on your schedule and understand the expectations that you put on yourself, and how you are diligent enough to plan in this way, then they will respect your time more and it will help to manage their expectations as well.

And then finally, schedule in your 'time-wasting' time too. Perhaps you schedule in 15 minutes to aimlessly scroll through social media or video sites. It's not guilt-ridden time spent on these things. It's already been scheduled in. It's like when I was a kid and my parents never denied me eating chocolate, but we had a 'sweet day' which was Sundays when we were allowed one or two pieces of Ferrero Roche.

3. Reduce External Triggers

The third part of the framework is to start to reduce those external triggers. That's only once parts one and two above have been done. This is the part that participants in my workshops often want to jump to. They want the shiny new app to help them manage their time and smartphone addictions, or a snazzy new technique. While they are valid – and that's why I include them here, they don't work unless steps one and two are in place. Technologies to manage digital 'addiction' are always changing so it's more useful to give you general strategies, rather than specific apps.

1. **Don't reach for the phone** first thing in the morning. The only thing you should be reaching for is a large glass of water, or your significant other. Give yourself at least 30 minutes (ideally 90+ minutes) without looking at any tech.

2. Keep your smartphone **out of sight** when focussing on a task. Out of sight, really is out of mind. You might think that you would continue to think about it, but you really do forget about it.

3. **Leave your phone at home** when you take your kids (if you have them) to the park. Be in the moment with them. Or if you don't have kids, then leave the smartphone at home when you go for a walk round the park/neighbourhood or head to the shops.

4. Buy a **separate camera**. If you have a camera that is just a camera, you can still capture all the moments you want to, but you won't be distracted by everything else on the smartphone.

5. Consider putting your phone into **grayscale**. It will make the phone less appealing, and you won't spend as long on it. Some operating systems on phones now have a Digital Wellbeing component, that can do this automatically at set times.

6. Keep your **phone on silent**. This will allow you to stay focussed. Some phones have a Do Not Disturb mode that will still allow you to assign select callers that can still get through to you. It's worth exploring if your phone has such a feature.

7. One step further is to keep your phone in **airplane mode**. I know this is a tough one for most people, but it's worth trying for at least a couple of hours each day. Especially when working on something important. This works better than just hiding the phone because when you do look at your phone, you won't see any new notifications. If you don't have it in airplane mode, then you are more likely to feel obligated to check and/or respond.

8. Set a technology **curfew**. **Nein for ninety**. This means that for 90 minutes when waking up, before bed and at least once during the day, you have no access to tech. This is a variation on the 'nein,, after nine' approach that I've spoken about before.

9. **Turn off your WIFI** at night. I mentioned this as something I do as part of my evening ritual. It has the benefit of meaning you won't check things online most likely (unless you use your data) but also you won't have unnecessary EMF's around overnight. Yes, you might still pick up a neighbours EMF's but remembering what I said earlier. Control what you can control.

10. **Keep mobile devices outside of the bedroom overnight**. At very least, put into airplane mode, and across the room in the bottom drawer.

11. **Use an old-fashioned alarm clock.** This will mean it's easier for you not to look at the phone first thing in the morning.

12. **Re-order** your apps and **clean the home screen** of your phone. I have made sure that when I press the "home" button on my phone, there are no apps present. Some essential apps are on the other main screens (like camera, calendar, Google Keep, Evernote etc), but all other apps I must 'work at' to get to. If you make it harder to get to the app by accident, then you're less likely to dive into them. When looking for the app, type the app name in rather than scrolling. It will stop you getting distracted by an app you were not planning to open.

13. Consider installing a **newsfeed blocker** for Facebook. Search for "Facebook newsfeed blocker + Chrome/Safari/Firefox/Edge" to find suitable solutions. I did this a few years ago, and when you start, you think that you'll just turn it off and still look at things, but I really didn't. Now, I turn it off from time to time and give myself a bit of time to look at the newsfeed (say 10 minutes) but often I just get bored with it and turn it back on again. I know Facebook aren't going to like me suggesting this one. In fact, no-one who relies on ads or connecting with their audience via the newsfeed is going to like that suggestion. I get it. I am shooting myself in the foot with it too, as I create a lot of content that goes out to people via the feed.

14. Look into **temptation stopping tools** that can prevent you from going on to certain websites. There are both extension add-ons for browsers like 'Waste no Time' and 'Stay Focussed' as well as websites like mindfulbrowsing.com[§]. Also, DF Tube is an add on that will remove suggested YouTube videos, so you don't scroll endlessly[**].

[§] Note that the internet and tools like this are rapidly changing so you might find these suggestions have been superseded by other ones. A bit of research should give you the latest ones to check out though.

[**] By the time you are reading this, the apps might have changed but I'm sure there will be replacements.

15. **Turn off all notifications.** The number of people I see with all these notifications turned on for the most pointless things baffles me. Every two seconds there's notifications to distract them. Turn them all off, except for the absolute essential ones. Perhaps just leaving text messages. Certainly, turn off email, social media sites, news sites and so on. If you have WhatsApp and are in group chats, then mute the notifications for a duration of time. That is, if you don't want to stop all notifications permanently.

16. Give yourself **tech time**. Allow a certain period each day that you will check your notifications. Perhaps, you can check your email once per hour for five minutes and respond to quick emails then. Any longer responses and you can set aside a bigger chunk of time and schedule it in to respond to emails then.

17. **Close your desktop email** application when doing focused work.

18. Schedule in some daily **"power down" periods** when you are away totally from tech. This could be just 5 - 10 minutes, one or two times per day. Go to the bathroom without your phone, or outside for an 'air break' without your phone or other distractions.

19. Make it a rule to **turn off phone when in the company of friends** - no phubbing[††]. Be present with them. Have the phone off and in a bag, not on the table. Remember, out of sight, out of mind.

20. **Unsubscribe** from all unnecessary emails.

21. **Monitor** your app usage. Consider using an app like https://www.rescuetime.com to see how you are spending your time. It will give you a break-down of which applications you are using the most. Some smartphone operating systems are starting to have this integrated into their software now too, as manufacturers start to (outwardly at least) show concern for how their products are affecting people's wellbeing.

22. **Block Time.** Specify a period where you will focus on just one thing (25 - 45 mins work best). Then take five minutes to move your body and breathe. Reward yourself after completing your main task for the day by allowing a *specified and timed* break on digital media.

23. **Plan your day** the night before. Start on your most important task before checking emails for the day. In fact, emails are effectively a list of other people's priorities. Not yours.

[††] Phubbing is a new term, according to the English Dictionary Online. The act of snubbing someone with your mobile phone.

24. Consider using a **permanent 'Out of Office'** autoresponder. Automatically reply to people with a suitable message. Perhaps informing them that you only check emails at certain points of the day, and if it's urgent for them to feel free to pick up the phone and call, but otherwise, in the interest of best serving your clients you don't respond immediately. Or whatever works for you.

25. **Unfollow people** that don't serve you. The old school friend who always makes you feel bad because their life looks so perfect. The celebrity who's views you never like. The acquaintance you met once seven years ago and only posts rubbish.

4. Rules Allow Freedom

The fourth and final point to consider when it comes to rescuing you from technology jail is to think about the hero pilots of World War Two – the RAF. Except this RAF doesn't stand for the Royal Air Force. Rather:

Rules Allow Freedom (RAF)

People often think that having structure, pre-planning or 'rules' in place sounds restrictive. In fact, I have found that by having 'rules', it allows me more freedom. I don't feel guilty when I'm 'time-wasting' if it's already scheduled in. Even if I don't always follow my own 'rules', they give me structure. Also remembering the idea to allow for *flexibility within the framework*. I remember when I started working for myself, I didn't have any structure to my week. So, I created a 'rule' that every Sunday I would release a YouTube video, no matter what was going on. Then on Monday I would re-post it to Facebook, Tuesday I would write a blog on my website and then an article about the video on LinkedIn. Wednesday I would upload the video directly to Facebook's native video system. All of these 'rules' gave me structure and comfort. And although I was quite rigid in the beginning (for around three years), I gave myself more flexibility with the release schedule as the habit became more ingrained.

Rules are a bit like pre-commitments. Remember all the way back in chapter 1.1 when we looked at the unconscious mind and habits? If not, take another look at that chapter. In essence we are saying, ahead of time, what we are committing to. In the case of digital technology, here are some of the rules or commitments I put in ahead of time.

1. **Blocking Apps** These apps I set ahead of time so that I can't access certain websites at pre-defined periods. The most intense app I use is one that won't allow me to turn the feature off even after rebooting my laptop. It means that I really can't waste time on those websites until the timer runs out. The tool I use is called Self-Control (for Mac) but who knows when you are reading this, and whether it's still available, so investigate current similar apps. Other apps are less intense, but easier for you to turn off, which can defeat the point.

2. **Pomodoro** This is a time commitment or rule. The Pomodoro Technique® was developed by Francesco Cirillo in the late 1980s. The technique uses a timer to break down work into intervals. Traditionally 25 minutes in length, separated by short breaks. Each interval is known as a *pomodoro*, from the Italian word for 'tomato', after the tomato-shaped kitchen timer that Cirillo used as a university student. I typically set my timer for 40 minutes. You can use a stopwatch, or there are several apps that incorporate additional features.

3. **State Breaking Apps** These are softer versions of totally blocking you out of a website. When you click to go on the website you will be interrupted with a message (which often you can set) such as "are you sure you want to go on Facebook. You said you wanted to go for a walk on your break." I have in the past used a site like Mindful Browsing for this. Again, you set the websites that you want to give yourself a warning about. This is simply to 'break your state'. The state being the automatic process of just visiting the website without thinking about it. By interrupting the automatic process - or 'breaking your state' - it shocks you out of the behaviour.

4. **Selective Deletion** One of the best things I installed was finding an app that would remove suggested videos from YouTube. YouTube can be a 'rabbit hole' for me. If I get an email with a link to a video that I do need to watch, or I search for something specific, before I know it, I've spent half an hour, or more on YouTube. By removing the suggested videos, I simply watch what I needed to and don't get distracted by other videos. Of course, I can turn this feature off, but it takes effort. If I have a scheduled 'time-wasting' period, I launch an alternative browser where the app isn't activated and view on there. The tool I use also works for feeds in other social media sites like Facebook, X, and Instagram which I also use. I typically only go onto those sites to post or check messages and notifications but not

get sucked into their feeds. If you search online for something like "YouTube suggested video blocker", or "newsfeed blocker" you should find something that will work for your systems.

5. **Nine for Ninety** This is a variation on the 'nein, after nine' principle I've outlined. You say 'no' (or 'nein' as no is in German) to technology for ninety minutes. Ninety minutes upon waking up, at least one 90-miute period in the day, and 90 minutes before bed. If you can't do 90 minutes, start with 15 minutes, and build up.

Although many people don't want to put 'rules' into place for their lives as they feel they are going to limit freedom, or spontaneity. Nothing could be further from the truth. When you implement rules, you will find that you have more time, more energy and you don't get bogged down in triviality. And of course, when you have a set of rules that create a framework for your life, it's always important to remember what I said before – *flexibility within the framework.*

Remember these are the four stages to managing technology:

1. Master your state and emotions.
2. Schedule and plan your time.
3. Reduce external triggers.
4. Rules allow freedom.

Again, jumping to stages three and four won't give you success in limiting technology long term. You must first look at stages one and two.

Digital Nutrition

When it comes to watching what you consume, just like with food, be wary of what you put into your body/mind. Just like junk food isn't going to be beneficial for you, junk media isn't either. I suggest heavily curating your personal news feeds. Choose carefully who you follow on social media and which sites you visit. Do they inspire you? Do they make you feel good about yourself? Do they give you a new way of seeing the world in a good light? Do they move you forward?

If you find that you feel worse about yourself, then unfollow those people. Watch how you consume your media. My strong suggestion is to avoid the news in the first or last 30 minutes (ideally 90 – 120 minutes) of the day.

In 2011, I read in Tim Ferriss' book, *The 4-Hour Workweek*, about a 30-day media fast. That meant not consuming media for 30 days. At first, I thought that was crazy. Especially not looking at the news. How on earth would I know what was going on in the world? Nevertheless, I gave it a go. And you know what. I really didn't miss much. I felt much better about myself and the world around me. The thing is that the news is not an accurate reflection of society. It's usually the worst bits. To grab our attention. And attention is the new currency. We are hooked on bad news stories. If the news accurately reported what was happening in the world, then 99.9% of it would be good news stories. These don't grab our attention though. And, if it's commonplace and not unusual, then it's not news.

Some people think it's crazy not to follow the news, and for about four years I didn't follow it at all. Although it will find you anyway. People will chat, you'll see the headlines of someone else's newspaper, the TV will be on in the lobby of a hotel or reception area. The big news will find you.

I remember in 2011 when there were riots in London which started on a Saturday night. And unlike most news - which isn't even local to you, and you can really do nothing about and therefore feel powerless, just scared or worried – this was local to me. About two miles away. The thing is though; I didn't even know about the riots until Tuesday when they closed our building early because the riot was heading close to our workplace. You might think that I was a bit ignorant not to know about them, but really, what did I miss out on? Three extra days of feeling frightened and worried? When it was relevant for me, and there was something I could do about it, I acted, i.e., leaving work early. And this was one extreme example in the last 14 years.

Nowadays I do get the news in, but I do it differently from before. Occasionally I will visit the BBC website but only in the middle of the day. Not at the beginning or end. Your unconscious mind is more susceptible to inputs at the beginning and end of the day, and you must be protective of what goes in. I also prefer to read rather than watch the news as the way newscasters may present the news, or the images/video presented can be more emotive. Reading it takes the sting out of it[‡‡].

[‡‡] As of 16 March 2020, the world is in a grip of the coronavirus (Covid-19) situation. The last three days I've been as absorbed as anyone and watched/read more news in three days than I have in the last ten years. As a result, I noticed getting more and more stressed with the situation. As a result, I have temporarily deleted the BBC app, and have stricter rules around consumption to protect my own mental health. Even after just a day of doing this I am feeling

It's up to you really. If you have news that you must consume because your job depends on it, then curate it. Still leave it 30 minutes after waking up to get it. Just don't pick up pointless news that really isn't relevant to you. Years ago, the news we would get would be very local to us, and now it's worldwide. It's not to say have no knowledge on world affairs, but you don't need to hear about it three times a day, every day.

In my talks, this is always a pointy issue and divides opinion. As with many of the principles in *The Leadership BEAT Model*™, I looked at what many successful people were doing and a common theme for many (certainly not all), was heavy news curation, if any news was allowed in at all. And in general, they had a wider media curation. All I can suggest is that you might like to experiment like I did. Test out 30 days of no news/media. After that, you might find you can manage it differently and still get what you need out of it. Your choice.

Final Health Considerations with Tech

Researchers (and this might come as no surprise) have found that high levels of screen time are linked to increased cancer and heart disease risk[477]. Not only that but looking down at devices creates an increased load of weight on the spine. By comparison when the head is at different angles the effective weight on the spine is as follows[478].

- 0° = 12 lb (5.4 kg)
- 15° = 27 lb (12.2 kg)
- 30° = 40 lb (18.1 kg)
- 45° = 49 lb (22.2 kg)
- 60° = 60 lb (27.2 kg)

With smartphone users now spending an average of two to four hours a day with their heads dropped down, this results in "700 to 1,400 hours a year of excess stresses seen about the cervical spine", according to the research[478].

And there are benefits to going tech free. One study conducted by Kovert Designs in Morocco (and reported in Fast Company magazine[479]) took 35

---

better. Still informed. Still focussed on what I can control, and how I can contribute to a safer, smaller situation. Just not obsessed. I really understand (again) how doing this (reading/watching news) every day, really can make people anxious and stressed. For the most part, I'd stay away. Situations like the coronavirus reach you anyway, and you can then opt-in to be informed to stay safe and well. (16 March 2020).

4.5 Digital Nutrition and Dieting

people out into the desert for four days without access to their smart devices. Kovert Designs also included five neuroscientists on the trip. What they noted after such a short period of time was better posture (obvious when considering what was mentioned above), deeper friendships (as they started to make better eye contact and opened up their posture even more), better conversations (as debate and contemplation on topics flourished because the answers weren't immediately available to them via some search engine), more efficient sleep (which again should come as no surprise having read the chapter on sleep in this book) and new perspectives (with people deciding to make big changes in career, relationships or personal health. Perhaps because of having more time to just 'be' with themselves, it gave them the opportunity to re-connect with another aspect of themselves).

These, I'm sure, are just a small list of benefits that will come from downing tech for some time. This chapter hasn't been about getting rid of tech altogether and you don't have to go out to the desert for four days to get similar benefits. Consider having tech windows, tech curfews, leaving the phone at home when with people you care about, respond on your timescale, have the phone in airplane mode or silent more often, and keep it out of sight when working. Digital nutrition and dieting are about being conscious, aware, and clever with your digital behaviour, not eliminating them altogether.

If you incorporate some of the advice in this chapter or look to amend your technology use in other positive ways, I'm sure you're going to reap countless benefits. Creating some simple rules for yourself will allow freedom. Remember what I said before:

Rules Allow Freedom (RAF)

Quick summary about digital nutrition and becoming superhuman...

1. Digital technology usage needs to be closely examined to ensure that you are the master of it, and not the other way around.

2. Most apps are built to zap your attention and create infinite dopamine/opioid loops that keep your distracted.

3. Remember that Rules Allow Freedom and that by instituting a few rules for how you use technology, you will become freer.

Action plan for becoming superhuman...

1. Commit to giving yourself at least one hour each day that you are tech free. And no, being asleep doesn't count. Ideally, make this during your working day, but if you really can't spare a whole hour without tech, at least do an hour without the phone, or emails.

2. Choose one of the tips that you can implement immediately and see how it works for you over the next ten days.

3. Go out to meet friends, or to the shops and leave your phone at home.

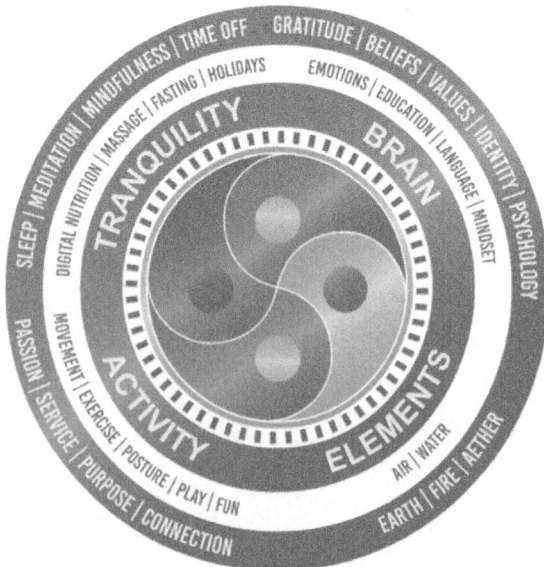

4.6 Time Off and Holidays
Have a break, have a holiday…

---

*"The purpose of a vacation is to have the time to rest.
But many of us, even when we go on vacation, don't
know how to rest. We may even come back more tired
than before we left."*

- Thich Nhat Hanh

As I write this chapter, I am sitting on a plane somewhere across Europe on my way to Cyprus for a couple of weeks in the sun and by the sea. When we are so focussed on achieving and getting our goals we can forget, or don't see the value in, scheduling time away from it all.

We need both short breaks and longer breaks to reset the system – mind, body, and spirit. Each week we should look to take one full day off from work. I mean, even God rested one day. If you are a user of *The Super Journal**, then you will know that in that journal it only has enough space for six days of entries each week.

It's not just each week that we should be taking time off. Our daily rhythm works according to an ultradian rhythm[†]. Much like overnight we have pattern of sleeping in 90-minute cycles, the ultradian rhythm also operates in 90-minute cycles. A bit like a game of football[‡]. Ideally, we would take time away from our work for several minutes every 90 minutes. In fact, I recommend taking short (2-5 minute) breaks every 25 – 45 minutes and a slightly longer one (10 – 15 minutes) after 90-minutes. Use that opportunity

---

[*] *The Super Journal* is the daily planner I created to help increase focus and productivity for entrepreneurs and professionals and is available at **www.thesuperjournal.com**
[†] In chronobiology – the study of timing of our biology and cells - an ultradian rhythm is a recurrent period or cycle repeated throughout a 24-hour day.
[‡] Soccer, in some countries.

to get outside, move, stretch, meditate or doing something different like tidying up, organising your desk or anything that takes you away from your work momentarily.

In addition to general time off, we need to be looking at longer holidays to allow our nervous system to properly reset. I don't think I need to convince you too hard that having a holiday is good for you. The right kind mind you. Not one where you are out late drinking and partying each night - although this can be fun in the moment - it won't give your body much time to recover and recharge. It might give your mind some much needed decompression but there are less destructive ways to do that. Consider going on an active holiday. A yoga retreat, hiking holiday, exploring nature or something else. Get plenty of sleep, movement, fresh air, sunshine, and nature and you'll reap even more benefits than simply lying by a beach sleeping off a hangover.

Have you ever noticed that often, the moment you go on holiday after an intense period of work, you suddenly get ill. It's not that strange. When you are working intensely and stressed you are perpetually in a fight-or-flight mode and the body is keeping you focussed, alert and active ready to deal with what you need to do. Then, the moment you get some downtime, the body will realise this, and as you have been depleting your energy balance, the body decides to shut down to give you time to rest. And to force you to rest, it will get ill. It's intelligent really.

There was a joint study from the Global Commission on Ageing and Transamerica Centre for Retirement Studies, and it highlighted interesting results on the potential health benefits of traveling more often. According to the study, women who went on holiday at least twice a year had significantly less risk of having a heart attack or dying from heart failure compared to women who rarely took a holiday and travelled. In the same study, men who did not take a holiday each year were shown to have a 20% higher risk of death from all causes and about a 30% greater risk of death from heart disease[480].

Furthermore, the longitudinal Framingham Heart Study, found that women who holidayed every six years or less had a significantly higher risk of developing a heart attack or coronary death compared to women who went on holiday at least twice per year[481]. And yet another study of 1500 women, which was published in the Wisconsin Medical Journal showed that women who took annual holidays were less likely to suffer from depression and other mental health issues[482].

Having time off is essential. A lot of people who are game changers in the world, people looking to create impact, make a difference, deliver great change are perhaps guilty of not taking enough time off. Their passion behind their greater purpose can give them all the fuel they need to appear to have superhuman energy and endurance. And while that may be true, it will only be true for a while. Without proper rest and relaxation, there exists the strong possibility that something will break for them in the future. Don't be like that. Schedule and prioritize your time off. In fact, wherever possible, schedule that in first.

Each week or month, plan out your days off – at least by blocking the time off. Plan out and block time during the day for time off. Plan your holidays (even if not the exact destination) in advance. Yes, you want to also be spontaneous too, and allow room for that, but if you don't plan anything, you might get to December and realise the whole year has gone by without any extended breaks.

If it's not scheduled, it is likely that it won't get done.

Quick summary about time-off and holidays and becoming superhuman...

1. Working continuously is not good for our physical or mental health and certainly not our productivity. You can only become superhuman if you recharge regularly.

2. Our body operates on an ultradian cycle which means that throughout the day it needs rest as well as times of activity. The ultradian rhythm operates in 90-minute cycles.

3. When you overwork yourself and finally get time to rest on holiday the body often forces you to slow down and so you will (rather irritatingly) get ill.

Action plan for becoming superhuman...

1. Commit to having one complete day off work each week. Yep, even God rested one day a week. That means no work emails (not even a peek) and no work calls.

2. Take a longer two-day break (or three) from work – a city-break or break in the countryside (even better) every two to three months.

3. Look to have a more extended break (one week or more) every four to six months. Schedule something in your diary today for a big holiday.

4.7 Stress Management 101
Chill out dude…

"I wanted to sell a million records, and I sold a million records. I wanted to go platinum; I went platinum. I've been working nonstop since I was 15. I don't even know how to chill out."

- Beyoncé Knowles

According to Dr Rangan Chatterjee, a UK doctor and best-selling author and popular podcast host, stress is the number one underlying reason for most of his patients' visits which he estimates to be around 80%[483]. And this falls into broad agreement with other figures out there[484,485]. At the root cause of many diseases might well be a stress component in some form or another – mental or physical. This book has already given you numerous stress reducing ideas such as meditation, breathing exercises, sleep, mindfulness, grounding/earthing, exercise and so on. This chapter offers even more modalities and therapies worth looking into which help with things like anxiety, stress, past unresolved trauma, and relaxation.

MASSAGE

The benefits of skin-on-skin massage are often underestimated. Not only just useful for the easing of tension, but this kind of touch has been proven to raise the level of Natural Killer (NK) cells, which help fight cancer[486]. Even a single session was shown to reduce inflammatory compounds in the body[487], with even more benefits on repeated sessions[488]. A reason to get a massage every few weeks - as if a reason was needed!

And of course, from a physical perspective massage can ease muscle pain, soreness and stiffness and provide a feeling of relaxation and help induce sleep. Massage is a great addition to any tranquility practices you might already employ – like sleep, fasting, meditation and mindfulness.

When I worked for Sainsbury's HQ, there was an on-site masseuse who came in weekly, and I had 30-minute massage every three weeks. Of course, if I could, I would have one daily. It can be seen as a luxury, but I usually use money from an account I set up specifically for treats. See the next paragraph on the Money Jar System.

FINANCIAL STRESS - MONEY JAR SYSTEM

"Havin' money's not everything; not havin' it is"

– Ye (Kanye West)

Financial strain can be a stress for many. The following is advice and strategies that I've learnt over the years that might help you.

I went to a wealth seminar in 2011 and was introduced to an idea on money allocation that I liked. It's called the Money Jar System. You take the money that you earn and distribute it into six different (virtual) jars. If you are self-employed or a business owner paying yourself, then take 20% (or whatever you need to, aside) for paying tax. Then the remainder is the income that you receive and distribute into six different jars.

The jars are set up as follows (although exact percentages can vary depending on you):

Necessities – 55%

This is where 55% of your income goes. It's your current account used for things like daily travel, bills, mortgage, haircuts, food and so on.

Financial Freedom Fund – 10%

This is money that you are investing in for your long-term future. It might be in Index Funds, bonds, ISA's, stocks, and shares. Ideally investing in things that will one day bring a healthy return that you can live on and become financially independent. So, this might include money that goes to buying rental properties.

Long-term Saving for Spending (LTSS) – 10%

This account is for big spending items that you want. It might be the big holiday, fancy car, big screen TV, new smartphone, or any other luxury item.

Education – 10%

This is for your continued growth. Attending seminars, hiring a coach, going to university, and taking a course. Things like that.

Charity – 5%

This is to give to charity. It might be that you wait on this one until you have your basic needs met. But beyond the basic needs, if you can give something it will be good for you to develop the habit, if nothing else. Let's say you earn £100,000 a year and begrudge giving £5,000 away, will it be any easier to give £500,000 away when you earn £10,000,000?

Play – 10%

This is the one that was most difficult for me. The idea with this one is that you are supposed to spend this *all*, each month. On things that are just for fun. It might be that you spend it on going out for a fancy meal, going to a concert, treating your friends to a game of LazerTag[*], paintballing, cryotherapy, or massages (unless these last two come under your necessities account. This might be the case if you are someone who depends on their physical body for your job – e.g., professional footballer, yoga teacher, dancer). The reason for spending this all is to enjoy your money in the moment. And not waiting for some distant future or only spending on things you need. If you do this, then subconsciously you'll never see the benefit of earning more money and so you won't. By spending and enjoying it, you teach your mind that it can bring fun to your life, and you'll re-program yourself to want to earn more of it.

Most bank accounts will let you automate a lot of this, so you don't even have to think about it once it's been set up. And you'll get used to living on 55% (or whatever the percentages are for you – these were the ones suggested at the seminar).

---

[*] As a kid we used to go to something called Laser Quest where you shoot your mates with laser guns and when they 'died' their packs would vibrate. I've recently been watching *How I Met Your Mother*, and one of the main characters, Barney, loves LazerTag, hence it is popping into my head.

T - TRANQUILITY

General Principles

1. **Spend less than you earn**. When you get a pay rise, just keep the same car, house, TV – whatever it is. You don't have to 'keep up with the Joneses'. If you keep increasing your spending in line with your pay increases, then you'll never become financially free or secure.
2. Don't use **credit cards** unless you can **pay off the balance in full** each month.
3. **Pay yourself first**. This means, even if you have debt, invest a small portion (say 10%) to your own education and projects to get yourself out of debt. Then pay your debtors.
4. The best financial investment you can make is in **The Bank of Self** (i.e., yourself. Your own continued education, development and health).
5. **Don't invest in things you don't understand**. And that goes for understanding yourself too. As the ancient Greek philosopher, Socrates, once said:

"Know thyself"

- Socrates

HEARTMATH

Heartmath is an interesting technique. It's deceptively simple and yet very powerful and well researched. It's a method of getting the mind and body synced up to allow an anxious or stressful situation to diffuse.

Before going into the main technique from Heartmath that I use, some background information. More detail on the techniques is available at the Institute of Heartmath and by reading the book *The Heartmath Solution*.

We are electromagnetic beings. We emit electromagnetic frequencies ourselves. The brain emits a field that extends beyond the body (about one foot away), but another part of the body emits a more powerful field that extends about 6 – 8 feet away. And that organ is the heart. The heart has its own independent nervous system referred to as "the brain in the heart" by neuroscientists. The heart has at least forty thousand neurons (nerve cells) – as many as are found in the subcortical centres of the brain[489]. The heart also transmits more messages to the brain than the other way around[490].

Both the heart and brain (and every other part of you and the universe) emit a frequency. These can be measured using EEG for the brain (electroencephalogram) and ECG for the heart (electrocardiogram). This will show up as a wave of some sort. If you are in a calm relaxed state, the waves will be nice and smooth with equal spacing between the peak-to-peaks and trough-to-throughs. If, however, you are in a state of stress, anger, frustration, or similar states then you will find a jagged and erratic pattern.

The shape of the heart waves comes from something called Heart Rate Variability (HRV). HRV is the beat-to-beat differences in your heart rhythm. For example, if you have a resting heart rate of 60 beats per minute (bpm), you might think that your heart beats once every second. The reality is that it might beat at 1.1 seconds then 0.9 seconds and then back to 1.1. If it's like this, and the variation is consistent then you will have a smooth consistent curve. If it's more like 1.1, 0.8, 1.3, 0.99, 1.02, 0.78 – i.e., more inconsistent, then you will get a jagged picture. In fact, having quite a high, but smooth HRV is deemed healthy. For example, 0.7, 1.3, 0.7, 1.3, 0.7, 1.3 and so on[†]. It's almost like saying that you can go from one extreme to another very quickly and with control. An analogy might be going from a standing start on the 100m running race and shoot out the blocks and then come back to the starting line to do it all again, quickly, and effortlessly.

What causes the HRV pattern to be in an erratic state? Well, being in an anxious, stressed, angry or similar state will. As will being overly fatigued or getting ill. What the scientists at the Institute of Heartmath have discovered over the last 30+ years of research are many fascinating things, including this. When you are in a state of stress, your HRV is erratic and jagged. This also tallies up with your brain wave measurements. Your EEG will look erratic too. However, when you do some simple practices to get yourself into a better state of being, your heart patterns start to smooth out (becoming coherent) and through a process of entrainment, so do your brainwaves. And having more coherent brain and heart patterns allows you to become a better leader as you start to make better decisions from a state of balance and not stress, anxiety, or frustration.

The scientists at the Institute of Heartmath have also discovered that a person can influence another person's field, especially if the people are emotionally close (e.g., family member) or touching. So, if you are in a stressed state, your

---

[†] The numbers I'm using are arbitrary and just used to illustrate the point.

field (remembering that it extends several feet away from you) might exert an influence on others and change their field – depending on whose is strongest.

This makes intuitive sense to me. Have you ever entered a room, and you can "feel" the energy in there isn't right. Even if no-one has said anything to you. I also think that is why being encased in a metal tube (the London Underground) with lots of overlapping energy fields isn't a great idea. People are already crammed in, frustrated, hot and possibly late for work. Their heart fields are very jagged and imposing that effect on those around them. Even our tendency to live in flats (or apartments) where there are so many competing energy fields can't be great for us as we become exposed to other people's feelings all too easily and frequently. Not to mention artificial electromagnetic frequencies coming from wiring, WiFi, Bluetooth, TV's, computers and more.

Why is knowing about heart fields important? Core heart feelings affect both branches of the autonomic nervous system. They can help reduce the activity of the fight or flight side (the sympathetic nervous system) and increase the activity of the rest and digest side (the parasympathetic nervous system). Positive emotions such as love, happiness, compassion, gratitude, appreciation, care will not only change the nervous system but in turn reduce the level of cortisol (stress hormone) in your body[491,492]. Interestingly, the same pre-cursor hormone (Pregnenolone) that is used for cortisol[493] is also used for the longevity hormone DHEA[494,495], and so if there's no need for cortisol, the DHEA production is increased. And DHEA has many protective and regenerative effects on the body[495]. These positive emotions also increase the level of IgA[496], an important secretory antibody which is the immune system's first line of defence and increasing IgA can make us more disease and infection resistant[497].

The Heartmath Solution is well worth reading to get a fuller picture of all this, but for now I'll explain the first technique (taken from the book) and the one I use the most, to get out of a stressful anxious state.

Freeze-Frame

1. Recognise the stressful situation. Take a "freeze-frame" on it. As if you are pausing a movie.
2. Move your attention away from your head and take it to your heart. You do this by pretending to be breathing in and out through your heart. Putting a hand on your heart can help imagine this and shift

your focus to your heart. Keep your focus there for at least ten seconds.

3. Recall a positive, fun feeling or time from your past. Do your best to re-experience it. Imagine you are there. Looking through your own eyes at the positive experience.
4. Now, allowing your intuition or common sense to contribute, ask your heart what a more effective response to the situation would be. What would minimise future stress?
5. Listen to your heart's "response".

That's it. Simple, yet it takes a bit of practice to do, especially to catch yourself in that moment and freeze-frame on it. After a while though, it will become easier. For more detail on Heartmath and further techniques I refer you to *The Heartmath Solution* book.

FORGIVENESS

"Forgiveness is for me; forgiveness sets me free."

I once heard it said that holding a grudge, anger, or resentment towards someone who you perceived has wronged you, is like drinking poison and expecting the other person to die. That sentiment might have even come from the Buddha many centuries ago. And we still need to learn it today. Harbouring this anger creates unnecessary stress on the body and may tend to hurt you.

Just "let it go". In fact, that's often a tactic that I use on myself to release the burden of events that seem to have wronged me. I just keep saying to myself "let it go". Especially recognising that it's for my benefit that I'm doing it. If you've just been cut off by someone in traffic as you drive to work, do you really think that the other person is giving you a second thought? They probably didn't even register that they had done anything. And besides, do you know their unique situation. Maybe they were rushing home to look after a loved one, or they just received terrible news. Or maybe they are just an inconsiderate driver. I remember one time when at a set of traffic lights someone who clearly had a short fuse trying to cut me off as we crossed the lights and then getting abusive (through the window of his car) as he veered to get in front of me. I did get a bit irritated at him but then I did think to myself "poor guy, he's obviously so little in control of his emotions that he loses it like that." However, years later (we're talking over five years), I was at the same set of lights, and I suddenly realised that where I had been positioned before at the lights was for a right turn only lane and I went straight ahead without realising it was a right turn only lane. Now, his response seems to make a little more sense – even if probably over the top and extreme. I hadn't even considered that I might have played a part in that incident. Either way, at the time I forgave him to spare me.

I know it's a silly example, but the point is valid all the same. How did Nelson Mandela manage to unite a nation and become such an inspiration to millions? He was able (amongst other things) to forgive the people and country that imprisoned him for 27 years. Hate begets hate. Resentment begets resentment. Anger begets anger. You don't put out a fire with more fire. You put it out with water (or another stifling agent)[‡].

Immaculee Illabagiza, best-selling author of *Left to Tell*, and advocate for peace and forgiveness, and survivor of the Rwandan genocide from 1994, shows that forgiveness can happen in even the direst of circumstances. Illabagiza, witnessed her whole family (except for one brother) murdered. She only survived by hiding for 91 days in a 3-by-4-foot bathroom with seven other women. After she survived and the French arrived, officially ending the dire situation in her part of Rwanda, she found out that the man who had killed her mother (and was personally known to her family) was being held in prison. She felt compelled to visit him. She wasn't sure what was going to happen, but her faith helped her forgive him. Her act of forgiveness even had the killer cry. The official in charge of the jail was angry that she could forgive him at first. Encouraging her to spit on the killer, slap him, hit him. She refused and her act of forgiveness even had a dramatic effect on the official. Illabagiza's story is extreme. One which, I hope, you and I will never have the misfortune of experiencing. Forgiveness set her free. I really don't know if I would ever be that strong, but I'd like to think that this story of forgiveness will rub off on me.

[‡] And yes, sometimes wildfires are curbed by setting more controlled fires. These however just allow the main fire not to spread any further, and it is not the fire itself that is putting the fire out. You create space and allow the fire to run out of fuel. The metaphor still stands in my view.

This idea of forgiveness isn't just directed at other people of course. It would be wise to learn to forgive yourself as well. Forgive yourself for being less than perfect. For your 'faults' or anything else that you berate yourself for. I also like what Oprah said about forgiveness.

"Forgiveness is giving up the hope that the past could have been any different."

– Oprah Winfrey

EMOTIONAL FREEDOM TECHNIQUE

Emotional Freedom Technique (EFT) or 'Tapping' as it is also commonly known is best described as "acupuncture without the needles". Effectively, there's quite a bit of back story to how EFT came to be which isn't exactly important for this section but well worth looking up if you are keen to know more on EFT. Studies show that EFT works by regulating the expression of genes that contribute to the overall health in the body, shutting down stress genes and upregulating stress-reduction genes[498].

In one recent study, EFT reduced symptoms of pain by 57 per cent, anxiety by 40 per cent, depression by 35 per cent and posttraumatic stress disorder (PTSD) by 32 per cent. All while increasing happiness by 31 per cent and lowering resting heart rate, blood pressure and cortisol levels[499]. There are also countless other studies showing effectiveness of EFT on weight loss[500], mental health, insomnia and immune system[501]. Even fibromyalgia symptom reduction[502].

EFT is a therapy where you tap, using your fingers, different parts of your body while repeating a phrase. These phrases vary depending on the issue but typically will be talking about the issue that you are facing. I'll give an example below, so you have an idea. In essence you just talk about the issue while tapping on the points I'm about to reveal.

Tapping Points

1. Crown of the head.
2. Side of the top of nose, where eyebrow meets nose.
3. Temple (other side of eyebrow).
4. In-between upper lip and nose.

T - TRANQUILITY

5. In-between lower lip and chin. Crease of chin.
6. Just beneath the collar bone.
7. Side of ribs. Where the bra strap would be. About where the bicep would touch the ribs.

Set-Up Statement

Prior to tapping through that cycle, you start the process off with a set-up statement. You also tap while saying this. You take four fingers from one hand and tap on the 'karate-chop' side of the other hand while saying the statement.

For example,

"Even though I'm really anxious about this presentation, I completely and totally (love and) accept myself."

The basic parts are this,

"Even though _____, I _____"

Where the first 'blank' is about the problem, and the second 'blank' is about something positive about you. Some people might find it hard to say, "I completely love and accept myself", so you can try these alternatives instead:

- I am worthy of loving and accepting myself even if I don't right now.
- I give myself permission to one day love and accept myself.
- I give myself permission to believe that is it is possible to love and accept myself.
- There is a part of me that fully loves and accepts myself even if I don't have access to that part at this moment.
- I accept that's what I am feeling.
- I am open to the possibility that I can (or I am trying or learning to) accept myself.
- I'm a good person.
- I'm OK.
- I accept myself and all my feelings.
- I love myself.
- I choose to release and surrender any attachment that I have to this.
- I forgive myself and any others who have contributed to this problem.

Say this set-up statement three times and then using a shortened version start tapping on each of the points. Tap around 6-8 times repeating the simple statement, then on the next cycle you would continue to talk but change the language up a little. See example below.

Why these points of the body? Trial and error. EFT was born from something called TFT (Though Field Therapy) which itself is essentially the same, only the tapping was done in different places and different protocols for different issues, before being simplified and becoming EFT. TFT itself was an accidental discovery too. Again, it's not too important for the scope of this book, as my main aim is just to give you the basics and hope that you explore further if interested.

You can use EFT for several different things. Emotional and even physical pain. Yes, it's a little spooky to think that tapping on your body can help with physical pain, but it really can help to do so.

How to Start

1. First identify what it is that is bothering you.
2. Give it an impact rating 1- 10. 10 being the worst and 1 being not even there.
3. Repeat the set-up statement three times while doing the karate chop onto the four fingers of opposite hand.
4. Tap from crown of the head to under the armpit (bra-strap area) resting on each area for around 6 – 8 taps while saying the shortened statement focussing on the area that is bothering you.
5. Repeat the tapping (without the set-up statement) another 1 – 2 times through. This time just speaking whatever comes to mind.
6. After 2 – 3 cycles take a deep breath in and out.
7. Gauge where you are on a scale of 1 – 10 now.
8. Continue to repeat until down to a manageable number.

I'll give you an example below of what one might say but the method above is the super short succinct version with no bells and whistles. I recommend looking into EFT further. Either working with a practitioner, or there are some great YouTube videos giving tuition on EFT as well as several books.

Example

Let's say this is about anxiety about giving a presentation. The set-up statement might be: "Even though I'm anxious about giving this presentation,

407

I know I'll be doing my best and that's all I can do." Tap on each tapping point 6 – 8 times. Tap on the karate chop for as many times as it takes to say the set-up statement three times.

1. Assess how anxious you are on scale of 1 – 10.
2. Karate Chop tapping while saying set-up statement three times.
3. Tap on crown of head. *"Anxious about presentation."*
4. Eyebrow/Nose point. *"Anxious about presentation."*
5. Temple/side of head. *"So anxious right now."*
6. Under nose. *"Anxious about this presentation."*
7. Above chin. *"Anxious about presentation."*
8. Beneath collar bone. *"So anxious. Anxious."*
9. Under armpit/bra-strap line. *"Anxious about presentation."*
10. Back to crown. *"I wonder why I'm so anxious."*
11. Eyebrow/Nose point. *"I wonder what it could mean?"*
12. Temple/side of head. *"This anxiety is here for a reason."*
13. Under nose. *"What could that reason be?"*
14. Above chin. *"I recognise this anxiety."*
15. Beneath collar bone. *"And I'm ready to release it now."*
16. Under armpit/bra-strap line. *"Yes, I'm ready to release it now."*
17. Big exhale.
18. Assess where you are on scale of 1 – 10.

The words above are just examples. You can say whatever it is you are feeling, or your inner chatter is saying – just verbalise it outwards. You don't have to say that you are ready to release it or anything like that. You can repeat this over and over and see how you do. If, after 15 minutes or so, it's not working for you, then that's fine. Sometimes it takes longer or doesn't work for that situation.

I've only touched on the process, so I would explore EFT in greater detail. It can be a useful tool to add to your toolbox.

This Too Shall Pass

I mentioned this phrase before when I wrote about my Vipassana experience in chapter 4.2. The realisation through experiential means, that all things in life and the universe are transient. Meaning that they pass. Whenever I start to get stressed about something in life (and yes, I still do get unwanted stress), I simply remind myself of this axiom of life:

"This too, shall pass."

Even as I write this, I have re-triggered a bad injury to my knee, a torn meniscus originally experienced in 2015, and then again at the end of 2018. And then as it was healing I re-did it demonstrating a move while teaching a yoga class. What is it that I think about though? ***This too, shall pass.*** I won't always be on crutches, or unable to go up and down the stairs. Things never stay the same. I know that for some people this might sound like a platitude of sorts.

The reality is just that, though. Things *do* come and go. The way we are feeling – good or bad, is just transient. Recognising this, is possibly one of my main go-to stress-busting techniques. To the point, that, although I don't currently have a tattoo, if I ever get one, one of the (three) phrases that I've decided I would make part of the artwork would be this.

"This too, shall pass."

In case you're wondering, the other two that I would add would be: "Thank You" and "Never Do, Never Know". Each having significance to me. "Thank You" is about having gratitude in life – for all things. Good and bad that might happen. And "Never Do, Never Know" is an abbreviated version of a saying I came across while travelling in Malaysia (as part of my longer 25-month long travels). I was originally contemplating a tattoo back then (something tells me I won't finally get one). The original phrase was in Chinese and loosely translates to "without having had experience, one cannot gain wisdom."

BREATHING – BELLY

In chapter 2.1 we looked at breathing. Breathing into the belly diaphragmatic breathing helps to activate the parasympathetic nervous system response. The rest and digest part. Most people breathe into the upper chest (and mouth), and not deep into the belly (and through the nose). When you breathe into the chest (and mouth) you are unnecessarily adding stress. We each have a threshold for stress, and when we exceed it, we snap. Many activities that we experience day-to-day will add to our baseline stress levels. If they are already high, things that shouldn't take us over the threshold, might. Ideally, we have stressful points in the day, and the stress goes down. Review the charts below. In the first chart, although we have stressful points throughout the day, we can cope with them. In the second chart, because of other factors adding to our stress levels anyway, for example, poor breathing, our baseline stress level is already elevated. So, things that shouldn't take us above our threshold might do.

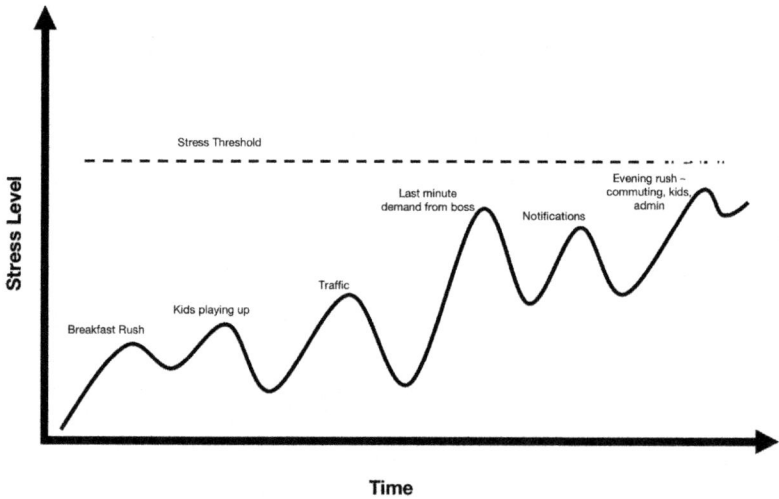

Figure 22 - Natural Stress Wave Throughout the Day (without additional baseline stress)

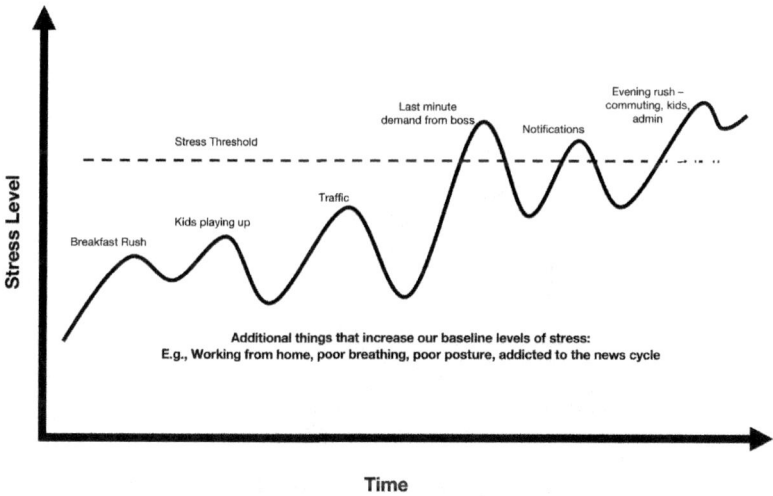

Figure 23 - Natural Stress Wave Throughout the Day (with additional baseline stress)

Check out chapter 2.1 for more on breathing techniques. The main thing from a stress response perspective, is to focus on deep belly breaths and in and out of the nose. This will help stress releasing.

And speaking of releasing…

Re-lease, let go, etc….

When I am doing my belly breaths (above), I add the mantra 're-lease' or 'let go'. Focussing on whatever the stressful 'thing' might be. I just remind myself of it when breathing to let it go and release it.

CCC

The Stoics were first around over 2000 years ago. Stoicism is a life philosophy and one that resonates with me. There's a lot to it, but one of the essential tenants for leading a good and happy life is to focus on what you can control in life. Which in effect, is very little. Only really your attitude and actions. Way back in the beginning of the book, in chapter 1.6, I talked about:

ATTENTION
A
ASSIGN ACTION

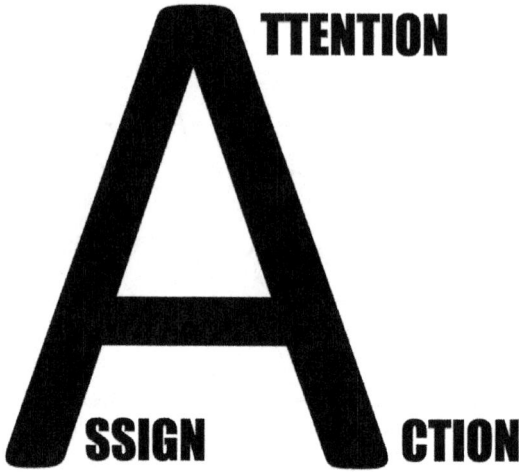

Figure 24 - The Three Things That Dictate Your Mood or State

That's only what you can control in life. What you pay attention to. The meaning/language you decide to assign to what you pay attention to, and the actions you decide to take.

The idea of focussing on what you can control in life will allow you to manage stress better. It's summed up by this statement (which I heard author Craig Ballantyne first say):

Control what you can control.

Cope with what you can't, and

Concentrate on what's important.

Many things that people worry about are beyond their control. Deciding what you can control in any given situation is going to make life easier. See below for some examples. We can't control the things on the left. We can influence them, by focussing our energy and efforts on the things in the right column.

What people worry about but have no control over	What you can control in this situation
Health	What you eat. How much you move. Paying attention to sleep and all the things in this book.
What other people think of you	Being friendly. Smiling. Being honest. Being true to who you are and so on.
Job Security or Promotion	Embracing all training given to you. Self-training if needed. Whether or not you take interest and roles in other departments. Volunteering for extra projects. Speaking up in meetings.
Weather	Whether you decide to pack an umbrella, or wet weather gear. Putting a gazebo up for your BBQ party and so on.
Climate change	Whether you recycle, walk or cycle instead of using the car. Whether or not you cut back on meat consumption. Eat locally. Turn off water when brushing teeth. And so on.
Being late	Leaving on time or earlier. Perhaps getting accommodation near to where you need to be. Finding alternate routes. Travelling under you own steam rather than relying on public transport. Getting to bed earlier and so on.

T - TRANQUILITY

The truth is that there is very little we can control in life. And most of what we worry about we can't control. If you just identify which is which and start to focus on what you can control, well, that might be the secret to a less stressful life for you.

It's simple. Not easy, mind you. Even knowing this I still worry or stress about things I can't control. Like what score I'll be given in feedback forms from delegates. What I can control is giving my best. Being prepared. Being present for them. A welcoming personality, giving them lots of examples, value and so on. What they put down in that box at the end of the day is beyond my control.

E+R=O

As I say above, we have very little control about things that occur in life. The events of our life. People often think that the event is the outcome though. You lose your job (E, the event) that must be bad (O, the outcome). The reality is different though. This equation – which I first heard from Jack Canfield (although I'm not sure if it's his or not) sums it up nicely.

$$E + R = O$$

E does not equal O. The event does not equal the outcome. Losing your job does not mean it's bad, or good. There is a third variable, R. The response – not reaction – you have to the event. We can't control the event. We lose the job. Fine. We might react negatively. We post bad things about our employer on social media, talk badly about them to others, wallow in self-pity at home watching daytime TV. Drink too early in the day, and six months, a year or two passes and we have no more job. Or we decide to *respond*[§]. We decide that perhaps now is the time to start that blog, change career, write a book, or we spend the mornings looking for jobs and then the afternoon we spend quality time with our children, finally being able to pick them up from school.

[§] We want to respond and not react. To react is automatic and often not thought out. To respond is measured. I often use this as an example in my workshops. Imagine going to a doctor when you are ill and they say to you "Here's this pill, come back in a week." And when you come back, they say to you "Your body has been *reacting* to the pill. Here's this other pill. Come back in a week." And then you go back a week later, and they say, "Your body has been *responding* to the pill." Which would you rather hear?

414

After a couple of months, we get the interview, and the interviewer is really impressed with our blog, or we found a new career to pursue.

BIG PICTURE – WILL IT MATTER IN FUTURE

The other technique I use a lot is to imagine the future. I do my best to step outside of my current reality, propel myself to a future time – be that six months, six years, or sixty years in the future. And then I ask myself "will I be concerned about this situation, I'm currently experiencing, in the future?" I know this takes a lot of rational and creative thinking, but if you can manage it, it can be quite powerful. I often think of this phrase doing this:

"One 'day' we'll look back on this and laugh. Why not make that 'day' today?"

OTHER TECHNIQUES

There are plenty of different ways to get some tranquility in your life and below I just list some more that you can investigate in more detail. They all help with release tension and stress from the body and mind.

- **Tai Chi, Yoga and Qigong**
  - I may have lumped them together here, but they are all slightly different from one another. Although you can learn some basics online, I would recommend committing to a live in-person course to get the basics right. They all help with balancing the mind and body. One study involving an intervention and control group for tai chi found that 12 weeks of twice a week practice helped significantly reduce depression in moderate to major depression participants. Without the use of any medication, as compared to the control group who were waiting to get on the tai chi program[503].
- **Floatation Tanks**
  - These are sensory deprivation pods. They are filled with water (about one foot deep) with plenty of Epsom (Magnesium) salts The concentration of salt is similar to that in the Dead Sea, which means you float on the surface. The temperature of the water is the same as your inner temperature. The idea being that when the pod is put in complete darkness (although you can usually have a little

415

light on if you so wish), you can't tell where your body ends, and the water begins. It's quite a surreal (almost transcendental) experience that I'd really recommend checking out. You open your eyes and all you can see is blackness. My first experience in a flotation tank I had a massive release of tension from different places on my body that went through me like a pulse wave and exited my mouth.

- **Matrix Re-Imprinting**
  - o This takes EFT a step further and regresses you back to a childhood time when a particular trauma took place. And we all have trauma in our childhood, even if we don't realise it. Maybe your parents were on the phone when you wanted to show them something and they said "not now!" Your younger self creates a belief about the world at that point. It could be that you are not important enough, you are annoying, you are unloved or something else. The point is, that Matrix Re-Imprinting helps resolve those traumas and you move forward in life. Even when you don't realise that something back in your childhood is impeding you now.

- **Reiki**
  - o Reiki uses a hands-off (or very gentle touch) to help rebalance energy in your body. I know, some of this stuff might sound a bit 'woo woo' for a book aimed at professionals and change-makers, but seriously, don't knock it just yet. My philosophy is just to give things a go. There's no real downside. If it works, then great. If it doesn't, so be it. There's unlikely to be any negative side effects. Unlike most medications, that often have many negative side effects, even if they do work.

Other things worth exploring could be Marma Point therapy, acupuncture hypnosis, Regression therapy and Craniosacral Therapy.

This is not meant to be an exhaustive list of course, but by checking out a few of these practices, it will lead you to discover more. Some will work for some people, and others will work for other people. We are all different. And the practitioner will also be pivotal in whether it works for you or not, not just the therapy itself. As well as what period of your life you are in. Just because something didn't work for you today with someone, it doesn't mean that the same approach won't work for you in six months' time – even with the same practitioner. It just might.

The main idea of this chapter is just to let you know that there are countless ways in which to chill out a little. Beyond what you might have already considered. Ways such as taking a walk into nature, exercising or having a vacation. Those options are great of course, and far better ways of relaxing than using alcohol, drugs, or medications. There are just so many ways to think about stress management, as we've just explored, and you could also consider.

Quick summary about stress management and becoming superhuman...

1. Stress can be at the root cause of most visits to the doctor's and is a global pandemic.

2. Although a bit of acute stress now and then can be beneficial, chronic low-level stress continually bombarding us is generally not a good thing.

3. There are many ways that one can de-stress from avoiding stressful situations, planning, following some stress management practices like walking, spending time in nature, yoga, qigong, tai chi, EFT, Heartmath, massage and more.

Action plan for becoming superhuman...

1. Explore different stress release techniques and see which work for you and fit into your schedule. It could be deep belly breathing, the re-lease mantra, taking up yoga or walking in the woods. Or any of the suggestions in this book you've found, or elsewhere.

2. Go back and re-read the principles around AAA – Attention, Assign and Action as well as the formula E + R = O and make sure you fully understand their significance.

3. Sit and contemplate this idea. "This too, shall pass." See how it can be applied to something in your life that you are currently stressed about. Or, if there's someone in your life that needs forgiveness (including you), find a way to forgive.

5.0 Following the BEAT

It's not the end, just the opposite in fact…

"The best time to plant a tree was 20 years ago. The second-best time is now."

– Chinese Proverb

The Beginning of Something

Congratulations! You've reached the end of this book. That is a superhuman effort. I know because writing it took me over ten years! However, it was important for me to pack as much into it as possible. I know that is contrary to what most people will tell you to do when writing a book. Keep it to one topic, save the other things for other books. Well, I wanted to give you as much as I could and not leave out anything. And you've made it through. Awesome job my friend. So, what now?

The Leadership BEAT Model™ is the blueprint that you need to optimise your own health, vitality, wellbeing and unlock your inner superhuman. *The*

Leadership BEAT Model™ is both simple and comprehensive and can be summarised with the framework below.

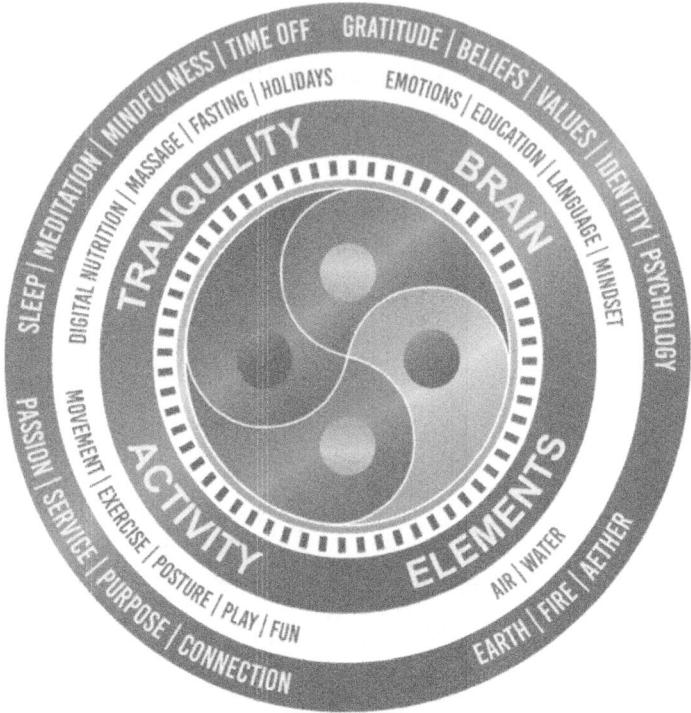

Figure 25 - The Leadership BEAT Model™

Using *The Leadership BEAT Model*™

Now that you have a blueprint at your fingertips, what do you do? How do you practically use the teachings from *The Leadership BEAT Model*™. Put in the simplest of terms you can simply look at each section and ask yourself some basic questions.

BRAIN: *Where are my thoughts and emotions right now? Am I in charge of my inner voice and living in line with my values? Am I learning and growing today?*

ELEMENTS: *Am I breathing into the belly, drinking plenty of water, eating lots of veg and getting outside in the natural light enough today?*

ACTIVITY: *Am I using every opportunity to get up and move, run, jump, crouch, and crawl? Do I have passion for what I am doing and spending time with people that inspire me?*

TRANQUILITY: *Have I had time away from technology today and some quiet alone and reflective time? Am I resting enough and sleeping well?*

In the appendix there are more structured questions for you, and supplementary resources. You can receive downloads of the resources in the appendix by going to **https://thethoughtgym.com/supervitality**.

Moving Forward

Moving forward, it's up to you what you do. Hopefully you are inspired and educated enough now to decide what action you need to take. If this is all new to you, then I suggest jumping into a section that appeals to you and revisiting it. Make sure you do some of the suggested exercises in that chapter and then master those new habits. Additionally, if you want a quick way to assess which areas of your life need focus then I suggest completing *The Energy Audit*, which can be found at **https://thethoughtgym.com/supervitality**. *The Energy Audit* is an extremely comprehensive assessment comprising of around 80 questions focussed on the four main areas of *The Leadership BEAT Model*™. It will help you identify which areas you need to focus on and give you the solutions as to what you need to do. It can do this because unlike traditional questionnaires which simply ask you questions, and you provide your responses, and the results just tell you back what you told it, *The Energy Audit* uses a solution-focussed approach whereby the question reveals within it what you could be doing to improve that area. For example, prior to *The Energy Audit*, a typical wellbeing questionnaire might state something like this:

"I feel stressed on a daily basis."

And then ask you whether you 'strongly agree', 'agree', 'neither agree nor disagree', 'disagree' or 'strongly disagree' with the statement. This really tells you nothing when you get the results back as it just tells you what you already know. E.g., if you stated you strongly agree with that statement, then the questionnaire results will just tell you that you are stressed daily but not tell you what you *actually* need to do.

However, a typical statement from *The Energy Audit* might say:

"I spend 15-20 minutes each day in quiet alone time, contemplation, prayer, meditation or similar."

In effect, for each question, you are being given a practice that will help you improve your energy, health, wellbeing and vitality.

I'm proud of *The Energy Audit* and its development over the course of several years. In addition, *The Energy Audit* has been confirmed as a valuable tool for increasing personal energy levels as part of my final year dissertation in my master's degree in Health & Wellbeing.

Small Steps

To instil any new habit, it's vitally important for success for most people that these initial steps are small. Really small. Tiny, in fact. For example, if your ambition is to run a marathon, the first step might not even be to walk around the block. The first step might be just to put on your trainers and then just go about your day. Then, it will be to leave the house in your trainers. Following that, it might then be to simply walk around the block.

Of course, everyone is individual with unique motivations and traits. In my experience though, for sustained habit change, it's good to start small, anchor those habits to existing ones and rather than scrub a bad habit out of your life, replace it with a new empowering one. As the space filled from the 'bad' habit will need to be filled with something. So, make sure it's a 'good' habit. I put good and bad in quotes purely because this might be subjective and in truth, I'm not sure there are good or bad habits, but really ones that get certain results for you. If the result you're looking for is to have low energy, susceptible to illness and become overweight, then maybe the habit of eating junk food and drinking too much is a good habit for you! Of course, I'm being a bit flippant here, but the reality is that it really depends on what you personally think about the habit. Does it serve you positively or not. Do you want to replace it with something else or not. The reason for the change is super important.

Stay Strong, Stay Super

Now you have completed the book, that's just the beginning. It's up to you to make the changes that will really improve your health, energy, vitality, business, focus and relationships. Your life. What you decide to do from this moment forward will decide your destiny. I trust you'll decide well and continue to stay strong and stay super!

Be sure to take *The Energy Audit*. This is the 80+ questionnaire that will help show you *exactly* what you personally could focus on to increase your own sense of health, wellbeing, and vitality. It's available, for free, at **https://thethoughtgym.com/supervitality.**

And share with me all your successes as I'd love to hear from you and connect further. You can connect with me on all the usual social media places like Facebook, Instagram, X, and YouTube with the username **TheThoughtGym.**

Wishing you every success!

"The future depends on what you do today."

– Mahatma Gandhi

FURTHER EDUCATION

As mentioned in the BRAIN section of this book, learning, growth, and education is vital for staying healthy and becoming superhuman. Whether that being enrolled in formal education courses, online courses or reading in and around your topics (and others). Below are some ways to continue your education on the topics discussed in this book, plus a few that just expand your awareness a little.

ONLINE BEAT MODEL Course and Book Resources

For additional resources to supplement the learning in this book, head over to **https://thethoughtgym.com/supervitality**. From there you will be able to access the free resources as well as a comprehensive online course where I will be able to coach you personally further on these topics.

BOOKS

I've read over 500 books in the last 10 years so it's really challenging to recommend just one or two. If you've made it to the end of this book, then chances are that you are really into optimising yourself to become superhuman.

Therefore, I'm going to list a few books that should keep you occupied for the next year or two (although some of these are very well known, so you may well have read a few already).

I've divided them up into roughly where they might fit into the teaching of *The Leadership BEAT Model*™. Some of these books were published quite some time ago, so naturally some of what they talk about has moved on. And of course, you don't have to (and neither do I) buy into everything they say, but I believe they are good foundational reading all the same. Check for more recent editions.

BRAIN

1. **The Thought Gym®** – *Train the Mind, and the Body Will Follow*; Hari Kalymnios
2. **Mind Over Medicine** - *Scientific Proof That You Can Heal Yourself*; Lissa Rankin, M.D.
3. **How Your Mind Can Heal Your Body**; David R. Hamilton, Ph.D.
4. **The Biology of Belief** - *Unleashing the Power of Consciousness, Matter & Miracles*; Bruce Lipton, Ph.D.
5. **As a Man Thinketh**; James Allen
6. **The Chimp Paradox** – *The Science of Mind Management for Success in Business and Life*; Steven Peters, M.D.
7. **Quantum Healing** - *Exploring the Frontiers of Mind/Body Medicine*; Deepak Chopra, M.D.
8. **Unlimited Power** – *The New Science of Personal Achievement*; Tony Robbins
9. **Introducing NLP** - *Psychological Skills for Understanding and Influencing People*; Joseph O'Conner
10. **The Holographic Universe**; Michael Talbot

ELEMENTS

1. **The Oxygen Advantage** - *The Simple, Scientifically Proven Breathing Techniques for a Healthier, Slimmer, Faster, and Fitter You*; Patrick McKeown
2. **Breath** - *The New Science of a Lost Art Plant Based Solution*; James Nestor
3. **Earthing** – *The Most Important Health Discovery Ever?*; Clint Ober
4. **The China Study** - *The Most Comprehensive Study of Nutrition Ever Conducted and the Startling Implications for Diet, Weight Loss and Long-term Health*; T. Colin Campbell, Ph.D.
5. **The pH Miracle** - *Balance Your Diet, Reclaim Your Health*; Robert O. Young, Ph.D.
6. **How Not to Die** - *Discover the foods scientifically proven to prevent and reverse disease*; Michael Gregor, M.D.
7. **Food: What the Heck Should I Eat?** – *The No-nonsense Guide to Achieving Optimal Weight and Lifelong Health*; Mark Hyman, M.D.
8. **The Food Revolution** – *How Your Diet Can Help Save Your Life and Our World*; John Robbins
9. **The Omnivores Dilemma** – The Search for a Perfect Meal in a Fast-Food World; Michael Pollan

SUPER VITALITY

10. **Radiation Nation** – *The Fallout of Modern Technology*; Daniel DeBaun, Ryan DeBaun

ACTIVITY

1. **Working Well** – *What You Need to Know to Live a Longer, Happier, Healthier Life*; Hari Kalymnios, Professor Andrew Sharman
2. **The Super Journal** – *Daily Planning and Goal Achieving*; Hari Kalymnios
3. **Pain Free** - *A Revolutionary Method for Stopping Chronic Pain*; Pete Egoscue
4. **Warrior Pose** – *How Yoga (Literally) Saved My Life*; Brad Willis
5. **The One Thing** - *The Surprisingly Simple Truth Behind Extraordinary Results*; Gary Keller, Jay Papasan
6. **The Mindful Athlete**; George Mumford
7. **Boundless** – *Upgrade Your Brain, Optimize Your Body & Defy Aging*; Ben Greenfield
8. **The TB12 Method**; Tom Brady
9. **Born to Run**; Christopher McDougall
10. **How Life Works**; Andrew Matthews

TRANQUILITY

1. **Meditation for Dummies**; Stephan Bodian
2. **Power vs. Force** - *The Hidden Determinants of Human Behaviour;* David R Hawkins
3. **Man's Search for Meaning -** *The Classic Tribute to Hope from the Holocaust*; Victor Frankl
4. **Conversations with God (Books 1-4)**; Neale Donald Walsh
5. **Sleep Smarter** - *21 Essential Strategies to Sleep Your Way to a Better Body, Better Health, and Bigger Success*; Shawn Stephenson
6. **Indistractable** - *How to Control Your Attention and Choose Your Life*; Nir Eyal
7. **The Heartmath Solution** - *The Institute of Heartmath's Revolutionary Program for Engaging the Power of the Heart's Intelligence*; Doc Childre, Howard Martin, Donna Beech
8. **A Guide to the Good Life** – *The Ancient Art of Stoic Joy*; William B. Irvine
9. **The Bhagavad Gita** – A Walkthrough for Westerners; Jack Hawley
10. **Sacred Hoops** – Phil Jackson

PODCASTS

I've been a big fan of podcasts since 2014, subscribing to several of them and listening to them for at least an hour a day. Podcasts are like your own bespoke radio station with just the topics you're interested in.

Podcasts I listen to most, if not all, episodes are:

1. **The Model Health Show** – Shawn Stephenson
2. **The Lucas Rockwood Show** – Lucas Rockwood
3. **Zestology** – Tony Wrighton
4. **Feel Better, Live More** – Dr Rangan Chatterjee
5. **The Mindful Paths Podcast** – Nick Day & Hari Kalymnios (yes, this is my podcast!)

Others that I dip in and out of are:

1. **The Joe Rogan Experience** – Joe Rogan
2. **Superhuman Academy** – Jonathan Levi
3. **Human Upgrade Radio** – Dave Asprey
4. **The Tony Robbins Podcast** – Tony Robbins
5. **Impact Theory** – Tom Bilyeu
6. **Success Talks** – Success Magazine
7. **The Rich Roll Podcast** – Rich Roll
8. **The Fat-Burning Man Show** – Abel James
9. **The Urban Monk Podcast** – Pedram Shoji
10. **The TED Radio Hour** – NPR
11. **The Tim Ferriss Show** – Tim Ferriss
12. **London Real** – Brian Rose
13. **The School of Greatness** – Lewis Howes
14. **The Gary Vee Audio Experience** – Gary Vaynerchuck
15. **Star Talk Radio** – Neil Degrasse Tyson
16. **Ben Greenfield Life** – Ben Greenfield
17. **The Art of Charm** – Jordan Harbinger
18. **Entrepreneur on Fire** – John Lee Dumas
19. **The Unbeatable Mind Podcast** – Mark Devine
20. **Diary of a CEO** – Steven Bartlett

MEDITATIONS

Instead of meditation apps, I tend to find meditations that I like and upload the audio directly to an old smartphone. That way there are no potential distractions from other apps or the internet.

1. **Getting Into the Vortex** – Ester and Jerry Hicks
2. **Soul Sync Meditation** – Preethaji
3. **Ong Namo (Guru Dev Namo)** – Mirabai Ceiba
4. **30 Day Meditations** – Deepak Chopra & Oprah Winfrey

DOCUMENTARIES

I've been a big fan of documentaries over the last few years. I always thought that for me to enjoy watching documentaries means I must be old. Well, I guess I have matured a bit since I was 20 years old as I've watched close to 100 over the last few years. Here are some of my picks for you to get started with.

1. Zeitgeist Movie (and its sequels Addendum and Moving Forward)
2. What the BLEEP Do We Know?
3. The Secret
4. Hungry for Change
5. Food Matters
6. Forks Over Knives
7. Fat, Sick and Nearly Dead
8. Food, Inc.
9. Simply Raw
10. What the Health?
11. Fed Up
12. That Sugar Film
13. Cowspiracy
14. Thrive
15. Resonance, Beings of Frequency
16. Vitality
17. DMT: The Spirit Molecule
18. The C Word Movie
19. Super-Size Me
20. Inside Job
21. The Game Changers
22. Unacknowledged
23. The Social Dilemma

GLOSSARY

A3	Attention, Assign, Action
ABC to Success	Awareness, Behaviour change, Consistency
A.B.L.E.	Always Be Learning and Evolving
A.S.E. Training	Adaptive Situational Exercise Training
A.S.K.	Always Seek Knowledge
BEAT	Brain, Elements, Activity, Tranquility
B.M.W.	Breathing, Movement, Water
C.I.A.	Choices in Advance
E3 Baby Mindset	Explore, Enjoy and Evolve
G.I.F.T.	Gratitude, Inspire (others), Forgive (self/others), Touch
H.A.B.I.T.	Habit and Behaviour Improvement Transformation
K.I.S.S.	Keep It Solution Simple
L.I.F.E.	Little Inconsequential Futile Events
LINNER	Lunch and Dinner (around 3-5pm)
N.A.P.	Non-Activity Period
N.E.A.T.	Non-Exercise Activity Thermogenesis
Nein, after nine	No tech after 9pm (and before 9am)
Nein, for ninety	No tech for 90 minutes upon waking/prior to bed
N.E.W.S.	Never-Ending Wasted Stress
O.W.N.	Oxygen, Water, Nutrients
PANLO 80/20	Plant-Based, Alkaline, Natural, Live, Organic
PSPC	Passion, Service, Purpose, Connection
RAF	Rules Allow Freedom
S9 Sport Selection Criteria	Strength, Suppleness, Stability, Size/Shape, Speed, Stamina, Skill, Spirit, Significance
SMASH	Sardines, Mackerel, Anchovies, Salmon, Haddock
Stoic 3C	Control (what you can control), Cope (with what you can't) and Concentrate (on what's important)
T.E.A.R. Model (The Thought Cycle)	Thoughts -> Emotions -> Actions -> Results

Appendix

You will find items from the appendices available for download at
https://thethoughtgym.com/supervitality for easier reading.

Appendix 1 - *The Leadership BEAT Model*™

Appendix 2 - *The Leadership BEAT Model*™ Core Sections

Appendix 3 - *The Leadership BEAT Model*™ Sub Sections

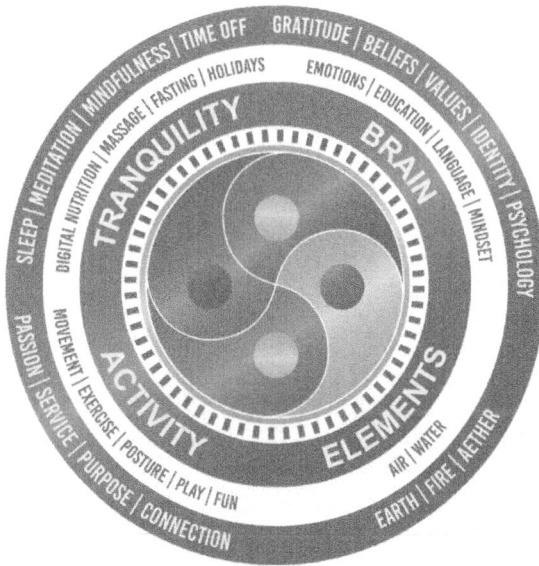

Appendix 4 - *The Leadership BEAT Model*™ Daily Questions

TRANQUILITY

1. Did I get 7 - 9 hrs quality uninterrupted sleep last night?
2. Have I shut down from all communication and electrical devices for at least 1 hour today?
3. Have I spent time in some kind of quiet alone time today (meditation, focused breathing, prayer, hypnosis etc)?
4. When was my last day off completely from work? And longer holiday?
5. Have I had a massage, bodywork or flotation in the last month?

BRAIN

1. Where is my **A**ttention, what language/meaning have I **A**ssigned, and what **A**ctions am I taking?
2. Am I living and making decisions in line with my highest values today?
3. Am I A.B.L.E.™ (Always Be Learning & Evolving) and living with the E3 Baby Mindset™ - Explore, Enjoy, Evolve?
4. What am I grateful for in my life right now?
5. Am I in charge of my inner voice today?

ACTIVITY

1. Am I moving my body for a few minutes each hour?
2. Am I positioned physically for optimal body alignment and energy?
3. Have I done 'Intentional' exercise today or some 'Integrative' or A.S.E.™ training?
4. Do I have passion and purpose in what I'm doing today? Have I laughed yet today?
5. Am I spending enough time with energy angels today? Or too long with energy vampires?

ELEMENTS

1. Have I done deep diaphragmatic breathing?
2. Have I drunk 3 -5 litres of quality water today? Is my pee almost clear?
3. Am I following the P.A.N.L.O. 80/20™ approach to eating today?
4. Have I been outside in sunlight today? Have I spent time outside and in nature?
5. How clean is my environment today? Physical, cosmetic products, EMF's?

431

Appendix 5 - Acid/Alkaline Food Chart

Alkaline Food Chart[1]

20% of your diet ← → ← 80% of your diet →

Food Type	Highly Acidic	Medium Acidic	Mildly Acidic	Mildly Alkaline	Medium Alkaline	Highly Alkaline
Drinks	Alcohol Coffee & Black Tea Fruit Juice (sweetened) Colas & Energy drinks Milk	Fresh, Natural Juice, Carbonated water	Rice, Soy, & Coconut Milk, Tap Water	Almond Milk , Distilled Water, Tap Water	Fresh Coconut Water, Herbal tea (alkalinity dependant on water too)	High pH water , Green Drinks (e.g. wheatgrass, barley grass, and green powder mixes of these and other greens like chlorella)
Condiments	Cocoa, Honey, Jam, Jelly, Mustard, Miso, Rice Syrup, Vinegar, Yeast, Artificial Sweeteners, Syrup, Processed Sugar	Ketchup Mayonnaise Butter		Herbs & Spices		Himalayan Salt, Real Salt
Fruits	Dried Fruit	Apple, Apricot, Banana, Blackberry, Blueberry, Cranberry, Grapes, Guava, Mango, Orange, Peach, Papaya, Pineapple, Strawberry	Cantaloupe, Fresh Dates, Nectarine, Plum, Sweet Cherry, Watermelon	Coconut, Grapefruit, Pomegranate, Tomato (cooked)	Lemon, Lime, Rhubarb	Tomato (raw)
Vegetables				Artichokes, Asparagus, Brussels Sprouts, Cauliflower, Comfrey Kohlrabi, Lamb's Lettuce Leeks New Baby Potatoes, Peas, Pumpkin, Onion, Rutabaga, Swede, Sweet Potato, Squash (Butternut, Summer, etc.), Watercress, White Cabbage	Arugula, Beets, Basil Capsicum/Pepper, Cabbage, Lettuce, Carrot, Chives, Collard/Spring Greens, Coriander, Endive, Ginger, Green Beans, Leeks, Lettuce, Mustard Greens, Okra, Radish, Red Cabbage, Red Onion, Turnip, Zucchini/Courgette	Avocado, Broccoli, Cabbage, Celery, Cucumber, Endive, Garlic, Grasses (alfalfa, kamut, straw, shave, wheatgrass, etc.), Kale, Parsley, Sprouts (alfalfa, bean, pea, soy, etc.), Spinach
Grains & Legumes	White Rice	Brown Rice Rye Bread Wheat Wholemeal Bread Wild Rice Wholemeal Pasta	Black Beans, Garbanzo Beans, Kidney Beans, Seitan, Amaranth, Buckwheat, Buckwheat Pasta, Millet, Oats/ Oatmeal, Soybeans, Spelt, Cous Cous	Lentils	Butter Beans, Lima Beans, Soy Beans (fresh), White (Navy) Beans, Quinoa (not technically a grain, but often used like one)	
Nuts & Seeds		Walnuts	Brazil Nuts, Cashews, Flax Seeds, Hazelnuts, Macadamia Nuts, Pecans, Pumpkin Seeds, Sunflower Seeds	Sesame Seeds Almonds Fennel Seeds	Chia Seeds, Hemp Seeds	
Meats & Fish and other 'typical' proteins	Beef, Chicken, Eggs, Farmed Fish, Pork, Shellfish	Ocean Fish	Freshwater Wild Fish	Tofu		
Other	Cheese & Dairy Chocolate Mushrooms	Goat's Cheese Vegan Cheese	Sunflower Oil	Avocado Oil, Coconut Oil, Flaxseed Oil, Grapeseed Oil, Hemp Oil, Olive Oil		

[1] Sample list. You will be able to find more foods, and depending on which chart you look at, there may be some variation. Review a few and observe common thread.

TheThoughtGym.com

Appendix 6 - Total Health Blueprint

The *Total Health Blueprint* is a 'cheat sheet' for you. In essence, it looks at all the activities that help make someone feel 'superhuman' and tells you – depending on your experience level – how often I suggest doing them. If you just followed this plan and didn't read any more books it would tell you what you need to know. Download to read properly.

TOTAL BODY BLUEPRINT FOR HEALTH & LONGEVITY

This Total Body Blueprint details the main activities and practices that help boost energy, health & longevity. They are based on the Leadership Beat Model created by Hari Kalymnios. The model identifies four main areas to focus on: Mindset (Brain) Nourishment (Elements) What occupies your time (Activity) and how you recuperate (Tranquility). Incorporating as many of the listed principles as you can, depending on where you currently are in your development, will help boost your wellbeing significantly.

TRANQUILITY - REST & REPAIR

	BASIC	INT.	ADV.
Sleep: morning sun for 5 mins (between 6am - 8:30am)	30 MIN	60 MIN	90 MIN
Sleep: low-red light for several minutes before bed	30 MIN	60 MIN	90 MIN
Sleep: bedtime wind down routine (e.g. read, stretch, prep bag, talk, sex, bath, music)	✓	✓	✓
Sleep: 7-8 hours quality sleep with consistent wake up and bed time	✓	✓	✓
Sleep: No TV/internet before bed (no clock, no computer, wifi, lights off)	✓	✓	✓
Sleep: morning movement of 15 minutes or more (e.g. rebounding, walking, yoga)	✓	✓	✓
Sleep: totally black out room (no sheets, light/led blinkers)	✓	✓	✓
Meditation / mindfulness practice (or similar e.g. prayer, focussed breathing)	M	D	2xD
Regular relaxing holiday (time between holidays)	Y	6M	3M
One day off (minimum) per week	Y	Y	Y
Fasting: overnight intermittent fast (15 days or more per week)	12H	14H	16H
Fasting: weekly longer fast	16H	24H	36H
Fasting: multiple day fast (3 - 7 days) every few months	12M	6M	3M
Daily technology off device (screen free time)	60 MIN	2H	4H
Sauna therapy	40 MIN	4xW	4xW
Cold water therapy (e.g. cold showers or cold showers of chill shower / ice baths / swims / baths)	M	W	D
Restorative therapies (e.g. cryotherapy chamber / floatation tanks)	6M	M	W
Bodywork (e.g. massage, acupuncture, physiotherapy, osteopathic, colonics etc)	3M	M	W

ACTIVITY - THE THINGS THAT YOU DO

	BASIC	INT.	ADV.
Daily step count	2K	5K	10K
Movement breaks every few minutes throughout the day	60 MIN	30 MIN	45 MIN
Stretching 3 x a week	D	3xW	D
Strength training (weights / assistance training)	2xW	2xW	3xW
Balance & stability training	2xW	2xW	3xW
Cardio training	2xW	2xW	5xW
High intensity interval training	M	2xW	2xW
Mental work (e.g. solving puzzles / crosswords & chess)	M	M	W
Passion: engaging in passionate work or hobbies	M	M	W
Serving / volunteering in some capacity	M	M	W
Purpose: having a greater purpose in life that moves you forward	✓	✓	✓
Connection: spending time with great family and/or friends (including physical touch)	2xW	2xW	2xW
Laughing and having fun	2xW	2xW	2xW

BRAIN - MINDSET NOURISHMENT

	BASIC	INT.	ADV.
Deliberate spending time doing as you really wanted	✓	✓	✓
Spending time reading non-fiction and non-fiction books	AD HOC	4xW	D
Identification of most important (4 values) & living to them	✓	✓	✓
Identification of helpful and hindering personal beliefs	✓	✓	✓
Identification of key areas for self-development	✓	✓	✓
Learning something new (e.g. languages, music, dance, skills)	✓	✓	✓
Emotional self regulation (being able to respond and not react to situations / others)	✓	✓	✓
Use of visualisations, affirmations, incantations and goals	✓	✓	✓

ELEMENTS - BODY NOURISHMENT

	BASIC	INT.	ADV.
Daily diaphragmatic breathing throughout the day	✓	3xW	.5M
Structured breathing practice	2L	3L	4L
Daily water intake	19.8 L	12.9.2	15.9.3
Portions of vegetables & fruit	2xW	4xW	D
Healthy fats & quality clean protein every day	40.99C	3xW	D
Handful of nuts and seeds	AD HOC	2xW	D
Fermented foods	AD HOC	AD HOC	D
Herbs & spices in food	AD HOC	2xW	D
Sea vegetables	AD HOC	3xW	5xM
Vegetables juices and/or vegetables smoothies	D	5xW	D
Grounding (earthing) for at least 20 minutes (on earth or using grounding tech)	D	D	D
Supplements: vitamin D (taken with vitamin K2), omega-3, topical magnesium	D	D	D
Supplements: probiotics, B-complex, turmeric, spirulina, super-green blend, MSM	D	D	D
Supplements: collagen, medicinal mushrooms, grapefruit seed extract, astaxanthin	D	2xM	D
Daily daylight exposure. (non sun burning exposure)	20 MIN	40 MIN	60 MIN
Red light therapy / infrared light therapy	W	W	3xM
A walk in nature, or parks (shinrin yoku)	W	3xW	✓
No skin/body toxic products (e.g. sulfates, parabens, phthalates, emf's)	✓	✓	✓

REFERENCES

1.   Smith H. NASA and Scouting. NASA. Accessed 25 September, 2020.
https://www.nasa.gov/audience/foreducators/informal/features/F_NASA_and_Scouting.html
2.   Maričić V. Longest time breath held voluntarily underwater (male). Accessed 21
August 2025, 2025. https://www.guinnessworldrecords.com/world-records/longest-time-
breath-held-voluntarily-(male)
3.   Smith KS, Virkud A, Deisseroth K, Graybiel AM. Reversible online control of habitual
behavior by optogenetic perturbation of medial prefrontal cortex. *Proceedings of the National
Academy of Sciences*. 2012;109(46):18932. doi:10.1073/pnas.1216264109
4.   Job V, Walton GM, Bernecker K, Dweck CS. Beliefs about willpower determine the
impact of glucose on self-control. *Proceedings of the National Academy of Sciences*.
2013;110(37):14837. doi:10.1073/pnas.1313475110
5.   Lally P, van Jaarsveld CHM, Potts HWW, Wardle J. How are habits formed:
Modelling habit formation in the real world. *European Journal of Social Psychology*.
2010;40(6):998-1009. doi:10.1002/ejsp.674
6.   Lawrence EM, Rogers RG, Wadsworth T. Happiness and longevity in the United
States. *Social science & medicine (1982)*. 2015;145:115-119.
doi:10.1016/j.socscimed.2015.09.020
7.   Avey H, Matheny KB, Robbins A, Jacobson TA. Health care providers' training,
perceptions, and practices regarding stress and health outcomes. *J Natl Med Assoc*. Sep
2003;95(9):833, 836-45.
8.   Crum AJ, Salovey P, Achor S. Rethinking stress: the role of mindsets in determining
the stress response. *J Pers Soc Psychol*. Apr 2013;104(4):716-33. doi:10.1037/a0031201
9.   Wikipedia. Biosphere 2. Wikipedia. Accessed 28 May, 2020.
https://en.wikipedia.org/w/index.php?title=Biosphere_2&oldid=955814309 .
10.   Cuddy A. Your body language may shape who you are. TED. Accessed 28 May,
2020.
https://www.ted.com/talks/amy_cuddy_your_body_language_may_shape_who_you_are?ut
m_campaign=tedspread&utm_medium=referral&utm_source=tedcomshare
11.   Wemm SE, Wulfert E. Effects of Acute Stress on Decision Making. *Applied
psychophysiology and biofeedback*. 2017;42(1):1-12. doi:10.1007/s10484-016-9347-8
12.   Hannibal KE, Bishop MD. Chronic stress, cortisol dysfunction, and pain: a
psychoneuroendocrine rationale for stress management in pain rehabilitation. *Physical
therapy*. 2014;94(12):1816-1825. doi:10.2522/ptj.20130597
13.   Whitworth JA, Williamson PM, Mangos G, Kelly JJ. Cardiovascular consequences of
cortisol excess. *Vascular health and risk management*. 2005;1(4):291-299.
doi:10.2147/vhrm.2005.1.4.291
14.   Santos-Longhurst A, Ernst H. High Cortisol Symptoms: What Do They Mean?
Healthline.com. Accessed 31 October, 2020. https://www.healthline.com/health/high-
cortisol-symptoms#symptoms
15.   Yaribeygi H, Panahi Y, Sahraei H, Johnston TP, Sahebkar A. The impact of stress on
body function: A review. *EXCLI journal*. 2017;16:1057-1072. doi:10.17179/excli2017-480
16.   Salleh MR. Life event, stress and illness. *The Malaysian journal of medical sciences :
MJMS*. 2008;15(4):9-18.
17.   Chatterjee R. 80% of Doctors Visits Stress Related. Twitter. Accessed 28 May, 2020.
https://twitter.com/drchatterjeeuk/status/1073495163677347840?lang=en
18.   Tyagi V, Scordo M, Yoon RS, Liporace FA, Greene LW. Revisiting the role of
testosterone: Are we missing something? *Reviews in urology*. 2017;19(1):16-24.
doi:10.3909/riu0716

19.   Oby ER, Golub MD, Hennig JA, et al. New neural activity patterns emerge with long-term learning. *Proceedings of the National Academy of Sciences of the United States of America*. 2019;116(30):15210-15215. doi:10.1073/pnas.1820296116

20.   Park DC, Lodi-Smith J, Drew L, et al. The impact of sustained engagement on cognitive function in older adults: the Synapse Project. *Psychological science*. 2014;25(1):103-112. doi:10.1177/0956797613499592

21.   Liu PZ, Nusslock R. Exercise-Mediated Neurogenesis in the Hippocampus via BDNF. *Frontiers in neuroscience*. 2018;12:52-52. doi:10.3389/fnins.2018.00052

22.   Sisti HM, Glass AL, Shors TJ. Neurogenesis and the spacing effect: learning over time enhances memory and the survival of new neurons. *Learning & memory (Cold Spring Harbor, NY)*. 2007;14(5):368-375. doi:10.1101/lm.488707

23.   Narushima M, Liu J, Diestelkamp N. Lifelong learning in active ageing discourse: its conserving effect on wellbeing, health and vulnerability. *Ageing and society*. 2018;38(4):651-675. doi:10.1017/S0144686X16001136

24.   Field J. *Wellbeing and Happiness:IFLL Thematic Paper 4*. 2009. Accessed 30 March 2019. https://www.learningandwork.org.uk/wp-content/uploads/2017/01/Well-being-and-Happiness-Thematic-Paper-4.pdf

25.   Emmons RA, McCullough ME. Counting blessings versus burdens: An experimental investigation of gratitude and subjective well-being in daily life. *Journal of Personality and Social Psychology*. 2003;84(2):377-389. doi:10.1037/0022-3514.84.2.377

26.   Emmons R. Why Gratitude Is Good. University of California, Berkeley. Accessed 29 May, 2020. https://greatergood.berkeley.edu/article/item/why_gratitude_is_good

27.   Achor S. The happy secret to better work. TED. Accessed 29 May, 2020. https://www.ted.com/talks/shawn_achor_the_happy_secret_to_better_work?language=en

28.   Kim ES, Hagan KA, Grodstein F, DeMeo DL, De Vivo I, Kubzansky LD. Optimism and Cause-Specific Mortality: A Prospective Cohort Study. *American Journal of Epidemiology*. 2017;185(1):21-29. doi:10.1093/aje/kww182

29.   Bornstein MH. *The SAGE Encyclopedia of Lifespan Human Development*. SAGE Publications Inc; 2018:2564.

30.   Armellino D, Hussain E, Schilling ME, et al. Using High-Technology to Enforce Low-Technology Safety Measures: The Use of Third-party Remote Video Auditing and Real-time Feedback in Healthcare. *Clinical Infectious Diseases*. 2012;54(1):1-7. doi:10.1093/cid/cir773

31.   Kini P, Wong J, McInnis S, Gabana N, Brown JW. The effects of gratitude expression on neural activity. *Neuroimage*. Mar 2016;128:1-10. doi:10.1016/j.neuroimage.2015.12.040

32.   Zahn R, Moll J, Paiva M, et al. The neural basis of human social values: evidence from functional MRI. *Cerebral cortex (New York, NY : 1991)*. 2009;19(2):276-283. doi:10.1093/cercor/bhn080

33.   Mosely M. The Truth About Personality. BBC. Accessed 29 May, 2020. https://www.bbc.co.uk/programmes/b036ypxw

34.   Lyubomirsky S, King L, Diener E. The benefits of frequent positive affect: does happiness lead to success? *Psychol Bull*. Nov 2005;131(6):803-55. doi:10.1037/0033-2909.131.6.803

35.   Diener E, Chan MY. Happy People Live Longer: Subjective Well-Being Contributes to Health and Longevity. *Applied Psychology: Health and Well-Being*. 2011/03/01 2011;3(1):1-43. doi:10.1111/j.1758-0854.2010.01045.x

36.   Dfarhud D, Malmir M, Khanahmadi M. Happiness & Health: The Biological Factors-Systematic Review Article. *Iranian journal of public health*. 2014;43(11):1468-1477.

37.   Williams LA, Bartlett MY. Warm thanks: gratitude expression facilitates social affiliation in new relationships via perceived warmth. *Emotion*. Feb 2015;15(1):1-5. doi:10.1037/emo0000017

38.   Digdon N, Koble A. Effects of Constructive Worry, Imagery Distraction, and Gratitude Interventions on Sleep Quality: A Pilot Trial. *Applied Psychology: Health and Well-Being*. 2011/07/01 2011;3(2):193-206. doi:10.1111/j.1758-0854.2011.01049.x

39.   Kashdan TB, Uswatte G, Julian T. Gratitude and hedonic and eudaimonic well-being in Vietnam war veterans. *Behav Res Ther*. Feb 2006;44(2):177-99. doi:10.1016/j.brat.2005.01.005

40.   Emmons R. Gratitude Works!: The Science and Practice of Saying Thanks. The Table | Biola CCT. Accessed 31 October, 2020. https://www.youtube.com/watch?v=BF7xS_nPbZ0

41.   Patino M. Oxygen Levels and Brain Function. Lung Health Institute. Accessed 30 May, 2020. https://lunginstitute.com/blog/oxygen-levels-brain-function/

42.   Zaccaro A, Piarulli A, Laurino M, et al. How Breath-Control Can Change Your Life: A Systematic Review on Psycho-Physiological Correlates of Slow Breathing. *Frontiers in human neuroscience*. 2018;12:353-353. doi:10.3389/fnhum.2018.00353

43.   Kox M, van Eijk LT, Zwaag J, et al. Voluntary activation of the sympathetic nervous system and attenuation of the innate immune response in humans. *Proceedings of the National Academy of Sciences of the United States of America*. 2014;111(20):7379-7384. doi:10.1073/pnas.1322174111

44.   Khanum A, Khan S, Kausar S, Mukhtar F, Kausar S. Effects of Diaphragmatic Breathing Exercises on Blood Sugar Levels in Working Class Females with Type-2 Diabetes Mellitus. *International Journal of Medical Research & Health Sciences*. 2019;8(1)

45.   McKeown P. *The Oxygen Advantage*. Piatkus; 2015.

46.   Zieliński J, Przybylski J. [How much water is lost during breathing?]. *Pneumonol Alergol Pol*. 2012;80(4):339-42. Ile wody tracimy z oddechem?

47.   Surtel A, Klepacz R, Wysokińska-Miszczuk J. [The influence of breathing mode on the oral cavity]. *Pol Merkur Lekarski*. Dec 2015;39(234):405-7. Wpływ toru oddechowego na jamę ustną.

48.   Sender R, Fuchs S, Milo R. Revised Estimates for the Number of Human and Bacteria Cells in the Body. *PLoS Biol*. Aug 2016;14(8):e1002533. doi:10.1371/journal.pbio.1002533

49.   Bertram R, Gram Pedersen M, Luciani DS, Sherman A. A simplified model for mitochondrial ATP production. *J Theor Biol*. Dec 21 2006;243(4):575-86. doi:10.1016/j.jtbi.2006.07.019

50.   Warburg O. On the Origin of Cancer Cells. *Science*. 1956;123(3191):309. doi:10.1126/science.123.3191.309

51.   Goldblatt H, Cameron G. Induced malignancy in cells from rat myocardium subjected to intermittent anaerobiosis during long propagation in vitro. *The Journal of experimental medicine*. 1953;97(4):525-552. doi:10.1084/jem.97.4.525

52.   Streeter CC, Gerbarg PL, Whitfield TH, et al. Treatment of Major Depressive Disorder with Iyengar Yoga and Coherent Breathing: A Randomized Controlled Dosing Study. *J Altern Complement Med*. Mar 2017;23(3):201-207. doi:10.1089/acm.2016.0140

53.   Mayer EA. Gut feelings: the emerging biology of gut–brain communication. *Nature Reviews Neuroscience*. 2011/08/01 2011;12(8):453-466. doi:10.1038/nrn3071

54.   Twal WO, Wahlquist AE, Balasubramanian S. Yogic breathing when compared to attention control reduces the levels of pro-inflammatory biomarkers in saliva: a pilot randomized controlled trial. *BMC Complementary and Alternative Medicine*. 2016/08/18 2016;16(1):294. doi:10.1186/s12906-016-1286-7

55.   Various. How much water is there on, in, and above the Earth? The United States Geological Survey Accessed 1 June, 2020. https://www.usgs.gov/special-topic/water-science-school/science/how-much-water-there-earth?qt-science_center_objects=0#qt-science_center_objects

56.   Mitchell HH, Hamilton TS, Steggerda FR, Bean HW. The chemical composition of the adult human body and its bearing on the biochemistry of growth. *Journal of Biological Chemistry*. 1945;158(3):625-637.

57.   Péronnet F. Healthy Hydration for Physical Activity. *Nutrition Today*. 2010;45(6)

58.   Armstrong LE, Ganio MS, Casa DJ, et al. Mild Dehydration Affects Mood in Healthy Young Women. *The Journal of Nutrition*. 2011;142(2):382-388. doi:10.3945/jn.111.142000

59.	Ganio MS, Armstrong LE, Casa DJ, et al. Mild dehydration impairs cognitive performance and mood of men. *British Journal of Nutrition*. 2011;106(10):1535-1543. doi:10.1017/S0007114511002005
60.	Khesbak H, Savchuk O, Tsushima S, Fahmy K. The Role of Water H-Bond Imbalances in B-DNA Substate Transitions and Peptide Recognition Revealed by Time-Resolved FTIR Spectroscopy. *Journal of the American Chemical Society*. 2011/04/20 2011;133(15):5834-5842. doi:10.1021/ja108863v
61.	Feng B, Sosa RP, Mårtensson AKF, et al. Hydrophobic catalysis and a potential biological role of DNA unstacking induced by environment effects. *Proc Natl Acad Sci U S A*. Aug 27 2019;116(35):17169-17174. doi:10.1073/pnas.1909122116
62.	Gayen D, Gayali S, Barua P, et al. Dehydration-induced proteomic landscape of mitochondria in chickpea reveals large-scale coordination of key biological processes. *J Proteomics*. Feb 10 2019;192:267-279. doi:10.1016/j.jprot.2018.09.008
63.	Anti M, Pignataro G Fau - Armuzzi A, Armuzzi A Fau - Valenti A, et al. Water supplementation enhances the effect of high-fiber diet on stool frequency and laxative consumption in adult patients with functional constipation. (0172-6390 (Print))
64.	Britannica TEoE. Cerebrospinal fluid. Encyclopædia Britannica, inc. Accessed 1 June, 2020. https://www.britannica.com/science/cerebrospinal-fluid
65.	Admin TO. WANT HEALTHY JOINTS? HYDRATE! Tuscon Orthopaedic Institute. Accessed 1 June, 2020. https://www.tucsonortho.com/want-healthy-joints-hydrate/
66.	Blau JN, Kell CA, Sperling JM. Water-deprivation headache: a new headache with two variants. *Headache*. Jan 2004;44(1):79-83. doi:10.1111/j.1526-4610.2004.04014.x
67.	Stanton AMD. *The Complete Idiot's Guide to Hormone Weight Loss* :. Penguin Random House; 2011:368.
68.	An R, McCaffrey J. Plain water consumption in relation to energy intake and diet quality among US adults, 2005–2012. *Journal of Human Nutrition and Dietetics*. 2016/10/01 2016;29(5):624-632. doi:10.1111/jhn.12368
69.	Pollack G. The Fourth Phase of Water: Beyond Solid, Liquid, and Vapour. University of Colorado. Accessed 4 June, 2020. https://ecee.colorado.edu/~ecen5555/SourceMaterial/Pollack13.pdf
70.	Stephenson S. Hydration and Water Masterclass. The Model Health Show. Accessed 1 March, 2018. http://theshawnstevensonmodel.com/best-water-filter-best-bottled-water/
71.	Luntz T. U.S. Drinking Water Widely Contaminated. Scientific American. Accessed 4 June, 2020. https://www.scientificamerican.com/article/tap-drinking-water-contaminants-pollutants/
72.	Rose J. *Talk of the Nation*. Study Finds Drugs Seeping Into Drinking Water. https://www.npr.org/transcripts/88062858
73.	Stephenson S. *The Model Health Show*. Truth About Water Supply & How Water Controls Your Health. https://themodelhealthshow.com/truth-water-supply/
74.	Hooper R. Top 11 compounds in US drinking water. New Scientist. Accessed 4 June, 2020. https://www.newscientist.com/article/dn16397-top-11-compounds-in-us-drinking-water/#
75.	Khan S, Beattie TK, Knapp CW. Relationship between antibiotic- and disinfectant-resistance profiles in bacteria harvested from tap water. *Chemosphere*. Jun 2016;152:132-41. doi:10.1016/j.chemosphere.2016.02.086
76.	Vighi G, Marcucci F, Sensi L, Di Cara G, Frati F. Allergy and the gastrointestinal system. *Clinical and experimental immunology*. 2008;153 Suppl 1(Suppl 1):3-6. doi:10.1111/j.1365-2249.2008.03713.x
77.	Stoller-Conrad J. Microbes Help Produce Serotonin in Gut. California Institute of Technology. Accessed 4 June, 2020. https://www.caltech.edu/about/news/microbes-help-produce-serotonin-gut-46495

78.   Council NR. *Fluoride in Drinking Water: A Scientific Review of EPA's Standards*. The National Academies Press; 2006:530.

79.   Grandjean P, Landrigan PJ. Neurobehavioural effects of developmental toxicity. *The Lancet Neurology*. 2014;13(3):330-338. doi:10.1016/S1474-4422(13)70278-3

80.   Bassin EB, Wypij D, Davis RB, Mittleman MA. Age-specific fluoride exposure in drinking water and osteosarcoma (United States). *Cancer Causes Control*. May 2006;17(4):421-8. doi:10.1007/s10552-005-0500-6

81.   Newbrun E. Topical fluorides in caries prevention and management: a North American perspective. *J Dent Educ*. Oct 2001;65(10):1078-83.

82.   Bottled Water Quality Investigation (Environmental Working Group) (2008).

83.   Heindler FM, Alajmi F, Huerlimann R, et al. Toxic effects of polyethylene terephthalate microparticles and Di(2-ethylhexyl)phthalate on the calanoid copepod, Parvocalanus crassirostris. *Ecotoxicol Environ Saf*. Jul 2017;141:298-305. doi:10.1016/j.ecoenv.2017.03.029

84.   Planelló R, Herrero O, Martínez-Guitarte JL, Morcillo G. Comparative effects of butyl benzyl phthalate (BBP) and di(2-ethylhexyl) phthalate (DEHP) on the aquatic larvae of Chironomus riparius based on gene expression assays related to the endocrine system, the stress response and ribosomes. *Aquat Toxicol*. Sep 2011;105(1-2):62-70. doi:10.1016/j.aquatox.2011.05.011

85.   Yousif E, Haddad R. Photodegradation and photostabilization of polymers, especially polystyrene: review. *SpringerPlus*. 2013;2:398-398. doi:10.1186/2193-1801-2-398

86.   Clorox. Brands Owned by Clorox. Accessed 4 June, 2020. https://www.thecloroxcompany.com/brands/

87.   Brita. What We Filter Out. Brita. Accessed 4 June, 2020. https://www.brita.com/why-brita/what-we-filter/

88.   Schwalfenberg GK. The alkaline diet: is there evidence that an alkaline pH diet benefits health? *Journal of environmental and public health*. 2012;2012:727630-727630. doi:10.1155/2012/727630

89.   Tanaka Y, Saihara Y, Izumotani K, Nakamura H. Daily ingestion of alkaline electrolyzed water containing hydrogen influences human health, including gastrointestinal symptoms. *Medical gas research*. 2019;8(4):160-166. doi:10.4103/2045-9912.248267

90.   LeBaron TW, Sharpe R, Ohno K. Electrolyzed-Reduced Water: Review I. Molecular Hydrogen Is the Exclusive Agent Responsible for the Therapeutic Effects. *Int J Mol Sci*. Nov 25 2022;23(23)doi:10.3390/ijms232314750

91.   Salt R. Are Your Facts Real? Real Salt. Accessed 26 November, 2020. https://realsalt.com/are-your-facts-real/

92.   Reams CD. Why Use the Lemon. Biological Immunity Research Institute. Accessed 26 November, 2020. https://www.biri.org/pdf/recipes/lemon-why-use-it.pdf

93.   Eweis DS, Abed F, Stiban J. Carbon dioxide in carbonated beverages induces ghrelin release and increased food consumption in male rats: Implications on the onset of obesity. *Obes Res Clin Pract*. Sep-Oct 2017;11(5):534-543. doi:10.1016/j.orcp.2017.02.001

94.   Health Survey for England 2016 (UK Government) 19 (2017).

95.   Gallagher J. Ultra-processed foods 'make you eat more'. BBC. Accessed 5 June, 2020. https://www.bbc.co.uk/news/health-48280772

96.   Guideline: sugars intake for adults and children (United Nations) (2015).

97.   Chang CY, Ke Ds Fau - Chen J-Y, Chen JY. Essential fatty acids and human brain. (1028-768X (Print))

98.   Madhusoodanan J. The Secret Life of Fat Cells. *ACS central science*. 2018;4(9):1078-1080. doi:10.1021/acscentsci.8b00633

99.   Sisson M. A Metabolic Paradigm Shift, or Why Fat Is the Preferred Fuel for Human Metabolism. Marks Daily Apple. Accessed 26 November, 2020. https://www.marksdailyapple.com/a-metabolic-paradigm-shift-fat-carbs-human-body-metabolism/

ABOUT THE AUTHOR

ABOUT THE AUTHOR

ABOUT THE AUTHOR

ABOUT THE AUTHOR

100.	Meites S, Rogols S. Amylase isoenzymes. *CRC Crit Rev Clin Lab Sci*. Jan 1971;2(1):103-38. doi:10.3109/10408367109151305
101.	Pigman W, Reid AJ. The organic compounds and enzymes of human saliva. *J Am Dent Assoc*. Sep 1952;45(3):326-38.
102.	Raus FJ, Tarbet WJ, Miklos FL. Salivary enzymes and calculus formation. *J Periodontal Res*. 1968;3(3):232-5. doi:10.1111/j.1600-0765.1968.tb01925.x
103.	Zhu Y, Hollis JH. Increasing the number of chews before swallowing reduces meal size in normal-weight, overweight, and obese adults. *J Acad Nutr Diet*. Jun 2014;114(6):926-31. doi:10.1016/j.jand.2013.08.020
104.	Suthar NN, Verma AP. Alkaline Diet and Health - A Brief Review. *International Journal of Basic & Applied Physiology*. 2014;3(1):22-30.
105.	Ribeiro MdLC, Silva AS, Bailey KM, et al. Buffer Therapy for Cancer. *Journal of nutrition & food sciences*. 2012;2:6-6.
106.	Young R. *The PH Miracle: Balance Your Diet, Reclaim Your Health*. Piatkus Books; 2009:416.
107.	Petre A, Meeks S. Lemon Juice: Acidic or Alkaline, and Does It Matter? Healthline. Accessed 29 October, 2022. https://www.healthline.com/nutrition/lemon-juice-acidic-or-alkaline#TOC_TITLE_HDR_4
108.	Torrens K. Raw vs cooked. BBC. Accessed 5 June, 2020. https://www.bbcgoodfood.com/howto/guide/raw-vs-cooked
109.	Barański M, Średnicka-Tober D, Volakakis N, et al. Higher antioxidant and lower cadmium concentrations and lower incidence of pesticide residues in organically grown crops: a systematic literature review and meta-analyses. *British Journal of Nutrition*. 2014;112(5):794-811. doi:10.1017/S0007114514001366
110.	Baudry J, Assmann KE, Touvier M, et al. Association of Frequency of Organic Food Consumption With Cancer Risk: Findings From the NutriNet-Santé Prospective Cohort Study. *JAMA Intern Med*. Dec 1 2018;178(12):1597-1606. doi:10.1001/jamainternmed.2018.4357
111.	Hal A. What Happened After One Family Went Organic For Just Two Weeks. *The Huffington Post*. Accessed 5 June 2020. https://www.huffingtonpost.co.uk/entry/the-organic-effect_n_7244000
112.	Silanikove N, Leitner G, Merin U. The Interrelationships between Lactose Intolerance and the Modern Dairy Industry: Global Perspectives in Evolutional and Historical Backgrounds. *Nutrients*. 2015;7(9):7312-7331. doi:10.3390/nu7095340
113.	Grand RJ, Montgomery RK, Chitkara DK, Hirschhorn JN. Changing genes; losing lactase. *Gut*. 2003;52(5):617-619. doi:10.1136/gut.52.5.617
114.	Mäkelä M. Milk and wheat allergy, and celiac disease. *Clinical and Translational Allergy*. 2011;1(Suppl 1):S37-S37. doi:10.1186/2045-7022-1-S1-S37
115.	Olsen N, Iftikhar N. What's the pH of Milk, and Does It Matter for Your Body? Healthline. Accessed 29 October, 2022. https://www.healthline.com/health/ph-of-milk
116.	Hidden J. Phosphorous. Oregon State University: Linus Pauling Institute. Accessed 29 October, 2022. https://lpi.oregonstate.edu/mic/minerals/phosphorus
117.	iPhysio. Scientists link drinking milk with Osteoporosis. iPhysio. Accessed 29 October, 2022. https://iphysio.io/osteoporosis/
118.	Michaëlsson K, Wolk A, Langenskiöld S, et al. Milk intake and risk of mortality and fractures in women and men: cohort studies. *BMJ : British Medical Journal*. 2014;349:g6015. doi:10.1136/bmj.g6015
119.	Feskanich D, Willett WC, Stampfer MJ, Colditz GA. Milk, dietary calcium, and bone fractures in women: a 12-year prospective study. *American journal of public health*. 1997;87(6):992-997. doi:10.2105/ajph.87.6.992
120.	Bolland MJ, Leung W, Tai V, et al. Calcium intake and risk of fracture: systematic review. *BMJ*. 2015;351:h4580. doi:10.1136/bmj.h4580

SUPER VITALITY

121.   Feskanich D, Willett WC, Colditz GA. Calcium, vitamin D, milk consumption, and hip fractures: a prospective study among postmenopausal women. *Am J Clin Nutr*. Feb 2003;77(2):504-11. doi:10.1093/ajcn/77.2.504
122.   Hegsted DM. Calcium and Osteoporosis. *The Journal of Nutrition*. 1986;116(11):2316-2319. doi:10.1093/jn/116.11.2316
123.   Pike RA. Adhesive. Encyclopædia Britannica. Britannica.com: Encyclopædia Britannica, inc.; 2015.
124.   Appleton BS, Campbell TC. Effect of high and low dietary protein on the dosing and postdosing periods of aflatoxin B1-induced hepatic preneoplastic lesion development in the rat. *Cancer Res*. May 1983;43(5):2150-4.
125.   Karpf A. Dairy monsters. The Guardian. Accessed 8 June, 2020. https://www.theguardian.com/lifeandstyle/2003/dec/13/foodanddrink.weekend
126.   Crowe FL, Key TJ, Allen NE, et al. The association between diet and serum concentrations of IGF-I, IGFBP-1, IGFBP-2, and IGFBP-3 in the European Prospective Investigation into Cancer and Nutrition. *Cancer Epidemiol Biomarkers Prev*. May 2009;18(5):1333-40. doi:10.1158/1055-9965.epi-08-0781
127.   Grimberg A. Mechanisms by which IGF-I may promote cancer. *Cancer biology & therapy*. Nov-Dec 2003;2(6):630-635.
128.   WHO Technical Report Series Protein and Amino Acid Requirements (World Health Organisation) (2002).
129.   BBC. Breast milk ice cream goes on sale in Covent Garden. BBC. Accessed 5 June, 2020. https://www.bbc.co.uk/news/uk-england-london-12569011
130.   Medicine PCfR. USDA Panel Backs Doctors' Complaints against Milk Ads. Newswise. Accessed 29 October, 2022. https://www.newswise.com/articles/usda-panel-backs-doctors-complaints-against-milk-ads
131.   Hyman M. Dairy: 6 Reasons You Should Avoid It at All Costs. HuffPost (The Huffington Post). Accessed 29 October, 2022. https://www.huffpost.com/entry/dairy-free-dairy-6-reason_b_558876
132.   Willett WC, Ludwig DS. Milk and Health. *N Engl J Med*. Feb 13 2020;382(7):644-654. doi:10.1056/NEJMra1903547
133.   Peters SL, Biesiekierski JR, Yelland GW, Muir JG, Gibson PR. Randomised clinical trial: gluten may cause depression in subjects with non-coeliac gluten sensitivity – an exploratory clinical study. *Alimentary Pharmacology & Therapeutics*. 2014/05/01 2014;39(10):1104-1112. doi:10.1111/apt.12730
134.   Fasano A. Zonulin, regulation of tight junctions, and autoimmune diseases. *Ann N Y Acad Sci*. Jul 2012;1258(1):25-33. doi:10.1111/j.1749-6632.2012.06538.x
135.   Hollon J, Puppa EL, Greenwald B, Goldberg E, Guerrerio A, Fasano A. Effect of gliadin on permeability of intestinal biopsy explants from celiac disease patients and patients with non-celiac gluten sensitivity. *Nutrients*. Feb 27 2015;7(3):1565-76. doi:10.3390/nu7031565
136.   Biesiekierski JR. What is gluten? https://doi.org/10.1111/jgh.13703. *Journal of Gastroenterology and Hepatology*. 2017/03/01 2017;32(S1):78-81. doi:https://doi.org/10.1111/jgh.13703
137.   contributors W. Green Revolution. Wikipedia, *The Free Encyclopedia* en.wikipedia.org: Wikipedia; 2022.
138.   Searcy B. Modern Day Wheat & Autoimmunity. Rain Oganica. Accessed 30 October, 2022. https://rainorganica.com/blogs/podcast/modern-day-wheat-autoimmunity
139.   Buzzelli A. Get Out Of The Gluten Glut (Part 1): Get to Know Gluten. Udemy; 2014. https://www.udemy.com/course/glutenglut/learn/lecture/780218?start=15#overview
140.   Junker Y, Zeissig S, Kim SJ, et al. Wheat amylase trypsin inhibitors drive intestinal inflammation via activation of toll-like receptor 4. *J Exp Med*. Dec 17 2012;209(13):2395-408. doi:10.1084/jem.20102660

141.   de Punder K, Pruimboom L. The dietary intake of wheat and other cereal grains and their role in inflammation. *Nutrients*. Mar 12 2013;5(3):771-87. doi:10.3390/nu5030771

142.   Freire RH, Fernandes LR, Silva RB, et al. Wheat gluten intake increases weight gain and adiposity associated with reduced thermogenesis and energy expenditure in an animal model of obesity. *Int J Obes (Lond)*. Mar 2016;40(3):479-86. doi:10.1038/ijo.2015.204

143.   Travis RC, Key TJ. Oestrogen exposure and breast cancer risk. *Breast Cancer Res*. 2003;5(5):239-47. doi:10.1186/bcr628

144.   NHS. Breast Cancer in Women. National Health Service (NHS) UK. Accessed 30 October, 2022. https://www.nhs.uk/conditions/breast-cancer/causes/

145.   Organisation WH. Healthy Diet. WHO. Accessed 30 October, 2022. https://www.who.int/news-room/fact-sheets/detail/healthy-diet

146.   Control CfD. Get the Facts: Added Sugars. Centres for Disease Control (CDC). Accessed 30 October, 2022. https://www.cdc.gov/nutrition/data-statistics/added-sugars.html

147.   Waterson L. Is five a day enough? The Guardian. Accessed 17 August, 2022. https://www.theguardian.com/lifeandstyle/2006/may/25/healthandwellbeing.health

148.   **Gallagher J.** Fruit and veg: For a longer life eat 10-a-day. BBC. Accessed 17 August, 2022. https://www.bbc.com/news/health-39057146

149.   Godoy-Matos AF, Silva Júnior WS, Valerio CM. NAFLD as a continuum: from obesity to metabolic syndrome and diabetes. *Diabetology & Metabolic Syndrome*. 2020/07/14 2020;12(1):60. doi:10.1186/s13098-020-00570-y

150.   Ouyang X, Cirillo P, Sautin Y, et al. Fructose consumption as a risk factor for non-alcoholic fatty liver disease. *J Hepatol*. Jun 2008;48(6):993-9. doi:10.1016/j.jhep.2008.02.011

151.   Freeman AM, Pennings N. Insulin Resistance. *StatPearls*. StatPearls Publishing Copyright © 2022, StatPearls Publishing LLC.; 2022.

152.   Schulze MB, Manson JE, Ludwig DS, et al. Sugar-Sweetened Beverages, Weight Gain, and Incidence of Type 2 Diabetes in Young and Middle-Aged Women. *JAMA*. 2004;292(8):927-934. doi:10.1001/jama.292.8.927

153.   Cheng C, Ru P, Geng F, et al. Glucose-Mediated N-glycosylation of SCAP Is Essential for SREBP-1 Activation and Tumor Growth. *Cancer Cell*. 2015;28(5):569-581. doi:10.1016/j.ccell.2015.09.021

154.   Page KA, Chan O, Arora J, et al. Effects of Fructose vs Glucose on Regional Cerebral Blood Flow in Brain Regions Involved With Appetite and Reward Pathways. *JAMA*. 2013;309(1):63-70. doi:10.1001/jama.2012.116975

155.   Lenoir M, Serre F, Cantin L, Ahmed SH. Intense sweetness surpasses cocaine reward. *PLoS One*. Aug 1 2007;2(8):e698. doi:10.1371/journal.pone.0000698

156.   Schaefer EJ, Gleason JA, Dansinger ML. Dietary fructose and glucose differentially affect lipid and glucose homeostasis. *J Nutr*. Jun 2009;139(6):1257s-1262s. doi:10.3945/jn.108.098186

157.   Swarbrick MM, Stanhope KL, Elliott SS, et al. Consumption of fructose-sweetened beverages for 10 weeks increases postprandial triacylglycerol and apolipoprotein-B concentrations in overweight and obese women. *Br J Nutr*. Nov 2008;100(5):947-52. doi:10.1017/s0007114508968252

158.   Yang Q, Zhang Z, Gregg EW, Flanders WD, Merritt R, Hu FB. Added sugar intake and cardiovascular diseases mortality among US adults. *JAMA Intern Med*. Apr 2014;174(4):516-24. doi:10.1001/jamainternmed.2013.13563

159.   Fontana L, Eagon JC, Trujillo ME, Scherer PE, Klein S. Visceral Fat Adipokine Secretion Is Associated With Systemic Inflammation in Obese Humans. *Diabetes*. 2007;56(4):1010. doi:10.2337/db06-1656

160.   Esposito K, Nappo F, Marfella R, et al. Inflammatory cytokine concentrations are acutely increased by hyperglycemia in humans: role of oxidative stress. *Circulation*. Oct 15 2002;106(16):2067-72. doi:10.1161/01.cir.0000034509.14906.ae

161.   Dregan A, Charlton J, Chowienczyk P, Gulliford MC. Chronic inflammatory disorders and risk of type 2 diabetes mellitus, coronary heart disease, and stroke: a population-based cohort study. *Circulation*. Sep 2 2014;130(10):837-44. doi:10.1161/circulationaha.114.009990

162.   Johnson RJ, Segal MS, Sautin Y, et al. Potential role of sugar (fructose) in the epidemic of hypertension, obesity and the metabolic syndrome, diabetes, kidney disease, and cardiovascular disease. *The American Journal of Clinical Nutrition*. 2007;86(4):899-906. doi:10.1093/ajcn/86.4.899

163.   Hamamichi R, Asano-Miyoshi M, Emori Y. Taste bud contains both short-lived and long-lived cell populations. *Neuroscience*. Sep 15 2006;141(4):2129-38. doi:10.1016/j.neuroscience.2006.05.061

164.   Miura H, Barlow LA. Taste bud regeneration and the search for taste progenitor cells. *Arch Ital Biol*. Jun 2010;148(2):107-18.

165.   Schiermeier Q. Eat less meat: UN climate-change report calls for change to human diet. *Nature*. 2019:291-292. vol. 7769.

166.   Milman O. Meat accounts for nearly 60% of all greenhouse gases from food production, study finds. *The Guardian*. https://www.theguardian.com/environment/2021/sep/13/meat-greenhouses-gases-food-production-study

167.   Harvey F. EU's farm animals 'produce more emissions than cars and vans combined'. *The Guardian*. https://www.theguardian.com/environment/2020/sep/22/eu-farm-animals-produce-more-emissions-than-cars-and-vans-combined-greenpeace

168.   Data OWi. Per Capita Meat Consumption, by Type - World, 1961 - 2013. 2013. https://ourworldindata.org/grapher/per-capita-meat-consumption-by-type-kilograms-per-year

169.   Herald TSM. Food: Fact of Fiction? *The Sunday Morning Herald*. https://www.smh.com.au/lifestyle/health-and-wellness/food-fact-or-fiction-20140113-30q1s.html

170.   Cappelletti S, Piacentino D, Sani G, Aromatario M. Caffeine: cognitive and physical performance enhancer or psychoactive drug? *Curr Neuropharmacol*. Jan 2015;13(1):71-88. doi:10.2174/1570159x13666141210215655

171.   Langton N. How Much Red Wine Do You Need to Get Enough Resveratrol? Livestrong. Accessed 7 June, 2020. https://www.livestrong.com/article/411745-how-much-red-wine-do-you-need-to-get-enough-resveratrol/

172.   NHS. Statistics on Alcohol, England 2019. National Health Service (NHS). Accessed 7 June, 2020. https://digital.nhs.uk/data-and-information/publications/statistical/statistics-on-alcohol/2019/content

173.   Scheer R, Moss D. Dirt Poor: Have Fruits and Vegetables Become Less Nutritious? Scientific American. Accessed 7 June, 2020. https://www.scientificamerican.com/article/soil-depletion-and-nutrition-loss/

174.   Davis DR, Epp MD, Riordan HD. Changes in USDA food composition data for 43 garden crops, 1950 to 1999. *J Am Coll Nutr*. Dec 2004;23(6):669-82. doi:10.1080/07315724.2004.10719409

175.   Greger M. How to Get Enough Antioxidants Each Day. Nutrion Facts. Accessed 7 June, 2020. https://nutritionfacts.org/2014/12/04/how-to-get-enough-antioxidants-each-day/

176.   Carlberg C. Vitamin D: A Micronutrient Regulating Genes. *Curr Pharm Des*. 2019;25(15):1740-1746. doi:10.2174/1381612825666190705193227

177.   Charoenngam N, Holick MF. Immunologic Effects of Vitamin D on Human Health and Disease. *Nutrients*. Jul 15 2020;12(7)doi:10.3390/nu12072097

178.   Botelho J, Machado V, Proença L, Delgado AS, Mendes JJ. Vitamin D Deficiency and Oral Health: A Comprehensive Review. *Nutrients*. May 19 2020;12(5)doi:10.3390/nu12051471

179.   Chakraborti CK. Vitamin D as a promising anticancer agent. *Indian journal of pharmacology*. 2011;43(2):113-120. doi:10.4103/0253-7613.77335

180.	Garland CF, Garland FC, Gorham ED, et al. The role of vitamin D in cancer prevention. *American journal of public health.* 2006;96(2):252-261. doi:10.2105/AJPH.2004.045260

181.	Nwosu BU, Parajuli S, Jasmin G, et al. Ergocalciferol in New-onset Type 1 Diabetes: A Randomized Controlled Trial. *Journal of the Endocrine Society.* 2022;6(1):bvab179. doi:10.1210/jendso/bvab179

182.	Hutter CD, Laing P. Multiple sclerosis: sunlight, diet, immunology and aetiology. *Med Hypotheses.* Feb 1996;46(2):67-74. doi:10.1016/s0306-9877(96)90002-x

183.	Munger KL, Levin LI, Hollis BW, Howard NS, Ascherio A. Serum 25-Hydroxyvitamin D Levels and Risk of Multiple Sclerosis. *JAMA.* 2006;296(23):2832-2838. doi:10.1001/jama.296.23.2832

184.	Wang TJ, Pencina MJ, Booth SL, et al. Vitamin D deficiency and risk of cardiovascular disease. *Circulation.* Jan 29 2008;117(4):503-11. doi:10.1161/circulationaha.107.706127

185.	Urashima M, Segawa T, Okazaki M, Kurihara M, Wada Y, Ida H. Randomized trial of vitamin D supplementation to prevent seasonal influenza A in schoolchildren. *Am J Clin Nutr.* May 2010;91(5):1255-60. doi:10.3945/ajcn.2009.29094

186.	Menon V, Kar SK, Suthar N, Nebhinani N. Vitamin D and Depression: A Critical Appraisal of the Evidence and Future Directions. *Indian J Psychol Med.* Jan-Feb 2020;42(1):11-21. doi:10.4103/ijpsym.ijpsym_160_19

187.	Anglin RE, Samaan Z, Walter SD, McDonald SD. Vitamin D deficiency and depression in adults: systematic review and meta-analysis. *Br J Psychiatry.* Feb 2013;202:100-7. doi:10.1192/bjp.bp.111.106666

188.	Armstrong DJ, Meenagh GK, Bickle I, Lee AS, Curran ES, Finch MB. Vitamin D deficiency is associated with anxiety and depression in fibromyalgia. *Clin Rheumatol.* Apr 2007;26(4):551-4. doi:10.1007/s10067-006-0348-5

189.	Endocrinology ESfP. Vitamin D supplements may promote weight loss in obese children. European Society for Paediatric Endocrinology. Accessed 8 June, 2020. www.sciencedaily.com/releases/2018/09/180927215656.htm

190.	Tazzyman S, Richards N, Trueman AR, et al. Vitamin D associates with improved quality of life in participants with irritable bowel syndrome: outcomes from a pilot trial. *BMJ Open Gastroenterol.* 2015;2(1):e000052. doi:10.1136/bmjgast-2015-000052

191.	Sotirchos ES, Bhargava P, Eckstein C, et al. Safety and immunologic effects of high- vs low-dose cholecalciferol in multiple sclerosis. *Neurology.* Jan 26 2016;86(4):382-90. doi:10.1212/wnl.0000000000002316

192.	Meena N, Singh Chawla SP, Garg R, Batta A, Kaur S. Assessment of Vitamin D in Rheumatoid Arthritis and Its Correlation with Disease Activity. *Journal of natural science, biology, and medicine.* Jan-Jun 2018;9(1):54-58. doi:10.4103/jnsbm.JNSBM_128_17

193.	EFSA. Vitamin D: EFSA sets dietary reference values. European Food Safety Authority. Accessed 31 October, 2022. https://www.efsa.europa.eu/en/press/news/161028

194.	Raed A, Bhagatwala J, Zhu H, et al. Dose responses of vitamin D3 supplementation on arterial stiffness in overweight African Americans with vitamin D deficiency: A placebo controlled randomized trial. *PLoS One.* 2017;12(12):e0188424. doi:10.1371/journal.pone.0188424

195.	Vieth R. How much vitamin D should I take? Vitamin D Society Canada. Accessed 31 October, 2022. https://www.vitamindsociety.org/blog-detail.php?id=8

196.	Vieth R. Are Adult Vitamin D Recommendations Too Low? Vitamin D Society Canada. Accessed 31 October, 2022. https://www.vitamindsociety.org/press_release.php?id=18

197.	Baik HW, Russell RM. Vitamin B12 deficiency in the elderly. *Annu Rev Nutr.* 1999;19:357-77. doi:10.1146/annurev.nutr.19.1.357

198.   Tucker KL, Rich S, Rosenberg I, et al. Plasma vitamin B-12 concentrations relate to intake source in the Framingham Offspring study. *Am J Clin Nutr*. Feb 2000;71(2):514-22. doi:10.1093/ajcn/71.2.514

199.   Norris J, Messina G, Wolfram T, Mangels R. Vitamin B12 Absorption. Vegan Health. Accessed 31 October, 2022. https://veganhealth.org/vitamin-b12/vitamin-b12-absorption/#fn5

200.   Abbott A. Scientists bust myth that our bodies have more bacteria than human cells.

201.   Wiertsema SP, van Bergenhenegouwen J, Garssen J, Knippels LMJ. The Interplay between the Gut Microbiome and the Immune System in the Context of Infectious Diseases throughout Life and the Role of Nutrition in Optimizing Treatment Strategies. *Nutrients*. Mar 9 2021;13(3)doi:10.3390/nu13030886

202.   Quigley EM. Gut bacteria in health and disease. *Gastroenterol Hepatol (N Y)*. Sep 2013;9(9):560-9.

203.   Eisenstein M. The hunt for a healthy microbiome. *Nature*. 2020:S6-s8. vol. 7792.

204.   Almeida A, Mitchell AL, Boland M, et al. A new genomic blueprint of the human gut microbiota. *Nature*. 2019/04/01 2019;568(7753):499-504. doi:10.1038/s41586-019-0965-1

205.   Overview of Human-Microbial Reactions. 2021/1/3/

206.   Yan F, Polk DB. Probiotics and immune health. *Curr Opin Gastroenterol*. Oct 2011;27(6):496-501. doi:10.1097/MOG.0b013e32834baa4d

207.   Falagas ME, Betsi GI, Tokas T, Athanasiou S. Probiotics for prevention of recurrent urinary tract infections in women: a review of the evidence from microbiological and clinical studies. *Drugs*. 2006;66(9):1253-61. doi:10.2165/00003495-200666090-00007

208.   Shi LH, Balakrishnan K, Thiagarajah K, Mohd Ismail NI, Yin OS. Beneficial Properties of Probiotics. *Trop Life Sci Res*. Aug 2016;27(2):73-90. doi:10.21315/tlsr2016.27.2.6

209.   Sun S, Chang G, Zhang L. The prevention effect of probiotics against eczema in children: an update systematic review and meta-analysis. *J Dermatolog Treat*. Jun 2022;33(4):1844-1854. doi:10.1080/09546634.2021.1925077

210.   Amalaradjou MA, Bhunia AK. Modern approaches in probiotics research to control foodborne pathogens. *Adv Food Nutr Res*. 2012;67:185-239. doi:10.1016/b978-0-12-394598-3.00005-8

211.   Nilsson AG, Sundh D, Bäckhed F, Lorentzon M. Lactobacillus reuteri reduces bone loss in older women with low bone mineral density: a randomized, placebo-controlled, double-blind, clinical trial. *J Intern Med*. Sep 2018;284(3):307-317. doi:10.1111/joim.12805

212.   Kazlauskiene A. Probiotics – a closer look at gut health. Haven Pharmacy. Accessed 31 October, 2022. https://havenpharmacy.ie/probiotics-a-closer-look/

213.   Peirce JM, Alviña K. The role of inflammation and the gut microbiome in depression and anxiety. *J Neurosci Res*. Oct 2019;97(10):1223-1241. doi:10.1002/jnr.24476

214.   Lorenzo D, GianVincenzo Z, Carlo Luca R, et al. Oral-Gut Microbiota and Arthritis: Is There an Evidence-Based Axis? *J Clin Med*. Oct 22 2019;8(10)doi:10.3390/jcm8101753

215.   Canakis A, Haroon M, Weber HC. Irritable bowel syndrome and gut microbiota. *Curr Opin Endocrinol Diabetes Obes*. Feb 2020;27(1):28-35. doi:10.1097/med.0000000000000523

216.   Rani V, Singhal S, Sharma K, et al. Human Gut Microbiome: A New Frontier in Cancer Diagnostics & Therapeutics. *Curr Pharm Des*. 2021;27(45):4578-4592. doi:10.2174/1381612827666211006152112

217.   Maldonado Galdeano C, Cazorla SI, Lemme Dumit JM, Vélez E, Perdigón G. Beneficial Effects of Probiotic Consumption on the Immune System. *Ann Nutr Metab*. 2019;74(2):115-124. doi:10.1159/000496426

218.   Kechagia M, Basoulis D, Konstantopoulou S, et al. Health benefits of probiotics: a review. *ISRN Nutr*. 2013;2013:481651. doi:10.5402/2013/481651

219.   Barkhidarian B, Roldos L, Iskandar MM, Saedisomeolia A, Kubow S. Probiotic Supplementation and Micronutrient Status in Healthy Subjects: A Systematic Review of Clinical Trials. *Nutrients*. Aug 28 2021;13(9)doi:10.3390/nu13093001

220. Mundula T, Ricci F, Barbetta B, Baccini M, Amedei A. Effect of Probiotics on Oral Candidiasis: A Systematic Review and Meta-Analysis. *Nutrients*. Oct 14 2019;11(10)doi:10.3390/nu11102449

221. Zeng L, Yu G, Wu Y, Hao W, Chen H. The Effectiveness and Safety of Probiotic Supplements for Psoriasis: A Systematic Review and Meta-Analysis of Randomized Controlled Trials and Preclinical Trials. *J Immunol Res*. 2021;2021:7552546. doi:10.1155/2021/7552546

222. Kang EJ, Kim SY, Hwang IH, Ji YJ. The effect of probiotics on prevention of common cold: a meta-analysis of randomized controlled trial studies. *Korean J Fam Med*. Jan 2013;34(1):2-10. doi:10.4082/kjfm.2013.34.1.2

223. Leyer GJ, Li S, Mubasher ME, Reifer C, Ouwehand AC. Probiotic effects on cold and influenza-like symptom incidence and duration in children. *Pediatrics*. Aug 2009;124(2):e172-9. doi:10.1542/peds.2008-2666

224. Rao RK, Samak G. Protection and Restitution of Gut Barrier by Probiotics: Nutritional and Clinical Implications. *Curr Nutr Food Sci*. May 1 2013;9(2):99-107. doi:10.2174/1573401311309020004

225. Zhang Q, Wu Y, Fei X. Effect of probiotics on body weight and body-mass index: a systematic review and meta-analysis of randomized, controlled trials. *Int J Food Sci Nutr*. Aug 2015;67(5):571-80. doi:10.1080/09637486.2016.1181156

226. Gao C, Ganesh BP, Shi Z, et al. Gut Microbe-Mediated Suppression of Inflammation-Associated Colon Carcinogenesis by Luminal Histamine Production. *Am J Pathol*. Oct 2017;187(10):2323-2336. doi:10.1016/j.ajpath.2017.06.011

227. de Baaij JH, Hoenderop JG, Bindels RJ. Magnesium in man: implications for health and disease. *Physiol Rev*. Jan 2015;95(1):1-46. doi:10.1152/physrev.00012.2014

228. Axe J. 9 Signs You Have Magnesium Deficiency and How to Treat It. Dr Axe. Accessed 31 October, 2022. https://draxe.com/nutrition/9-signs-magnesium-deficiency/

229. Kirkland AE, Sarlo GL, Holton KF. The Role of Magnesium in Neurological Disorders. *Nutrients*. Jun 6 2018;10(6)doi:10.3390/nu10060730

230. University H. Magnesium. Harvard School of Public Health. Accessed 31 October, 2022. https://www.hsph.harvard.edu/nutritionsource/magnesium/

231. NIH. Magnesium. National Institute of Health. Accessed 31 October, 2022.

232. Pickering G, Mazur A, Trousselard M, et al. Magnesium Status and Stress: The Vicious Circle Concept Revisited. *Nutrients*. Nov 28 2020;12(12)doi:10.3390/nu12123672

233. Kowal A, Panaszek B, Barg W, Obojski A. The use of magnesium in bronchial asthma: a new approach to an old problem. *Arch Immunol Ther Exp (Warsz)*. Jan-Feb 2007;55(1):35-9. doi:10.1007/s00005-007-0008-8

234. Strambi M, Longini M, Hayek J, et al. Magnesium profile in autism. *Biol Trace Elem Res*. Feb 2006;109(2):97-104. doi:10.1385/bter:109:2:097

235. Rosique-Esteban N, Guasch-Ferré M, Hernández-Alonso P, Salas-Salvadó J. Dietary Magnesium and Cardiovascular Disease: A Review with Emphasis in Epidemiological Studies. *Nutrients*. Feb 1 2018;10(2)doi:10.3390/nu10020168

236. Lu JF, Nightingale CH. Magnesium sulfate in eclampsia and pre-eclampsia: pharmacokinetic principles. *Clin Pharmacokinet*. Apr 2000;38(4):305-14. doi:10.2165/00003088-200038040-00002

237. Nuytten D, Van Hees J, Meulemans A, Carton H. Magnesium deficiency as a cause of acute intractable seizures. *J Neurol*. Aug 1991;238(5):262-4. doi:10.1007/bf00319737

238. Patrick L. Nutrients and HIV: part two--vitamins A and E, zinc, B-vitamins, and magnesium. *Altern Med Rev*. Feb 2000;5(1):39-51.

239. Yasui M, Ota K. Experimental and clinical studies on dysregulation of magnesium metabolism and the aetiopathogenesis of multiple sclerosis. *Magnes Res*. Dec 1992;5(4):295-302.

240. Facchinetti F, Borella P, Sances G, Fioroni L, Nappi RE, Genazzani AR. Oral magnesium successfully relieves premenstrual mood changes. *Obstet Gynecol*. Aug 1991;78(2):177-81.

241.   Phd TJRM. Magnesium Deficiency in Systemic Lupus Erythematosus. *Journal of Nutritional & Environmental Medicine*. 1997/01/01 1997;7(2):107-112. doi:10.1080/13590849762691

242.   Jahnen-Dechent W, Ketteler M. Magnesium basics. *Clin Kidney J*. Feb 2012;5(Suppl 1):i3-i14. doi:10.1093/ndtplus/sfr163

243.   Gröber U, Schmidt J, Kisters K. Magnesium in Prevention and Therapy. *Nutrients*. Sep 23 2015;7(9):8199-226. doi:10.3390/nu7095388

244.   Castiglioni S, Cazzaniga A, Albisetti W, Maier JA. Magnesium and osteoporosis: current state of knowledge and future research directions. *Nutrients*. Jul 31 2013;5(8):3022-33. doi:10.3390/nu5083022

245.   Raman R. What Does Magnesium Do for Your Body? Healthline. Accessed 2 November, 2022. https://www.healthline.com/nutrition/what-does-magnesium-do

246.   Yousef AA, Al-deeb AE. A double-blinded randomised controlled study of the value of sequential intravenous and oral magnesium therapy in patients with chronic low back pain with a neuropathic component. *Anaesthesia*. Mar 2013;68(3):260-6. doi:10.1111/anae.12107

247.   Curry JN, Yu ASL. Magnesium Handling in the Kidney. *Adv Chronic Kidney Dis*. May 2018;25(3):236-243. doi:10.1053/j.ackd.2018.01.003

248.   Institute LP. Essential Fatty Acids. Oregon State University: Linus Pauling Institute. Accessed 2 November, 2022. https://lpi.oregonstate.edu/mic/other-nutrients/essential-fatty-acids

249.   Hjalmarsdotti F. 17 Science-Based Benefits of Omega-3 Fatty Acids. Healthline. Accessed 2 November, 2022. https://www.healthline.com/nutrition/17-health-benefits-of-omega-3#TOC_TITLE_HDR_8

250.   Virtanen JK, Wu JHY, Voutilainen S, Mursu J, Tuomainen T-P. Serum n–6 polyunsaturated fatty acids and risk of death: the Kuopio Ischaemic Heart Disease Risk Factor Study. *The American Journal of Clinical Nutrition*. 2018;107(3):427-435. doi:10.1093/ajcn/nqx063

251.   Price A. 6 Grapefruit Seed Extract Benefits You Won't Believe. Dr Axe. Accessed 2 November, 2022. https://draxe.com/nutrition/grapefruit-seed-extract/

252.   Krajewska-Kułak E, Lukaszuk C, Niczyporuk W. [Effects of 33% grapefruit extract on the growth of the yeast--like fungi, dermatopytes and moulds]. *Wiad Parazytol*. 2001;47(4):845-9. Ocena wpływu 33% ekstraktu z grejfruta na wzrost grzybów drozdzopodobnych, dermatofitów i pleśni.

253.   Sharma A, Maurya AK. Aggregate Frequencies of Body Organs. *International Journal Of Electrical, Electronics And Data Communication*. 2017;5(11):102-106.

254.   Hospital AM. The Digestive Process: Digestion Begins in the Mouth. Alton Memorial Hospital. Accessed 30 October, 2022. https://www.altonmemorialhospital.org/Health-Library/View-Content?contentTypeId=134&contentId=193

255.   Oschman JL. Can electrons act as antioxidants? A review and commentary. *J Altern Complement Med*. Nov 2007;13(9):955-67. doi:10.1089/acm.2007.7048

256.   Oschman JL. Chronic disease: are we missing something? *Journal of alternative and complementary medicine (New York, NY)*. 2011;17(4):283-285. doi:10.1089/acm.2011.0101

257.   Chevalier G, Sinatra ST, Oschman JL, Sokal K, Sokal P. Earthing: health implications of reconnecting the human body to the Earth's surface electrons. *Journal of environmental and public health*. 2012;2012:291541-291541. doi:10.1155/2012/291541

258.   Chevalier G, Sinatra ST, Oschman JL, Delany RM. Earthing (grounding) the human body reduces blood viscosity-a major factor in cardiovascular disease. *J Altern Complement Med*. Feb 2013;19(2):102-10. doi:10.1089/acm.2011.0820

259.   Chevalier G, Patel S, Weiss L, Chopra D, Mills PJ. The Effects of Grounding (Earthing) on Bodyworkers' Pain and Overall Quality of Life: A Randomized Controlled Trial. *Explore (NY)*. May-Jun 2019;15(3):181-190. doi:10.1016/j.explore.2018.10.001

260.	Ghaly M, Teplitz D. The biologic effects of grounding the human body during sleep as measured by cortisol levels and subjective reporting of sleep, pain, and stress. *J Altern Complement Med*. Oct 2004;10(5):767-76. doi:10.1089/acm.2004.10.767

261.	Sokal K, Sokal P. Earthing the human body influences physiologic processes. *Journal of alternative and complementary medicine (New York, NY)*. 2011;17(4):301-308. doi:10.1089/acm.2010.0687

262.	Brown D, Chevalier G, Hill M. Pilot study on the effect of grounding on delayed-onset muscle soreness. *Journal of alternative and complementary medicine (New York, NY)*. 2010;16(3):265-273. doi:10.1089/acm.2009.0399

263.	Khazai N, Judd SE, Tangpricha V. Calcium and vitamin D: skeletal and extraskeletal health. *Current rheumatology reports*. 2008;10(2):110-117. doi:10.1007/s11926-008-0020-y

264.	Mitsuo T, Nakao M. Vitamin D and anti-aging medicine. *Clin Calcium*. Jul 2008;18(7):980-5.

265.	Coles ME, Wirshba CJ, Nota J, Schubert J, Grunthal BA. Obsessive compulsive disorder prevalence increases with latitude. *Journal of Obsessive-Compulsive and Related Disorders*. 2018/07/01 2018;18:25-30. doi:https://doi.org/10.1016/j.jocrd.2018.04.001

266.	Wang G, Liu X, Bartell Tami R, Pearson C, Cheng Tina L, Wang X. Vitamin D Trajectories From Birth to Early Childhood and Elevated Systolic Blood Pressure During Childhood and Adolescence. *Hypertension*. 2019/08/01 2019;74(2):421-430. doi:10.1161/HYPERTENSIONAHA.119.13120

267.	Lindqvist PG, Epstein E, Landin-Olsson M, et al. Avoidance of sun exposure is a risk factor for all-cause mortality: results from the Melanoma in Southern Sweden cohort. *Journal of Internal Medicine*. 2014/07/01 2014;276(1):77-86. doi:10.1111/joim.12251

268.	Paul DS. *Superhuman Academy*. Yes, You Can Alter Your Genes. Accessed 11 January 2021. https://superhumanacademy.com/podcast/dr-sharad-paul-genetics-skin-cancer/

269.	Wang DH, Yamada A, Miyanaga M. Changes in Urinary Hydrogen Peroxide and 8-Hydroxy-2'-Deoxyguanosine Levels after a Forest Walk: A Pilot Study. *Int J Environ Res Public Health*. Aug 29 2018;15(9)doi:10.3390/ijerph15091871

270.	Hansen MM, Jones R, Tocchini K. Shinrin-Yoku (Forest Bathing) and Nature Therapy: A State-of-the-Art Review. *International journal of environmental research and public health*. 2017;14(8):851. doi:10.3390/ijerph14080851

271.	Morita E, Fukuda S, Nagano J, et al. Psychological effects of forest environments on healthy adults: Shinrin-yoku (forest-air bathing, walking) as a possible method of stress reduction. *Public Health*. 2007/01/01 2007;121(1):54-63. doi:https://doi.org/10.1016/j.puhe.2006.05.024

272.	White MP, Alcock I, Grellier J, et al. Spending at least 120 minutes a week in nature is associated with good health and wellbeing. *Scientific Reports*. 2019/06/13 2019;9(1):7730. doi:10.1038/s41598-019-44097-3

273.	BBC. The Truth About Boosting Your Immune System. In: Barret M, editor. The Truth About. England: BBC iPlayer; 2021. p. 30 minutes.

274.	Carrell S. Scottish GPs to begin prescribing rambling and birdwatching. The Guardian. Accessed 8 June, 2020. https://www.theguardian.com/uk-news/2018/oct/05/scottish-gps-nhs-begin-prescribing-rambling-birdwatching

275.	van Maanen A, Meijer AM, van der Heijden KB, Oort FJ. The effects of light therapy on sleep problems: A systematic review and meta-analysis. *Sleep Med Rev*. Oct 2016;29:52-62. doi:10.1016/j.smrv.2015.08.009

276.	Rybak YE, McNeely HE, Mackenzie BE, Jain UR, Levitan RD. An open trial of light therapy in adult attention-deficit/hyperactivity disorder. *J Clin Psychiatry*. Oct 2006;67(10):1527-35. doi:10.4088/jcp.v67n1006

277.	Fargason RE, Fobian AD, Hablitz LM, et al. Correcting delayed circadian phase with bright light therapy predicts improvement in ADHD symptoms: A pilot study. *J Psychiatr Res*. Aug 2017;91:105-110. doi:10.1016/j.jpsychires.2017.03.004

278.	Fifel K, Videnovic A. Light Therapy in Parkinson's Disease: Towards Mechanism-Based Protocols. *Trends in neurosciences.* 2018;41(5):252-254. doi:10.1016/j.tins.2018.03.002

279.	Rutten S, Vriend C, van den Heuvel OA, Smit JH, Berendse HW, van der Werf YD. Bright light therapy in Parkinson's disease: an overview of the background and evidence. *Parkinson's disease.* 2012;2012:767105-767105. doi:10.1155/2012/767105

280.	Willis GL, Moore C, Armstrong SM. A historical justification for and retrospective analysis of the systematic application of light therapy in Parkinson's disease. *Reviews in the Neurosciences.* 2012;23(2):199-226. doi:doi:10.1515/revneuro-2011-0072

281.	Willis GL, Turner EJD. Primary and Secondary Features of Parkinson's Disease Improve with Strategic Exposure to Bright Light: A Case Series Study. *Chronobiology International.* 2007/01/01 2007;24(3):521-537. doi:10.1080/07420520701420717

282.	Vigh B, Manzano MJ, Zádori A, et al. Nonvisual photoreceptors of the deep brain, pineal organs and retina. *Histol Histopathol.* Apr 2002;17(2):555-90. doi:10.14670/hh-17.555

283.	News B. Sunbathing ups men's testosterone. BBC. Accessed 7 April, 2021. http://news.bbc.co.uk/1/hi/health/8493042.stm

284.	Myerson A, Neustadt R. INFLUENCE OF ULTRAVIOLET IRRADIATION UPON EXCRETION OF SEX HORMONES IN THE MALE11. *Endocrinology.* 1939;25(1):7-12. doi:10.1210/endo-25-1-7

285.	Stausholm MB, Naterstad IF, Joensen J, et al. Efficacy of low-level laser therapy on pain and disability in knee osteoarthritis: systematic review and meta-analysis of randomised placebo-controlled trials. *BMJ Open.* Oct 28 2019;9(10):e031142. doi:10.1136/bmjopen-2019-031142

286.	de Morais NC, Barbosa AM, Vale ML, et al. Anti-inflammatory effect of low-level laser and light-emitting diode in zymosan-induced arthritis. *Photomed Laser Surg.* Apr 2010;28(2):227-32. doi:10.1089/pho.2008.2422

287.	Ferraresi C, Kaippert B, Avci P, et al. Low-level laser (light) therapy increases mitochondrial membrane potential and ATP synthesis in C2C12 myotubes with a peak response at 3-6 h. *Photochem Photobiol.* Mar-Apr 2015;91(2):411-6. doi:10.1111/php.12397

288.	Li WH, Seo I, Kim B, Fassih A, Southall MD, Parsa R. Low-level red plus near infrared lights combination induces expressions of collagen and elastin in human skin in vitro. *Int J Cosmet Sci.* Jun 2021;43(3):311-320. doi:10.1111/ics.12698

289.	Demidova-Rice TN, Salomatina EV, Yaroslavsky AN, Herman IM, Hamblin MR. Low-level light stimulates excisional wound healing in mice. *Lasers in Surgery and Medicine.* 2007/10/01 2007;39(9):706-715. doi:10.1002/lsm.20549

290.	Geneva II. Photobiomodulation for the treatment of retinal diseases: a review. *International journal of ophthalmology.* 2016;9(1):145-152. doi:10.18240/ijo.2016.01.24

291.	Use Feng Shui To Become Abundant Today |. https://youtu.be/GW0cMaC3Fp0. MindValley University.

292.	2022 Interior Landscape Plants For Indoor Air Pollution Abatement (NASA) (1989).

293.	Vartanian LR, Kernan KM, Wansink B. Clutter, Chaos, and Overconsumption: The Role of Mind-Set in Stressful and Chaotic Food Environments. *Environment and Behavior.* 2017/02/01 2016;49(2):215-223. doi:10.1177/0013916516628178

294.	Agency EE. Noise pollution is a major problem, both for human health and the environment. European Environment Agency. Accessed 23 October, 2022. https://www.eea.europa.eu/articles/noise-pollution-is-a-major

295.	EWG. Exposures add up – Survey results. Environment Working Group. Accessed 23 October, 2022. https://www.ewg.org/news-insights/news/2004/12/exposures-add-survey-results

296.	Matta MK, Zusterzeel R, Pilli NR, et al. Effect of Sunscreen Application Under Maximal Use Conditions on Plasma Concentration of Sunscreen Active Ingredients: A Randomized Clinical Trial. *JAMA.* 2019;321(21):2082-2091. doi:10.1001/jama.2019.5586

297.   Barrett Julia R. Chemical Exposures: The Ugly Side of Beauty Products. *Environmental Health Perspectives.* 2005/01/01 2005;113(1):A24-A24. doi:10.1289/ehp.113-a24

298.   Calafat AM, Ye X, Wong LY, Bishop AM, Needham LL. Urinary concentrations of four parabens in the U.S. population: NHANES 2005-2006. *Environ Health Perspect.* May 2010;118(5):679-85. doi:10.1289/ehp.0901560

299.   Datta S, He G, Tomilov A, Sahdeo S, Denison Michael S, Cortopassi G. In Vitro Evaluation of Mitochondrial Function and Estrogen Signaling in Cell Lines Exposed to the Antiseptic Cetylpyridinium Chloride. *Environmental Health Perspectives.* 125(8):087015. doi:10.1289/EHP1404

300.   Tun MH, Tun HM, Mahoney JJ, et al. Postnatal exposure to household disinfectants, infant gut microbiota and subsequent risk of overweight in children. *Canadian Medical Association Journal.* 2018;190(37):E1097. doi:10.1503/cmaj.170809

301.   Svanes Ø, Bertelsen RJ, Lygre SHL, et al. Cleaning at Home and at Work in Relation to Lung Function Decline and Airway Obstruction. *American Journal of Respiratory and Critical Care Medicine.* 2018/05/01 2018;197(9):1157-1163. doi:10.1164/rccm.201706-1311OC

302.   Agency EE. Living healthily in a chemical world. European Environment Agency. Accessed 23 October, 2022. https://www.eea.europa.eu/signals/signals-2020/articles/living-healthily-in-a-chemical-world

303.   High Exposure to Radio Frequency Radiation Associated With Cancer in Male Rats. National Institute of Health (NIH); 2018. https://www.niehs.nih.gov/news/newsroom/releases/2018/november1/index.cfm

304.   Kwon MS, Vorobyev V, Kännälä S, et al. GSM Mobile Phone Radiation Suppresses Brain Glucose Metabolism. *Journal of Cerebral Blood Flow & Metabolism.* 2011/12/01 2011;31(12):2293-2301. doi:10.1038/jcbfm.2011.128

305.   Pearson H. Mobile-phone radiation damages lab DNA. *Nature.* 2004/12/21 2004;doi:10.1038/news041220-6

306.   Zhang G, Yan H, Chen Q, et al. Effects of cell phone use on semen parameters: Results from the MARHCS cohort study in Chongqing, China. *Environment International.* 2016/05/01 2016;91:116-121. doi:https://doi.org/10.1016/j.envint.2016.02.028

307.   Foerster M, Thielens A, Joseph W, Eeftens M, Röösli M. A Prospective Cohort Study of Adolescents' Memory Performance and Individual Brain Dose of Microwave Radiation from Wireless Communication. *Environmental Health Perspectives.* 126(7):077007. doi:10.1289/EHP2427

308.   Li D-K, Chen H, Ferber JR, Odouli R, Quesenberry C. Exposure to Magnetic Field Non-Ionizing Radiation and the Risk of Miscarriage: A Prospective Cohort Study. *Scientific Reports.* 2017/12/13 2017;7(1):17541. doi:10.1038/s41598-017-16623-8

309.   Wyde M, Cesta M, Blystone C, et al. Report of Partial findings from the National Toxicology Program Carcinogenesis Studies of Cell Phone Radiofrequency Radiation in Hsd: Sprague Dawley[®] SD rats (Whole Body Exposures). *bioRxiv.* 2018:055699. doi:10.1101/055699

310.   Basso JC, Suzuki WA. The Effects of Acute Exercise on Mood, Cognition, Neurophysiology, and Neurochemical Pathways: A Review. *Brain Plast.* Mar 28 2017;2(2):127-152. doi:10.3233/bpl-160040

311.   Slentz CA, Duscha BD, Johnson JL, et al. Effects of the amount of exercise on body weight, body composition, and measures of central obesity: STRRIDE--a randomized controlled study *Arch Intern Med.* Jan 12 2004;164(1):31-9. doi:10.1001/archinte.164.1.31

312.   Santos L, Elliott-Sale KJ, Sale C. Exercise and bone health across the lifespan. *Biogerontology.* Dec 2017;18(6):931-946. doi:10.1007/s10522-017-9732-6

313.   Wender CLA, Manninen M, O'Connor PJ. The Effect of Chronic Exercise on Energy and Fatigue States: A Systematic Review and Meta-Analysis of Randomized Trials. *Front Psychol.* 2022;13:907637. doi:10.3389/fpsyg.2022.907637

SUPER VITALITY

314.   Stamatakis E, Ahmadi MN, Gill JMR, et al. Association of wearable device-measured vigorous intermittent lifestyle physical activity with mortality. *Nature Medicine*. 2022/12/08 2022;doi:10.1038/s41591-022-02100-x
315.   Hamasaki H. Daily physical activity and type 2 diabetes: A review. *World J Diabetes*. Jun 25 2016;7(12):243-51. doi:10.4239/wjd.v7.i12.243
316.   Exercise. Stop Colon Cancer Now. Accessed 14 December, 2022. https://www.stopcoloncancernow.com/colon-cancer-facts/preventing-colon-cancer/exercise
317.   NHS. Benefits of Exercise. National Health Service (NHS). Accessed 14 December, 2022. https://www.nhsinform.scot/healthy-living/keeping-active/benefits-of-exercise
318.   Breast Cancer Risk: Exercise (Physical Activity). Susan G Komen. Accessed 14 December, 2022. https://www.komen.org/breast-cancer/risk-factor/lack-of-exercise/
319.   Xie Y, Liu S, Chen XJ, Yu HH, Yang Y, Wang W. Effects of Exercise on Sleep Quality and Insomnia in Adults: A Systematic Review and Meta-Analysis of Randomized Controlled Trials. *Front Psychiatry*. 2021;12:664499. doi:10.3389/fpsyt.2021.664499
320.   White JR, Case DA, McWhirter D, Mattison AM. Enhanced sexual behavior in exercising men. *Arch Sex Behav*. Jun 1990;19(3):193-209. doi:10.1007/bf01541546
321.   Gremeaux V, Gayda M, Lepers R, Sosner P, Juneau M, Nigam A. Exercise and longevity. *Maturitas*. Dec 2012;73(4):312-7. doi:10.1016/j.maturitas.2012.09.012
322.   Bassett DRJ, Wyatt HR, Thompson H, Peters JC, Hill JO. Pedometer-Measured Physical Activity and Health Behaviors in U.S. Adults. *Medicine & Science in Sports & Exercise*. 2010;42(10)
323.   Wilmot EG, Edwardson CL, Achana FA, et al. Sedentary time in adults and the association with diabetes, cardiovascular disease and death: systematic review and meta-analysis. *Diabetologia*. Nov 2012;55(11):2895-905. doi:10.1007/s00125-012-2677-z
324.   Owen N, Healy GN, Matthews CE, Dunstan DW. Too much sitting: the population health science of sedentary behavior. *Exercise and sport sciences reviews*. 2010;38(3):105-113. doi:10.1097/JES.0b013e3181e373a2
325.   Rutten GM, Savelberg HH, Biddle SJH, Kremers SPJ. Interrupting long periods of sitting: good STUFF. *International Journal of Behavioral Nutrition and Physical Activity*. 2013/01/02 2013;10(1):1. doi:10.1186/1479-5868-10-1
326.   Boreham CAG, Kennedy RA, Murphy MH, Tully M, Wallace WFM, Young I. Training effects of short bouts of stair climbing on cardiorespiratory fitness, blood lipids, and homocysteine in sedentary young women. *British Journal of Sports Medicine*. 2005;39(9):590. doi:10.1136/bjsm.2002.001131
327.   Heisz JJ, Clark IB, Bonin K, et al. The Effects of Physical Exercise and Cognitive Training on Memory and Neurotrophic Factors. *J Cogn Neurosci*. Nov 2017;29(11):1895-1907. doi:10.1162/jocn_a_01164
328.   Heath R. Sitting Ducks – Sedentary Behaviour and its Health Risks: Part One of a Two Part Series. British Journal of Sports Medicine. Accessed 8 June, 2020. https://blogs.bmj.com/bjsm/2015/01/21/sitting-ducks-sedentary-behaviour-and-its-health-risks-part-one-of-a-two-part-series/
329.   Rehfeld K, Lüders A, Hökelmann A, et al. Dance training is superior to repetitive physical exercise in inducing brain plasticity in the elderly. *PLoS One*. 2018;13(7):e0196636. doi:10.1371/journal.pone.0196636
330.   Standing GB. Top 10 Health Risks to Sedentary Behaviour. Get Britain Standing. Accessed 22 June, 2020. http://www.getbritainstanding.org/health-risks.php
331.   Patel AV, Hildebrand JS, Campbell PT, et al. Leisure-Time Spent Sitting and Site-Specific Cancer Incidence in a Large U.S. Cohort. *Cancer Epidemiol Biomarkers Prev*. Sep 2015;24(9):1350-9. doi:10.1158/1055-9965.epi-15-0237
332.   Cardiology ACo. Excess sitting linked to coronary artery calcification, an early indicator of heart problems. Science Daily. Accessed 9 June, 2020. https://www.sciencedaily.com/releases/2015/03/150305205959.htm

333.   Al-Dirini RM, Reed MP, Thewlis D. Deformation of the gluteal soft tissues during sitting. *Clin Biomech (Bristol, Avon)*. Aug 2015;30(7):662-8. doi:10.1016/j.clinbiomech.2015.05.008

334.   Labonté-LeMoyne É, Santhanam R, Léger P-M, Courtemanche F, Fredette M, Sénécal S. The delayed effect of treadmill desk usage on recall and attention. *Computers in Human Behavior*. 2015/05/01/ 2015;46:1-5. doi:https://doi.org/10.1016/j.chb.2014.12.054

335.   Thosar SS, Bielko Sl Fau - Mather KJ, Mather Kj Fau - Johnston JD, Johnston Jd Fau - Wallace JP, Wallace JP. Effect of prolonged sitting and breaks in sitting time on endothelial function. 2015;(1530-0315 (Electronic))

336.   Beers EA, Roemmich JN, Epstein LH, Horvath PJ. Increasing passive energy expenditure during clerical work. *Eur J Appl Physiol*. Jun 2008;103(3):353-60. doi:10.1007/s00421-008-0713-y

337.   Oppezzo M, Schwartz DL. Give your ideas some legs: the positive effect of walking on creative thinking. *J Exp Psychol Learn Mem Cogn*. Jul 2014;40(4):1142-52. doi:10.1037/a0036577

338.   Aberg MA, Pedersen NL, Torén K, et al. Cardiovascular fitness is associated with cognition in young adulthood. *Proc Natl Acad Sci U S A*. Dec 8 2009;106(49):20906-11. doi:10.1073/pnas.0905307106

339.   Weiler R, Aggio D, Hamer M, Taylor T, Kumar B. Sedentary behaviour among elite professional footballers: health and performance implications. *BMJ Open Sport & Exercise Medicine*. 2015;1(1):e000023. doi:10.1136/bmjsem-2015-000023

340.   Schmid D, Colditz G. Sedentary behavior increases the risk of certain cancers. *JNCI: Journal of the National Cancer Institute*. 2014;106(7)doi:10.1093/jnci/dju206

341.   Patel AV, Bernstein L, Deka A, et al. Leisure time spent sitting in relation to total mortality in a prospective cohort of US adults. *American journal of epidemiology*. 2010;172(4):419-429. doi:10.1093/aje/kwq155

342.   Vlahos J. Is Sitting a Lethal Activity? New York Times. Accessed 8 June, 2020. https://www.nytimes.com/2011/04/17/magazine/mag-17sitting-t.html?_r=1&

343.   NHS. Why we should sit less. National Health Service (NHS). Accessed 8 June, 2020. https://www.nhs.uk/live-well/exercise/why-sitting-too-much-is-bad-for-us/

344.   van Uffelen JGZ, van Gellecum YR, Burton NW, Peeters G, Heesch KC, Brown WJ. Sitting-Time, Physical Activity, and Depressive Symptoms in Mid-Aged Women. *American Journal of Preventive Medicine*. 2013;45(3):276-281. doi:10.1016/j.amepre.2013.04.009

345.   Diaz KM, Duran AT, Colabianchi N, Judd SE, Howard VJ, Hooker SP. Potential Effects on Mortality of Replacing Sedentary Time With Short Sedentary Bouts or Physical Activity: A National Cohort Study. *Am J Epidemiol*. Mar 1 2019;188(3):537-544. doi:10.1093/aje/kwy271

346.   Heron L, Neill C, McAneney H, Kee F, Tully MA. Direct healthcare costs of sedentary behaviour in the UK. *Journal of Epidemiology and Community Health*. 2019;73(7):625. doi:10.1136/jech-2018-211758

347.   Garrett G, Benden M, Mehta R, Pickens A, Peres SC, Zhao H. Call Center Productivity Over 6 Months Following a Standing Desk Intervention. *IIE Transactions on Occupational Ergonomics and Human Factors*. 2016/07/02 2016;4(2-3):188-195. doi:10.1080/21577323.2016.1183534

348.   Bey L, Hamilton MT. Suppression of skeletal muscle lipoprotein lipase activity during physical inactivity: a molecular reason to maintain daily low-intensity activity. *J Physiol*. Sep 1 2003;551(Pt 2):673-82. doi:10.1113/jphysiol.2003.045591

349.   Wood G. Ask The Doctor. In: Victoria WEABCF, editor. Exercise. Australia: Netflix; 2017. p. 30 minutes.

350.   Pesola AA-O, Laukkanen A, Heikkinen R, Sipilä S, Sääkslahti A, Finni T. Accelerometer-assessed sedentary work, leisure time and cardio-metabolic biomarkers during one year: Effectiveness of a cluster randomized controlled trial in parents with a sedentary occupation and young children. (1932-6203 (Electronic))

SUPER VITALITY

351. Bergouignan A, Legget KT, De Jong N, et al. Effect of frequent interruptions of prolonged sitting on self-perceived levels of energy, mood, food cravings and cognitive function. *International Journal of Behavioral Nutrition and Physical Activity*. 2016/11/03 2016;13(1):113. doi:10.1186/s12966-016-0437-z

352. Dohrn I-M, Kwak L, Oja P, Sjöström M, Hagströmer M. Replacing sedentary time with physical activity: a 15-year follow-up of mortality in a national cohort. *Clinical Epidemiology*. 01/25 2018;10:179-186. doi:10.2147/CLEP.S151613

353. Celis-Morales CA, Welsh P, Lyall DM, et al. Associations of grip strength with cardiovascular, respiratory, and cancer outcomes and all cause mortality: prospective cohort study of half a million UK Biobank participants. *BMJ*. 2018;361:k1651. doi:10.1136/bmj.k1651

354. Burandt P, Porcari JP, Cress ML, Doberstein S, Foster C, Green DJ. *Putting mini-trampolines to the test*. 2016. https://acewebcontent.azureedge.net/certifiednews/images/article/pdfs/ACE_MiniTrampoline.pdf?

355. Bhattacharya A, McCutcheon EP, Shvartz E, Greenleaf JE. Body acceleration distribution and O2 uptake in humans during running and jumping. *J Appl Physiol Respir Environ Exerc Physiol*. Nov 1980;49(5):881-7. doi:10.1152/jappl.1980.49.5.881

356. Nazroo J, Matthews K. *The impact of volunteering on well-being in later life*. 2012:10. https://www.royalvoluntaryservice.org.uk/Uploads/Documents/Reports%20and%20Reviews/the_impact_of_volunteering_on_wellbeing_in_later_life.pdf

357. Littlepage L, Obergfell E, Zanin G. Family Volunteering: An Exploratory Study of the Impact on Families. 2003:

358. Stephenson S. *The Model Health Show*. The Surprising Benefits of Helping Others & the Truth about Thirst. Accessed 8 June 2020. https://themodelhealthshow.com/scott-harrison/

359. Anderson ND, Damianakis T, Kröger E, et al. The benefits associated with volunteering among seniors: a critical review and recommendations for future research. *Psychol Bull*. Nov 2014;140(6):1505-33. doi:10.1037/a0037610

360. Musick MA, Wilson J. Volunteering and depression: the role of psychological and social resources in different age groups. *Soc Sci Med*. Jan 2003;56(2):259-69. doi:10.1016/s0277-9536(02)00025-4

361. Tabassum F, Mohan J, Smith P. Association of volunteering with mental well-being: a lifecourse analysis of a national population-based longitudinal study in the UK. *BMJ open*. 2016;6(8):e011327-e011327. doi:10.1136/bmjopen-2016-011327

362. Yeung JWK, Zhang Z, Kim TY. Volunteering and health benefits in general adults: cumulative effects and forms. *BMC public health*. 2017;18(1):8-8. doi:10.1186/s12889-017-4561-8

363. Inagaki TK, Ross LP. Neural Correlates of Giving Social Support: Differences Between Giving Targeted Versus Untargeted Support. *Psychosomatic Medicine*. 2018;80(8)

364. Reblin M, Uchino BN. Social and emotional support and its implication for health. *Current opinion in psychiatry*. 2008;21(2):201-205. doi:10.1097/YCO.0b013e3282f3ad89

365. Windsor TD, Curtis RG, Luszcz MA. Sense of purpose as a psychological resource for aging well. *Developmental Psychology*. 2015;51(7):975-986. doi:10.1037/dev0000023

366. Kimiko T. Relationship of Having Hobbies and a Purpose in Life With Mortality, Activities of Daily Living, and Instrumental Activities of Daily Living Among Community-Dwelling Elderly Adults. article. *Journal of Epidemiology, Vol 26, Iss 7, Pp 361-370 (2016)*. 2016;(7):361. doi:10.2188/jea.JE20150153

367. Alimujiang A, Wiensch A, Boss J, et al. Association Between Life Purpose and Mortality Among US Adults Older Than 50 Years. *JAMA Network Open*. 2019;2(5):e194270-e194270. doi:10.1001/jamanetworkopen.2019.4270

368. Mineo L. Good genes are nice, but joy is better. Harvard University. Accessed 9 June, 2020. https://news.harvard.edu/gazette/story/2017/04/over-nearly-80-years-harvard-study-has-been-showing-how-to-live-a-healthy-and-happy-life/

369. Goldstein P, Weissman-Fogel I, Dumas G, Shamay-Tsoory SG. Brain-to-brain coupling during handholding is associated with pain reduction. *Proceedings of the National Academy of Sciences*. 2018;115(11):E2528. doi:10.1073/pnas.1703643115

370. Grewen KM, Anderson BJ, Girdler SS, Light KC. Warm Partner Contact Is Related to Lower Cardiovascular Reactivity. *Behavioral Medicine*. 2003/01/01 2003;29(3):123-130. doi:10.1080/08964280309596065

371. Ardiel EL, Rankin CH. The importance of touch in development. *Paediatrics & Child Health*. 04/29/accepted 2010;15(3):153-156.

372. Nelson CA, 3rd, Zeanah CH, Fox NA, Marshall PJ, Smyke AT, Guthrie D. Cognitive recovery in socially deprived young children: the Bucharest Early Intervention Project. *Science*. Dec 21 2007;318(5858):1937-40. doi:10.1126/science.1143921

373. Szalavitz M. How Orphanages Kill Babies-- and Why No Child Under 5 Should Be in One. The Huffington Post. Accessed 9 June, 2020. https://www.huffpost.com/entry/how-orphanages-kill-babie_b_549608?

374. Chatterjee R. Getting in touch with human touch: 4 ways to rediscover intimacy. Accessed 24 October, 2022. https://drchatterjee.com/easy-ways-reconnect-partner-christmas/

375. De Couck M, Caers R, Spiegel D, Gidron Y. The Role of the Vagus Nerve in Cancer Prognosis: A Systematic and a Comprehensive Review. *J Oncol*. 2018;2018:1236787. doi:10.1155/2018/1236787

376. Gladwell M. Outliers. *The New York Times*. https://www.nytimes.com/2008/11/30/books/chapters/chapter-outliers.html

377. Griffin J. *The Lonely Society*. 2010:9.

378. Cherry K. What You Should Know About Loneliness: Causes and Health Consequences of Feeling Lonely Very Well Mind. Accessed 16 October, 2018. https://www.verywellmind.com/loneliness-causes-effects-and-treatments-2795749

379. Focus on Families (UK Government) (2007).

380. Cousins N. Anatomy of an Illness (as Perceived by the Patient). *New England Journal of Medicine*. 1976/12/23 1976;295(26):1458-1463. doi:10.1056/NEJM197612232952605

381. Foley E, Matheis R, Schaefer C. Effect of forced laughter on mood. *Psychol Rep*. Feb 2002;90(1):184. doi:10.2466/pr0.2002.90.1.184

382. Kuiper NA, Martin RA. Laughter and stress in daily life: Relation to positive and negative affect. *Motivation and Emotion*. 1998;22(Special issue on affect and self-regulation):133-153.

383. Szabo A, Ainsworth SE, Danks PK. Experimental comparison of the psychological benefits of aerobic exercise, humor, and music. Germany: Walter de Gruyter; 2005. p. 235-246.

384. Louie D, Brook K, Frates E. The Laughter Prescription: A Tool for Lifestyle Medicine. *American journal of lifestyle medicine*. 2016;10(4):262-267. doi:10.1177/1559827614550279

385. Stephenson S. *The Model Health Show*. 5 Things Kids Can Teach Us About Living A Happy, Healthy Life. Accessed 10 June 2020. https://themodelhealthshow.com/kids-can-teach-us-about-living-a-happy-healthy-life/

386. Laukkanen JA, Laukkanen T, Kunutsor SK. Cardiovascular and Other Health Benefits of Sauna Bathing: A Review of the Evidence. *Mayo Clinic Proceedings*. 2018;93(8):1111-1121. doi:10.1016/j.mayocp.2018.04.008

387. Hof W. Benefits of Cold Shower. Wim Hof. Accessed 22 June, 2020. https://www.wimhofmethod.com/benefits-of-cold-showers

388.		Levi J. *Superhuman Academy*. How to Get Everything You Want in Life with Alex Charfen, Coach to Billionaire Entrepreneurs. https://superhumanacademy.com/podcast/how-to-get-everything-you-want-in-life-w-alex-charfen-coach-to-billionaire-entrepreneurs/

389.		Raichle ME, Gusnard DA. Appraising the brain's energy budget. *Proceedings of the National Academy of Sciences of the United States of America*. 2002;99(16):10237-10239. doi:10.1073/pnas.172399499

390.		Milne S, Orbell S, Sheeran P. Combining motivational and volitional interventions to promote exercise participation: protection motivation theory and implementation intentions. *Br J Health Psychol*. May 2002;7(Pt 2):163-84. doi:10.1348/135910702169420

391.		Walker M. *Why We Sleep*. Penguin Random House UK; 2017:360.

392.		Milewski MD, Skaggs DL, Bishop GA, et al. Chronic lack of sleep is associated with increased sports injuries in adolescent athletes. *J Pediatr Orthop*. Mar 2014;34(2):129-33. doi:10.1097/bpo.0000000000000151

393.		Bergeron MF, Mountjoy M, Armstrong N, et al. International Olympic Committee consensus statement on youth athletic development. *Br J Sports Med*. Jul 2015;49(13):843-51. doi:10.1136/bjsports-2015-094962

394.		Van Cauter E, Plat L. Physiology of growth hormone secretion during sleep. *J Pediatr*. May 1996;128(5 Pt 2):S32-7. doi:10.1016/s0022-3476(96)70008-2

395.		Reddy OC, van der Werf YD. The Sleeping Brain: Harnessing the Power of the Glymphatic System through Lifestyle Choices. *Brain Sci*. Nov 17 2020;10(11)doi:10.3390/brainsci10110868

396.		Stephenson S. *Sleep Smarter*. Hay House UK; 2016:296.

397.		Czeisler CA, Duffy JF, Shanahan TL, et al. Stability, precision, and near-24-hour period of the human circadian pacemaker. *Science*. Jun 25 1999;284(5423):2177-81. doi:10.1126/science.284.5423.2177

398.		Camilleri M. Serotonin in the gastrointestinal tract. *Curr Opin Endocrinol Diabetes Obes*. Feb 2009;16(1):53-9. doi:10.1097/med.0b013e32831e9c8e

399.		Hadhazy A. Think Twice: How the Gut's "Second Brain" Influences Mood and Well-Being. Scientific American. Accessed 10 June, 2020. https://www.scientificamerican.com/article/gut-second-brain/

400.		Chen C-Q, Fichna J, Bashashati M, Li Y-Y, Storr M. Distribution, function and physiological role of melatonin in the lower gut. *World journal of gastroenterology*. 2011;17(34):3888-3898. doi:10.3748/wjg.v17.i34.3888

401.		Hegarty S. The myth of the eight-hour sleep. BBC. Accessed 11 June, 2020. https://www.bbc.co.uk/news/magazine-16964783

402.		Lucassen EA, Coomans CP, van Putten M, et al. Environmental 24-hr Cycles Are Essential for Health. *Curr Biol*. Jul 25 2016;26(14):1843-53. doi:10.1016/j.cub.2016.05.038

403.		Rångtell FH, Ekstrand E, Rapp L, et al. Two hours of evening reading on a self-luminous tablet vs. reading a physical book does not alter sleep after daytime bright light exposure. *Sleep Medicine*. 2016/07/01/ 2016;23:111-118. doi:https://doi.org/10.1016/j.sleep.2016.06.016

404.		Kleszczynski K, Fischer TW. Melatonin and human skin aging. *Dermatoendocrinol*. Jul 1 2012;4(3):245-52. doi:10.4161/derm.22344

405.		Tan DX, Manchester LC, Fuentes-Broto L, Paredes SD, Reiter RJ. Significance and application of melatonin in the regulation of brown adipose tissue metabolism: relation to human obesity. https://doi.org/10.1111/j.1467-789X.2010.00756.x. *Obesity Reviews*. 2011/03/01 2011;12(3):167-188. doi:https://doi.org/10.1111/j.1467-789X.2010.00756.x

406.		Li Y, Li S, Zhou Y, et al. Melatonin for the prevention and treatment of cancer. *Oncotarget*. Jun 13 2017;8(24):39896-39921. doi:10.18632/oncotarget.16379

407.		Kochman J, Jakubczyk K, Antoniewicz J, Mruk H, Janda K. Health Benefits and Chemical Composition of Matcha Green Tea: A Review. *Molecules*. Dec 27 2020;26(1)doi:10.3390/molecules26010085

408.   Jehan S, Zizi F, Pandi-Perumal SR, et al. Obstructive Sleep Apnea and Obesity: Implications for Public Health. *Sleep Med Disord*. 2017;1(4)

409.   Jiang SZ, Lu W, Zong XF, Ruan HY, Liu Y. Obesity and hypertension. *Exp Ther Med*. Oct 2016;12(4):2395-2399. doi:10.3892/etm.2016.3667

410.   News A. Early morning exercise is best for reducing blood pressure and improving sleep. Appalachian State University. Accessed 15 April, 2018. http://newsarchive.appstate.edu/2011/06/13/early-morning-exercise/

411.   Melrose S. Seasonal Affective Disorder: An Overview of Assessment and Treatment Approaches. *Depress Res Treat*. 2015;2015:178564. doi:10.1155/2015/178564

412.   Thompson A, Jones H, Gregson W, Atkinson G. Effects of dawn simulation on markers of sleep inertia and post-waking performance in humans. *European Journal Of Applied Physiology*. 2014;114(5):1049-1056. doi:10.1007/s00421-014-2831-z

413.   DiNicolantonio JJ, O'Keefe JH, Wilson W. Subclinical magnesium deficiency: a principal driver of cardiovascular disease and a public health crisis. *Open Heart*. 2018;5(1):e000668. doi:10.1136/openhrt-2017-000668

414.   Martyka Z, Kotela I, Blady-Kotela A. [Clinical use of magnesium]. *Przegl Lek*. 1996;53(3):155-8. Kliniczne zastosowanie magnezu.

415.   Schutte-Rodin S, Broch L, Buysse D, Dorsey C, Sateia M. Clinical guideline for the evaluation and management of chronic insomnia in adults. *Journal of clinical sleep medicine : JCSM : official publication of the American Academy of Sleep Medicine*. 2008;4(5):487-504.

416.   Russo MA, Santarelli DM, O'Rourke D. The physiological effects of slow breathing in the healthy human. *Breathe (Sheffield, England)*. 2017;13(4):298-309. doi:10.1183/20734735.009817

417.   Komori T. The relaxation effect of prolonged expiratory breathing. *Mental illness*. 2018;10(1):7669-7669. doi:10.4081/mi.2018.7669

418.   Sinha AN, Deepak D, Gusain VS. Assessment of the effects of pranayama/alternate nostril breathing on the parasympathetic nervous system in young adults. *Journal of clinical and diagnostic research : JCDR*. 2013;7(5):821-823. doi:10.7860/JCDR/2013/4750.2948

419.   Telles S, Nagarathna R, Nagendra HR. Breathing through a particular nostril can alter metabolism and autonomic activities. *Indian J Physiol Pharmacol*. Apr 1994;38(2):133-7.

420.   Gavin M. Common Sleep Problems. Kids Health. Accessed 27 October, 2022. https://kidshealth.org/en/teens/sleep.html

421.   Hegarty S. The Myth of the Eight-Hour Sleep. BBC. Accessed 7 May, 2018. http://www.bbc.co.uk/news/magazine-16964783

422.   Gorvett Z. The forgotten medieval habit of 'two sleeps'. BBC. Accessed 20 January, 2023. https://www.bbc.com/future/article/20220107-the-lost-medieval-habit-of-biphasic-sleep

423.   Dutheil F, Danini B, Bagheri R, et al. Effects of a Short Daytime Nap on the Cognitive Performance: A Systematic Review and Meta-Analysis. *Int J Environ Res Public Health*. Sep 28 2021;18(19)doi:10.3390/ijerph181910212

424.   Cairney S, Clough AR, Maruff P, Collie A, Currie BJ, Currie J. Saccade and Cognitive Function in Chronic Kava Users. *Neuropsychopharmacology*. 2003/02/01 2003;28(2):389-396. doi:10.1038/sj.npp.1300052

425.   Thaiss CA, Zeevi D, Levy M, et al. Transkingdom control of microbiota diurnal oscillations promotes metabolic homeostasis. *Cell*. Oct 23 2014;159(3):514-29. doi:10.1016/j.cell.2014.09.048

426.   Panda S. *The Circadian Code*. Vermilion; 2018:288.

427.   Ponte Márquez PH, Feliu-Soler A, Solé-Villa MJ, et al. Benefits of mindfulness meditation in reducing blood pressure and stress in patients with arterial hypertension. *J Hum Hypertens*. Mar 2019;33(3):237-247. doi:10.1038/s41371-018-0130-6

428.   Black DS, Slavich GM. Mindfulness meditation and the immune system: a systematic review of randomized controlled trials. *Annals of the New York Academy of Sciences*. 2016/06/01 2016;1373(1):13-24. doi:10.1111/nyas.12998

429.   Hoge EA, Bui E, Palitz SA, et al. The effect of mindfulness meditation training on biological acute stress responses in generalized anxiety disorder. *Psychiatry Res.* Apr 2018;262:328-332. doi:10.1016/j.psychres.2017.01.006

430.   Paudyal P, Jones C, Grindey C, Dawood R, Smith H. Meditation for asthma: Systematic review and meta-analysis. *J Asthma.* Jul 2018;55(7):771-778. doi:10.1080/02770903.2017.1365887

431.   Burnett-Zeigler IE, Satyshur MD, Hong S, Yang A, T. Moskowitz J, Wisner KL. Mindfulness based stress reduction adapted for depressed disadvantaged women in an urban Federally Qualified Health Center. *Complementary Therapies in Clinical Practice.* 2016/11/01/ 2016;25:59-67. doi:https://doi.org/10.1016/j.ctcp.2016.08.007

432.   Levine GN, Lange RA, Bairey-Merz CN, et al. Meditation and Cardiovascular Risk Reduction: A Scientific Statement From the American Heart Association. *J Am Heart Assoc.* Sep 28 2017;6(10)doi:10.1161/jaha.117.002218

433.   Zeidan F, Emerson NM, Farris SR, et al. Mindfulness Meditation-Based Pain Relief Employs Different Neural Mechanisms Than Placebo and Sham Mindfulness Meditation-Induced Analgesia. *The Journal of Neuroscience.* 2015;35(46):15307. doi:10.1523/JNEUROSCI.2542-15.2015

434.   Gu Q, Hou JC, Fang XM. Mindfulness Meditation for Primary Headache Pain: A Meta-Analysis. *Chin Med J (Engl).* Apr 5 2018;131(7):829-838. doi:10.4103/0366-6999.228242

435.   Mehta R, Sharma K, Potters L, Wernicke AG, Parashar B. Evidence for the Role of Mindfulness in Cancer: Benefits and Techniques. *Cureus.* May 9 2019;11(5):e4629. doi:10.7759/cureus.4629

436.   Lutz J, Brühl AB, Scheerer H, Jäncke L, Herwig U. Neural correlates of mindful self-awareness in mindfulness meditators and meditation-naïve subjects revisited. *Biol Psychol.* Sep 2016;119:21-30. doi:10.1016/j.biopsycho.2016.06.010

437.   Zanesco AP, King BG, MacLean KA, Saron CD. Cognitive Aging and Long-Term Maintenance of Attentional Improvements Following Meditation Training. *Journal of Cognitive Enhancement.* 2018/09/01 2018;2(3):259-275. doi:10.1007/s41465-018-0068-1

438.   Wu R, Liu LL, Zhu H, et al. Brief Mindfulness Meditation Improves Emotion Processing. *Front Neurosci.* 2019;13:1074. doi:10.3389/fnins.2019.01074

439.   Carpenter JK, Sanford J, Hofmann SG. The Effect of a Brief Mindfulness Training on Distress Tolerance and Stress Reactivity. *Behav Ther.* May 2019;50(3):630-645. doi:10.1016/j.beth.2018.10.003

440.   Schutte NS, Malouff JM, Keng SL. Meditation and telomere length: a meta-analysis. *Psychol Health.* Aug 2020;35(8):901-915. doi:10.1080/08870446.2019.1707827

441.   Johns SA, Von Ah D, Brown LF, et al. Randomized controlled pilot trial of mindfulness-based stress reduction for breast and colorectal cancer survivors: effects on cancer-related cognitive impairment. *Journal of Cancer Survivorship.* 2016/06/01 2016;10(3):437-448. doi:10.1007/s11764-015-0494-3

442.   Lardone A, Liparoti M, Sorrentino P, et al. Mindfulness Meditation Is Related to Long-Lasting Changes in Hippocampal Functional Topology during Resting State: A Magnetoencephalography Study. *Neural Plast.* 2018;2018:5340717. doi:10.1155/2018/5340717

443.   Grossman P, Niemann L, Schmidt S, Walach H. Mindfulness-based stress reduction and health benefits. A meta-analysis. *J Psychosom Res.* Jul 2004;57(1):35-43. doi:10.1016/s0022-3999(03)00573-7

444.   Hoge EA, Bui E, Palitz SA, et al. The effect of mindfulness meditation training on biological acute stress responses in generalized anxiety disorder. Article. *Psychiatry Research.* 2018;262:328-332. doi:10.1016/j.psychres.2017.01.006

445.   Kollias H. A calorie isn't a calorie. Precision Nutrition. Accessed 22 June, 2020. https://www.precisionnutrition.com/digesting-whole-vs-processed-foods

446.   Grande Covián F. [Energy metabolism of the brain in children (author's transl)]. *An Esp Pediatr.* Mar 1979;12(3):235-44. El metabolismo energético del cerebro en la infancia.

447.   Mizushima N, Levine B, Cuervo AM, Klionsky DJ. Autophagy fights disease through cellular self-digestion. *Nature*. Feb 28 2008;451(7182):1069-75. doi:10.1038/nature06639

448.   Alirezaei M, Kemball CC, Flynn CT, Wood MR, Whitton JL, Kiosses WB. Short-term fasting induces profound neuronal autophagy. *Autophagy*. Aug 2010;6(6):702-10. doi:10.4161/auto.6.6.12376

449.   Goldhamer AC, Lisle DJ, Sultana P, et al. Medically supervised water-only fasting in the treatment of borderline hypertension. *J Altern Complement Med*. Oct 2002;8(5):643-50. doi:10.1089/107555302320825165

450.   Horne BD, Muhlestein JB, Lappé DL, et al. Randomized cross-over trial of short-term water-only fasting: metabolic and cardiovascular consequences. *Nutr Metab Cardiovasc Dis*. Nov 2013;23(11):1050-7. doi:10.1016/j.numecd.2012.09.007

451.   Safdie FM, Dorff T, Quinn D, et al. Fasting and cancer treatment in humans: A case series report. *Aging (Albany NY)*. Dec 31 2009;1(12):988-1007. doi:10.18632/aging.100114

452.   Sears ME. Chelation: harnessing and enhancing heavy metal detoxification--a review. *ScientificWorldJournal*. 2013;2013:219840. doi:10.1155/2013/219840

453.   Srasra E, Bekri-Abbes I. Bentonite Clays for Therapeutic Purposes and Biomaterial Design. *Curr Pharm Des*. 2020;26(6):642-649. doi:10.2174/1381612826666200203144034

454.   Campbell NR, Wickert W, Magner P, Shumak SL. Dehydration during fasting increases serum lipids and lipoproteins. *Clin Invest Med*. Dec 1994;17(6):570-6.

455.   Slater M. Fasting Away Lyme Disease. What Doctors Don't Tell You. What Doctors Don't Tell You: What Doctors Don't Tell You; 2022. p. 66.

456.   Longo VD, Mattson MP. Fasting: molecular mechanisms and clinical applications. *Cell Metab*. Feb 4 2014;19(2):181-92. doi:10.1016/j.cmet.2013.12.008

457.   Choi IY, Piccio L, Childress P, et al. A Diet Mimicking Fasting Promotes Regeneration and Reduces Autoimmunity and Multiple Sclerosis Symptoms. *Cell Rep*. Jun 7 2016;15(10):2136-2146. doi:10.1016/j.celrep.2016.05.009

458.   Bruce-Keller AJ, Umberger G, McFall R, Mattson MP. Food restriction reduces brain damage and improves behavioral outcome following excitotoxic and metabolic insults. *Ann Neurol*. Jan 1999;45(1):8-15.

459.   Mihaylova MM, Cheng CW, Cao AQ, et al. Fasting Activates Fatty Acid Oxidation to Enhance Intestinal Stem Cell Function during Homeostasis and Aging. *Cell Stem Cell*. May 3 2018;22(5):769-778.e4. doi:10.1016/j.stem.2018.04.001

460.   Cheng C-W, Adams GB, Perin L, et al. Prolonged fasting reduces IGF-1/PKA to promote hematopoietic-stem-cell-based regeneration and reverse immunosuppression. *Cell stem cell*. 2014;14(6):810-823. doi:10.1016/j.stem.2014.04.014

461.   Wisinger S. The benefits of fasting. Accessed 22 June, 2020. http://www.wisinger.co.uk/fasting/

462.   Trepanowski JF, Kroeger CM, Barnosky A, et al. Effect of Alternate-Day Fasting on Weight Loss, Weight Maintenance, and Cardioprotection Among Metabolically Healthy Obese Adults: A Randomized Clinical Trial. *JAMA Internal Medicine*. 2017;177(7):930-938. doi:10.1001/jamainternmed.2017.0936

463.   Gabel K, Hoddy KK, Haggerty N, et al. Effects of 8-hour time restricted feeding on body weight and metabolic disease risk factors in obese adults: A pilot study. *Nutrition and healthy aging*. 2018;4(4):345-353. doi:10.3233/NHA-170036

464.   Moro T, Tinsley G, Bianco A, et al. Effects of eight weeks of time-restricted feeding (16/8) on basal metabolism, maximal strength, body composition, inflammation, and cardiovascular risk factors in resistance-trained males. *Journal of Translational Medicine*. 2016/10/13 2016;14(1):290. doi:10.1186/s12967-016-1044-0

465.   Sutton EF, Beyl R, Early KS, Cefalu WT, Ravussin E, Peterson CM. Early Time-Restricted Feeding Improves Insulin Sensitivity, Blood Pressure, and Oxidative Stress Even without Weight Loss in Men with Prediabetes. *Cell Metabolism*. 2018/06/05/ 2018;27(6):1212-1221.e3. doi:https://doi.org/10.1016/j.cmet.2018.04.010

466.   Antoni R, Robertson TM, Robertson MD, Johnston JD. A pilot feasibility study exploring the effects of a moderate time-restricted feeding intervention on energy intake, adiposity and metabolic physiology in free-living human subjects. *Journal of Nutritional Science.* 2018;7:e22. e22. doi:10.1017/jns.2018.13

467.   McHill AW, Phillips AJ, Czeisler CA, et al. Later circadian timing of food intake is associated with increased body fat. *The American journal of clinical nutrition.* 2017;106(5):1213-1219. doi:10.3945/ajcn.117.161588

468.   Kogevinas M, Espinosa A, Castelló A, et al. Effect of mistimed eating patterns on breast and prostate cancer risk (MCC-Spain Study). *Int J Cancer.* Nov 15 2018;143(10):2380-2389. doi:10.1002/ijc.31649

469.   Sato S, Solanas G, Peixoto FO, et al. Circadian Reprogramming in the Liver Identifies Metabolic Pathways of Aging. *Cell.* 2017;170(4):664-677.e11. doi:10.1016/j.cell.2017.07.042

470.   Solanas G, Peixoto FO, Perdiguero E, et al. Aged Stem Cells Reprogram Their Daily Rhythmic Functions to Adapt to Stress. *Cell.* 2017;170(4):678-692.e20. doi:10.1016/j.cell.2017.07.035

471.   Weir HJ, Yao P, Huynh FK, et al. Dietary Restriction and AMPK Increase Lifespan via Mitochondrial Network and Peroxisome Remodeling. *Cell Metabolism.* 2017;26(6):884-896.e5. doi:10.1016/j.cmet.2017.09.024

472.   Felix L. Technology: Quick Stats. Digital Detox. Accessed 29 June, 2020. https://www.digitaldetox.com

473.   Goodin T. Digital Detox Research. It's Time to Log Off. Accessed 28 June, 2020. https://www.itstimetologoff.com/digital-detox-facts/

474.   Talks M. Digital Detoxing: Vital Statistics. Digital Detoxing. Accessed 28 June, 2020. https://www.digitaldetoxing.com/#vital-statistics

475.   Tigre Moura F. Dopamine: More Than Pleasure, The Secret is the Anticipation of a Reward. Live In Innovation. Accessed 29 October, 2022. https://liveinnovation.org/dopamine-more-than-pleasure-the-secret-is-the-anticipation-of-a-reward/

476.   Szczypka MS, Rainey MA, Kim DS, et al. Feeding behavior in dopamine-deficient mice. *Proc Natl Acad Sci U S A.* Oct 12 1999;96(21):12138-43. doi:10.1073/pnas.96.21.12138

477.   Celis-Morales CA, Lyall DM, Steell L, et al. Associations of discretionary screen time with mortality, cardiovascular disease and cancer are attenuated by strength, fitness and physical activity: findings from the UK Biobank study. *BMC Medicine.* 2018/05/24 2018;16(1):77. doi:10.1186/s12916-018-1063-1

478.   Khaleeli H. Text neck: how smartphones are damaging our spines. The Guardian. Accessed 28 June, 2020. https://www.theguardian.com/lifeandstyle/shortcuts/2014/nov/24/text-neck-how-smartphones-damaging-our-spines

479.   Segran E. What Really Happens To Your Brain And Body During A Digital Detox. Fast Company. Accessed 28 June, 2020. https://www.fastcompany.com/3049138/what-really-happens-to-your-brain-and-body-during-a-digital-detox

480.   Aging GCo. *Destination Healthy Aging:The physical, cognitive and social benefits of travel* 2018:15. https://globalcoalitiononaging.com/wp-content/uploads/2018/07/destination-healthy-aging-white-paper_final-web-1.pdf

481.   Eaker ED, Pinsky J, Castelli WP. Myocardial Infarction and Coronary Death among Women: Psychosocial Predictors from a 20-Year Follow-up of Women in the Framingham Study. *American Journal of Epidemiology.* 1992;135(8):854-864. doi:10.1093/oxfordjournals.aje.a116381

482.   Chikani V, Reding D, Gunderson P, McCarty CA. Vacations improve mental health among rural women: the Wisconsin Rural Women's Health Study. *Wmj.* Aug 2005;104(6):20-3.

483.   Chatterjee DR. *The Doctors Farmacy.* Is There An Antidote To Stress? https://drhyman.com/blog/2019/12/31/podcast-ep87/

484.   Beckman T. Citations for "60-90% of all doctor's office visits are for stress-related ailments and complaints.". LinkedIn. Accessed 29 June, 2020.

https://www.linkedin.com/pulse/citations-90-all-doctors-office-visits-stress-related-tom-beckman/

485.   Nerurkar A, Bitton A, Davis RB, Phillips RS, Yeh G. When Physicians Counsel About Stress: Results of a National Study. *JAMA Internal Medicine*. 2013;173(1):76-77. doi:10.1001/2013.jamainternmed.480

486.   Hernandez-Reif M, Field T, Ironson G, et al. Natural killer cells and lymphocytes increase in women with breast cancer following massage therapy. *Int J Neurosci*. Apr 2005;115(4):495-510. doi:10.1080/00207450590523080

487.   Rapaport MH, Schettler P, Breese C. A preliminary study of the effects of a single session of Swedish massage on hypothalamic-pituitary-adrenal and immune function in normal individuals. *Journal of alternative and complementary medicine (New York, NY)*. 2010;16(10):1079-1088. doi:10.1089/acm.2009.0634

488.   Rapaport MH, Schettler P, Bresee C. A preliminary study of the effects of repeated massage on hypothalamic-pituitary-adrenal and immune function in healthy individuals: a study of mechanisms of action and dosage. *J Altern Complement Med*. Aug 2012;18(8):789-97. doi:10.1089/acm.2011.0071

489.   Childre D, Martin H. *The Heartmath Solution*. HarperCollins Publishers; 1999:281.

490.   Lacey J, Lacey B. *Physiological Correlates of Emotion*. Some autonomic-central nervous system interrelationships. Academic Press; 1970:205-227.

491.   Brummett BH, Boyle SH, Kuhn CM, Siegler IC, Williams RB. Positive affect is associated with cardiovascular reactivity, norepinephrine level, and morning rise in salivary cortisol. *Psychophysiology*. Jul 2009;46(4):862-9. doi:10.1111/j.1469-8986.2009.00829.x

492.   Pauly T, Drewelies J, Kolodziejczak K, et al. Positive and negative affect are associated with salivary cortisol in the everyday life of older adults: A quantitative synthesis of four aging studies. *Psychoneuroendocrinology*. Nov 2021;133:105403. doi:10.1016/j.psyneuen.2021.105403

493.   USADA. Pregnenolone: What You Need to Know. USADA. Accessed 29 October, 2022. https://www.usada.org/spirit-of-sport/education/pregnenolone/

494.   Pellecome. Is Pregnenolone the Same As DHEA? Pellecome. Accessed 29 October, 2022. https://pellecome.com/2020/04/25/is-pregnenolone-the-same-as-dhea/

495.   Yen SS. Dehydroepiandrosterone sulfate and longevity: new clues for an old friend. *Proc Natl Acad Sci U S A*. Jul 17 2001;98(15):8167-9. doi:10.1073/pnas.161278698

496.   Dillon KM, Minchoff B, Baker KH. Positive emotional states and enhancement of the immune system. *Int J Psychiatry Med*. 1985;15(1):13-8. doi:10.2190/r7fd-urn9-pq7f-a6j7

497.   Woof JM, Kerr MA. The function of immunoglobulin A in immunity. *J Pathol*. Jan 2006;208(2):270-82. doi:10.1002/path.1877

498.   Feinstein D. Energy psychology: Efficacy, speed, mechanisms. *EXPLORE*. 2019/09/01/ 2019;15(5):340-351. doi:https://doi.org/10.1016/j.explore.2018.11.003

499.   Bach D, Groesbeck G, Stapleton P, Sims R, Blickheuser K, Church D. Clinical EFT (Emotional Freedom Techniques) Improves Multiple Physiological Markers of Health. *J Evid Based Integr Med*. Jan-Dec 2019;24:2515690x18823691. doi:10.1177/2515690x18823691

500.   Stapleton P, Sheldon T, Porter B. Clinical benefits of Emotional Freedom Techniques on food cravings at 12-months follow-up: A randomized controlled trial. *Energy Psychology: theory, research, practice, training*. 2012;4(1):1-12.

501.   Babamahmoodi A, Arefnasab Z, Noorbala AA, et al. Emotional Freedom Technique (FFT) Effects on Psychoimmunological Factors of Chemically Pulmonary Injured Veterans. *Iran J Allergy Asthma Immunol*. Feb 2015;14(1):37-47.

502.   Brattberg G. Self-administered EFT (Emotional Freedom Techniques) in Individuals With Fibromyalgia: A Randomized Trial. *Integrative Medicine: A Clinician's Journal*. 2008;7(4):30-35.

503.   Yeung AS, Feng R, Kim DJH, et al. A Pilot, Randomized Controlled Study of Tai Chi With Passive and Active Controls in the Treatment of Depressed Chinese Americans. *J Clin Psychiatry*. May 2017;78(5):e522-e528. doi:10.4088/JCP.16m10772

INDEX

Y

Z

ABOUT THE AUTHOR

Hari Kalymnios is a renowned author, speaker, and expert in health, well-being, and personal development. With a passion for unlocking individual potential, Hari empowers others to live vibrant lives.

Raised in London, Hari holds a First-Class degree in Physics with Astrophysics from The University of Manchester. After extensive worldwide travel, he gained experience working for notable companies like Accenture and the London Stock Exchange. Hari has authored previous titles, including *The Thought Gym* (2013) and *Working Well* (2018). He has also created *The Super Journal*, a day planner for productivity and goal attainment. In 2017, Hari obtained a master's degree in Health & Wellbeing from Leeds Trinity University.

As a leading authority on vitality and energy, Hari integrates mindset, mindfulness, and self-leadership principles to inspire extraordinary levels of health and success. His multidisciplinary background in psychology, neuroscience, and leadership enables a holistic approach to well-being, encompassing nutrition, exercise, sleep, and stress management.

Recognized for his dynamic speaking style, Hari captivates audiences worldwide with his storytelling and practical insights. Through his content creation, including videos, blogs, and online courses, he shares ideas and philosophies to thousands. He can be reached on social media via the handle: **thethoughtgym**.

With an unwavering commitment to helping others thrive, Hari guides individuals on the path to becoming their best selves. He reminds us that true vitality and personal mastery are achievable through the transformative journey he facilitates.

In addition to being a part-time yoga teacher, Hari loves cycling around Europe each summer, undertaking multi-country, multi-day social rides. He's also partial to getting a sweat on with boxing, Thai boxing, kettlebells, circuits, and anything else that moves his body. He's still working on his handstands but is oh so close!

www.TheThoughtGym.com
www.HariKalymnios.com

FURTHER TRAINING
Workshops, Coaching and Consulting

Healthy employees, business owners and change-makers who have an abundance of vitality are highly valuable in today's economy. Therefore, concepts, ideas and philosophies in this book have been developed into a series of workshops, talks, keynotes and coaching programs.

Hari is a popular and in-demand trainer, speaker and consultant on these ideas, and his sessions are always well-received and invaluable. Using a blend of science & data, practical exercises, storytelling, jargon-free language and real-life examples, Hari makes the content useful, engaging and accessible to everyone.

Please reach out to discuss your unique requirements.

Printed in Dunstable, United Kingdom